MEMOIRS OF MY PEOPLE

MEMOIRS OF MY PEOPLE

*Jewish Self-Portraits from the
11th to the 20th Centuries*

SELECTED AND EDITED BY
LEO W. SCHWARZ

SCHOCKEN BOOKS · NEW YORK

First Schocken Paperback edition, 1963

CONTENTS

INTRODUCTION

THE anthologist, like the historian and the novelist, is an autobiographer in disguise. He is driven into the jungles and watering places of literature by instinct as well as by design. The ultimate form in which he exhibits his loot is dictated not only by public taste; it is above all the expression of those fundamental impulses and habits that lead him to the library-cubicle rather than to the market-place. For this reason, and for weightier ones that will soon appear evident, I shall endeavor to explain autobiographically, in part at least, the genesis and character of this book.

My preoccupation with autobiography for many years has convinced me that personal narratives of experience, aside from being a mine of entertainment, are the clearest mirrors of character and culture. Certainly this is true of the stream of experience of which the autobiographers in this book are a part. To be sure, their accounts are slices of history and frequently pages of literature. But the personalities that people these pages and the hundred little dramas they enact are essentially human nature in action with its infinite range of tragedy and joy, of absurdity and nobility. In what other form of expression can one find a deeper consciousness of the community of human beings? Or the meaning of human bondage and human freedom?

If you are in doubt, ponder for a moment the motives that impelled these men and women to record their experiences. With some it is vanity, imitation, profit, discipline, with others the urge for immortality, but with the majority it is the overpowering need to express themselves. A shattering event has broken their lives, inner pain tortures their spirits, an historic upheaval has cast them from their moorings—they must willy nilly write down their reactions. "These notes of mine," writes Theodor Herzl, "are no labor to me but merely relief." That wonderful lady of Hameln, Glückel, driven no less inexorably by the pain of bereavement, recounts her tale "in the hope of distracting my soul from the burdens laid upon it" so that she may "live through many wakeful nights."

Natural catastrophes also incite the memory. Leone da Modena, one of the most curious autobiographers in the gallery, tells us that when he was seven months old his parents fled Ferrara because of a great earthquake. An older survivor of the disaster, the distinguished scholar Azariah dei Rossi, was impelled to describe the experience in the introduction to his classic work, *Light of the Eyes*. "Friday, the 18th of November, 1571, was a memorable day. At about ten o'clock, when folks were peacefully asleep, the rumbling of a violent earthquake was heard. It lasted about three minutes. Nothing like it has happened in our time nor have our forebears reported anything to match it for centuries. Every moment brought new horrors, forcing upon one the belief that the earth was cracking open and the world coming to an end."

These recordings constitute spiritual exchange of a high order. The quality of the writer's character is refracted in the confession. Autobiography is the product of psychological conditions that express the core of culture as art represents its aspiration.

As to the pervasive assumption that personal expression in Jewish historical experience is neither continuous nor characteristic, the merest glance at the available autobiographical materials will cast doubt upon it. Begin with the earliest source. While literary or critical studies of the Hebrew Bible rarely treat autobiographical passages as separate texts, no one will deny they exist. And there is good reason to believe that the successive editors of the Hebrew Bible omitted similar material as extraneous to their policies. Surely this must have been true in the Prophetic literature. Apart from the prose passages of a personal character, the poetic self-portraits—such as those in Jeremiah and Isaiah—indicate not only intense personal feelings but a certain ambivalence in the use of "I." (Parenthetically, the tendency among modern scholars to identify the "I" of the Psalms with the community of Israel needs reappraisal. Some of the Psalms are too intensely personal to be anything else than a word-portrait of an individual's experience or mood—that is, autobiographical poetry.) Certainly the excerpts in Ezra-Nehemiah suggest that they were taken from longer memoirs.

In Hellenistic Jewish literature—though surviving items such as the *Autobiography* of Josephus and the *Epistles* of Paul are scanty—there must have been more such books and letters which did not survive. Recall, for example, the moving autobiographical passage in *De Specialibus Legibus* where Philo of Alexandria talks about a personal crisis arising out of the need to turn aside from the placid life of a student to meet the exigencies of a statesman. There is also his *Legatio ad Gaium,* an extraordinary account of his stewardship as head of the Jewish embassy in connection with the pogrom that was instigated by the Greeks in Alexandria and the Emperor's order to place his statue in the Temple there. We know from Eusebius's description of the original that the extant account is only a fragment of what was five books.

Undoubtedly there were personal and family documents during the first centuries of the Common Era, as well as correspondence among literate business men and adventurers. But, as far as we know now, there were no official means for their preservation. The discovery of the Bar-Kochba letters among the recent archeological finds at the Dead Sea, like the letters in the Cairo *Genizah,* gives us hope that more such material may come to light.

In any case, within the period ranging from the ninth century to the eighteenth—say, beginning with Donnolo's brief autobiography (in the form of an introduction to the *Sefer Yezirah*) and his relative Ahimaaz's *Sefer Yuhasin* to Solomon Maimon's masterpiece—there is enough material to warrant the statement that expression in subjective literature was both indigenous and continual. This applies without question to the modern and contemporary epoch.

Thus we may conclude that, despite the apparent breaks in continuity in earlier epochs, there is strong evidence that autobiographical literature is in the main coextensive with the whole of Jewish historical experience. A critical study of this body of data might prove as fruitful to the historian as it would be fascinating to the layman.

Discussing the motivation for autobiographical literature in Jewish history, the late Dr. Jacob Shatsky—in his essays in *Zukunft* (1925-1926)—concludes that it is primarily catastrophe. He notes the outbursts of personal documents particularly during such upheavals as the Crusades, the Spanish expulsion in 1492, the Chmielnitzki Revolt, and so on. But in contrast to general history, he notes further, there is a dearth of Jewish autobiography written under peaceful conditions—what he designates as *"shtilleben literatur."* The evidence appears to bear out Dr. Shatsky's first conclusion; the experience of the catastrophe of 1939-1945 dramatically underscores it. However, there is a margin of doubt about his second conclusion.

In general there is a paucity of autobiographical literature altogether until the Renaissance. Now it is precisely around that period that Jewish personal documents also begin to flourish—though certainly they never compared in output with those written by European Christians and humanists. As soon as autobiography became a standard form of literary expression in modern times, Jews became almost as prolific in this field as their Gentile contemporaries. It seems to me that, irrespective of external conditions, individuals undergo traumatic experiences in normal times, so to speak, as intense as those suffered in times of catastrophe, and as a consequence seek expression, escape and consolation in autobiography.

In picturing Gentile-Jewish relations in other times and cultures, official documents—such as codes, laws, decrees, bulls and the like—are essential; but they do not always describe living situations. The actual living relations at a specific time and place are portrayed with far more reality and vividness in diaries, letters and other forms of communication among Jews themselves and between Jews and Gentiles.

Consider, for example, the Jewish communities of the Mediterranean littoral and especially Palestine of the fifteenth century. Their social and economic circumstances are most truly and vividly described in the personal letters of Jewish travelers and immigrants to the Holy Land, like Obadiah of Bertinoro and many others included in J. D. Eisenstein's *Ozar Massaoth (Treasury of Travels)*. You find not only a good deal of intercommunication between Jews and their neighbors; you find surprisingly peaceful relations under nominally coercive regimes.

Moreover, other intricate patterns and relevant concepts emerge. The solidarity of Jewish communities appears to have been maintained by continual accretions from one another; so that the unity of Judaism may almost be said to have been preserved because of, and indeed by very means of, the dispersion. And personal documents show more clearly than do the more conventional records that the lively participation of Jews in general culture was in fact a method of assimilation for survival.

If you are seeking the eternally human element in the mainstream of Jewish life and history, you will find it in the torrent of memory overflowing in the pages of this volume. You will find flesh-and-blood beings— martyrs and merrymakers, rabbis and rapscallions, sages and sinners— with all their virtues as well as their faults laid bare. They go through life, as we do, facing every conceivable problem, living tragically and joyfully, forgiving "wrongs darker than death or night" and hoping "till hope creates from its own wreck the thing it contemplates." These men and women are tough with a spiritual fibre that the best histories could hardly portray, and they tell their tales with heart-throb and spirit. You will note also the strong sense of community feeling and prodigious attachment to intellectual effort.

As I reread these pages, a question posed itself relentlessly: Do these personalities really exhibit only a people of the Book? Does not the life they reveal transcend the Book, and even the Word? I do not pretend to have a ready answer; but an answer must be found if the love of life and joy in wisdom and beauty, that are reflected in the highest moments of this millennial experience, are to continue. I wonder whether the sovereign achievement of Jews lies in their extraordinary religious and intellectual attainments, or in the high order of social life they achieved in chronically hostile states and cultures.

This pageant of personal history underlines the dangers of black-and-white judgments. The historian, the apologist and the journalist have given us a set of neat labels that for the most part portray Jews as angels or devils. But Jews, like other historical families, like life itself, elude generalization; they are human natural, so to speak, reflecting all the complications and all the contradictions that characterize the struggle for survival and self-expression. Matthew Arnold's classic distinction between Hellenism and Hebraism does not square with experience: there is as much "sweetness and light" in the character of Jews as there is "fire and strength" in the Greek mind. Nor does Israel Zangwill's superlative epigram, when put to the test, fare any better: the sons of Hellas lived in "the beauty of holiness" just as the sons of Jacob felt the "holiness of beauty." Indeed, what does seem to shine out of the literature of personal experience is the fundamental unity of the human spirit.

Leo W. Schwarz

January, 1963

FAMILY ALBUM

AHIMAAZ BEN PALTIEL (1017-?)

It was with good reason that Ahimaaz, a poet of distinction, fixed his thoughts on the exploits of his illustrious ancestors. He was the scion of an Italian family whose traditions reached back a thousand years and whose great lights had been ministers to the potentates of the Byzantine Empire and the Fatimid Caliphate. Accordingly he collected every scrap of written and oral information to compose this record, extended himself to arrange the material in orderly sequence, and then cast the memory portraits into the literary form then in vogue—rhymed prose. Despite an occasional lapse into the miraculous, characteristic of his times, his story is a saga of valiant men, devoted to the faith of their fathers and respected by the powerful rulers they served. It is a pity that Ahimaaz' wholehearted veneration of his notable forebears prevented him from telling us more about his own experiences. Nevertheless, the tales are welcome flashlight rays in the darkness that veils those distant times.

* * *

I, AHIMAAZ, the son of Paltiel ben Samuel ben Hananel ben Amittai, sought God's aid and guidance in order to find the lineage of my family and He bountifully granted my request. I concentrated my mind and soul upon this work; I put the family documents and traditions in order, and I narrated the story in rhymed form. I began with the earliest tradition during the time of the destruction of Jerusalem and of the Temple by the Romans; then I traced it through the settlement of the exiles in the city of Oria in Italy (where I am now living) and the arrival of my ancestors in Capua; and finally, I have concluded with my own generation. I have written it all in this book for the use of future generations. I completed it in the month of Sivan and I praise and I honor and thank God for helping me to finish the book in the spirit and form I desired.

Wherefore, I will now carefully relate the traditions of my fore-

3

fathers. Carried upon a vessel with the captives whom Titus took from Jerusalem, they went to the city of Oria. There they established a community, and by deeds of labor and love they grew and prospered. Among their descendants there arose a great light whose name was Rabbi Amittai. He was both scholar and poet, and eminent for his piety and learning. His three sons were no less distinguished, being deeply versed in the Bible and the Talmud, as well as in the mystical and philosophic lore of their times. Worthy disciples of an eminent father were these learned men: Rabbi Shephatiah, seeker after wisdom; Rabbi Hananel, master of Torah; and Eleazar, expert in law.

In the 800th year after the destruction of Jerusalem (868), King Basil I was elevated to the throne of the Byzantine Empire. He seized the kingdom by bloodshed and treachery and, in his zeal for the Christian faith, he was determined to destroy Israel or compel the people to forsake the Law of Moses and adopt the religion of Jesus. He sent cavalrymen to the furthest corners of his empire to compel the Jews to change their religion. They arrived at the port of Otranto, embarked for the province of Apulia, and announced the fearsome report throughout the land. They also came to Oria, bearing an epistle with the Chrysobulla—the royal seal of gold—from the Emperor to Rabbi Shephatiah.

I give herewith the contents of the epistle:

"I, King Basil, request that you, Rabbi Shephatiah, come to visit me. Pray do not refuse to come, for I have heard of your great wisdom and knowledge and I yearn to see you. I swear by my life and my crown that your coming and returning will be in peace. I will receive you with the same honor as my own kith and kin and I will grant in bountiful affection whatsoever you request."

Whereupon Rabbi Shephatiah sailed to Constantinople, the city that was built by Emperor Constantine—may God destroy its glory and power!—and God granted that he win the favor of the King and the people.

Then the King engaged Rabbi Shephatiah in a discussion of religious matters. He questioned him regarding the Temple in Jerusalem and the Church called the Hagia Sophia in Constantinople, inquiring which building had required greater wealth. The King contended that the Church was the greater of the two inasmuch as untold wealth and treasure had been used to build it. Rabbi Shephatiah appropriately asked that a copy of the Scriptures be placed before them.

"There you will find the facts," he said, "by which you can judge which structure consumed more wealth."

The King immediately procured the Scriptures and, by comparing the figures recorded by David and Solomon, he was satisfied that the treasure used in building the Temple was greater by 120 talents of gold and 500 talents of silver. Whereupon the King exclaimed, "The wisdom of Rabbi Shephatiah has prevailed against me."

And the Rabbi graciously replied, "My Lord, it is the Scriptures, not I, that have prevailed against you."

Afterwards the King invited him to a royal banquet. The table was overflowing with delicacies and fruits, and food was served to Rabbi Shephatiah in golden dishes so that he might eat in accordance with the dietary laws. These dishes were lowered on chains of precious silver and the place from which they were lowered was invisible.

Now Basil had a daughter whom he loved as the apple of his eye. She was tormented by a demon and no cure could be found for her.

The King spoke to the Rabbi secretly, imploring his aid. "Help me, Shephatiah; cure my daughter of her sickness."

He replied that he would do so with the help of the Almighty, but he must have a place free of the impurities of idol worship. The King offered the beautiful garden of Bukoleon, the palace on the walls facing the Sea of Marmora. After examining it thoroughly, the Rabbi approved the Bukoleon, which means "Mouth of the Lion." He took the girl there and conjured up the demon in the name of God who dwells on high and who founded the earth in his wisdom.

And the demon cried aloud, "Why are you helping the daughter of a wicked man who wreaks his wickedness upon your people? God has placed her in my power so that I may humble her. Now depart because I will not leave her body."

But the Rabbi replied, "I refuse to listen to your words. Come out, in the name of God, so that the King may know there is a God in Israel."

The demon came forth and attempted to flee but Rabbi Shephatiah seized it, enclosed it in a leaden vessel which he sealed with the name of God, and then threw the vessel to the bottom of the sea. Thereupon the girl became calm and poised and returned to the King and the Queen.

Then Shephatiah sought the King's permission to depart. The King came forth to greet him, put his arm around his shoulders, and led him into his private chambers. There he tried, by offering huge rewards, to induce Shephatiah to abandon his faith. He walked up and down with him, urging him zealously to embrace his heathen faith. He offered him treasures and appointed companions to influence him. Shephatiah, oppressed by the King's zeal and insolence, objected vehemently.

"O Mighty Lord," he cried, "you are subjecting me to violence!"

Whereupon the King descended from his throne, took Rabbi Shephatiah from the midst of the people, and granted him permission to depart. He sent him to the Queen so that she might give him gifts and a blessing. The Queen asked him whether he had any children, and he replied, "Your servant has a son and two daughters."

The Queen offered him her earrings and her girdle and urged him to accept them. "I give them to you as a token of my regard for your wisdom. They are priceless; give them to your daughters." The weight of the earrings was a litra of gold and the girdle was of equal worth.

Before his departure the King summoned him and said, "Shephatiah, ask of me whatsoever you desire. If it is not wealth you wish, you shall have an inheritance of cities and provinces. I wish to fulfill my promise."

"If my Lord wishes to favor Shephatiah," he replied, filled with pain and almost in tears, "allow those engaged in the study of our Law to continue without interference. Do not oppress them and make their lives sorrowful. If my Lord cannot grant me this, then it is my wish that at least my city be free from religious persecution."

The King replied angrily, "If I had not given you my word, I would make an example of you here and now. But I wrote the letter and cannot break faith with you."

Consequently the King issued an edict sealed with a seal of fine gold, and commanded that there should be no religious persecution in the city of Oria. And he sent Rabbi Shephatiah home in peace and honor.

But that wicked King continued to send his representatives throughout the empire in order to compel the people to accept the errors of the pagan faith. For a quarter of a century—until the day of his death—the sun and the moon were darkened. May his end be cursed and may his evil and sin be remembered!

In the days when Basil's son Leo the Wise (886-912) succeeded him to the throne—may his memory be blessed—and the Arabs began to overrun Calabria and Apulia, capturing and plundering many cities, Sudan, their leader, who ruled the country, was in Bari. He sent couriers to Oria to make a covenant of peace, guaranteeing that the land would not be laid waste but only tribute would be exacted. However, this covenant was merely a trick whereby he hoped to plunder and destroy our famous city.

Now the Governor of Bari sent Rabbi Shephatiah as an ambassador to discuss the pact and arrange that the conditions be incorporated in a written document officially sealed. Sudan received him with signal honor and spoke with him in a friendly manner in the presence of his assembled chieftains. He purposely delayed almost until evening so that Shephatiah might not be able to return by reason of the Sabbath and thus inform the Governor of his stratagem.

Shephatiah finally grew aware of his deceit and asked for permission to leave. "You have tricked me," he declared angrily, "let me go."

"Where will you go now?" asked Sudan. "It is almost Sabbath."

But Shephatiah persisted, saying that Sudan need not be anxious about him. At last Sudan let him go. Invoking the aid of God Almighty, Rabbi Shephatiah wrote a formula on the horse's hooves in order to speed the journey. Then he uttered the name of God imploringly and the ground shrank before him.

As soon as he reached the outer sections of the city, he urged the people to flee. "Sudan, leader of the Arabs, and his hosts are coming to loot and destroy," he announced.

The Governor came to meet him at the gates of the city. He told him what the situation was and they held counsel in regard to what steps should be taken. Then Shephatiah entered the city before darkness had fallen, made his ablutions, put on his holiday garments, and, as custom prescribed, welcomed the Sabbath with joy, food, drink and study.

Sudan, puffed up with pride, defiant in his arrogance, reached the city with his hosts by forced marches. He found the country deserted and, infuriated by this disappointment, he summoned Rabbi Shephatiah.

"Hand over that man who desecrated the Sabbath and thus by his own Law is worthy of death," were his ominous words.

But Shephatiah, strong with the power of God, replied, "Why do you make a false accusation? Heaven is my witness, and the whole population of the city too, that I entered the city while it was still day, and before the sun had gone down I had prepared myself for the Sabbath and welcomed the holy day fittingly in accordance with the commandment of my King and Redeemer, the Holy One of Israel."

Rabbi Shephatiah had a daughter of rare beauty named Cassia. He was anxious that the girl should be wedded but her mother stood in the way. Whensoever anyone asked her hand in marriage, her haughtiness acted as a damper. She would say, "She is the daughter of a great man and a girl of exceptional qualities. I will not allow her to leave this house unless a man like him can be found. I will let her marry only a man of equal scholarly accomplishments."

One night, as Rabbi Shephatiah engaged in prayer and study, the girl arose from her bed and in her dressing gown prepared the water for his ablutions. As she stood before him, he noticed that she had a fully developed body and was ripe for marriage. After prayers he returned to his wife and rebuked her for her behavior.

"We have a beautiful dove who is without blemish and ready for marriage, and my brother has asked her hand for his son Hasadiah. By listening to you I have transgressed our laws and interfered with her happiness."

On the way to the synagogue the next morning he met his brother Rabbi Hananel and told him that it was his wish to have Hasadiah become the husband of Cassia. His brother showed his gratitude and esteem by falling upon his knees before him. After the service he invited the congregation to his house and blessed the children in marriage. Rabbi Amittai, brother of the radiant bride, wrote in her honor the poem *O Lord, Who Telleth of the End from the Beginning* . . . to crown the occasion with splendor.

God blessed Shephatiah with long life, deep learning, great wealth, and favored him with a worthy son. Both he and his son were upright and perfect men. Rabbi Shephatiah died in peace, first among the learned, and ever devoted to the just and righteous God.

Rabbi Hananel, the brother of Shephatiah, was no less distinguished and upright. I will now tell of his wonderful deeds.

One day the Archbishop and Hananel were discussing religious subjects and treated of the calculations regarding the appearance of the new moon. It happened that the next day would be the first day of the new moon which is sanctified by Israel. The Archbishop asked him in how many hours the moon would make its appearance and the Rabbi named the exact hour. But he had erred.

The Archbishop, differing with him, said, "If your answer is an example of your calculations, you certainly are not an expert."

Rabbi Hananel had not calculated carefully, but the Archbishop had and would have caught him in his net had not God come to his rescue.

For the Archbishop said, "O wise Hananel, if my calculation is accurate, then you will do my bidding. You must abandon your religion and accept the faith of the Gospel. On the other hand, if your calculation is accurate, then I will do as you bid. I will give you my New Year's gift of a horse valued at three hundred gold coins. If you prefer, you may take the money instead."

They accepted the terms and agreed, before the magistrates and the ruling prince, to abide by the pact.

That night the Archbishop ordered men stationed on the city-wall and the towers to observe the exact time of the moon's appearance and what fraction of it appeared.

When Rabbi Hananel returned to his house, he checked his calculation and discovered that he had made an error. His heart melted within him, his strength left him. However, he found courage and appealed to God to lift him out of the pit. He revealed his plight to his brothers and his family, entreating them to pour out their supplication to God in the hope that He would hear their prayers and perform a miracle as He had done for their ancestors in Egypt. What night came, he went to his roof and kept his eyes fixed on Him to whom great praise is due. As the time of the waxing of the moon approached, he appealed, in pain and tears, to the loving God for succor and, in fervent devotion and prayer, sought His intervention.

God heard his prayers and hid the moon behind the clouds until the following night. When the Rabbi went to hear the decision in the morning, the Archbishop said to him in the presence of all the people, "You know as well as I that I was correct and the moon appeared at the time I stated. But who can punish you? You have won grace from your God even as an erring son escapes punishment by cajoling his father."

Whereupon he paid him the three hundred gold coins which Rabbi Hananel did not keep, but distributed among the needy. Then his brothers and friends assembled and gave praise to God who saves His servants from distress and brings them from darkness to light.

Rabbi Amittai, the beloved son of Shephatiah, became his worthy successor. The day before his death, the father requested his son to maintain the collegium of scholars and administer it wisely so that both teachers and students might continue their studies. Amittai carried out his father's wish, expounding reverently and brilliantly on all branches of religious and legal knowledge in association with the rabbis and scholars. All the days of his life he lamented the destruction of the Temple in Jerusalem and was deeply concerned over the persecution of his people.

Once he had gone to his estate in the suburbs, and it happened that a pious and learned pilgrim died in the city. The elders of the community summoned Rabbi Amittai to participate in the burial services. He informed them he would join the procession when it passed beyond the city and would recite the prayers at the burial place. The whole community was present when Rabbi Amittai intoned the service and recited an elegy which he had composed in honor of the deceased. It opened with the words, "O Soul in Exile! He who knows thee not reviles thee; he who knows thee laments thy fate."

Rabbi Moses, a brother of the deceased, who was a teacher of children, happened to be there and made an offensive pun on the verse. Rabbi Amittai overheard him and the teacher's cut remained fresh in his mind.

Years later a married woman was suspected of committing a transgression and the community, gathered to investigate the evidence and judge her guilt, found that this same Rabbi Moses was the only witness against her.

Rabbi Amittai thereupon asked him, "Have you another witness, as our law requires?"

As another witness could not be produced, Amittai pronounced the sentence prescribed for a false witness: he put Rabbi Moses under a ban and exiled him from Oria. He went first to Capua and then to Pavia.

I will now tell of Rabbi Paltiel who was a master astrologer. He was the son of Cassia, a great-granddaughter of Shephatiah.

In his time an Arab army under Caliph Abu Tamim Mead Al Muizz overran Italy and devastated the province of Calabria. The invader put Oria under siege and, wearing down the resistance of its defenders, took the city by storm, slaughtered most of the inhabitants and took the rest captive. The Caliph summoned the descendants of Rabbi Shephatiah. God let Paltiel win his favor and Al Muizz later made him his astrologer and, later on, his Vizir.

One night the Caliph and Paltiel were observing the stars, and lo and behold! the Caliph's star devoured three stars in succession. He asked Paltiel to interpret the phenomenon.

"First let me hear your interpretation," said Paltiel.

"The three stars that were devoured," the Caliph declared, "symbolize the cities of Tarento, Otranto and Bari which I am destined to vanquish."

"No, my Lord," replied Paltiel, "I see a greater destiny. The three stars symbolize three countries which you will rule: Sicily, Africa and Egypt."

No sooner had he spoken than Al Muizz embraced him, gave him a ring from his finger, and swore that if his prophecy proved true he would appoint him Vizir.

In less than a week emissaries from the princes of Sicily informed Al Muizz that the Emir had died and invited him to become their ruler. Whereupon he sailed to Sicily with his army and became the lord of the country. As a consequence, he had complete faith in Paltiel and appointed him Vizir.

Afterwards the Caliph went to Africa with Paltiel, leaving his brother behind to rule in his stead. Paltiel's influence became second only to that of the Caliph and his renown reached everywhere.

Now at that time there came a deputation from the Emperor of Macedonia, impressively arrayed and bearing gifts in accordance with their custom, to seek an audience with the Caliph. The ambassador inquired for the steward of the royal household, and an Arab attendant replied, "A Jew has authority over the whole realm and he decides who may or may not see the Caliph. You must have his permission to obtain an audience."

"Why, I would rather return to my lord in Constantinople," the ambassador replied contemptuously, "than appeal to a Jew for permission to speak with the Caliph!"

When the report of his remarks reached Paltiel, he issued an order forbidding anyone to approach the ambassador's quarters or to pay the slightest attention to him and his suite.

The thwarted Greek kept to himself, fuming and cursing, for ten days. Then he humbly and penitently returned, pleading that Paltiel forgive his offensive behavior. The Vizir made him cool his heels for three days. When at last he did receive him, it was in a manner befitting a royal envoy: The whole palace, from the gate to the banquet hall, was luxuriously decorated. The walls were hung with scarlet tapestries and precious ornaments; the floors were covered with silk rugs; and all was resplendent with the brilliance of treasures of onyx and opal, and sweetened with the fragrance of rare perfume. In this setting of splendor Paltiel welcomed the ambassador and honored him with rich gifts. As the envoy entered he saw the Vizir reclining upon a couch, and he was given a chair wrought of gold. They conversed amiably about the Jewish religion and about Paltiel's native country and lineage.

After a festive repast, a prearranged incident added another surprise. Paltiel ordered a servant to bring the washing-bowl. The servant appeared with a delicately wrought bowl and plate of onyx and jasper, and, after pouring water over his lord's hand, he suddenly stumbled and fell, in accordance with Paltiel's orders, and broke the costly utensils into bits.

As the envoy jumped up and turned pale, Paltiel simply smiled and said, "Why do you appear so shocked?"

"Because," answered the envoy, "I have just witnessed irreparable damage. To see priceless plates smashed to pieces!"

Paltiel then asked him whether the Emperor used plates of precious stones or merely those of gold. When the envoy replied that the Emperor possessed only plates of gold, Paltiel remarked, "Of course dishes wrought of precious stones are infinitely more valuable than those of gold and cannot be mended if broken. Yet many plates of even rarer gems than the one you have just seen smashed are broken in the palace of my Lord, the Caliph."

After this Paltiel dismissed the ambassador with honor and sent him away with gifts for his lord in Constantinople.

When the Caliph of Egypt died, his subject princes sent a deputation of dignitaries with an epistle to Caliph Al Muizz, inviting him to become the ruler of Egypt.

"We have heard," the letter read, "of your prowess and wisdom which surpasses that of our former ruler, and our princes and nobles are unanimous in their desire to become your loyal subjects."

After consulting with Paltiel, it was decided that the Vizir should depart in advance and set up encampments because of the length of the journey, the starkness of the country, and the scarcity of victuals. Paltiel carried out these orders, establishing way stations where the Caliph's entourage, as well as the warriors, could lodge and eat. As the Caliph bivouacked three miles outside of Cairo, the nobles and the people joyfully marched out to present themselves to the new monarch. They prostrated themselves as they took an oath of allegiance and made the traditional exchange of noble hostages. Then the Caliph, preceded by a body of warriors who were stationed at all the points of vantage and in all public places, marched into the city at the head of his army and ascended the throne. The nation swore fealty to the Caliph, presenting him with the sceptre and crown. Thereupon he ruled Egypt with honor and glory, and Paltiel, now the Vizir of the lands of the East, including Egypt, Syria, Palestine and Babylonia, shared his riches and power.

It befell once on the awesome Day of Atonement that when Paltiel was elected to read a passage from the scrolls of the Torah, the whole congregation rose in unison as a gesture of respect. But, although he appreciated the honor, he was loath to strain their energies and said, "Unless the aged sit down and only the young remain standing, I will not accept the honor of reading from the Torah."

After the reading, he made a pledge before God and his holy congregation to have 5,000 gold dinars be distributed as follows: 1,000 to the President and Faculty of the Academy; 1,000 to those who had dedicated their lives to mourning in the Holy Land; 1,000 to the Academies of Babylonia; 1,000 to the poor; and 1,000 for the purchase of oils to light up the splendor of the Torah. The very next morning, lest anything interfere with his charitable intentions, he hired a number of fully equipped and guarded caravans to deliver the donations to those he had designated.

When Al Muizz was afflicted with the illness that ultimately killed him, he appointed his son Al Azizz as his successor and Paltiel his regent. Al Azizz ruled after his father's death, but the native officials slandered Paltiel and intrigued against him. The young Caliph, furious at their behavior, rebuked them and disclosed their charges to his Vizir. Taking counsel together, they devised a plan to put a stop to these machinations.

Paltiel removed his family and household to a magnificent country estate which he had received from the Caliph as a gift.

Soon thereafter, Al Azizz inquired, "Where is our beloved Rabbi Paltiel?"

The court attendants replied, "He is at his country estate with his kith and kin, seeking rest and relaxation."

Whereupon the Caliph summoned all the nobles and officials and declared, "Our dear friend Paltiel, sage and Vizir of our realm, is at his country estate. Let us all show our admiration and respect for him by visiting him in state."

He immediately set out in the royal chariot, followed by all the lords of the realm. Instead of waiting for Paltiel to make obeisance to him as he approached the palace, Al Azizz ordered the runners not to announce his arrival, stepped down from the chariot, and went to meet the venerable Vizir. He embraced Paltiel affectionately and, in order to show his esteem and love as a shining example to his detractors, he walked off arm and arm to a place apart from the whole assemblage. Then the court musicians and jesters entertained with music, dance, and jesting until evening, when the Caliph returned to Cairo. In this way the tongues of his enemies were silenced once and for all, praise be to God.

One night, as Paltiel and the Caliph were taking a stroll under the canopy of heaven, they watched three brilliant stars disappear simultaneously. Paltiel ventured this interpretation: "The stars that were blacked out symbolize those who will die within the year: King John of Macedonia, the King of Baghdad. . . ."

"And you," added the Caliph, interrupting him, "the king of the East, are the third."

"Oh no, my Lord," said Paltiel, "That cannot be, for I am a Jew. The third star represents the Caliph of Spain."

But the Caliph persisted. "Truly you are the third as I have said."

And in that very year, 976, as the Caliph had predicted, Paltiel died. May his soul repose in Eden. His son Samuel, who succeeded him in greatness and wisdom and benificence, took the remains of his parents as well as those of his grand-uncle Hananel in coffins to Jerusalem. He made gifts totalling 20,000 gold drachmas for religious, educational and charitable purposes. May he be granted a long life and may his name be remembered for a blessing!

Samuel had great influence in the palace of the rulers in Capua (where I was born). He was appointed Minister of Finance, administering the customs of the port and the budgets of all the city departments. He followed Paltiel's illustrious example by dispensing his wealth for educational and religious purposes and he showed reverence for his forefathers by rebuilding his grandfather's synagogue. All his other children died when they were infants, but God was merciful and left him an only son whom he called Ahimaaz. He gave this child every advantage of education so that, like his illustrious ancestors, he might live in the spirit of the teachings of the divine commandments.

And I am that Ahimaaz, the son of Paltiel. I composed this book of my family history in the year 1054, not only by my own wisdom and intelligence, but also by the grace and aid of God. I glorify His majesty and give Him my thanks for helping me to complete the book as I had planned it, from beginning to end.

LOGBOOK OF A PHYSICIAN

MOSES MAIMONIDES (1135-1204)

When his octocentennial was celebrated in 1935, Maimonides was signally honored in Madrid by an official decree of the Government of Spain, the land of his birth. The world, too, recognized one of the very great spirits of medieval times. His philosophy influenced Western as well as Jewish thought, and his voluminous ethical, legal and medical writings are all stamped with genius. Driven from Spain when he was only thirteen, and later fleeing the same fanatical persecution of the Moorish sect of Almohades in Fez, he passed the remainder of his life in Egypt as the mentor of his people and the physician to Saladin's Vizir. Even these brief extracts from his letters bear witness to the deep humanity of a great mind.

❋ ❋ ❋

(1165)

I PUT to sea on Sunday, the fourth day of the second month, and on the following Sabbath we encountered very rough weather. The storm was so fierce that I vowed to observe annually these two days as strict fast days together with my people and the whole household. I also ordered my children always to observe these fasts in our home, and laid upon them the duty of making charitable donations as liberal as their means permitted. As for myself, I vowed solemnly that as on this occasion I was alone with God on the tempestuous sea and succored by Him alone, so every year on this day I will cease all work, withdraw from men, and devote myself completely to study and prayer in His presence.

On Sunday night, the 3rd of Sivan, I landed safe and happy in Acco and thereby escaped enforced apostasy. So at last we arrived in the Land of Israel, and I also vowed to set aside this day of our arrival as an annual family holiday to be celebrated festively with a banquet and the distribution of gifts to the poor. We left Acco on Wednesday, the 4th of

Marheshvan, and reached Jerusalem after a perilous journey. I spent the entire day, as well as the following two days, praying at the remains (the Wailing Wall) of the ancient Temple. On Sunday, the 9th of Marheshvan, I left Jerusalem for Hebron where I prayed at the graves of the Patriarchs in the Cave of Machpelah. These two days, the 6th and 9th of Marheshvan, I appointed as festivals for me and mine, which should be passed in prayer and in feasting. May God help me and bring to fulfillment in me the words of Psalmist, "My vows will I pay unto the Lord."

(1167) When storms threatened in the past, I wandered from place to place, but now, by God's mercy, I have been enabled to find a sanctuary in Cairo. Upon my arrival, I perceived to my great distress that the learned of the city were at loggerheads, unmindful of what was happening in the community. I therefore felt it my duty to undertake the task of guiding the holy flock, of reconciling the hearts of the fathers to their children, and of correcting their false ways. Great is the evil, but I may succeed in curing it; and in accordance with the prophetic prescription, "I will seek the lost one, and that which has been cast out I will bring back, and the broken one I will heal."

(1172) The news that the government ordered all the Jews in Yemen (Southern Arabia) to apostatize in the same manner as the ruling powers in western countries have acted toward us, filled us with terror. A whole community shares your grief; we are bewildered; we feel unable to think calmly, so terrible is the alternative in which Israel has been placed on all sides, in the East and in the West. That, on the one hand, several among our people have become restive and unsettled in their ideas, and on the other hand others continue unshaken in their beliefs is precisely what was predicted by Daniel; namely, that when our captivity would be prolonged and we be made to suffer severely, many would leave our fold because of the oppression. They would sink into a sea of doubts and be lost; while others would entertain no misgiving nor would they be confused. Be assured, however, that our main opponents—oppression, intellectual confusion, and false authority—will vanish away. They may prosper for a limited period, but their supremacy will be fleeting. We have the certain promise of the Almighty that decrees aiming at our apostacy or destruction will be brought to naught.

I am not at all surprised to hear of the conduct of our coreligionist in South Arabia, who proclaims himself the Messiah, nor of the credulity of his followers. The man is beyond doubt demented. His actions are consequently the effect of his disease over which he has no control, and those who have faith in him are misguided and cannot form a right idea of the character of the Messiah. But I am surprised at you who possess learning, who must have read what the rabbis have taught. Are you not aware that the Prince who is to redeem Israel from their suffering must prove himself greater than all prophets, with the exception of Moses? Are you not also aware that one who proclaims himself a prophet and is shown to be false by subsequent circumstances should be put to death? Besides, tradition requires three requisites in the character of the redeemer of the outcasts; namely, wisdom, vigor, and riches. He must be wise in forecasting consequences; vigorous in holding his actions under proper control, and rich in mental resources. But when a person who lacks these attainments declares himself a prophet, we give no heed to his assertions. How much less so if he is an ignoramus! In no way does he who arose in your country show such characteristics as I have just described. Can anyone who is in his right senses even entertain the idea that he is the Messiah? No: you must make a laughingstock of the simpleton. In short, if he were perfectly sane, his conduct would, I think, be deserving of death. But I am fully persuaded that he is mad and his thoughts lack foundation. I will give some good advice, useful to him as well as to yourselves: put the brainless fellow away for a time, and meanwhile take care to circulate the news of his insanity among the gentiles; then, set him at large, and he will not be hurt for having styled himself the Messiah. In that manner you will also have saved the people from the persecution of our religious enemies.

I must add that in the first era of Islam a Jew arose in Syria, who declared himself to be the Messiah. Ten thousand Jews espoused his cause. He offered as evidence of his mission the capacity he possessed to cure himself at will: he could go to bed a leper and rise in the morning as healthy as a newborn child. His ridiculous endeavors failed. He forswore his faith, but his dupes, and unhappily many others, suffered terribly. Again in Africa, in the city of Fez, forty-five years ago another man pretended to be the herald of the Messiah, commissioned to announce that within twelve months the Redeemer would come to Zion. This promise was not fulfilled, and through it our people were exposed to innumerable sorrows. I heard this from an eyewitness. Ten years before that, a Jew of Spain stood forth in Cordova and declared himself the Messiah. Nearly all the Jews of that country ran the risk of being exterminated. The same plan was tried, thirty years previous to that, in

France. The fool performed wonders—as many believed—but he could not save himself from the block; and, what is worse, he could not deliver from persecution and death many of the congregation of Jacob.

(1176) A few months after I left my friend Japhet ben Elijah, my father, may his memory be blessed, died, and I received letters of consolation from the distant parts of Spain and North Africa. I too suffered great personal misfortunes here in Egypt from illness, loss of money, and the activities of informers who would bring about my death. Then followed the saddest blow that I have suffered to this day: the death of my righteous and beloved brother David. He was drowned on a business voyage in the Indian Ocean, and with him was lost a fortune which belonged to me and him and others. His little daughter and widow were left in my care. From the day that I heard the evil tidings I was stricken in bed with fever. I was plagued with despair and mourned like a child. Almost eight years have passed, yet still I mourn and nothing will console me. He grew up on my knees, he was my brother and my pupil—how shall I be consoled? He engaged in trade, sailing the seas, so that I might devote myself to religious and intellectual pursuits at home without worry. He was learned in biblical and talmudic lore and well-versed as a grammarian. What a joy it was merely to see him! He has gone to his eternal abode and left me bewildered in a strange land. Whenever I look at a page with his handwriting or one of his books, my heart throbs and my grief is reawakened. In short, I should have died of grief, were it not for the Torah which is my delight and the sciences in the study of which I forget my sorrow.

(1191) Know that in my capacity as a physician I have won high regard among the powers that be in this land. I refer to the Judges, the Emir, and the palace of the Vizir Al Fadhel. Since I am so occupied with the great, the plain folk cannot gain access to me. My official position requires that I devote my entire day to my patients in Cairo, and when I return to Fostat I am too fagged out to spend the remainder of the day or part of the night looking into medical literature. Medicine, as you know, is an unbounded field of study. The lot of one who is faithful and conscientious, who will not pass an opinion unless there is reasonable evidence for its validity, who cannot continue reading if he does not know the author and the method by which he has demonstrated his point, is a particularly hard one. It follows that I can hardly find a moment for my religious studies except on the Sabbath. Nor can I make any progress with the other sciences. This predicament causes me great sorrow.

(1192) My heart is pained in your pain, dear friend Joseph, but you will please me better by actively propagating to men what is true than by setting yourself as my champion against the untrue. Teach, do not recriminate. Remember that you have injured this man, that his revenues are at stake. Shall such a man, being stricken, not cry? He concerns himself with what the multitude holds highest. Leave him to his trivialities. What does he know of the soul and of philosophy? Remember he is old and occupies a position of dignity, and you are young and owe his age and position respect. You ask me as to your plan of opening a school in Baghdad in which you will teach the Law with my *Code* as the textbook. I have already sanctioned your proposal. Yet I fear two things. You will be constantly embroiled with these men. Or, if you assume the duty of teaching, you will neglect your own business affairs. I counsel you to take nothing from them. Better in my eyes is a single dirhem gained by you as a weaver, a tailor, or a carpenter, than a whole revenue enjoyed under the auspices of the Head of the Captivity.

(1199) My day is occupied in the following manner: I live in Fostat and the Sultan dwells in Cairo. These two palaces are two Sabbath days' journey (about one mile and a half) distant from each other. My duties to the Sultan are very heavy. I am obliged to visit him every day, early in the morning; and when he or any of his children, or any of the inmates of his harem, are indisposed. I dare not quit Cairo, but must stay during the greater part of the day in the palace. It also frequently happens that one or two of the royal officers fall sick, and I must attend to their healing.

Hence, as a rule, I repair to Cairo very early in the day, and even if nothing very unusual happens, I do not return to Fostat until the afternoon. Then I nearly perish of hunger. I find the antechambers filled with people, both Jews and gentiles, nobles and common people, judges and bailiffs, friends and foes—a mixed multitude, who await the time of my return.

I dismount from my animal, wash my hands, go forth to my patients, entreat them to bear with me while I partake of some slight refreshment, and the only meal I take in twenty-four hours. Then I attend to my patients, write prescriptions and give directions for their various ailments. Patients go in and out until nightfall, and sometimes even later.

I converse with and prescribe for them while lying down from sheer fatigue, and when night falls I am so exhausted that I can scarcely speak.

In consequence of this, no Israelite can have any private interview with me except on the Sabbath. On that day the whole congregation, or at least the majority of the members, come to me after the morning service when I instruct them as to their proceedings during the whole week; we study together a little until noon, when they depart. Some of them return, and read with me after the afternoon service until evening prayers. That is how I spend the Sabbath. I have here related to you only part of what you would see if you were to visit me.

EVERY MAN HIS OWN MESSIAH

ABRAHAM ABOULAFIA (1240-1292)

Some measure of the completeness with which the mystical passion took hold of Aboulafia's spirit is revealed in his serious attempt to convert Pope Nicholas III to Judaism. His family was one of the most distinguished in Spanish Jewry—it is still in existence in Palestine and elsewhere—and his incredible activities aroused the curiosity and animosity of his contemporaries. Especially did he leave his impress on the Kabbalah, creating a whole school of disciples. Aboulafia developed a system which had much in common with Indian Yoga. "His teachings can be put into effect by practically everyone who tries," writes Professor Scholem, the greatest living authority on Kabbalah. "That is probably one of the reasons why the kabbalists refrained from publishing them." He represented himself as the Messiah both to Christians and Jews. As a result of his own spiritual experiences and researches, he gave a new interpretation to the function of the Messiah, which he declared himself prepared to fulfil; but, as the following confessions indicate, it seems to have comprised the propagation of a method of individual spiritual regeneration rather than of political salvation. Aboulafia's account has been combined with that of an anonymous disciple who reflects the immense influence of the master.

✳ ✳ ✳

IT HAS been my purpose in all that I have written to reach that which I shall reveal to you herein. I was born at Saragossa in the Kingdom of Spain, where I dwelt until I was weaned, with my mother, brothers and sisters. I grew up on the Ebro, which is the river passing between Saragossa and Tudela; and I began to study Scriptures with commentaries and grammar with my father and teacher of blessed memory. In addition I learnt a little Mishna and a little Talmud with him; for most of what I learnt comes from him. But when I was eighteen years old he died.

I remained in Spain for two more years after the death of my father. Then when I was twenty years old, the spirit of the Lord roused me and set me on the move; and I went forth from there to the Land of Israel by land and sea; for it was my purpose to go to the River Sambatyon.* But I could go no further than Acre. So I departed by reason of the strife that increased between the Moslems and the Crusaders, and I returned through the Kingdom of Greece where I was married.

Then the spirit of the Lord roused me and I took my wife with me and set my face to reach my people. My desire was to learn Torah; and when I was in the city of Capua, five days' journey from Rome, I found a worthy man, wise, understanding, a philosopher and experienced physician. His name was Rabbi Hillel of blessed memory; and I made companionship with him, learning from him something of the science of philosophy. Straightway it became exceedingly sweet to me and I endeavored to achieve the knowledge of it with all my strength. I devoted myself to it by day and night; and my desire was not satisfied until I had studied Maimonides' *Guide to the Perplexed* many times. I also taught it in many places; to four students in Capua, but they took to bad courses, for they were young fellows without knowledge. At another place there were ten and not one of them succeeded. At Azriepo there were four, who also did not succeed; for views are very different among men, and all the more so as regards the depths of wisdom and the secrets of the Torah. I found not a single one among them who was worthy of being given even the chapter headings of the actual truth.

In Rome I taught the two elders, Rabbi Zedekiah and Rabbi Isaiah, my friends of blessed memory. They succeeded therein somewhat but passed away, for they were very old. In Barcelona there were two. One was old and went by the name of Rabbi Kalonymos of blessed memory, a great man; and the other was an intelligent and understanding and very worthy youth of good family, whose name was Rabbi Judah, known as Solomon, who succeeded therein very greatly. At Burgos there were two, a rabbi and a student. The rabbi's name was Moses Sianpo of blessed memory, a great, wise and worthy man; that of the student was Rabbi Shem Tob, also a fine and good lad, but his youth made him

---

* A mystical river that plays an important role in Jewish legendry. In an autobiographical letter, Eldad the Danite, a picturesque globe-trotter who flourished in the ninth century, writes, "Now the breadth of the Sambatyon River is two hundred cubits; the waters are glut with large and small stones and the noise they make sounds like a great storm and during the night the sound of it is heard a day's journey away. The river runs and the stones and sand rumble during the six weekdays, but it rests on the seventh day and is quiet until the close of the Sabbath."

unsuitable for the study, so that neither he nor his master learnt more from me than a few external traditions.

At Celi there were two, one of them Rabbi Samuel, the prophet, who received certain kabbalistic traditions from me, and the other Rabbi Joseph Gikitila (one of the leading kabbalists of the thirteenth century), who undoubtedly succeeded to a remarkable degree in what he learnt from me, and who added from his own knowledge and power; and the Lord was with him. And in this town, to be sure, where I am today, namely Messina, I found six men and I was the seventh. From me they learnt for a very short while, and each of them received from me as much as he could absorb, whether little or much. But they all parted from me with the exception of the first; and he is the first cause of all that each of his companions learnt from me. His name is Rabbi Saadiah bar Isaac Sinalmafi of blessed memory; he was followed by Rabbi Abraham ben Shalon, who was followed by his son Jacob, and he in turn by his friend Isaac, who was also followed by a friend of theirs. Three of them were of three grades of initiation, and three of lower grades of initiation. The name of the seventh was Rabbi Natronai, the Frenchman, of blessed memory, and the grades of initiation and revealed knowledge vanished at once, and he diverted it from them. The reasons for this were in the nature of their wills and temperaments; then there were some that were accidental and some that were inevitable.

Now when I was thirty-one years old, the Lord awakened me from my sleep in the city of Barcelona. I studied *The Book of Creation* (one of the earliest kabbalist or possibly pre-kabbalist works in Hebrew literature) with its commentaries; and the hand of the Lord was on me and I wrote a book that was wiser yet than those, and books of strange prophecies. My spirit became quick within me, and the spirit of the Lord reached my mouth and the Holy Spirit worked through me so that I manifested many dread and awful sights with signs and wonders. And on account of them jealous sprites gathered around me and I saw imaginary things and errors; and my ideas were confused because I found no man of my kind to teach me the way to go. Therefore I did grope like a blind man at noon for fifteen years, with Satan at my right hand to lead me astray; and I became crazed at the things my eyes saw, fifteen years ere the Lord, vouchsafed to me knowledge and counsel.

From the year 1281 to 1285 the Lord was with me to deliver me from all troubles. At the beginning of the year 1285 the Lord brought me into the Holy Temple (i.e., I became fully acquainted with the whole of mystic lore) and that was the time when I completed this book which

I wrote here at Messina for my precious, honorable, wise and understanding pupil, who longs to know the incorruptible Torah, namely, Saadiah, who is the first-mentioned of my seven disciples. I wrote the book because I do see that he loves me greatly and in order that it may serve as a memorial of what he learnt with me.

For forgetfulness is always present, and also I know that if he possesses the book, it will be useful to his companions aforementioned, for their understanding; likewise for those resembling them as concerns the greater part of what is written therein. And I know that were it not for the matter of false visions, the aforementioned would not have departed from me; and the false visions which were the cause of their departure were for me myself divine trials to make me aware of my qualities and to try me, in order at last to give light to the eyes of my heart.

For on account of them I guarded my mouth and tongue and restrained them from speech and my heart from purposeless thought. I returned unto the All-Present, who is worthy of such return; and I kept the covenant made, and I recognized and grasped what had been too much for me before this time. Therefore I praise the name of my God and the God of my fathers, who did not forsake His loving kindness and truth at any time, in whose mercies I trust. He set in my heart by His grace that which is too wondrous for me.

For it came into my mind, when I saw the happenings that were coming about in the world, to bring back the heart of the fathers to the sons, and hearts of the sons to the father (i.e. to act as the Messiah).

There is no doubt that among the Christians there are certain sages who know this secret. They spoke to me in secret and revealed to me that this was their opinion without any doubt. Thereupon I reckoned them likewise among the pious of the nations of the world. And there is no point in paying attention to the fools of any nation; for the doctrine is given only to those who know.

At thirty-nine, after having studied diligently the secrets of the Kabbalah for nine years, I wrote my first real prophetic book, which I entitled *The Book of the Righteous*. The year—5039 since the Creation, the place—Patras, Greece. A year later, under very trying circumstances, I came to write *The Book of Testimony*. I had been inspired by the Lord to go to Rome and there to convert Pope Nicholas III to Judaism. On the way I passed through Trani where I was beset by a band of ruffians who had been incited by malevolent Jews, and only through the intervention of God did I manage to escape them. Next I passed through Capua where I stayed long enough to compose *The Book of Life*.

Finally, in the month of Ab, ten years after having left Barcelona, I arrived in Rome.

My plans were to look up the Pope the day before Rosh Hashana, 1280. The Pontiff, however, who was then in Suriano, a day's distance from Rome, upon being informed of my coming, arranged for a stake to be erected near the inner gate of the town so as to be spared the inconvenience of an audience with me. When I heard of these solicitous preparations in my behalf, I retired to a lonely chamber where I beheld the most wondrous visions. It was then that I composed *The Book of Testimony,* a sacred confirmation of my constant alacrity to give my life for God's commandments, and of His promptitude in rescuing me from my enemies. I proceeded to Suriano. But just as I was passing through the outer gate a herald came running toward me and announced that the Pope had died suddenly during the preceding night. Returning to Rome two days later, I was seized by some Franciscan friars and imprisoned for twenty-eight days, being finally released on the first day of Heshvan.

Such have been the glorious miracles that the Lord has wrought with me and his faithful servants.

Know, friends, that from the beginning I felt a desire to study Torah and learned a little of it and of the rest of Scripture. But I found no one to guide me in the study of the Talmud, not so much because of the lack of teachers, but rather because of my longing for my home, and my love for father and mother. At last, however, God gave me strength to search for the Torah, and I went out and sought and found, and for several years I stayed abroad studying Talmud. But the flame of the Torah kept glowing within me, though without my realizing it.

I returned to my native land and God brought me together with a Jewish philosopher with whom I studied some of Maimonides' *Guide to the Perplexed* and this only added to my desire. I acquired a little of the science of logic and a little of natural science, and this was very sweet to me for, as you know, "nature attracts nature". And God is my witness: If I had not previously acquired strength of faith by what little I had learned of the Torah and the Talmud, the impulse to keep many of the religious commands would have left me, although the fire of pure intention was ablaze in my heart. But what this teacher communicated to me in the way of philosophy (on the meaning of the commandments) did not suffice me, until the Lord had me meet a godly man, a kabbalist who taught me the general outlines of the Kabbalah. Nevertheless, in consequence of my smattering of natural science, the way of Kabbalah seemed all but impossible to me. It was then that my teacher said to me:

"My son, why do you deny something you have not tried? Much rather would it befit you to make a trial of it. If you then should find that it is nothing to you—and if you are not perfect enough to find the fault with yourself—then you may say that there is nothing to it."

But, in order to make things sweet to me until my reason might accept them and I might penetrate into them with eagerness, he used always to make me grasp in a natural way everything in which he instructed me. I reasoned thus within myself: There can only be gain here and no loss. I shall see; if I find something in all of this that is sheer gain; and if not, that which I have already had will still be mine. So I gave in and he taught me the method of the permutations and combinations of letters and the mysticism of numbers and the other "Paths of the book of *Yetsirah*". In each path he had me wander for two weeks until each form had been engraven in my heart, and so he led me on for four months or so and then ordered me to "efface" everything.

He used to tell me: "My son, it is not the intention that you come to a stop with some finite or given form, even though it be of the highest order. Much rather is this the 'Path of the Names': The less understandable they are, the higher their order, until you arrive at the activity of a force which is no longer in your control, but rather your reason and your thought is in its control."

I replied: "If that be so (that all mental and sense images must be effaced), why then do you, Sir, compose books in which the methods of the natural scientists are coupled with instruction in the holy names?"

He answered: "For you and the likes of you among the followers of philosophy, to allure your human intellect through natural means, so that perhaps this attraction may cause you to arrive at the knowledge of the Holy Name."

And he produced books for me made up of (combinations of) letters and names and mystic numbers (*Gematrioth*), of which nobody will ever be able to understand anything for they are not composed in a way meant to be understood.

He said to me: "This is the (undefiled) 'Path of the Names'."

And indeed, I would see none of it as my reason did not accept it. He said: "It was very stupid of me to have them shown to you."

In short, after two months had elapsed and my thought had disengaged itself (from everything material) and I had become aware of strange phenomena occurring within me, I set myself the task at night of combining letters with one another and of pondering over them in philosophical meditation, a little different from the way I do now, and so I continued for three nights without telling him. The third night, after midnight, I nodded off a little, quill in hand and paper on my knees. Then I noticed that the candle was about to go out. I rose to put it right, as oftentimes happens to a person awake. Then I saw that the light continued. I was greatly astonished, as though, after close examination, I saw that it issued from myself. I said: "I do not believe it." I walked to and fro all through the house and, behold, the light is with me; I lay on a couch and covered myself up, and behold, the light is with me all the while. I said: "This is truly a great sign and a new phenomenon which I have perceived."

The next morning I communicated it to my teacher and I brought him the sheets which I had covered with combinations of letters.

He congratulated me and said: "My son, if you would devote yourself to combining Holy Names, still greater things would happen to you. And now, my son, admit that you are unable to bear not combining. Give half to this and half to that, that is, do combinations half of the night, and permutations half of the night."

I practiced this method for about a week. During the second week the power of meditation became so strong in me that I could not manage to write down the combinations of letters (which automatically spurted out of my pen), and if there had been ten people present they would not have been able to write down so many combinations as came to me during the influx. When I came to the night in which this power was conferred on me, and midnight—when this power especially expands and gains strength whereas the body weakens—had passed, I set out to take up the Great Name of God, consisting of seventy-two names, permuting and combining it. But when I had done this for a little while, behold, the letters took on in my eyes the shape of great mountains, strong trembling seized me and I could summon no strength, my hair stood on end, and it was as if I were not in this world. At once I fell down, for I no longer felt the least strength in any of my limbs. And behold, something resembling speech emerged from my heart and came to my lips and forced them to move. I thought—perhaps this is, God forbid, a spirit of madness that has entered into me? But behold, I saw it uttering wisdom. I said: "This is indeed the spirit of wisdom." After a little while my natural strength returned to me. I rose very much impaired and I still did not believe myself. Once more I took up the Name to do with it as before and, behold, it had exactly the same effect on me. Nevertheless I did not believe it until I had tried it four or five times. When I got up in the morning I told my teacher about it. He said to me: "And who was it that allowed you to touch the Name? Did I not tell you to permute only letters?" He spoke on: "What happened to you represents indeed a high stage among the prophetic degrees." He wanted to free me of it for he saw that my face had changed.

But I said to him: "In heaven's name, can you perhaps impart to me some power to enable me to bear this force emerging from my heart and to receive influx from it?" For I wanted to draw this force towards me and receive influx from it, for it much resembles a spring filling a great basin with water. If a man (not being properly prepared for it) should open the dam, he would be drowned in its waters and his soul would desert him.

He said to me: "My son, it is the Lord who must bestow such power upon you for such power is not within man's control."

That Sabbath night also the power was active in me in the same way. When, after two sleepless nights, I had passed day and night in meditating on the permutations or on the principles essential to a recognition of this true reality and to the annihilation of all extraneous thought—then I had two signs by which I knew that I was in the right receptive mood. The one sign was the intensification of natural thought on very profound objects of knowledge, a debility of the body and strengthening of the soul until I sat there, my self all soul. The second sign was that imagination grew strong within me and it seemed as though my forehead were going to burst. Then I knew that I was ready to receive the Name. I also that Sabbath night ventured at the great ineffable Name of God (the name JHWH). But immediately that I touched it, it weakened me and a voice issued from me saying: "Thou shalt surely die and not live! Who brought thee to touch the Great Name?" And behold, immediately I fell prone and implored the Lord God saying: "Lord of the universe! I entered into this place only for the sake of heaven, as Thy glory knowest. What is my sin and what my transgression? I entered only to know Thee, for has not David already commanded Solomon: Know the God of thy father and serve Him; and has not our master Moses, peace be upon him, revealed this to us in the Torah saying: Show me now Thy way, that I may know Thee, that I may there find grace in Thy sight?" And behold, I was still speaking and oil like the oil of the anointment anointed me from head to foot and very great joy seized me which for its spirituality and the sweetness of its rapture I cannot describe.

All this happened to your servant in his beginnings. And I do not, God forbid, relate this account from boastfulness in order to be thought great in the eyes of the mob, for I know full well that greatness with the mob is deficiency and inferiority with those searching for the true rank which differs from it in genus and in species as light from darkness.

Now, if some of our own philosophizers, sons of our people who feel themselves attracted towards the naturalistic way of knowledge and whose intellectual power in regard to the mysteries of the Torah is very weak, read this, they will laugh at me and say: See how he tries to attract our reason with windy talk and tales, with fanciful imaginations which have muddled his mind and which he takes at their face value because of his weak mental hold on natural science. Should, however, kabbalists see this, such as have some grasp of this subject or even better such as have had things divulged to them in experiences of their own, they will rejoice and my words will win their favor. But their difficulty will be that I have disclosed all of this in detail. Nevertheless, God is my witness that my intention is in *majorem dei gloriam* and I would wish that every single one of your holy nation were even more excellent herein and purer than I. Perhaps it would then be possible to reveal things of which I do not as yet know. . . . As for me, I cannot bear not to give generously to others what God has bestowed upon me. But since for this science there is no naturalistic evidence, its premises being as spiritual as are its inferences, I was forced to tell this story of the experience that befell me. Indeed, there is no proof in this science except experience itself. . . . That is why I say, to the man who contests this path, that I can give him an experimental proof, namely, my own evidence of the spiritual results of my own experiences in the science of letters according to *The Book of Creation*. I did not, to be sure, experience the corporeal (magic) effects (of such practices); and even granting the possibility of such a form of experience, I for my part want none of it, for it is an inferior form, especially when measured by the perfection which the soul can attain spiritually. Indeed, it seems to me that he who attempts to secure these (magic) effects desecrates God's name, and it is this that our teachers hint at when they say: Since license prevailed, the name of God has been taught only to the most reticent priests.

BY THE WATERS OF THE TAGUS

JUDAH ASHERI (1270-1349)

In this memoir the reader may gain an intimate picture of the personality and times of a luminary whose activities centered in Germany and Spain. His father, Asher ben Yehiel, and brother Jacob left an indelible imprint on talmudic literature and tradition, and he takes enormous pride in the family achievement. Despite his modest appraisal of his abilities, Judah was an ever busy, just, devout leader of his people; when his illustrious father died he was immediately elected in his place as rabbi of the important congregation of Toledo. He bemoans the need of accepting a salary, a measure that became a necessity in that period. This selfportrait is part of a long testament which he left for the guidance and inspiration of his family.

* * *

I WILL open with a voice of thanksgiving, I, Judah, to the Rock whose works are awe-inspiring, to whom appertain glory and greatness transcending man's capacity to express them; who, ere ever I was born, remembered me for good. My mother dreamed how she was told that she would bear a son, and was asked whether she wished him to be wise or wealthy? She chose wisdom. And though in reality dreams speak vain things, for I learned not wisdom, yet in a certain deceptive sense the dream was fulfilled. The world imagines that I am a scholar, one who giveth goodly words! Wealth, too, the Lord, blessed be He, hath bestowed upon me beyond the ordinary, in that He hath provided me with the measure of mine allotted bread. I rejoice in my portion.

When I was an infant about three months old, my eyes were affected, and were never completely restored. A certain woman tried to cure me when I was about three years of age, but she added to my blindness, to the extent that I remained for a year confined to the house, being unable to see the road on which to walk. Then a Jewess, a skilled oculist, appeared on the scene; she treated me for about two months, and then died.

Had she lived another month, I might have received my sight fully. As it was, but for the two months' attention from her, I might never have been able to see at all. Blessed be the Lord, who exercised marvelous loving-kindness toward me, and opened for me a lattice through which I might behold, with my own eye, the work of His hands.

I left Germany at the age of thirteen, and when fifteen I came to Toledo, in the new moon of Iyar in the year 1305. It is obvious that at my exodus when thirteen I possessed nothing; nor when I married first the daughter of R. Yehiel and later the daughter of R. Solomon, did I receive even enough to pay for the wedding garments and celebrations. From my lord, my father, of blessed memory, I inherited only a trifle as my share of his library. All that he owned at the time of his demise, together with all his household goods, did not suffice to carry out his testamentary bequests. Never in my life did I accept gifts from individuals, except about 1400 gold pieces which were given to me by three men, from whom I sought a loan but who insisted on making a gift. Because of their importance and position, I was unable to refuse their bounty. I used the money for my sister's marriage. I also lost money through those who transacted business for me, although that money was not my own. For 7000 gold pieces of borrowed capital were in the hands of my brother Eliakim, 8500 were deposited with R. Mordecai the Frenchman, who only returned to me 2000, 3000 were entrusted to R. Nissim, and the rest in the hands of others whom it would weary me to mention. I could not have survived till now but for the mercy of God, who put it in the heart of men to lend me capital, from the profits of which I maintained myself. For from the time of the death of my lord, my father, of blessed memory, that is to say for twenty-seven years and three months—I have not taken from the congregation (whom may God preserve!) under contract more than 1290 gold pieces. This I accepted for two years and four months, and I ceased to enter into any contract until the ten years mentioned were completed. Thereafter I received up to August (1340) from them 1500 pieces annually for nine years and ten months, a total of 14,750. Thenceforth they contracted to increase the annual payment to 3000 pieces. They agreed that after my death an annual pension of 1000 pieces should be paid for ten consecutive years to my wife and children or to any of them then living in Toledo. During my lifetime each of my sons was guaranteed 300 pieces a year for ten years, so long as he should pursue his studies and dwell in Toledo. A similar sum was appointed, under similar conditions, to be paid after my death to each of my sons out of the total of 1000 pieces mentioned above. I received from them from the August named to the end of November in this year 1348, for seven years and four months, 22,000 pieces. The total received by me from the congregation till the end of November has been 37,240 gold pieces. Of this sum, my son Solomon received, for two years and two months, 800 pieces in accordance with the arrangement already explained.

The contract which the congregation granted was not entered into because I demanded it of them (for I knew that I was unworthy of such consideration) but it was due to their abundant generosity and their affection for my lord, my father. But in the tenth year of my office, the congregation heard that it was my intention to seek a resting place elsewhere. They then fixed for me the payment of 1500 pieces annually. Had I been willing to accept more, they would have given it, as is expressly stated in their letter (which I still possess) of the year 1341. When the aforesaid Mordecai absconded I lost in his hand more than 6000, and it became known to the heads of the congregation that I designed emigrating to Seville. They besought me to remain, and they increased the sum payable under the contract to 3000 gold pieces a year. I am aware that all this was not due to my own deserts. It was due to the bounty of the Merciful One, the faithful God, and to the merit of my fathers, the repairers of the breach, the holy ones who were in the earth.

He who searcheth hearts knoweth that all my yearning desire for children in this world was solely dictated by my wish to raise up offspring which should fill my father's place in the study of the Law, in good works, and in the service of God. And in this sense I besought Him who is enthroned o'er the Cherubim, entreating God for myself, my children, and all our generations after us, that we may dwell in the house of the Lord all the days of our life, to behold the graciousness of the Lord and to pass our time in the inner shrine of His Law from morn to eve and from eve to morn, in the precious presence of God. I prayed that He would keep us far from men of vanity and frivolity, that we might maintain the example of our fathers, who, as our tradition assures us, were for many generations before us men of learning, of right-doing, and God-fearers—men from whom the Torah went forth unto Israel. And this has been my constant prayer at the graves of the righteous and perfect: "Lord of the Universe, King that sittest on the throne of mercy! It is revealed and known before Thee that all my desire for children was not out of my love for them, nor to gain honor through them, but only to perform that duty of continuing the race which Thou hast ordained. May it be Thy will to order us in all our affairs in good counsel before Thee. O may the fear of Thee be with us that we sin not, and may we live in Thy presence in reverence. Grant unto me sons who may grow into maturity, and may fill my father's place. And may God in His mercy raise up for us the merit of the righteous one buried in this grave. May my prayer be heard here, and may He too pray on our behalf, blessing us continually and at all hours."

One of the good methods which I desired for maintaining the family record was the marriage of my sons to members of my father's house. I had many reasons for this. First, it is a fair and fit thing to join fruit of vine to fruit of vine. It is indeed an important duty, for as our Sages said: "He who loves his relatives, he who marries his sister's daughter, and he who lends to the poor in the hour of his distress—to him applies the text. 'Then shalt thou call, and the Lord will answer; thou shalt cry and He will say, Here I am.' " Furthermore, the women of our family have grown accustomed to the ways of students, and the love of the Torah has entered their hearts, so that they are a help to their husbands in their scholarly pursuits. Moreover, they are not used to extravagant expenditure; they do not demand luxuries, the provision of which disturbs a man from his study. Then again, children for the most part resemble the mother's family. Finally, if with changing times a man see fit to seek his livelihood in another city, there will be none to place obstacles in the way of the wife accompanying her husband.

The second plan is for me to write something of the history of my saintly progenitors, for the edification of those that come after us. Seeing that the Lord, blessed be He, brought us to Toledo, that great and renowned city, and that a little later the Jews were expelled from France, possibly some may think that we were among the exiles, or that we left our country in consequence of some whispered suspicion. Therefore, it seems desirable to me to disabuse everyone of such an imputation. And further, when our posterity regards the upright lives of our ancestors, they will be ashamed if they walk not in the same paths. Rather will they strive in all things to imitate their fathers, thus finding grace and good favor in the sight of God and man. Otherwise, better were it for them never to be born, like infants who never see the light. As I left Germany when about thirteen years of age, I did not acquire exact information as to our fathers' righteous lives, except the little which I heard from my lord, my father of blessed memory, and from his sister and my grandmother, who related to me some of the family history. What little I heard of the doings of our first ancestors I set down here.

My grandfather, R. Yehiel ben Asher, was born in the year 1210.

When he was ten years old he had a firm friend in R. Solomon ha-Kohen. They entered into a pact that each should share the other's rewards, whether religious or secular. They held to this agreement all their days, and were unique in their generation for saintliness and benevolence. Now on the eve of the Day of Atonement in the year 1264, early in the night, the candle of my grandfather went out in the synagogue. For it was customary in Germany to kindle a wax candle for every male in the synagogue, on the eve of the Fast, and the candle was of a size to burn the whole day and night. Later (during the middle days of Tabernacles) my grandfather died and great honor was shown unto him at his death, people from neighboring places attending his funeral. Now it is the practice in Germany to set the coffin on a stone appointed for the purpose near the cemetery, and to open it to see whether the body has been dislocated by the jolting of the coffin. When they did this to him, R. Solomon ha-Kohen approached up to four cubits, and said in the presence of the assembly, "In your presence I call upon him to remember our covenant." Within the coffin a look of joy lit his face, most of those present saw him smile, and I testify on the evidence of my father and grandmother that this happened. A day came when R. Solomon ha-Kohen was studying in his college in the daytime, and lo! my grandfather of blessed memory was seated by his side. Amazed, R. Solomon asked how he fared, and he answered, exceeding well, and that a seat was ready at his side for his friend. "I wonder", said R. Solomon, "that thou art permitted to be visible to mortals." He answered: "I have liberty to go to my house as of aforetime, but I am unwilling that they should say: How this saint prides it over the other righteous men!" Six months after his death, at midnight on the Sabbath night, he appeared to his wife and said: "Haste and rise, take thy sons and daughters, and remove them hence, for tomorrow all the Jews of this place will be slain. So was it decreed against the whole neighborhood, but we prayed and our petition was successful except as regards this place." She rose and obeyed, but returning to save her belongings, she was killed with the congregation. She had previously rescued my lord, my father, R. Asher of blessed memory, and his brother, R. Hayyim, fellow disciple of R. Meir of Rothenburg, teacher of my father. They had another brother, by name R. Eleazar, who died at the age of twenty-seven. He was reported to be as fine a scholar as his brother R. Hayyim. They had six sisters, the whole family saintly—all bearing deservedly high reputations among their contemporaries. The nine of them escaped on the day and under the circumstances narrated above. All of them had large families of sons and daughters, and I have heard that one of the sons of my uncle R. Hayyim, of blessed memory, married in Germany, and that there were at his wedding about five hundred men and women, all relatives, the relationship reaching to that of third cousins.

The cause of my father's departure from Germany was due to the imprisonment of Rabbi Meir of Rothenburg, of blessed memory. Count Meinhard of Goiz, then head of the government, arrested him, and the congregation of Germany ransomed him for a considerable sum. The governor refused to accept as guarantor any other person than my lord, my father, of blessed memory. He was compelled to become security for a large amount. But before the contributions were apportioned to the various congregations, Rabbi Meir died in prison. The Governor unjustly refused to admit my father's plea that as Rabbi Meir died before his release, the guarantee had lapsed. Payment was still demanded from my father and the congregation, and my father escaped to another city; he left Germany altogether because of his fear of the authorities, and settled in the great city of Toledo. In the first year of his residence there, they sent him a written communication from the town council of the place where he formerly lived, inviting him to return home. They would dispatch fifty officers to meet him on the German frontier, and would give him a documentary safe-conduct from the Emperor. For they recognized his wisdom and excellence, and were wont to follow his advice in all matters. But in face of the frequent ill-treatment of the Jews there, he was unwilling to go back. This was the reason of the coming of my lord, my father of blessed memory, to this country. "This was the Lord's doing," to the end that my father might raise up many disciples on Spanish soil. "He executed the righteousness of the Lord, and His ordinances with Israel." For there were not in these lands any thorough commentaries. He also wrote commentaries and decisions to the Talmud. Wherever his commentaries, responsa and decisions reached, they made known the statutes of the Lord and His laws. His sons walked in his ways, and maintained his opinions. "As for Asher, his bread was fat;" his Rock guarded him with every care, because he was faithful to its charge. "And of Asher he said: blessed be Asher because of his sons"—all of them were interpreters of uprightness, who from the least to the greatest of them held fast to the law of God, the Lord of the Universe, and by what they wrought were a shield to their generation. I was by far the most insignificant of all of them; through His grace God raised me up in my father's place, a tendril of his stock, a shooting of his roots and planting, to maintain his School on its site, even better equipped than of yore. And also in what pertained to the affairs and organization of the community, we passed our time together in settlement of causes and judgments. Men of the government also agreed to abide by my decisions, not because of my wisdom or wit, for "I am brutish, unlike a man, and have not a man's understanding," but God filled them with a kindly disposition towards me, so that my words were acceptable to them, in that they deemed me in their thoughts an impartial judge.

As for me, my prayer is made before the Lord of the Universe, that He may requite with a good recompense this holy congregation for their labors, and for all the good which they as a body and as individuals have done unto me in granting all my requests and of their heart's generosity and not for any selfish motive. And so will it ever continue until I part from them in great love, "and my seed shall be established in their sight, and my offspring before their eyes." And may it be their good will to prepare a way for my progeny to settle among them as they did with my father and me, kindness after kindness. For what has passed and for what is to come, unto the Rock tremendous in His doing, Judah shall lead the thanksgiving. And may the bounty of God and the merit of our fathers cause that there never fail from us in Toledo—until the majestic and awful God establish Jerusalem and a Redeemer come unto Zion— one to fill the seat of my lord, my father, R. Asher of beloved memory; (may this be so) for all time until Shiloh cometh and people be gathered unto him, and there arise a priest with Urim and with Thummim.

Ended and completed, praise to the God of the Universe!

CASTILIAN VIGNETTE

MENAHEM BEN ZERAH (?-1385)

Menahem was an eyewitness to epoch-making events in France and Spain during the fourteenth century. Born into a family of scholars, he steadfastly continued his studious life despite the ravages of war, pestilence and want. This brief succinct account of his life, written in a preface to a book to explain its purpose, indicates how talmudic scholarship flourished even in chaotic times. He was typical of many modest, self-sacrificing scholars of the Middle Ages, whose industry and courage made possible the unbroken continuity of religious and social tradition.

❊ ❊ ❊

I MENAHEM BEN AARON BEN ZERAH, the humblest of my family, was born in the land of Navarre. My noble father was among those who were driven from France in the month of Ab in the year 5066 of the Creation (1306).* When I was about sixteen years old, I married a daughter of Rabbi Benjamin Abetz, may his soul rest in Eden. He spread the study of Torah in Etoile, and many of his students were of the house of Askra, a family distinguished for learning and wealth.

Now in the year 1322 the wrath of the Lord was kindled against His people. The King of France (Philip V, 1316-1322) who ruled over Navarre died, and the populace arose and decided to destroy, murder and devastate all the Jews in their realm. In Etoile and in other places of the land, they killed about six thousand Jews. My father, my mother and four younger brothers suffered martyrs' deaths for the sanctification

---

* This happened during the reign of Louis X who issued the decree of expulsion on June 21st. The crown seized both real and personal property of the Jews and permitted them a month to leave the country. Although they were recalled in 1315, this vandalism marked the beginning of the decline of French Jewry. Esthori Pharhi, who was studying at Montpellier at the time, left a brief account of his experience, "They yanked me out of the schoolroom," he wrote, "they stripped me of my very shirt. Naked, I left my father's house and my native land; I wandered as a mere lad from nation to nation without a knowledge of their tongues until I finally found peace in the Holy Land."

of God—may He avenge their blood! I alone, of my father's house, escaped —stricken, smitten of God, and afflicted. For twenty-five mobsters smote me mercilessly; I was thrown among the dead where I lay from evening till midnight on the 23rd of the month of Adar. At midnight, a certain knight who knew my father came and had mercy upon me. He took me from the dead and carried me to his house. When the Healer, may He be blessed, undeservedly healed my wounds, I decided to go to Toledo to study Torah.

Then a new King arose over Navarre (Charles IV, 1322-1328), and the children of those who had been slain complained to him of the oppression, asking that he punish those who had spilt the blood of our fathers. But he did not heed our request.

In those days I studied for about two years with my master, Rabbi Joshua ben Shoab, may he rest in Eden. Afterwards, I came to this land (Spain) in the year 1331. I dwelt in Alcala and studied there with Rabbi Joseph ibn Alayish, may he rest in Eden. He and I used to study continually, day and night: it was our custom to start a treatise of the Talmud from the beginning and read the entire text with the *Supplements* of Rabbi Perez. After his death in 1360, the leaders of the community asked me to teach in his place, and, although I was unworthy of this honor, I did as they requested.

While Rabbi Joseph ibn Alayish was still alive, I also studied in Toledo with my master, Rabbi Judah,* may he rest in Eden. We examined two sections of the Talmud—Seder Zeraim (Seeds) and Seder Toharoth (Purifications) according to the system of the Rosh, and I investigated with him the variant readings of the texts of Seder Moed (Festivals), Seder Nezikim (Damages) and the Gemara of Gittin (Divorce) arranging them in accordance with his interpretation. Between 1350 and 1368 I studied uninterruptedly with my associates and friends in Alcala, our studies being chiefly according to the method of our master, Rabbi Perez.

And it came to pass that the Lord awakened the spirit of Don Henry,** son of King Alfonso. He fought with his brother Don Pedro who ruled after the death of his father. He besieged the fortified cities and captured them. In the month of Iyar, 1368, he besieged Toledo. And it happened that at the end of that year Don Pedro went forth from

---

* Judah Asheri who in 1328 succeeded his father, Asher ben Yehiel (referred to as the "Rosh") as Rabbi of Toledo. See Judah's *vita*, pp. 30-36.

** This paragraph refers to the struggle between Pedro the Cruel (1350-1369) and Henry de Trastamond II (1369-1379).

Seville with his entire army to fight against his brother and to rescue Toledo from the siege; and the King, Don Henry, marched out to meet him and slew him in the city of Montilla. Thereupon the kingdom was secure in the hands of King Henry and his power was greatly strengthened.

Now, during this period of war the whole earth was chaotic and everyone did as he pleased. The populace pillaged and robbed most of the communities of Spain and pauperized Israel. It was a time of distress for Jews who dwelt throughout the kingdom of Castile, without parallel since the time they were exiled there. They died by the sword and were carried away as captive slaves. The holy community of Toledo suffered so severely during the siege that they ate the flesh of their sons and daughters. About eight thousand souls, young and old, died during the siege from hunger and dire want. And so heavily were they taxed by the King that hardly a crumb remained to an inhabitant. I, too, was completely bereft of all that I had; they despoiled, robbed and smote me. They took the clothes off my back and left me nothing of all my labor. Gone my books, my home, my land!

Then, with the aid of the eminent Don Samuel Abarbanel of Seville, may God watch over him, I was revived and enabled to support my old age. He helped me to extricate myself from the destruction, and I went to live in Toledo where some of the notables who survived and knew me before entreated me to remain. So I consented to stay with them, may the Lord of Hosts have mercy upon the remnant of our people. They gave me, as well as my companion scholars, our allotted bread.

All the good which the eminent Don Samuel did for me, I remembered. I found him an intelligent man, fond of learned men whom he fed and to whom he was devoted. Even though the times gave him no peace, he longed to study the works of authors. And I saw that those who served in the courtyard of the King, may his glory be exalted, those who, in accordance with their excellency and station, were the shield and refuge of their people, tended to neglect the observance of the obligatory commandments (prayer, blessings, Sabbath, festivals and the like) because of the great unrest and the lust for privilege. For this reason and on account of my love for Don Samuel, may God watch over him, I followed the footsteps of our teachers and sages: I sharpened my quill, I entered into privacy and composed a book which I called *Provender for the Journey*. And I completed the work in the hope of the coming of the Messiah and of a portion in the World To Come.

ADVENTURE IN THE HOLY LAND

MESHULLAM BEN MENAHEM (FIFTEENTH CENTURY)

The traveler, the merchant and the pilgrim are among the most typical and most interesting of wandering Jews. From the patriarchs, A'braham and Joseph, to modern globe-trotters like Arminius Vambéry and Louis Golding, they have given to Jewish literature a strong aroma of the caravansary. Meshullam was a merchant of Volterra, Italy, who knew his way around in the fifteenth century, and left us a graphic account of a trip to the Levant in 1481. At Palermo he chanced upon Rabbi Obadiah of Bertinoro, a notable whom he accompanied through the Archipelago. But he also met with mishaps and adventures which he describes warmly and in detail. Admirers of Mark Twain's *Innocents Abroad* will recognize the same Holy Land in this tale out of Meshullam's letter, recording the cleverness with which he outwitted both cutthroats and customs.

❊ ❊ ❊

WE LEFT Hebron on Tuesday, the 28th cf July, 1481, and traveled in the company of two good and honored mamelukes, inasmuch as caravans of Christian merchants pass only occasionally between Hebron and Jerusalem. Thus we were obliged to accompany these two men and with them there was a bastard whose intention was to kill us. His name is Ali and he was a Moslem. We went with him and took our lives in our hands.

At nightfall we reached a village called Halibi, and Ali went into the village and persuaded three of his companions to rob us on the journey. Then that Ali came to us and spoke deceitfully. He said that we should accompany him and the two mamelukes and he would take us by an indirect road so that we should not have to pay tolls until we reached Jerusalem. The mamelukes believed him and so did we. We journeyed forth at midnight and he led us in a circle to a place ten miles from Hebron, where there was a house in ruins and a cave where Jesse, the father of David, was buried (they say that this cave reaches to the cave of Machpelah). And the cursed fellow led us by ways which nobody had passed before into a great wood on the hills, and when we reached the middle of the woods the cursed Ali said, "I now want the two ducats which you have promised me." My companion, the drago- man, replied, "We promised you only one golden ducat. Anyhow, we shall give you what you want when we reach Jerusalem. Now you may have half a ducat because we have no more." But he wanted to see our money and therefore made excuses.

He had a bow and arrows and was riding on a fine horse, a jennet, and he left us, went into the woods and called aloud. When the mame- lukes saw this they went after him and appealed to his heart. And Joseph, the dragoman, into whose mouth God had put the words, said to them, "Know that if this man does any wrong to us or kills us you will not escape for the Jews will know of it. We went with the Niepo, the Lord of Hebron, from his city and they will seek us through him and he knows that we went with you. What will you reply when the Niepo seeks us at your hands?" The good mamelukes who did not intend to harm us replied, "By our lives, we will kill him."

Now they also had bows and arrows and they went after the man and brought him back. And Joseph, the dragoman, went after them in stealth in order to listen to their conversation, and I and Raphael, my companion, were left alone in the woods. The dragoman heard Ali say, "Let me do this. I have three companions with whom I spoke last night in Halibi, and we will kill them and take their horses and all their possessions and divide it equally, because they are very rich. Who will seek them at our hands?" Then the mamelukes replied, "Do not think so for it is our duty to protect them. The Lord, the Niepo of Hebron, has entrusted them to us and we must account for them." Then Ali answered, "Tell the Niepo that you left them near Jerusalem or that the Orbanites slew them, and that you fled with their good horses and they pursued you, because they recognized that you were mamelukes, and you were not able to save them and are guiltless." All this Joseph heard when he went behind them in order to find out whether the mamelukes would consent after all the talk. When the mamelukes saw that Ali would not listen to them they said to him, "Choose one of two things: Either die here, for we will slay you, or come with us. We do not wish to call your companions because the responsibility for this rests upon us. If you come with us, we swear by the Life of our King that we will not betray your secret to anybody." And that is why he returned against his will.

Now the mamelukes said to us, "Let us go in front with this cursed fellow and you follow behind, near to us." Then there was much talk between them, and the mamelukes placed him between them so that he could not flee. And in this way we traveled at night by the light of the moon until dawn. When Ali saw that it was dawn he said to the mamelukes, "I wish to leave my horse here in the village." He was afraid to enter Jerusalem for fear that the mamelukes would betray him to the Emir of Jerusalem. So he disappeared.

And we hastened to Bethlehem and from there on the high road we found Rachel's tomb. It is a high monument of stones and the Moslems have erected above her grave an arch resting upon four pillars. They honor her, and both Jews and Moslems pray there. God protected us from the hands of that betrayer and robber, and we gave a ducat to each of the mamelukes instead of the villain; anyhow, we paid no tax because of the roundabout journey we made, for there are seven toll-houses between Hebron and Jerusalem.

On the same day we arrived in Jerusalem, the Holy City, in peace, thanks be to the Lord, who sent us those two mamelukes to save us from death. On the way we found at the Well of the Virgin more than ten thousand men who were proceeding against the Orbanites and none could go out and none could come in. You see, therefore, that if we had delayed a single day we should not have been able to get through and should have been in great danger. Blessed be He and blessed be His Name, Who doeth good to the undeserving.

TWILIGHT OF SPANISH GLORY

DON ISAAC ABRAVANEL (1437-1509)

Born in Lisbon of a distinguished family and the father of the poet Judah Leo Medigo and the scholar-diplomat Samuel Abravanel, Don Isaac played a great role during stirring times. He served as finance minister to the kings of Portugal, Spain, and Naples successively, and in each instance was rewarded with confiscation of his possessions and exile. What he experienced during the tragic destruction of Spanish Jewry and the expulsion of 1492 is touchingly described in his reminiscences. An interesting sidelight is provided in the diary of Columbus who incidentally was assisted by many Jews. "In the same month during which their Majesties decreed that all Jews should be driven out of the Kingdom and its territories," the diary begins, "they gave me the commission to undertake with sufficient men my expedition of discovery to the Indies." Abravanel was a prolific author, composing expansive commentaries on the Bible and eloquent speculations on the messianic salvation of his people.

❋ ❋ ❋

I ISAAC ABRAVANEL, am the son of that prince in Israel, Judah the son of Samuel ben Judah ben Joseph ben Judah of the house of Abravanel. All of my forebears, descended from King David, son of Jesse of Bethlehem, were worthy leaders of our people. May their memory be forever blessed.

I lived in the beautiful city of Lisbon, capital of the realm of Portugal, secure in the wealth of my family inheritance. My home was filled with God's blessings. I enjoyed honor, riches, and the joy of my fellow men. I builded myself a spacious home and made it a gathering place for the wise, a hall of justice and learning. How happy I was at the palace of King Alphonso V, who ruled justly over a realm that touched two seas, who prospered in all that he did! His throne was a veritable seat of justice and a wellspring of righteousness, for he trusted in the Almighty, eschewed evil, and ruled his people well. He was wise in his choice of leaders. Richly did he eat of the Tree of Knowledge, but the fullness of the Tree of Life the Lord did not grant him. In his power and prosperity were the safety and freedom of the Jews. Under his shadow I delighted to sit; I was near unto him and he delighted in me; so long as he lived I was in attendance at his palace.

Then came an evil day for all the people and especially Israel—a day of darkness, lamentation and oppression. Death quickly mounted his windows and terror gripped his palace. She filled the halls, grasped the knife to slay her son, and slew him as the divine sentence decreed. Thus a spirit passed and went unto his God even as the chaff blows from the threshing floor. And the Daughter of Zion was left as a booth in the vineyard without a support; her being departed with his soul. The people hungered and mourned, and great was the lamentation in the House of Judah. I too suffered woefully in my mourning; like Job, my soul was poured out within me and I became as dust and ashes.

In his place ruled his son Don Juan II (1481-1495), who knew not the greatness and wisdom of his father. His perverted heart hated the princes and deceived all who served him. He estranged himself from all those who had loved his father, nobles of the highest lineage throughout the realm as well as his own flesh and bone. "All of you are worthy of death," he said deceitfully. "You have conspired to surrender me and my country to the kings of Spain." He seized one of the greatest and most trustworthy nobles, Ferdinand, Duke of Braganza, who was second in rank to the King, and had him executed. (This occurred in 1483.) His brothers, seeing that the pride and glory of their family was dead and fearing for their lives, fled in haste and disappeared. The King confiscated their estates and possessions, and blotted out their whole royal house.

The King was also incensed with me because I would not be a party to deceit and oppression. He vented his wrath against me because in the good old days I had been a bosom friend of the princes who had fled and they had sought my counsel. The nobles of the country also made severe charges against me, accusing me of being one of the conspirators. They declared that the conspirators would certainly not have kept their secret from me. Other wicked men, desiring to overthrow me and seize my possessions, sharpened their tongues like serpents and attributed to me wickedness that could not even enter my mind.

In the midst of the turmoil, evil couriers brought me the following message, "The King commands that you appear before him at once." I obeyed, and innocently proceeded to the appointed place of meeting.

While stopping on the way at an inn, a certain man approached me. "Go not near that place of meeting," he warned. "These are evil times. Save yourself. Fear has gripped the country; ugly rumors are rife; your enemies have made a death-pact against you." I saw that the world was topsyturvy, that truth and kindness were driven underground and the fear of God was no more. I meditated: Whither shall I go? I know how greedy these men are for gain and how ready to plunder and rob. Who will stay the anger of the King and the lust of his henchmen? Who will say to him: What in the world are you doing? Of what use is gold and silver? They will pursue and destroy me. Even if I managed to survive, I would be mercilessly oppressed all the time. Consequently I abandoned my inheritance, my wife and children, and all that I possessed, and I escaped alone. I arose in the night and took to the road; I put on strength in the face of misfortune and fled. Suddenly my fate became as the chaff that the storm stealeth away. I was deprived of my all as a result of a ban and I escaped by the skin of my teeth. When the sun shone forth the next morning, I heard the tumult of Pharaoh's House; couriers pressed forward with the King's command to seize and kill me. At the same time the royal troops and cavalry pursued me all that day and night through the wilderness.

Through God's compassion, they were unable to harm me. At midnight I left that Egypt, the kingdom of Portugal, and entered the kingdom of Castile by way of the border town of Segura della Orden. I went the way the Lord sent me; when the King saw that he could not lay hands on me, he fumed and raged and took all that I possessed—silver, gold, princely treasures and estates. Out of the bowels of the netherworld I cried out: "Save me, O King! What good can come of your oppression? Is not the Judge of the world just? Why do you act evilly toward your servant? Why do you strive against me and persecute me? Why does not my lord test me?" But he was as silent as an adder; his ears were stopped. I look for justice but behold violence; for righteousness, but behold a cry.

So I escaped alone to the Kingdom of Castile from the sword of my oppressor. I came there as a sojourner, and in order to pay my debt to God for saving me, I turned my attention to an investigation of the Scriptures. I made notes on the books of Joshua, Judges, and Samuel. This took place in the year 1484. As I intended to begin a commentary on the books of Kings, I was summoned before Ferdinand, King of Spain, the mightiest of the kings of the earth, who ruled the kingdoms of Castile, Aragon, Catalonia, Sicily, and other Mediterranean islands. I went to the court of the King and the Queen, and for a long time I served them, finding grace in their eyes and in the eyes of the first princes of the realm. I was in their service for eight years, being blessed with wealth and honor. But as a result of my heavy duties to the King, my literary efforts slackened, and I abandoned my inheritance from the Kings of Israel and Judah for the King of Aragon and Castile.

In 1492 the King of Spain seized the great city of Granada,* together with the whole kingdom. His haughtiness brought a change of character; his power led him to sin against his God. He thought to himself: "How can I better show my gratitude to my God, Who gave victory to my army and put this city into my power, than by bringing under His wing the scattered flock of Israel that walks in darkness? How shall I better serve Him than to bring back to His faith the apostate daughter? Or, if they remain stiffnecked, to drive them to another land so that they will not dwell here nor be seen in my presence?" Consequently the King enacted a decree as fixed as the law of the Medes and the Persians. He commanded that the children of Israel could remain in the country only if they submitted to baptism; but if they were unwilling to embrace Christian faith, they must leave the territories of Spain, Sicily, Majorca, and Sardinia. "Within three months," he decreed,** "there must not remain in my kingdoms a single Jew."

I was at court when the decree was proclaimed. I was disconsolate with grief. Thrice I addressed the King, imploring his mercy: "O King, save your loyal subjects. Why do you act so cruelly toward us? We have prospered in this land and we would gladly give all we possess for our country." I begged my noble friends at court to intercede for my people. The King's most trusted counsellors pleaded desperately that he revoke the decree and turn from his design to destroy the Jews. But his ears were closed as though he were stone deaf.*** The Queen, seated at his right, opposed revoking the decree; she pressed him to complete the task he had begun. Our exertions were therefore without effect. Despite the fact that I neither rested nor relaxed, the thunderbolt struck.

When the dreadful news reached the people, they mourned their fate; and wherever the report of the decree spread, Jews wept bitterly.

* With the capture of that magnificent city passed the last foothold of Moslem power in Spain. Ferdinand and Isabella erected a large cross in the Alhambra on January 2nd.

** The decree was issued in Granada on March 31, making June 31 the *terminus ad quem*.

*** It is reported that the King, persuaded by a delegation headed by the author promising a payment of 300,000 ducats, was on the point of revoking the decree when Torquemada, the notorious Inquisitor, appeared on the scene and declared, "Judas Iscariot sold his Master for 30 pieces of silver. You want to sell him for 300,000 ducats. Here He is—take Him and sell Him!" The decree became irrevocable.

The terror and lamentation were greater than at any time since the expulsion of our forefathers from their own soil in Judah to foreign strands. However, they bravely encouraged each other: "Let us cling unflinchingly to our faith, holding our heads with pride before the voice of the enemy that taunts and blasphemes. If they let us live, we will live; if they kill us, we will perish. But we will not break our Divine Covenant nor shall we turn back. We will go forth in the name of the Lord our God."

In this spirit the people, old and young, women and children, a multitude of 300,000 from every province, went forth on one day, unarmed and afoot. I was among them. They went whithersoever the wind carried them. Some fled to the kingdom of Portugal, others to the kingdom of Navarre. Many chose the way of the sea and were lost, drowned, burnt to death, and sold into slavery. They suffered the curses written in our Scriptures: "The Lord will cause thee to be smitten before thine enemies; thou shalt flee seven ways before them; thou shalt be a horror to all the kingdoms of the earth." (Deuteronomy 28:25) Of this vast host, only a small number survived. Blessed be the name of the Lord!

I, too, chose the path of my people, departing on a seagoing vessel. I went into exile with my whole family and came to this glorious city of Naples, whose kings are merciful. Thereupon I decided to pay my vow to God by setting upon the task of writing a commentary on the books of Kings. It was a time to recall the destruction of our Holy Temple and the Exile of our people, which are recorded in these books. It was a time to remember our glories and our misfortunes.

THE ROAD TO ROME

DAVID REUBENI (?-1537)

Reubeni was a fabulous figure in a fabulous century. He was called Messiah, kabbalist, prophet and impostor—some modern historians cling to the last—but, in his own words, "I am a sinner and a man of war". He was a combined Herzl and Jabotinsky of the sixteenth century. Claiming that he was the brother, generalissimo and emissary of King Joseph of Habor (north of Medina in Arabia) who commissioned him to interest the Pope and the monarchs of Spain and Portugal in raising an armed force to recapture Palestine from the Turks, he traveled from Arabia via Egypt and the Mediterranean between 1522 and 1525. The following excerpt from his diary describes the journey to the gates of Rome. He was then accorded the status of an ambassador by Pope Clement, King John of Portugal and Charles V, and for a time enjoyed diplomatic triumphs, but in 1537 he was imprisoned by Charles and died there. The last years of his life were closely tied to the activities of a Marrano disciple, Solomon Molko, whose story is told in the next selection.

❊ ❊ ❊

I AM David, the son of King Solomon (may the memory of the righteous be for a blessing), and my brother is King Joseph, who is older than I, and who sits on the throne of his kingdom in the wilderness of Habor (Khorgbar), and rules over thirty myriads of the tribe of Gad and of the tribe of Reuben and of the half-tribe of Manesseh. I have journeyed from before the King, my brother and his counsellors, the seventy Elders. They charged me to go first to Rome to the presence of the Pope, may his glory be exalted.

I left them by way of the hills, ten days' journey, till I arrived at Jeddah, where I was taken with a great sickness and remained five weeks, until I heard that a ship was going to the land of Ethiopia. I embarked on the ship in the Red Sea and went three days, and on the fourth day we arrived at the city of Suakim, in Ethiopia. I took a house and stayed there two months, but I was ill, and being cupped lost fifty pounds of blood; for in order to get better I had more than one hundred applications of hot nails. Afterwards I met many merchants who were traveling by way of Mecca to the kingdom of Sheba, and I called the chief of them, a descendant of the Prophet of the Ishmaelites named Omar Abu Kamil. I took two camels to journey with them, and they were a great multitude with more than three thousand camels. I improved in health daily, and we passed through great deserts and forests and fields in which there are many good herbs and good pasturage and rivers, a journey of two months, until we arrived at the capital of the kingdom of Sheba in Ethiopia, where resides King Omara, who dwells on the Nile. He is a black king and reigns over black and white, and the name of his city is Lamula, and I stayed with him ten months. The King travels in his countries, every month a different journey. I traveled with the King and had as my servants more than sixty men of the sons of the Prophet riding on horses, and they honored me with great honor.

All the time that I stayed in the country of Ethiopia with the King I fasted daily, when I lay down and when I got up, and I prayed day and night and I stayed not in the company of scoffers nor of merry-makers. On every journey they prepared for me a wooden hut near the King's house. The King has maidservants and menservants and slaves, most of them naked, and the Queen and the concubines and the ladies are dressed in golden bracelets, two on the hands and two on the legs; and they cover their nakedness with a golden chain, hand-embroidered, and a cubit wide round their loins closed before and behind. But their body is quite naked and bare, and they wear a golden wreath in their noses. The males and females eat elephants and wolves, leopards, dogs, and camels, and they eat human flesh. The King called me every day before him and said, "What askest thou of us, thou son of the Prophet; if thou desirest slaves, camels, or horses, take them." And I replied, "I want nothing of thee, but I have heard of the glory of thy kingdom and I have brought thee this gift with love and pleasure, and behold, I give thee a garment of silk and seven hundred ducats, florins of gold. I love thee and I grant thee pardon and forgiveness and a full title to paradise, to thee and to thy sons and daughters, and all thy household, and thou shalt come to us next year to the city of Mecca, the place for the atonement of sins." After these things an Ishmaelite came from the city of Mecca and slandered me before the King and said, "This man in whom thou believest is not of the sons of the Prophet, but from the wilderness of Habor." When the King heard this and sent for Abu Kamil and told him the words and the slander, Abu Kamil answered and said, "I know neither one man nor the other, but I have seen that the first man is honorable and fasts every day and fears God, and does not go after merriment nor after women and does not love money. But the other man loves money and does many evil things and talks a great deal"; and the King said, "Thy words are true," and Abu Kamil left him and told me these matters. After that the King's wife heard the words of the slanderer and sent for me and said to me, "Do not remain in this country for this new man who has come from Mecca has slandered thee to the King in words unfitting, and he is taking counsel with many men to seek from the King to slay thee." And I said to her, "How can I go away without the King's permission?" But the Queen replied, "The King comes tonight to my house and I will send for thee, and thou shalt come before me and before the King and thou shalt ask permission from the King, and I shall help thee and thou shalt go tomorrow on thy way in peace." So when I came before the King I burst forth and said, "What is my transgression, and what is my sin?" Have I not come before thee with gifts and love and kindness, and desired not to receive from thee, either silver or gold or slaves or maidservants or menservants; but this knave who has slandered me to thee loves money and speaks falsehood, and behold, I have been with thee ten months. Call thy servants and thy lords and let them tell thee if they have found in me any sin or transgression or any fault. Therefore, in thy kindness and for God's sake, give me permission to go on my way and I shall pray for thee and bless thee." And the Queen also said, "Give him permission that he may go on his way, for he is honorable and trusty and we have found no blemish in him, but only good report." And the King answered and said to me, "What needest thou, slaves, or camels, or horses? Take them and go in peace;" and I said to the King, "I want nothing but permission from thee that I may go tomorrow at dawn, for I know that I have wicked enemies against me; therefore may it be good in thy sight to send with me one of thy honored servants to the place of the house of Abu Kamil."

Then the King called one of his servants and ordered him to go with him and gave us two horses and we rode to the house of Abu Kamil, and on the way we crossed many rivers and the feeding ground of elephants. There was one river of mud and water in which horses, when crossing it, sank in the mire up to their bellies, and many men and horses had been drowned in this place. But we crossed it on horseback, and thanked God we were safe. We traveled eighteen days until we arrived at Senaar, and next morning I and my servant journeyed on further five days on the River Nile until I reached the city of Sheba, but it is in ruins and desolate, and there are wooden huts in it, and Abu Kamil came to me and said, "How art thou come from the King and he did not give thee slaves? I know that the King loves thee, therefore stay in my house and I will go up to the King and will beg him for thee;" and I said, "I will do so." But that night I dreamt in the house of Abu Kamil, and I saw my father, on whom be peace, and he said to me, "Why has thou come to this far land? Go hence tomorrow in peace and no evil will come upon thee, but if thou waitest until Abu Kamil returns, know that thou wilt die;" and when I woke from my sleep I said to Abu Kamil, "Let me go, I do not wish thee to go to the King for me," and in the morning I journeyed from Sheba, and Abu Kamil sent his brother with me, and we went ten days' journey to the kingdom of Elgel. Elgel is in the kingdom of Sheba and under the rule of Omara, and the name of the King of Elgel is Abu Akrab, and we came before him and Abu Kamil's brother said to him, "The King has ordered us to conduct this our lord, the son of the Prophet, by this way;" and I stayed before that King three days, and afterwards I journeyed on, I and my servant, till we came to Mount Takaki, and I stood before a great lord called Abd Alohab, and he wished me to go by way of a short desert to the land of Dongola, and I stayed in his house six days and gave him twenty ducats and garments. They filled me six water skins and placed them on three camels, and I journeyed on, I and my servant and the servant of Alohab, ten days by the desert way, and we found many men on horses, and I said to the servant of Alohab, "Lead me to Masah, five days' distance from this land, which is at the end of the kingdom of Sheba, on the River Nile;" and he said to me, "I will do according to thy words, and if thou wishest I will go with thee to Egypt." Then I bowed myself down before the King of heaven and earth, when I heard the words of the man, for I feared to remain in the land of Sheba, and I and he went through the beginning of the desert, where there is much sand, and we went on the sand as upon hills and I fasted three days consecutively until I reached the city of al Habor; and afterwards I reached the River Nile and behold, there was an old Ishmaelite of the lords of Egypt in front of me, and he came and kissed my hands, and said, "Come, O blessed of the Lord, O lord the son of our lord, do me kindness and come into my house and I will take thy blessing. I have food and provender and place to lodge," and I went with that man whose name is Osman. He had a wife and children, and prepared the house for me and my servant, and then I sent away the servant of Alohab to his country, and I gave him ten ducats and he went home.

And in that land five young men came to me from the two tribes and gave me two little lions, and I took the lions to bring them to Egypt, and the men returned to their country; and I stayed in the house of the old man with my servant one month, and the honored old man said to me, "Behold thy camels are very weak and cannot travel in this desert; thou wilt have to feed them two or three months until they get fat and then they can travel the three days' journey in the desert, where camels can find neither grass nor food nor anything to eat until you get to Girgeh, on the River Nile near to Egypt." I bought from the old man a she-camel, good and fat, for twenty ducats, and the old man bought for me two strong camels for seventy ducats, and the camels which I had I gave at camel price in exchange, and afterwards the lords of that city and its surroundings came and brought me flour, barley, rye, lambs, and bullocks, by way of tithe to the house of the old man, and they filled his house. But of what they gave me I only took what the camels eat and the remainder I gave to the old man and to the poor as a gift, and I said to the old man, "Come with me to King Mehmel," and I went with him before the King and his servants, and he was drinking date-wine and eating mutton without bread. The King was pleased with me and said, "This day is blessed on which our lord, the son of our lord the Prophet, has come before us, and it is my will that thou shalt remain in my house and, if thou wilt, I will do thee honor and glory," and I said to the King, "Be thou blessed before the Lord, I will pray for thee and I will give thee pardon and atonement for all thy sins."

On the 14th day of the month of Kislev I journeyed with my servant from the house of the old man, with many men by way of the great desert, and I was always fasting and praying to God, when I lay down and when I got up, and when I went forth and when I journeyed; and I determined not to eat or drink, save only once in every three days and nights, and did not eat between one oasis and another, for in this desert even wells three days' distance from each other are reckoned near, and some wells are four days' journey apart, and some wells five days. We could only drink the water which was on our camels until we arrived at the city of Girgeh, after forty-five days, and we had a man with us who knew the way in the desert like a pilot in the sea, by way of the stars by night and through his knowledge by day, for this desert is like the great sea. That wise man said to me, "Come with me to my house until

I find thee a way to go to Egypt"; and the man's name was Shalom, in Arabic Selim. His house was a mile from the end of the desert and I went with him to his house, which is on the Nile, and he gave me a hut and bed, and one of his servants to do for me. My servant and I stayed with the man twenty days, and I sold my camels for one hundred golden florins and I sailed in a small boat on the River Nile until I reached the gates of Egypt. There the Ishmaelite Turks detained me, and wished to examine my stuff and boxes in order to take tithe from me, and they wanted twenty florins for the servants. But when the Turks saw the two lions I had with me, they asked them of me as a present, and they would free me from the customs and the tithe. So I gave them the lions and I had no other expenses, and they honored me with great honor and their joy was very great, for they said they wished to send the lions to the King of Turkey.

I entered Cairo on the New Moon of Adar, 5283 (1523). I had journeyed with a man who had friends in Cairo, who said to me, "Come to my house tonight and stay till morning, and tomorrow I will seek for you a suitable lodging." I went with this man, I and my slave, and all my stuff.

It was a big house with large trees, and they gave me a room and placed before me bread and cheese. I said, "I cannot eat cheese, give me eggs," and I ate and slept till the morning. That morning I took out my pieces of gold and said, "Come with me to sell the gold to the Jews, because they are better versed in business than the ordinary people." He came with me to the Jewish quarter, and I stood in front of the door of a shop in which were Jewish money-changers. I asked them in Hebrew, "Who is the chief among you?" so that the Ishmaelites should not understand. The Jew said, "I will come with thee," and I and he went till we came to the house of R. Abraham (De Castro), Chief of the Mint. He was the most esteemed in Cairo. I said to him, "I am a Jew, and wish to stay with thee three or four days, and I will tell you a secret. Put me on the way to go to Jerusalem. I want neither silver nor gold nor food from you, but only lodging." R. Abraham answered, "I cannot let thee come to my house, because thou hast come disguised as an Ishmaelite, and if thou didst stay in my house it would do me harm." I said to him, "Do me this kindness for the love of God and the love of the Elders, for one good deed leads to another." He answered, "It would be good for me and all the Israelites that live in Egypt if thou dost not come to my house." So I left his house and went with the Ishmaelite and came to the house of an Ishmaelite merchant, whose name in Hebrew was Zachariah and in Arabic Jahia, the son of Abdallah.

Then I sold my Ethiopian slave to the merchant for 200 broad florins, and traveled with several merchants from Cairo to Gaza. We came to a big khan like an encampment, and they gave me one of the upper rooms and in my room a Jewish merchant from Beyrouth was staying, called Abraham Dunaz. I stayed in that room two days and spoke nothing to him; all day I prayed and spoke to nobody. After that I called him and asked his name, and I asked, "What do you pray for at this season, for rain or dew?" He replied, "For rain," and also told me that he had seen many Ishmaelites, and even descendants of the Prophet, but never saw a man as wise as me. I said to him, "I know by calculation that today is a festival of yours, the day of Purim." He replied, "Yes, that is true," and asked me, "Who told you all this?" I replied that in my country there are many Jews and wise men, and their houses are near to my house, and I have friends among them who eat at my table of fruit but not meat, and they love me and I love them. And he said to me that in his country Jews cannot talk with any Ishmaelites nor any descendants of the Prophet, for they hate us and they love dogs more than Israelites. I told the Jew, "Fear not nor be dismayed, for speedily the end will come for you, and the Almighty will humble the wicked to the ground and raise up the lowly upon high, and speedily make you see great matters and much confusion among the kings. Now, Abraham, do me a kindness and seek for me merchants to conduct me to the Temple in Jerusalem, but first to Hebron." He told me that he would do so, and went and found a donkey man and made the bargain between him and me. I did not wish to reveal my secret to him, but when starting on my journey told him the beginning of the matter. The money changer, Joseph, the shopkeeper, came to me with his brother, Jacob, and their old father, who was still living. They were with me about two hours and I told them no more of my business than the barest headings. Through the Jew, Abraham, the Jews sent me meat and bread, and I stayed at Gaza five days.

On the 19th Adar, 5283 (1523), I journeyed from Gaza to Hebron, and traveled day and night until I arrived at Hebron at the site of the cave of Machpelah on the 23rd Adar at noon. The keepers of the cave came to kiss my hands and feet, and said to me, "Come in, O blessed of the Lord, our Lord, the son of our Lord;" and two of the guardians of the Mosque of Abraham who were wise and great and appointed over all the guardians and Judges in Hebron, took me by the hand and brought me to one grave and said to me, "This is the grave of Abraham, our father", and I prayed at that place; and then they showed me on the left hand a small chapel and therein is the tomb of Sarah, our mother, and between them is the Ishmaelites' praying chapel. Above Abraham's tomb is the tomb of Isaac in the great Mosque, and near to his tomb is Rebecca's, above the tomb of Sarah; and at the foot of Abraham's tomb is a plan of Jacob's tomb in another great Mosque, and near the plan of his grave is Leah's, alongside of Sarah's. I gave them ten florins charity to buy olive oil for the lamps and said to the guardians that this plan is not true, for Abraham, Isaac, and Jacob are in one cave underground, and they are not buried on the surface. They replied, "Thy words are true," and I asked them to show me the cave, and I went with them. They showed me a well with a lamp therein burning day and night, and lowered the lamp into the well by a rope, and I saw, from the mouth of the well, a door of man's height. I believed that this was the real cave and rejoiced in my heart, and sent the Ishmaelites away and prayed by that well until I had finished my prayer. After that I called the oldest of the guardians and said to them, "This is not the door of the well, but there is another door," and they replied, "It is so. In olden days the door of the cave was in the middle of the great Mosque, in which is the plan of Isaac's tomb." I asked them to show me the place of that door and went with them. They removed the carpets from the floor of the Mosque and showed me the place of the door, closed by big stones and leaden weights, and no man can remove that overburden. I told them to cover the ground again with the carpets, and asked them if they knew who built the door of the cave. They took out a book and read out before me that a king, the second after Mahomet, built the gate of the cave after the Ishmaelites had taken the holy place from the Christians. That King sent four men into the cave, each with a candle in his hand, and they stayed an hour in the cave and came out. Three of them died immediately after they came out, but the fourth survived for three days. The King asked what they had seen in the cave and the survivor replied, "I saw these forms; our father Abraham in his coffin in the place of the upper plan, and round Abraham's tomb many lamps and books and a covering of beautiful cloths over it; and near to our father Abraham, our mother Sarah and Isaac and Rebecca above at their head, and our father Jacob and our mother Leah at their feet; and there were lamps round each tomb, and on each was an image, a man on a man's tomb, and a woman on a woman's. The lamps in our hands were extinguished, and in the cave shone a great light like the light of the sun, and in the cave there was a pleasant odor like that of incense. When we passed Rebecca's tomb the man's image on Isaac's tomb called out to us in a great voice, and we remained breathless until we left the cave." The King commanded that the gate should be closed and it remains closed to this very day.

I stayed to pray at the mouth of the well and watched the door of the cave on Sabbath eve until dawn, and in the morning I stayed to pray until the evening, and on the Sunday night I prayed and did not sleep until the morning. The two Elders had told me that on the third day I should find a sign and I remained, wondering what I should see. On the Sunday morning the guardians called me with great joy and said to me, "Our Lord and Prophet, rejoice with us for we have had a great joy. Water has come to the bath of the Mosque, and it is now four years since water came to it"; and I went with them to see the water. It was good and clear and came to the bath from a distant land.

I journeyed from Hebron on the 24th Adar and came to Jerusalem, and there were robbers on the way. My companions said to me, "Our lord, son of the Prophet, there are enemies before us;" and I said to them, "Fear not nor be dismayed, they are afraid and you are safe." I was still speaking when, behold, the Turkish judge had come from Hebron with many servants. The robbers saw him and all of them fled, and I journeyed with him to Jerusalem. I entered it on the 25th Adar, 5283 (1523), and that day I entered the house of the Holy of Holies, and when I came to the sanctuary all the Ishmaelite guardians came to bow before me and to kiss my feet, and said to me, "Enter, Oh blessed of the Lord, our Lord, the son of our Lord," and the two chief among them came and took me to the cavern which is under the *Eben Shethiah,* and said to me, "This is the place of Elijah the Prophet, and this the place of King David, and this King Solomon's place, and this the place of Abraham and Isaac, and this the place of King David, and this King Solomon's place, and this the place of Abraham and Isaac, and this the place of Mahomet." I said to the guardians, "Now that I know all these places go ye on your way, for I wish to pray, and in the morning I will give you charity." They went away and I knew at once that all their words were false and vain. I prayed until all the Ishmaelites came to prayer. They left the Temple court after their prayer two hours after dark. I went below the *Eben Shethiah.* Then the guards extinguished all the lights in the court except four, and before they closed the gates they searched to see if any man were sleeping in the cavern, so as to turn him out. They found me, and said, "Leave this place, for we are the guards and may allow no one to remain to sleep here. We have so sworn to the King, and if thou wilt not go we shall ask the Governor to remove thee against thy will." When I heard these words, I came out of the court and they shut the doors, and I prayed outside the court all night, and fasted, and this was my fourth day. In the morning, when the Ishmaelites came to pray in the court, I entered with them, and when they had finished their prayer, I called out with a loud voice, "Where are the guards? Let them all come before me;" and I said to them, "I am your Lord, and the son of your Lord, the Prophet. I have come from a distant country to this holy house and my soul desireth to remain therein to pray and not to sleep." And after that four of the guards came to expel me, and I said to them, "I am your Lord, the son of your Lord, if you wish peace wish me well and I will bless you; but if not I will be avenged of you and will write to the King of Turkey your evil deeds." They replied, "Forgive us this time for we wish to serve thee and to be thy slaves as long as thou remainest in the holy house, and will do thy will." Then I gave them ten ducats for charity, and stayed in the sanctuary and fasted in the Holy of Holies five weeks. I ate no bread and drank no water except from Sabbath eve to close of Sabbath, and I prayed below the *Eben Shethiah* and above it. Afterwards ten messengers from King Joseph, my brother, and his Elders came before me, and they recognized and stood before me in the sanctuary.

The Ishmaelites have a sign on the top of the cupola of the court, and this sign is like a half-moon turned westward; and on the first day of Pentecost of 5283 (1523), it turned eastward. When the Ishmaelites saw this they cried out with a loud voice, and I said, "Why do you cry?" and they replied, "For our sins, this sign of the half-moon is turned eastwards, and that is an evil sign for the Ishmaelites"; and the Ishmaelite workmen went on the Sunday to restore the sign to its place, and on Monday the sign again turned eastward while I was praying, and the Ishmaelites were crying and weeping, and they sought to turn it round but they could not; and our Elders had already told me, "When thou seest this sign go to Rome," and I saw the gates of mercy and the gates of repentance, and walked in the sanctuary. It is a big structure like the upper buildings, and I did that which the Elders ordered me underneath the sanctuary, out of man's reach, and the turning of the sign took place after I had done what the Elders commanded beneath the sanctuary. I went up the Mount of Olives, and I saw two caves there and returned to Jerusalem and ascended Mount Zion. There are two places of worship there in the town; the upper place is in the hands of the Christians and the lower in that of the Ishmaelites. This the Ishmaelites opened for me and showed me a grave, and told me that it was the grave of King David, on whom be peace, and I prayed there. Then I left and went to the upper place of worship, which the Christians opened for me. I entered it and prayed there and returned to Jerusalem, and went to the house of a Jew called Abraham Hager. He was smelting near the synagogue, and there were women there cleaning the candlesticks of the synagogue. I asked him his name and he said, "Abraham"; and I sent the Ishmaelites away and said to them, "I have work to do with the smelter." They went away and I asked him, "At this season do you pray for rain or dew?" and he said, "Dew," and was astonished, and I spoke a good deal with him but did not tell him I was a Jew. But on the third time that I went to his house before leaving Jerusalem, I said to him, "Make me a model showing Venice, Rome, and Portugal." He made me such a model, being a Sefardi, who had come from there and I said I wished to go to Rome, and he said, "Why?" and I answered, "I am going for a good cause, but it is a secret which I cannot reveal, and I want thee to advise me how I should go"; and I then gave him a letter which I had written to Jerusalem and said to him, "Give this letter into the hand of R. Isaac the Nagid."

I left Jerusalem on the 24th Sivan, 5283, and a number of Ishmaelites came on horseback to accompany me five miles. I went on my way and arrived in Gaza in the month of Tammuz at the place where I stayed on the first occasion. An old Jew, a dealer in spices, called Ephraim, came to me and I said to him, "Go summon unto me Joseph, the money-changer, and let him bring with him weights for gold and silver and pictures of coins, and come together to me in the presence of Ishmaelites." The old man did so, and two of them came to me and I asked Joseph, the money-changer, as to the health of his old father, and his brother, Jacob, and he said, "They are well." Afterwards four old men came before me, and I said to them, "I am a Jew, and my father is King Solomon, and my brother, Joseph, who is my elder, is now King over thirty myriads in the wilderness of Habor." We ate and drank wine that night, though from the day I journeyed from the wilderness of Habor I had drunk no wine till that night. Afterwards I went with old Ephraim that night to the house of a Jew called R. Daniel. He is the richest of the Jews in Gaza and honest and pious, and he told me of all the Turkish governors who had come to Gaza. R. Daniel has a son valiant and handsome, called Solomon, but the Jews hate him because they say he is wild. I summoned him and rebuked him between ourselves and said, "Turn from thy evil ways before Jerusalem is taken; if thou dost not repent, thy blood be on thy head," and he swore that he would repent. Then the Rabbi, R. Samuel, sent me through old Ephraim a thousand greetings and begged me to take the Sabbath meal with him that night. I did so and stayed with him till midnight, and asked them to show me their synagogue, and I went and prayed therein about two hours. I returned to the house of the R. Ishmael and said to him, "If thou wilt do me a favor for the sake of God and thy love of the Elders and the rest of Israel, find me speedily a ship going to Alexandria." They told me that a ship was starting that week for Damietta with Jews from Jerusalem therein and this old man, R. Ephraim, would accompany me. I said to them, "Be blessed of the Lord, remove from you causeless hate and return to the Lord in order that he may speed our redemption and the redemption of the house of Israel, for thus said the Elders." I journeyed from Gaza on the 15th of Tammuz, 5283, and in two days reached Damietta, where I took a house, and then I went to the house of a Jew called R. Mordecai, whose brother, R. Samuel, lives in Cairo. I stayed with him over Sabbath, and on Sunday he took me to the seashore, and we rode on a camel for twenty days along the shore.

I embarked on a ship and reached Alexandria on the 24th Tammuz, and went to the khan, and the learned kabbalist, R. Mordecai, came to me and I said, "I am a Jew, the brother of the King of the wilderness of Habor, and I wish thee to direct me by sea to Rome." R. Mordecai said to me, "Go to the Consul and he will advise thee what to do, for he is an honorable man. Tell me what he tells thee." I went to the Consul and said to him, "I am the brother of the King of the wilderness of Habor, and I have come by the command of my brother, King Joseph, and the advice of the seventy Elders, and I wish to go to the Pope and then to the King of Portugal. Therefore advise me what I shall do and find me the ship in which I shall go." The Consul replied, "There is a ship going to Puglia, but I fear evil will come to me because of thee; therefore, I advise thee to wait till a galley goes to Venice, and the Ishmaelites will direct thee." I returned to my place and went to the house of the said R. Mordecai. A young man called Joseph, whose father and mother were of Naples, and who had a wife from Turkey, came there, and I asked R. Mordecai to let the young man go with me to Rome. He said to me, "Go, this young man will be thy interpreter in Rome." Then I went home and stayed until the eve of the New Year, 5284, and prayed in the little synagogue on New Year's eve. The name of the landlord was Isaac Bucapzi, and he and a Jew called R. Benjamin joined me in prayers. I stayed there the two days New Year, and then went home, and during the feast of Tabernacles I went to the house of R. Mordecai to stay with him the first two days. I remained in Alexandria until I heard the galley was about to start for Venice, and I went to the great Turkish Pasha to get his permission. There were mighty lords with him and I said to him, "I seek a kindness from you because of my love and the love of the Prophet, and I will pray to the Prophet for you that he may give you a right to paradise; speak to the captain of the galley and order him to conduct me in the ship to Venice." They did so, and they sent with me their servants and ordered the captain accordingly, and the captain said, "So will I do."

I and my servant, Joseph, traveled from Alexandria in the middle of Kislev, 5284 (November, 1523), and I fasted all day and prayed day and night, and took with me from Alexandria all kinds of food for Joseph. But it was no use, for all became mixed up with the food of the Christians. He ate from their utensils, and I cried out against him, but he cared not. When I reached Candia I bought many kinds of food, and the Christians and the captain complained to me of Joseph that he stole bread and wine from the people on the ship. I was ashamed of him but could not speak with him, for he regarded not my word.

When I reached Venice I went to the captain's house, where he gave me room, and I fasted in his house six days and six nights, and when I had finished prayers I saw a man behind me, and said in Hebrew, "Who art thou?" He replied, "I am a Jew," and I asked him who told him I was here. He replied, "Thy servant Joseph says that thou art a holy envoy." I asked him his name, and he replied Elchanan. Another time this Elchanan returned with another Jew called R. Moses Castilis, a painter. I said to R. Moses, "I am greatly in need of seven ducats, for my servant Joseph is poor and sick, and I have spent for him and in Alexandria much money." I went with R. Moses to the Ghetto (the place of the Jews) and a respected Jew called R. Mazliah came to me, and I spoke to him as to the expense, and he said he would go to the house of R. Hiyya. We went there and I said to him, "I am a Jew from the wilderness of Habor, a holy envoy sent by the seventy Elders." I was in his eyes as one who mocked, so I said to him, "I require seven ducats; speak with the wardens and find out if they will give this." He replied, "If the rest of the Jews will give, I will give my share." I told him this was the sixth day of my fast and I was only eating at nightfall, and asked him to send me some wine. I returned to my lodging at the captain's house, but he sent me nothing. So I only ate eggs, bread and

water, but the respected R. Mazliah had done his best, and R. Simon ben
Asher Meshullam came to me and said, "I hear that you are a holy
envoy from the seventy Elders and going to Rome; tell me wherefore
they have sent you and I will send two Jews with you and pay all the
expenses." I said to him, "I am going to the Pope and can say nothing
more than that I am going for the good of Israel. If thou wilt send two
men with me to Rome, thou wilt have a share in the good deed, and
they will bring you back good tidings." Afterwards I and R. Moses, the
painter, went to the captain's house and took leave of him, and took all
my things and went to the ghetto to the house of R. Moses, the painter;
and R. Mazliah came to me and I asked him to find me a ship for Rome.
He did so and that night I got into a small boat, and from there into
the ship, and I fasted. I and Joseph started on our journey on Friday, the
new moon of Adar, 5284 (about March, 1524), and stayed over Sabbath
on the ship until I reached Pesaro. Here I stayed in the house of
R. Foligno, and said to him, "Do me the kindness to put me on my way
to Rome, as I do not wish to sleep here overnight." He went and found
me horses, and I and Joseph rode to another city where there were
Jews; and so every evening from journey to journey, with many Jews,
until we arrived, on the eve of Purim, at midday at Castel Nuovo, near
Rome, at the house of a Jew called R. Samuel, and I stayed with him
over Purim; and on that day I bought the skipping hoop with which I
did what the Elders had ordered me and next day I left and arrived at
Rome, thank God!

POPE, EMPEROR, AND THE INQUISITION

SOLOMON MOLKO (?-1534)

Among those Marranos—crypto-Jews—who did not escape the fires of the Inquisition was the romantic figure of Solomon Molko. Born in Portugal of a family of Spanish emigrés, he already held a government post when David Reubeni flashed across his horizon like a messianic comet. He reverted to his ancestral religion, symbolically changed his Christian name (Diego Pires), initiated himself into the lore of Kabbalah, and joined Reubeni in his meteoric career. "I was constantly with him," he writes, "as a servant before a master." They appeared together before Charles V at Ratisbon in 1532, flying a banner with the Hebrew initials of the Maccabaean rallying cry, "Who is like unto Thee, O Lord, among the mighty?" Their appeal that Charles mobilize the Jews against the Turks led to their seizure. Soon afterwards, Molko was condemned to death by the Inquisition. The following account is excerpted from the famous historical work *Vale of Weeping* by a contemporary, Joseph Ha-Cohen. Molko's autobiographical letter is printed in Roman type.

❊ ❊ ❊

*N*OW *there came out of Portugal a noble whose name was Solomon Molko. He was of those who had fled there in the days of the Inquisition. While he was still a youth, he served as one of the secretaries of the king (John III, 1521-1557). But when he saw David Reubeni, the Lord touched his heart and he returned to the Lord, the God of our ancestors, and he was circumcised.*

At that time he knew nothing of the Law or the Scriptures. After he was circumcised, the Lord endowed him with wisdom. Soon he became the wisest of men, arousing much wonder. He went to Italy, and with great daring spoke of the Divine Law in the presence of kings. Thence he went to Turkey, and later returned to Rome. He spoke with Pope Clement (VII, 1523-1534) who, against the desire of his intimates, extended every kindness to him. The Pope gave him a letter of safe-

conduct, signed with his own hand, permitting him to live as he pleased, and without delay Solomon lived openly as a Jew.

Now Solomon became learned in the wisdom of the Kabbalah. From his lips came words of grace, for the spirit of the Lord was upon him and His word was constantly on his tongue. He continually drew forth marvelous words from the deep fountain of the Kabbalah and he wrote them upon tablets. But I have not yet seen them. He preached to large audiences in Bologna and in other places. Many followed him both to hear his wisdom and to test him with riddles, but Solomon answered all their questions. Nothing was hidden from him. When they heard Solomon's words of wisdom they said, "What we heard about you was a true report. You have gained wisdom even exceeding your fame."

Many clothed themselves with envy, but they could inflict no harm upon him in Italy, for he was beloved by the nobles. He united himself with David Reubeni; in those days they were as one.

And Solomon wrote to the sages a letter containing words of peace and truth, saying,

". . . It was rumored that Prince David Reubeni had come to Italy, and he too suffered from the malicious tongues of the slanderers. When we met, it was my design that I should sit at his feet as a disciple, but the contrary happened, for he inquired of me. Notwithstanding, I believed him to be a very learned man, and when he said that he did not know the law and the sciences, it was only to deceive the people and to see how I would behave towards him. In accordance with my intention, I was constantly with him, even as a servant is with his master.

"When I went to Venice to ask a printer to publish for me wonderful and profound things from the mysteries on the Holy Law, so that others might be encouraged to study the Book, I found a physician, a man of true faith, whose name was Jacob Mantino. He was engaged in a controversy with another physician, Elijah Halphon. I tried, without success, to make peace between them. As Dr. Halphon intended to go to Rome, I tried to prevail upon him not to do so. When I told him that the destruction of the city by the waters of the flood was nigh,* he went to another city, saying that he would not remain in the same city with his enemies. Seeing that I was friendly with Dr. Mantino, he too became my enemy. While these things occurred, the flood was upon the city of Rome. . . .

"After an attempt had been made by the enemies to poison me and I was healed, I went to Rome to observe the stars and interpret their

---

* The flood actually occurred as predicted, on October 8, 1530.

meaning. And before certain events took place I prophesied in a letter to the Pope, and also to some of the cardinals belonging to the court. I also wrote to the King of Portugal through this ambassador, for I had had a private conference with him. And when the earthquake actually came to pass (January 26, 1531), they were all astounded and marveled at my powers. The ambassador said to me, 'If the king had known how wise you are before you left Portugal, he would have given you permission to leave as you wish.'

"And daily he and his servants showed me great honor at his home and in the presence of the Pope. The cardinals held countless meetings and assemblies. When they saw the honors bestowed upon me by the Pope, some said, 'He should be killed. Did he not despise the waters of baptism in Portugal?' But others defended me, 'He should not be killed,' they said, 'for he is a sage. Did he not predict events that have actually occurred?' And with words and deeds they honored me before the people.

"The widespread report of this finally came to the ears of Dr. Jacob Mantino of Venice. He said to the Jews of that community, 'Now I shall go to Rome, and pursue that Solomon until I have injured him. Either he will return to Christianity or he shall be burned at the stake.' When Dr. Mantino came to Rome, he went first to the home of the ambassador of Portugal, and said to him, 'Why are you not zealous in honoring the King, your master? Is it because of that man who stands in the Pope's court, who was a servant and a scribe in the King's palace, before he became a Jew?' The ambassador answered, 'It is not our custom to go about condemning and slandering secretly. And it shall not be done here.'

"And Dr. Mantino left him in anger, and went before the judges, the great men of the city, 'with the voice of Jacob and the hands of Esau.' But the judges said, 'We cannot do anything without witnesses. When you bring witnesses, we will do all you desire.'

"And he went to and fro to seek witnesses among the Portuguese who were then in Rome. And after a diligent search, he found witnesses and brought them into the Court of Justice of the Inquisition. And they wrote out an accusation, condemning me, and called me before them to explain how I justified my claim to being a Jew after having belonged to another religion, and further by what right I preached the Law to the multitude. Then I showed them the security of the Pope, written and sealed, ordering that the permission to live as I pleased be respected. In great anger, they took it from me and brought it to the Pope, saying:

'Why does this come from you? If you pervert judgment, why have you appointed us judges?' And he answered, 'What you say is true. But I ask you to be silent, for we have a secret understanding between us. The times require this to be so.' And when this man saw that he could not prevail against me, he took with him the portion of my book dealing with the First Vision which I had sent to Dr. Joseph Titsak, and he translated it into the Italian language. He showed it to many cardinals so that they might be ashamed and blush at that which the Pope suffered against their own law. Finally, because of their continual urgings and intrigues, the Pope gave the nobles permission to do what the law required. But to me he said, 'Stay here with me lest these men seize you.' And the most high God, for the sake of His mercies and loving kindness which have not ceased, caused them to meet a man of my form and likeness, clothed in garments like mine; and they took him suddenly and burned him alive. And they came to the palace of the Pope, and said, 'The man in whose honor you delight is now a burning fire.' I, however, was hidden in the most secret chambers. And when I appeared, he feigned astonishment at my appearance. And he called to the Chief Justice, and said, 'What have you done? Look! There is Rabbi Solomon with us, and you have burned another in his stead. And now hasten and write in the judgment-place that the victim had reviled and blasphemed, and cursed his God and his King so that it may not be known that he was burned instead of Rabbi Solomon, lest trouble follow.' And they hastened to follow his orders.

"Then I said to the Pope, 'You have already observed the stars with your own eyes, just as I have told you from the beginning, as you know, as these stars show, what will happen to you; that weeping may endure for a night, but joy cometh in the morning. Send me away, now, I beg you, for I may no longer remain here on trial.' And he dismissed me in peace, and I rode away in the night on a fast horse, accompanied by a good escort provided by the Pope.

"You may recognize and know that everything which I have related to you is true, from the contents of the credentials of the heads of the communities of Rome and the Rabbis, which I send to you. And many are the trials I have suffered. I am weary of writing about them, for no book can contain them. And because my enemies say vain things and publish false writings, and quote words which I have never uttered and which I have not commanded, neither came into my heart, therefore do I warn you not to pay any attention to any writings except those which are written by mine own hand, and signed with my name and sealed with my seal. Regard not lies and misrepresentations, but only the words of truth which I utter. Stand fast, all ye who hope in the Lord, and your hearts will be strengthened. Blessed be the Lord forevermore! Amen, Amen!"

Now Solomon was accustomed to discuss the beliefs and faith with the emperor (Charles V). When the emperor was in Ratisbon (in 1532), he went there and talked with him. But the emperor was unresponsive and, because of his ill temper, he would not listen to him. The emperor commanded that he be clapped into prison, he and his friend Prince David and their followers. And they remained there several days.

After the Turks were repulsed there was a period of respite and the emperor left Ratisbon. He returned to Italy, and took all the prisoners, bound in fetters, in wagons, setting a special guard over them. Then, in accordance with his imperial custom, the emperor discussed them with his advisers. . . . They found Solomon guilty and condemned him to death. And they said, "Bring him forth, and let him be burned." In order to prevent him from addressing the people, they put a bridle on his jawbones, and thus he came before them. The whole population surged about him, as he stood facing the crackling flames. And one of the emperor's nobles said, "Take the bridle from between his teeth, for I have a message to him from the King." When this was done, he said to Solomon, "The emperor sent me to you to say this: 'If you repent, your repentance will be accepted and you shall live.' He shall provide for you and you shall be one of his court; but if not—death is your fate." He did not move an eyelash. Even as a saint or an angel of God, he said, "Because I have lived your religion, my heart is bitter and grieved. Now do as you please. My soul, I know, will return to her Father's house where it will be better off than here."

And they were incensed, and cast him upon the burning woodpile. He was as a burnt offering to the Lord, and He smelled the sweet savour, and took to Him his pure soul. Then they brought his servants from the prison and they suffered the same fate. None escaped the destruction, except the noble David Reubeni, his friend; over him they set a guard. Whereupon the emperor went to Bologna, and they brought along Reubeni, bound in fetters, in a wagon, and took him to Spain. There he lived for a long time and died in the prison house.

During these days there were many in Italy who believed that Solomon Molko had, by his wisdom, delivered himself from his enemies, and that the fire did not touch his body. Some even took an oath before the community and the assembly that he was in his home eight days after the auto-da-fé, and that he left there and was never again seen. Almighty God alone knows the truth. Would to God I could write down with certainty whether his words were true or false.

THE STORY OF MY IMPRISONMENT

YOMTOB LIPMANN HELLER (1579-1654)

The dramatic tale of this celebrity's imprisonment in 1629, due to the treachery of his enemies, has as its setting the first phase of the Thirty Years' War (1618-1648). Heller had been elected rabbi of Prague, the metropolis of Bohemia, as a youth two years earlier, and had published a number of notable legal commentaries which contained references to Christians, that were used as a basis of a charge of defamation. It is a tribute to his integrity that he would not compromise with his influential defamers and suffered the loss of his high office as well as exile in Poland, where he ultimately became rabbi and head of a talmudic academy in Cracow. This unusual memoir is the simple, honest story of a noble man.

* * *

BY REASON of the continued war round the city of Prague between the armies of Emperor Ferdinand II and Duke Frederick von der Pfalz, wealth declined and taxations and levies increased. As a result the members of the community were compelled to raise many loans at high rates of interest. When the time of repayment arrived, disputes became numerous in Israel regarding the share to be paid by each, and hearts were torn asunder; those close together became distant; plots were hatched in secret and some even openly as well. And all my toil as rabbi to bring them together with gentle words and entreaties were of no avail. On account of this bad situation I shall not mention the names of the people who sinned against their souls. May they be blotted out of the Book of Life, and may the Exalted Name atone for them all, and the name of the Lord be blessed for ever.

When I was warned that a plot was being hatched against the leaders and against me as well, I did not believe it, because I knew that I had done no harm to anybody, that I had never twisted judgment and that I had done nobody any ill. Yet as for me, who am a worm and not a man—why, even with regard to King David, we find that he had enemies for no reason and false foes. How much more so should it be the case for me, the lowly and contemptible, who am not worthy to be mentioned in the same breath as our lord King David, may he rest in peace.

On Monday, the 4th of July, 1629, at the time of the afternoon service, a Jew came to tell me that the Imperial Judge had asked him about me, and whether I was at home, as he had a secret matter to discuss with me. This man had told him, "I do not know: maybe he is in the House of Study, or teaching at the school after his fashion." Further he said, "Why should Your Honor go to him? If you so desire, I shall tell him that you wish to talk with him, and then the Rabbi will come to your house." But the Imperial Judge said, "No, I shall go to him myself."

That was as much as this Jew told my sons. When I heard it, I was concerned, but went to the synagogue; and upon my return I brought with me the leaders and outstanding folk, and told them of the incident. While we were talking, the Imperial Judge came in a coach to the house of a Jew just opposite my house, and remained there till about one o'clock in the morning. Then he came to my house and sent to the winter house to ask permission to enter my rooms. The leaders and fine folk who had come with me, and I myself, all invited him in. And when he entered he gave his hand to each of us in friendly fashion. I had already prepared two chairs. He set me on his right hand side and sat to my left, and began chatting about one thing and another. Thereafter the gentleman said to me that he had a private matter to talk over. So I conducted him to an inner chamber, kept for my studies.

Now letters which I had received that day from the Holy Congregation of Vienna had informed me that the Kaiser had ordered his regent in Prague to have me conducted to Vienna in iron chains. And so when the Judge came alone and said that he had a private matter to discuss. I guessed that matter was connected with this, and replied,

"Please say what you have to say in the house of our communal head His Honor Rabbi Jacob Shmilas."

He asked me to go in his coach with him to the house in question, but I requested him to ride while I walked so that we should not be seen together. (The truth was that I feared that he would take me to prison and not to the house of Rabbi Jacob.)

Thereupon he replied, "I shall accompany you afoot in order to do him honor."

So the leaders and fine folk accompanied us, and there too he set me on his right hand and spent a little time chatting. Then he asked

Rabbi Jacob to accompany him into another room, and there the Imperial Judge said: "I am very sorry, I have no words to tell the Rabbi how bad things are, because in my eyes he is a good man. So I shall tell you what the matter is, and you in your wisdom will put it to the Rabbi, so that he should not be upset and overwhelmed."

And this is what he told him: the Kaiser had ordered his regent by letter to take the Rabbi in iron chains and lead him thus to Vienna under close guard; the irons and fourteen guards were already waiting at his house. And the Viceroy had ordered the Imperial Judge to bring the Rabbi that same night.

Thereupon Rabbi Jacob was exceedingly startled and upset and besought him not to hurry.

"I myself," he said, "shall send some of our leaders to the Regent to entreat him about this thing."

"Do so," replied the Judge, "and I shall stay here all night long if necessary until I hear what the Viceroy has to say."

So the communal leaders, namely David Lurie, Reb Hena and Reb Israel Weisels went there. Now the dwelling of the Regent was in a small spot beyond the River Elbe in Prague. When they came there, the palace was closed and locked because it was midnight. They knocked at the door but there was no reply, because the deep slumber of the first watch of the night had fallen upon the watchmen. Nevertheless the emissaries did not return but knocked again on the door with all their force until the chamberlain of the Prince, who was on the watch that night and was on guard at the entrance to the Regent's bedroom, heard the noise of the knocking and looked out at them through the window, asking, "Why are you knocking like this? Can't you see that everybody is asleep and we are not to be awakened?"

Thereupon they asked him to open to them as they were the leaders of the Jews and had been sent to the Lord Viceroy on a very urgent matter. When he opened the door, they requested him to awaken the Prince and tell him that the leaders of the Jews had to speak to him on a matter of life or death. Then he went to the Prince's bedroom with a burning taper, awakened him and told him, claiming that it was a matter of life and death.

"Let them come in," said he.

When they entered, they prostrated themselves on the ground and said, "Your Lordship sent the Imperial Judge to arrest the Rabbi and lead him bound to Vienna under strong guard. But where shall we hide our reproach? Tomorrow people will say that he is the most important

of them, and that the only reason for arresting him is that the Jews have
rebelled against the Kaiser. And in every town where this report will be
spread, they will maltreat the Jews who are subject to our Imperial
Majesty the Kaiser, who himself can only lose as a result. Therefore we
beg and beseech that the Rabbi should be permitted to travel to Vienna
himself in order to appear before whomsoever Your Lordship may command. And we shall be security that he will hasten to carry out Your
Lordship's orders."

The Prince ordered his chamberlain to bring him the Kaiser's letter,
and read them the order. Then he said, "Return to your homes tonight
and come back tomorrow for my answer. Tonight I give you the Rabbi
on your security that he will not flee. And tell the Imperial Judge in my
name to go home and come here with you tomorrow."

On the morrow the leaders returned according to the order of the
Viceroy, together with the Imperial Judge; and he ordered the latter to
accept the security of the leaders that the Rabbi would within six days
be in Vienna and appear before the Chancellor of State; and if the Rabbi
were not there within the appointed time, they would be punished by a
great fine, and their bodies and money were offered in his stead. And all
this was written down. May God remember them for good by reason of
this good deed they did for me. And on Tuesday, the 8th day of Tammuz,
I started out.

On the following Sunday, which was before the appointed sixth day,
I reached Vienna. I was accompanied by the said Reb Hena for the
purpose of intercession. We went the same day to the Palace of the
Chancellor, but he was not there. On the following day I appeared
before him. He spoke harshly to me in the name of the Kaiser with
regard to my two works *Maadenai Melech* (The Sweets of the King)
and *Lehem Hamudoth* (Desirable Bread). For the Kaiser had been told
that in these works I had written against their faith. Of this he spoke at
very great length.

"God forbid," I replied, "that I should do any such thing. All our
books deal with the writing of the Talmud in accordance with the Torah
of Moses which is our faith, and this Talmud is an interpretation of the
written law decreed for us by His Blessed Name. These are foreign to
idolators and star worshippers, to whom the words of the Talmud apply;
and all the sages and authors since the compilation of the Talmud are
required not to depart from its words." .

It is unnecessary to repeat in detail the things said to me by the
Chancellor or the answers I gave him; but they all referred to matters of

religion, not, as I had heard, to the fact that my book was called *The Sweets of the King*. This was not the reason why the Kaiser was wroth with me, but the truth will appear further on.

When he had finished, he said to me, "Stay in your lodging, and do not go out of it under pain of punishment in money and body. For such is the order of the Kaiser."

When I entreated him, he replied that the Kaiser had desired to arrest me and imprison me immediately, but he had recommended that I should not be imprisoned.

"Further," said he to me, "the matter will be brought before a commission of scholars expert in the literature and language of the Jews, and they will report to the Kaiser in accordance with their findings."

On Sunday, the 17th of Tammuz, after the said commission had already held its meeting, the second town judge came to me with two beadles carrying an order from the Chancellor in the name of the Kaiser, to lead me to the prison kept for those sentenced to death. After much entreaty, he dismissed the beadles but accompanied me himself. Many of the honorable and important Jews of the town also accompanied me and endeavored to strengthen and encourage me. I stayed in that prison all the day and night, and no Jew was permitted to talk to me there, not even through the spy hole. Yet His Blessed Name showed me His loving-kindness, because all the prisoners treated me with honor, and each one endeavored to serve me as far as he could. Next day the Chief Judge gave me a special room in the building above, and permitted all the important Jews to visit me there. On the Tuesday the intermediaries succeeded in having me brought out of that building to the prison of the King's prisoners.

There I was comfortable because I had a bed, a table, a chair and a lamp. And the building was in the street of the Jews' warehouses. There was no lack of Jews to sit with me at any time. In addition the Chief Warder treated me well and provided me with anything for which I might ask.

On the 25th day of Tammuz, I was summoned to appear before the commission. To begin with, they asked me why I praised the Talmud in my introduction, despite the fact that it had been burnt by order of the Pope; and the Kaiser was required to go by the Pope's edict.

My reply was, "My praises were intended for my own people, who must hearken to all the words of our sages, that being an essential part of the Torah."

Then they asked me once again why I had written against their faith, in accordance with the questions asked me by the Chancellor. I replied to them as I had replied to him, and they dismissed me to my place in the prison.

On Thursday, the 27th of Tammuz, the judgment of the Kaiser was issued in the following terms: despite the fact that, in accordance with the findings of the commission, I should have been condemned to death, yet since the Kaiser like his forefathers before him was a merciful monarch, therefore he showed me the mercy of permitting me to redeem myself by the payment immediately of 12,000 reichsthalers, without any period of time in which to make the payment. As for the books, they were to be burnt. If I should refuse to give the said sum, no mercy would be shown and I would have to submit to the death penalty.

In my distress I prepared an appeal, saying, "I prostrate myself in gratitude for the favor shown me by His Majesty the Kaiser who permits me to live. Yet be it known unto him that his terms are equivalent to an order to mount aloft to the very heavens or to swallow a tube a hundred ells in length."

But he did not believe me because of the denunciations concerning me, in which much mention had been made of my wealth.

On Sabbath, the 18th of Ab, the Chancellor spoke as follows in the name of the Kaiser to the intercessor: "If he does not pay this sum of money, I shall send him back to the prison where he was at first, and from there he will be led to three squares in the city of Vienna, where he will be stripped naked, beaten on his naked body, and then led to Prague, where he will again be stripped and beaten in three public squares in order that he may be a shame and a reproach to all Israel; for no such thing has been done since the days when Israel was exiled from its land. For what will the onlookers say when they see the great shame done to their great Rabbi in this largest of cities, where there are so many Jews?"

Then the intercessors fell on their faces and said, "But it is impossible for us to pay this great fine demanded by the Kaiser."

To which the Chancellor replied, "But there are Jews who say that he is so rich that this fine is not even a fifth part of his wealth."

Then they entreated him, saying that they knew in all truth and verity that this was falsehood.

"Return to me afterwards," said he at length. "I shall recommend the Kaiser to treat him with even more favor."

So they went away and returned on the Sunday, on the Monday, and on the Tuesday, when he swore to them in anger that the Kaiser had ordered that the punishment of flogging was to be carried out, but he had acted as an intercessor and had won the Kaiser over to lessen the punishment.

"Therefore hearken to me and give 10,000 Rhenish gulden to redeem him. All the Jews are expected to redeem one another, particularly if it is the case of a man who is as great as he is according to your account. And I have heard say that not only the Jews who dwell in the countries and states of the Kaiser but also the Jews who dwell under the Moslem rule are ordered to help ransom and redeem one another."

To which the intercessors replied that our law forbade us to pay more than the actual value of a man as ransom.

He laughed in annoyance, saying, "Can you estimate the value of so great a man? Is he not worth the ten thousand? If you agree to this sum, it is good; I shall go to the Kaiser and may be able to mollify him with this gift. But if you do not listen to me, I shall be unable to raise the matter any more, and his judgment will be carried out."

On Thursday, the 6th of Ab, the Chancellor said that the Kaiser had agreed to this sum. Thereupon I requested that I might be given time for making the payments, for how could I pay at once? Following much entreaty, he gave me time for payment, namely 2,000 Rhenish gulden in ready money, 1,000 gulden six weeks later, while a further thousand reichsthalers of the remainder would be paid off every three months until the full sum had been paid. May God remember the upright Rabbi Jacob Shmilas, who sent me a bill for 2,000 Rhenish gulden in ready money from his own pocket and property. And the leaders of the Vienna congregation, who contributed 700 Rhenish gulden to help me; apart from my honorable and beloved kinsman by marriage Rabbi Enoch Schiff, who gave me 100 reichsthalers; and various other honorable men who stood security on my behalf for half of the balance. The other half had the security of Rabbi Hena, who had come to Vienna with me, and of my son-in-law Rabbi Wolf Slavis.

LIFE IN LOMBARDY

LEONE DA MODENA (1571-1648)

Born in Venice of the family of a physician whom Emperor
Charles V had dubbed a Knight of the Golden Fleece, Leone was a
personality of rare fascination. He showed great promise and versatility in his childhood, but his later development was somewhat
frustrated by the loss of the family fortune and his struggle to eke
out a living. He lists twenty-six occupations, ranging from tutor-
ing to matchmaking, which he pursued during the course of his
checkered existence. He could deal out a hand of cards with the
same expertness as he composed in Italian and Hebrew. His memoirs
afford a glimpse into the curious psychological nature of a mind
that was a battleground for the opposing elements of rationalism and
occultism.

❋ ❋ ❋

IN THE year 1569 Mistress Penina, my father's wife, died; and in the
same year at the Feast of Weeks he took to wife Mistress Rachel,
daughter of Johanan Halevy of blessed memory, who came from
Apulia but was of German stock. At the time she was the widow of
Mordecai, known as Gumpeln Parenzo, the brother of Meir Parenzo,
who is mentioned by name in sundry printed books. She had one son
from the aforesaid Master Mordecai, whose name was Abraham and who
was then about nine years old. Before the marriage my father asked Rabbi
Abraham da Rovigo, who was well versed in many wisdoms, whether
he would succeed if he took this woman, and the Rabbi told him that he
would not succeed with her in property, and if he took her, she should
change her name; so she changed her name to Diana. And the said
Mistress Diana conceived from him in the year 1571.

Now there was a very great and powerful earthquake in the city of
Ferrara, the like of which had not been known in any country, just as is

75

written in the book *Light of the Eyes* by the sage Azariah dei Rossi.*
And my father and his household fled for their very lives to Venice.

While they were there I, the bitter and hasty, was born on Monday
between the eighteenth and nineteenth hour on the 23rd of April, 1571.
Well-nigh like Job and Jeremiah may I curse that day, for wherefore did
I come forth to see toil and wrath, distress and straits and evil alone all
the while?

The birth was extremely hard for my mother, and when I came forth
I was doubled over with my breech facing outwards, even then having to
do with reverses. At the end of eight days I was circumcised with great
joy by the renowned scholar and kabbalist, Rabbi Menahem Azariah of
Fano, and my father and Mistress Sarah, daughter of my uncle Shemaiah,
were my godparents; and my Hebrew name was called Judah Arieh.
May the Lord have mercy on my soul and may the upsets of my life be
an atonement for my sins and transgressions.

They dwelt in Venice for about eight months and then returned to
Ferrara. While they were on the way to Francolino, near Ferrara, they
left the ship and gave me to a gentile porter, who fled and bore me away
in his bosom. As soon as they saw that I had vanished, his honor Master
Samson Meshullam of blessed memory, who was my father's guide,
pursued him about two miles and caught up with him and took me. Then
he thrashed him thoroughly, and brought me back to my parents; and we
came to Ferrara and dwelt there.

I began to learn the alphabet from a certain teacher known as
Hazaneto, afterwards from Rabbi Isaac Supino, and afterwards from the
Rabbi Azriel Basola. And though it is said, "Let a stranger praise thee
but not thine own mouth," I may admit since I am now fully grown and
it is no longer praise that in truth I did well with my studies from the
very beginning. When I was two and a half years old, I said the
Haphtarah in the synagogue, and when I was three I recognized my
Creator and the value of study and knowledge, and I would explain the
portion of the week and understand it. (There appears to have been an
ancient custom of this kind in the Italian Jewish Community, and other
sources also refer to it.) And so I passed from class to class.

One day I was walking about in the garden and fell from a stone
and twisted my hand and was sick for some time, to say nothing of the
worms which troubled me. A certain woman gave me rock oil, and I
fainted, and almost remained in that faint. A little later I became sick
with smallpox; and these were all things that happened to me before I

* Dei Rossi's account is quoted in the Introduction, pp. xx-xxi.

was four, yet are as clear in my mind and memory as if they happened yesterday; for I still know what my thoughts were then.

In 1575 we left Ferrara and went to live in Colonia, a small town belonging to Venice, to conduct a pawnshop. My father went to a great deal of trouble to prepare a ritual bath for the womenfolk in his house and to draw suitable water there. At the end of 1576 it was declared fitting, and at the time I was studying Mishna together with Rabbi Gershon Cohen, who is now the head of a Yeshibah in Poland, and was then a boy like me.

The teacher went somewhere, and both of us went down to the bath to play, as boys do; and I fell in to it when it was full to the brim, and the other boy ran away shouting, and the housefolk heard him and came dashing with my father and mother and looked for me here and there and did not know where I had fallen. And meanwhile an hour passed while I kept hold of a ledge round the bath until the housefolk came. Then a servant girl jumped into the water and took me out; and they carried me to bed as though I had been dead of dread and fear.

There at Colonia my brother Samuel was married to Mistress Giuditta, daughter of Angelo della Faggiani of Pesaro, with feasting and festival, and I spoke Torah at the table as my teacher had instructed me, so that everybody there was astonished. As teacher I had Malachi Gallico of blessed memory, a rabbi, a physician and a kabbalist. In those days a certain gentile named Priamo had been beaten and wounded and people were discussing in the presence of my father and various guests of our house, whether he would die or not. I jumped up and said that he certainly would, making a pun on a Bible verse in this connection which set them all laughing.

In the month of Elul (August-September) 1578, we left Colonia for Montagnana about five miles away, and father made a synagogue in his house, where it can still be found in the home of Master Zerah Halevy, long life to him. For during many years the men of the spot had not prayed in congregation, because of quarrels among themselves. But we put the matter in order.

Rabbi Malachi left us, and for a year my teacher was Rabbi Eliakim da Macerata of blessed memory, a kabbalist and holy. Soon after, Rabbi Malachi was murdered in Piedmont on the way by the servant of a horse-owner for the sake of his money. And since he took his red vest and put it on, the Jew whom he had left understood what had happened and the servant was arrested and executed. May the Lord avenge the blood of Rabbi Malachi. In Nisan, 1580, my father sent me to Ferrara to the house of his grandson, Mordecai de Modena, to study books and wisdom, and there I spent a year. For four months I studied with Rabbi Yehiel Taureolo, and for eight months with Rabbi Hezekiah Finzi. It was his practice that every Sabbath all the pupils who studied *Alfasi* (a talmudic compendium) should prepare a discourse of their own on the portion of the week. And at the house of study on the Sabbath Day he would gather a quorum and the boy would deliver his discourse to him. When it came to my turn it was the portion on heave offerings, and I took as my subject the words "gold and silver and copper," and the saying "Rabbi Simeon ben Gamliel says the world depends on three things: on the Torah, and on the temple service, and on mutual aid." And I compared the first three with the second three, these being the things which the Lord desires of men and wherein He let His Presence rest on Israel.

When I had finished Rabbi Hezekiah said to two old men who were there, "I am convinced that this boy will preach sermons in Israel, for his manner shows that he will succeed with them."

Later, in 1605, 1606, and 1607, when I delivered sermons at the Great Synagogue every Sabbath by order of the community, he would always come to hear me; and when they used to praise my words he would say, "I prophesied twenty-five years ago that he would be a preacher."

I also learnt to play instruments, to sing, to dance, to do fine penmanship, and a little Latin. But on account of two servant women who hated me and embittered my life, I returned home when the year was over. So in the spring of 1581 my father of blessed memory sent me to Padua to the house of Rabbi Samuel Archivolti of blessed memory, to board with him and learn Torah from him. From him I learnt the craft of versifying and how to write prose, and he loved me very much until the day of his death; for he used to say that I was one of the pupils who was his very likeness and image in wisdom.

I was there for a whole year and then my father summoned me home. Now since my parents wanted to keep me there, the Lord provided us in the spring of 1582 with a young man from Italy who, however, came at the time from Safed. His name was Moses, son of Benjamin della Rocca, a grandson of the scholar Rabbi Moses Basola and a knowledgeable and understanding man. And this Moses became my teacher and from him I learnt much. During two years he was with me, after which he left for Cyprus where he married. While still a fine young man, he was summoned to the Upper Assembly. When I heard this sad news, I wrote laments for him and particularly the Hebrew and Italian *ottava rima* which is printed in my volume of sermons *Midbar Yehudah;* at the time

I was thirteen years old. All the poets saw it and praised it, and up to the present it is a wonder for Christian and Jewish sages alike. Thereafter I ceased to study with any regular teacher, but only on my own, though I was not in a large city where comrades might have helped me to maintain my studies. Alas that I dwelt during the best period for study without a teacher and rabbi!

At that time my father began to send me from time to time to Ferrara to supervise business affairs and collect debts. There our affairs were conducted by Samson Meshullam of blessed memory and I would come in and go out and have nothing to do. In the month of Tishri, 1587, when my father Isaac was growing old, his eyes grew dim. For about six months he was blind, groping in the dark. After many treatments everybody said that there was no hope any longer. All the same he did not cease praying day and night unto the Lord, until the Lord heard his voice and set it in the heart of a certain physician to give him an easy water to put in his eyes; and he returned to his strength, and the light came back to his eyes. What was even more miraculous, previously he had been accustomed to read with spectacles (Hebrew literally "eye-houses") and afterwards he read and saw everything without them for the five years that he still lived. But all that time we were growing steadily poorer, eating and doing nothing; for my father was disturbed and affrighted and in dread from the constellations which fought against him; and his heart would not raise him to any decision to leave this unlucky spot and to travel elsewhere, or anything similar.

At that time my brother, my mother's son Abraham Parenzo, who had grown up in father's house in childhood and youth, came into bad company who incited him to gaming, and he lost both his own and father's money, yet father always had for him the father's mercy for his son and always treated him well. But when this said brother saw how badly he had behaved, he went to Ancona, where there were many families that were kin to my mother of blessed memory, and he found favor in their eyes, for he was handsome, good-looking and intelligent. So they gave him a wife and trained him for the right path, while he too repented and went the proper way without going wrong any more. He was beloved and esteemed by all the gentile merchants of the city and by the whole Jewish community, who honored him; and he succeeded and earned very much, gaining more than he had lost. He wrote to my father several times that the time had come to repay him for all the good he had done, and entreated him to remove thither, since he would be doing him a favor. In addition he promised to train me in business because he loved me very much. Despite his entreaties father did not wish to listen until he saw nothing but evil all the time and had lost all hope. Then he sent property there with flax and silk and household goods and synagogue requirements, and agreed to send me in advance.

Now that year there was a great plague at Ancona in which many householders died; and my brother lost two sons, and the two brothers of his wife also died, married men and fathers of children. In the month of Iyar, 1588, I left Montegnano for Ancona; when I reached Venice I heard that my brother's mother-in-law had also died while his wife was very sick. But I went on, made a very stormy passage by water, and reached Ancona on the new moon of Sivan, 1588, where I found that the Lord had held my brother's wife, but he was very bitter in spirit at all the mishaps which had befallen him. Still, when he saw me he rejoiced very much and felt a little better, esteeming me exceedingly, as the townsfolk also did.

But on the day after the Feast of Weeks, his head pained him and he went to bed; and from day to day his sickness grew worse though nobody knew what it was. While from the time that he took to his bed, he said that he was going to die and told dreams he had dreamt. And when flies buzzed round his bed, he used to say that they were death flies. Finally he lost his mind, and after fifteen days, on the eve of Sabbath, the 18th of June, 1588, as the morning star arose, he passed away, at the age of twenty-eight years. And the whole community honored me exceedingly at his death with sermons and laments. And they all bewailed him because he had been acceptable to all his brethren and acquaintances. I wrote a lament for him in rhyme with an echo. It is found among my poems and writings.

Then I remained perplexed and at a loss, for they warred against me from Heaven; and I went on a ship alone without any Jews with me, and I came to Venice and then returned home to Montegnano. Here I cannot describe the pain and grief which my mother suffered, for she had loved him with all her soul and did not forget him till the day of her death. My father of blessed memory also wept for him as a father weeps for his son. And in truth from that time all the well-being of our house vanished and our hope and support came to an end. Since that time the stars have decided that I shall not see anything good.

On the New Moon of Tammuz, 1589, in order that I should not remain idle, I began to teach Torah to the son of Manasseh Levy of blessed memory and to Joseph the son of Zerah Halevy; an employment with which I continued until 1612 in my own despite, for it was not proper in my own eyes.

After this my mother spoke to me every day, saying,

"If only you were to listen to me and comfort me in my grief! Take the daughter of my sister, namely Esther, daughter of Mistress Gioja, wife of Isaac Simha, for she is fitting for you in my opinion; then I shall have found a match for you among my kin, and there will be peace in our home."

And she also begged my father of blessed memory with all her might, and wrote to her sister about it; and her sister also replied suitably, and it came about.

Meanwhile I had undertaken a Query to Heaven by process of dream, by prayer but without conjuration, to see the woman who was intended as my match. And I dreamt: a certain old man took me by the hand and led me to a wall where there was a picture painted with a curtain in front of it. He removed the cover and I saw the likeness of Mistress Esther, daughter of my said aunt, and the very color and fashion of her clothes. Yet while I looked at her, that likeness was changed, and in its place there came another which my eyes could not clearly distinguish. Next morning I told the dream to my father and mother, but they did not believe it.

In the month of Elul, 1589, my mother and I came to Venice to journey to Ancona in order to recover the property and goods which had been in the hands of my brother of blessed memory; for his wife had taken them and we did not see as much as a shoelace. Still, afterwards we decided not to go, and stayed in Venice. While we were there, my mother and her sister and the kinsfolk again took up the matter of the match; and we came to an agreement and gave our hands on it, and I took possession at the betrothal with great joy, and to my mother I pointed out the color of the clothes and ornaments which I had described to her more than a year earlier, when I had seen her in my dream. She was indeed a beautiful woman and wise, and I said that the words of Proverbs would apply about her and not the words of Ecclesiastes. (In Proverbs there is a verse "He who finds a wife finds something good." In Ecclesiastes, however, there is a verse, "A woman more bitter than death I have found.")

When the time of the wedding came, which was on the 13th day of Sivan, 1590, I wrote to my father, who was then in Bologna, and he came. And I summoned all my friends and relations and we went immediately after Shebuoth, all of us rejoicing and merry at heart, to Venice.

When we got there, we found the bride in bed; but everybody said that there was nothing more serious than a little diarrhea, which would soon be cured. But from day to day the sickness grew worse, till she was on the verge of dying; but her heart was as the heart of a lion, and she was not frightened.

On the day of her death she called me and embraced and kissed me, saying, "I know that this is shamelessness. But God knows that during the whole year of our match we have not touched one another, even with the little finger. And now at the hour of death, the right of death is permitted me. I did not merit to be your wife. What shall I do if it is decreed from on high? Let the Lord do His Will."

Then she requested that a sage be called for her to confess; and he came and she said the death confession and requested the blessing of her parents and my mother. And on the eve of Sabbath, the 24th of Sivan, 1590, almost the anniversary of the time my brother died, my bride departed as the bride Sabbath came in, with a life of vanity to a life of eternity; and she passed away to her own place. There was much weeping in and out of the house among all who knew her; and she was laid to rest in all honor.

Immediately after she was buried all the kinsfolk came to my mother and me and said, "The sister who follows her is as good as she is. Why should we not maintain the kinship and give comfort to the father and mother of the girl?"

And they pressed me unceasingly to take her sister Rachel as my wife. So I wrote to my father, who replied to me as he always replied regarding this matter, as follows: "Do what you wish, for you have to make the choice. Today or tomorrow I shall be taken from you, but you and your children will stay with her. Therefore understand what lies before you and do as the hand of the Lord doth show you."

So in order to give satisfaction to my mother and the dead girl after the fashion she had hinted in her words, I agreed and took the aforesaid Mistress Rachel as my wife. And we immediately wrote the contract and made the wedding on Friday, the 5th of Tammuz, 1590, under a good star.

On the 10th of Tishri, 1615, my son Mordecai went away because a godless man troubled us; and he ceased to teach the pupils of the society. In the month of Kislev he returned and began to engage in the art of alchemy, together with the priest Joseph Grillo, a great sage; and he toiled therein exceedingly. He grew so wise in this art that all the followers of it, who had grown gray and aged thereat, were astonished that a lad like him should know so much. Finally in the month of Iyyar he prepared himself a house in the Old Ghetto and himself made all the preparations necessary for the work. Then he repeated a certain experiment which he had learnt and tried at the house of the priest; namely, to take nine onkias of lead and one of silver and transform them into ten onkias of pure silver. This I saw and tested on the two occasions it was done by him. I myself sold this silver for six and a half pounds the onkia. It stood the test of the *coppella* (a small instrument used at the period for testing gold and silver). And I knew that it was really so, although this work involved great labor and toil and took two and a half months each time.

It should finally have brought in about a thousand ducats a year. And this is not all; for I also devoted my life to understanding things like that and was not likely to deceive myself. But thanks to our sins, at the festival of Tabernacles, 1616, much blood suddenly descended from his head to his mouth. After that he ceased to engage in this work, for people said that this might be due to the vapors and smokes of the arsenic and the salts which entered his head and harmed him. So he remained engaged in trifles for two years until he died.

Here I wish to write down for a memorial the number of ways I sought to earn my living; and I tried and did not succeed:

1. Jewish pupils. 2. Gentile pupils. 3. Teaching how to write. 4. Sermons. 5. Sermons written for others. 6. Acting as cantor. 7. Secretary of charitable and other societies. 8. Officiating as rabbi. 9. Decisions in ritual law. 10. Officiating as judge. 11. Daily lessons in the synagogue. 12. Conferring rabbinical diplomas. 13. Letters written in the names of others. 14 Music. 15. Verses for weddings and tombstones. 16. Italian sonnets. 17. Writing comedies. 18. Producing them. 19. Drawing up legal documents. 20. Translation. 21. Printing my own writings. 22. Proofreading. 23. Teaching the writings of charms and talismans. 24. Selling books of charms. 25. Commercial agent. 26. Matchmaker.

MY DOUBLE LIFE AND EXCOMMUNICATION

URIEL DA COSTA (1590-1640)

Of the colorful array of Marrano personalities, there is none more fascinating than Uriel da Costa, the tragic younger contemporary of Spinoza. He was born in Oporto, Portugal, in 1590, escaped to Holland with his family in 1618, and there embraced Judaism. But his uncompromising struggle for religious freedom led to constant persecution and finally public disgrace. His revealing autobiography, written in Latin, is a moving document, and has become a classic in the literature of religious liberty. So tortured was he by the heartless treatment of the community that he is reported—there is no actual verification, however—to have committed suicide in 1640, soon after the writing of this testament.

❊ ❊ ❊

I WAS born in Portugal in a city of the same name but commonly called Oporto. My parents were of the nobility, originally descended from those Jews who were forced to embrace Christianity in that kingdom. My father was a true Christian and a man of unquestioned honor and integrity. I had a good education at home, servants always at my command, and I rode a Spanish jennet to perfect myself in horsemanship, an art in which my father was so skilled and in which I endeavored to follow his steps. At length, being grown up, and as well accomplished in the liberal arts as young gentlemen generally are, I applied myself to the study of law. As to my character and disposition, I was by nature very pious and compassionate. So much so that I could not hear the story of any person's misfortunes without melting into tears. I had so strong an innate sense of modesty that I dreaded nothing so much as to suffer disgrace. Not that I had the least degree of cowardice in my nature. When there was reasonable justification I was not free from resentment. It is for this reason that I always had an aversion to that haughty and insolent tribe of men who are inclined to despise and trample upon others, and I therefore took every opportunity to defend the oppressed and to make their cause my own.

Religion has brought incredible suffering into my life. According to the custom of the country, I was educated in Roman Catholicism. When I was but a youth the dread of eternal damnation made me anxious to observe all its doctrines punctiliously. I employed my leisure time in reading the Gospels, the Breviaries of the Confessors and other religious literature. But the more time I devoted to them, the more perplexed did I become. Little by little this caused me such difficulties, doubts and conflicts that I was overwhelmed with grief and melancholy.

Reflection led me to believe that the obtaining of a plenary absolution by the confession of sins and the fulfillment of all that the Church required was impossible. This consequently made me despair of salvation inasmuch as it was to be obtained only by such special rules. But as it was very difficult to shake off quickly a religion in which I had been educated from my infancy and which by a long unquestioning faith had taken deep root, I began, when I was about twenty years old, to question the teachings concerning the afterlife. I asked myself whether or not they were forgeries and whether belief in them was consistent with reason. My reason perpetually suggested to me conclusions that were just the contrary. Under the shadow of this doubt I continued for some time, and finally I was persuaded that salvation could not be obtained in the prescribed manner.

During this time I continued to apply myself to the study of law. When I was in my twenty-fifth year an opportunity presented itself whereby I obtained an ecclesiastical benefice as treasurer in the church. But I was unable to find the satisfaction I wanted in the Catholic church. I wanted, however, to attach myself to a religion and, aware of the great dispute between the Christians and the Jews, I made a study of the *Books of Moses* and of the *Prophets*. I found some things sharply contradictory to the doctrines of the New Testament. There seemed to be less difficulty in believing those things which were revealed by God Himself. Besides, the Old Testament was assented to by both Jews and Christians whereas the New Testament was believed only by Christians. Hence I decided to become a convert to the Law of Moses. As he declared himself to be only a deliverer of what was revealed by God Himself, being called to that mission or rather constrained to accept it, I thought it my duty to make the Law the rule of my life. Having made this decision and finding it unsafe to profess this religion in Portugal, I began to think of changing my residence and leaving my native home. In order to do this, I immediately resigned from my ecclesiastical benefice in favor of another, uninfluenced either by profit or honor, the two prevailing motives among the people of our country. I also left a beautiful house situated in the best part of the city, which my father had built. When I had concluded all the necessary arrangements, my mother, brothers and myself boarded a ship, not without danger for it is illegal for those who are descended from Jews to depart without a special permit from the King. I must tell the reader that out of natural affection, I had communicated to my family my sentiments on the falsity of our religion even though the discovery of it might have proved fatal to me—so dangerous is it in that country to speak freely on this subject, even to one's dearest friends. At the end of our voyage we arrived at Amsterdam where we found the Jews professing their religion with great freedom, as the Law directs them. We immediately fulfilled the precept concerning circumcision.

I had not been there very long before I observed that the customs and ordinances of the modern Jews were quite different from those commanded by Moses. Now if the Law was to be observed according to the letter, as it expressly declares, the Jewish interpreters are not justified in adding to it interpretations quite contrary to the original text. This provoked me to oppose them openly. Nay, I looked upon the open defense of the Law against such innovations as a service to God. The modern rabbis, like their ancestors, are an obstinate and stiffnecked race of men, vigorous advocates of the teachings and institutions of the Pharisees, not without a view to gain and, as is justly imputed to them, vainly fond of the conspicuous seats in the synagogue and greetings in the market place. Men of this character could not bear my differing with them in the slightest degree. They insisted that I follow unswervingly their prescribed regulations or else suffer exclusion from the synagogue and the full sentence of excommunication. But it would have been unworthy of him who had so recently left his native country and been content to forego many other temporal advantages for liberty of conscience to be overawed and to submit to men who had no right to such power. Besides, I thought it both sinful and beneath a man to be a slave in things pertaining to the conscience. Therefore I resolved to suffer the worst they could inflict rather than recant. Accordingly they excommunicated me from their congregation. Even my own brothers who before had looked upon me as their teacher, dared not take any notice of me as they passed me in the streets, for fear of the rabbis.

This state of affairs led me to write a tract in defense of myself and to prove plainly out of the Law of Moses the vanity and the invalidity of the traditions and ordinances of the Pharisees as well as their conflict with the Law. After I had begun this work (for I consider myself obliged to relate everything clearly and circumstantially), it so happened that I entirely agreed with the opinion of those who confine the rewards and punishments proposed in the Old Testament to this life only and are little concerned with the future life or the immortality of the soul. The following argument, among others, led to this viewpoint: The Law of Moses is completely silent as to the latter problems and proposes only temporal rewards and punishments to observers and transgressors thereof. The discovery that I entertained such opinions was no small triumph to my adversaries who felt that as a result they had the Christians as their allies, who by their faith in the Gospel which expressly mentions eternal rewards and punishments, do believe and preach the immortality of the soul. It was with the idea of rendering me odious to the Christians and of silencing me completely that, even before my tract went to press, they employed a certain scholar * to publish a book entitled *Of the Immortality of the Soul*. In it the scholar inveighed bitterly against me as one who defended the philosophy of Epicurus and who by denying the immortality of the soul disputed the very existence of God. At that very time I had, in reality, an incorrect idea of Epicurus and, prejudiced by my unsavory relations with other persons without even hearing what he had to say for himself, I did not scruple to censure him freely. But now that I have heard from impartial lovers of the truth some estimate of this philosopher and his teaching, I have found reason to change my opinion and to be sorry for the injustice I did him then when I pronounced him a ridiculous madman even though, being an utter stranger to his writings, I was far from being competent to judge his opinions.

The next step they took was to set their children upon me in the streets. They insulted me en masse as I walked along, abusing and railing at me. They cried out, "There goes a heretic, there goes an imposter." At other times they assembled before my doors, flung stones at the windows and did everything they could to disturb and annoy me so that I could not live at peace in my own house. After the above-mentioned book was published, I immediately set about my own defense. I wrote an answer in which I opposed with all the power at my command the doctrine of the immortality of the soul, incidentally dealing with the deviations of the Pharisees from Mosaic institutions. No sooner had this appeared in print than the elders and officials of the Jews agreed to make a complaint against me before the public magistrate. They asserted that

* Samuel da Silva. The book appeared in 1623.

I had published a book to disprove the immortality of the soul in order to subvert, not only the Jewish, but also the Christian religion. As a result, I was apprehended and sent to prison from which, after a confinement of eight or ten days, I was discharged upon giving security. For the magistrate fined me three hundred florins ($120) and confiscated my recently published books.

Let me here declare my mind freely. What should hinder a man from speaking the truth without reservation, who is just about to make his exit and to leave behind him a sad though true example of human misery? Sometime after this (as age and experience are apt to bring new discoveries to the mind of man and consequently to alter his judgment of things) I began to ask myself whether the law of Moses should be considered the law of God inasmuch as there were many arguments which seemed to persuade or rather determine the contrary. At length I came to the conclusion that it was nothing but a human invention, like many other religious and legal systems in the world, and that Moses was not really its author. I noted that it contained many things contrary to the laws of nature; and God, who was the author of those laws, could not contradict Himself, which He must have done had He given to mankind rules and regulations contrary to the laws of nature. Having thus determined this point, I began to reason with myself in the following manner (I wish I had never entertained such a thought!): What can it profit me to spend all my days in this melancholy state, isolated from the society of this people and their elders, especially since I am a stranger in this country without any acquaintance among its inhabitants or even any knowledge of its language? How much better will it be for me to return to their community and conform to their ways in compliance with the proverb which directs us to do in Rome as the Romans do. These considerations led me to return to their society. Accordingly, I made a formal recantation and subscribed to such regulations as they were pleased to impose upon me, after having lived for fifteen years in a state of separation from them. I must note that a certain cousin of mine helped to mediate this reconciliation.

A few days after this I was accused by my nephew, a lad whom I kept in my house, of breaking the dietary laws. New and cruel proceedings were begun against me. My cousin, whom I mentioned before as a kind of mediator between us, thinking that my behavior brought dishonor on his mediation and being a proud, bold fellow and very hasty, declared himself openly my inveterate enemy. He won all my brothers over to his side and left nothing undone that might ruin my reputation and fortune, and deprive me of life itself. He prevented a marriage which I was then just on the point of concluding, for I had lost my wife recently. He was also the cause for one of my brothers withholding my property which was in his possession. He also put a stop to the dealings which existed between us, as a result of which I suffered incredibly in my business affairs. In a word, he was a most implacable enemy to my reputation, fortune and life. Besides this domestic war, if I may so call it, another of a more public nature was carried on against me by the rabbis and the people who began to persecute me with fresh hatred, behaving with such insolence to me that I justly came to abhor and detest them.

About this time a new situation arose. One day I happened to be in the company of two men, one a Spaniard and the other an Italian, who came from London to Amsterdam. Both of them were Christians and not even related to Jews by descent. They revealed to me their present situation and asked my advice concerning the possibility of their becoming converts to Judaism. I dissuaded them from any such intention, advising them rather to bear the inconveniences of their present condition rather than to subject themselves to so burdensome a yoke with which they were unacquainted. At the same time I cautioned them not to make the least mention to the Jews of what had passed between us. This they faithfully promised me. These perfidious wretches, however, induced by the hope of filthy lucre, instead of repaying me with gratitude, went and disclosed everything to my dear friends, the Pharisees. The officers of the synagogue convened, the rabbis were inflamed with resentment and the insolent rabble cried out with one voice, "Crucify him!" In short, I was asked to appear before the rabbinical court where the charges against me were read with as much solemnity and impressiveness as though I had been on trial for life. Then it was decided that if I were really a Jew, I ought to submit to their sentence; otherwise I must be excommunicated again.

O just and equitable judges who take upon yourselves the power of condemnation and punishment! But when I appealed to your authority for protection against oppression and wrong then indeed you pretend that you have not the authority to interfere in such matters and are only servants of civil power. Of what validity, then, is your judgment that I should obey it? Then my sentence was read out of a little book. It declared that I must enter the synagogue dressed in the clothes of mourning, holding a black wax taper in my hand and there to read distinctly before the whole congregation a form of recantation in which they described in the blackest colors the magnitude of my crimes. Then I was to submit to a public whipping with a scourge made of leather thongs. After that I was to prostrate myself at the entrance of the synagogue that they might all pass over me. Moreover, I was to fast a certain number of days.

No sooner had I heard my sentence than I was fired with indignation and resentment. However, withholding my anger as well as I could, I answered only that I could not consent to undergo such a severe sentence. They consulted together and proceeded to excommunicate a second time. But not content with this, many of them spit upon me as they passed me in the streets and encouraged their children to do likewise. The only reason why they did not stone me was because they wanted power. This persecution lasted for a period of seven years, and should I relate all that I suffered it would seem incredible. For two parties violently persecuted me—the whole Jewish community and my family who sought their revenge in my disgrace. Nor would they be satisfied until they got me into their own power and jurisdiction, saying among themselves: "He is stubborn. He will do nothing until he is forced to, and therefore ought to be compelled." When I was sick nobody would attend me. If I suffered any other misfortune, it became a triumph and joy to them; if I proposed any one of them to act as judge between us the proposal was rejected. When I attempted to lay the whole case before a public magistrate, I found it very tedious and difficult, for judicial proceedings are at best both expensive and dilatory.

During these troubles they would often exhort me to submit, saying, "We are all your fathers and therefore you need not fear that we shall act unfairly or unkindly toward you. Only say that you are ready to perform whatever we ask of you, leave the rest to us and all shall be made easy." This was the very point in dispute, and I understood how disgraceful it would be to surrender out of discretion and depend upon their mercy. Yet I wanted to put an end to this long affair and after much reluctance I prevailed upon myself to submit to their terms and to test their honor. For I argued with myself thus: If they deal dishonorably with me they will stand convicted by their own behavior and exhibit their implacable enmity toward me and how little they are to be trusted. At length this execrable and detested people did plainly show what their religion and principles are by treating men of honor and character as though they had been the vilest slaves. In a word, I said to them, "I depend upon your mercy and I am ready to undergo whatsoever you are pleased to impose upon me." Now let every man of truth and humanity observe my situation and judge the sentence which a particular set of people, under foreign jurisdiction, passed upon an innocent man.

I entered the synagogue which was filled with curious spectators of both sexes. At the appointed time I walked up to the reading desk which was in the center and with a clear voice read aloud the form of confession which they had drawn up for me, namely, that I deserved to die a thousand deaths for the crimes I had committed such as the profanation of the Sabbath, the breach of my religious vows, etc., which I had carried so far as to dissuade others from being converts to Judaism. To atone for these violations I submitted to their sentence and was ready to undergo whatever they wished to lay upon me, promising not to be guilty of similar crimes in the future. When I had finished the reading I stepped down from the desk. The chief elder came up to me and, whispering in my ear, bid me go to a certain corner of the synagogue. When I had done this, the doorkeeper asked me to strip. Accordingly I stripped myself down to the waist, tied a kerchief about my head, pulled off my shoes and, holding up my arms above my head, clasped a kind of pillar in my hands, to which the doorkeeper tied them with a rope. Having thus prepared myself for my punishment, the verger stepped forward and with a scourge of leather thongs gave me nine and thirty stripes, according to the Jewish custom (it was a legal commandment that the number of stripes shall not exceed forty) for these very scrupulous and pious gentlemen take due care not to offend by overstepping their bounds. During the period of my whipping they sang a psalm. Then I was ordered to sit down on the ground whereupon an elder came forward and absolved me from my excommunication. So now the gates of heaven which were doubly locked and barred against me were suddenly flung wide open. O the ridiculous ideas and conceits of mortals! After this I dressed and went to the entrance of the synagogue where I prostrated myself. The doorkeeper held up my head while everyone, both young and old, passed over me, stepping with one foot on the lower part of my legs and making ridiculous gestures, more like monkeys than human beings. After they had all done this I got up and, being washed and made clean by a man who stood near me for that purpose, I went home.

Now let nobody say that they did not do me honor, for if they scourged me yet they lamented over me and stroked my head. O shameless race of men! O detested fathers! You from whom I had nothing dishonorable to fear! You who said, far be it from us to abuse you indecently! Now let anyone who has heard my story judge how decent a spectacle it was to see an old man, a person of no mean rank, and one who was by nature exceedingly modest, strip naked before a large assemblage of men, women and children and scourged by order of his judges and those who deserved rather to be called abject slaves. Let him imagine the confusion and anguish such a one must suffer by being obliged to lie at the feet of his bitterest enemies and to be trampled upon by those who had already loaded him with injuries and insults. Think of him seeing his own brothers (O monstrous, inhuman and shameful treatment) who were educated in the same house, joining in an unnatural confederacy with his persecutors and unmindful of that great affection with which I always loved them; and all this, regardless of the many good deeds I had done them, requiting all my kindness and tenderness with shameful injuries and disgrace.

My detestable persecutors said in their own defense that they only made me a public example in order to deter others of their faith from open violation of religious ordinances and from writing books against their rabbis. O wicked wretches and fathers of untruth! With how much more justice could I have made you a public example of punishment in order to deter you from practicing similar abuses on men who are sincere lovers of truth, haters of deceit and invariably the friends of all mankind. Of such men you are the common enemies, esteeming all others but as the beasts of the field and scum of the earth while you arrogantly extol yourselves with vain praises as the only favorites of Heaven. In reality, you really have nothing to boast of unless you regard it as praiseworthy to live as outcasts, isolated from the society of men, despised and hated by all for your absurd customs by means of which you distinguish yourselves from the rest of the world. . . .

Permit me at this point to propound the following question: If the groundless fears which you instill into the minds of men are contrived on purpose to restrain the natural evil which is inherent in them and thus to keep within the bounds of their duty those who would otherwise lead immoral lives, must you not at the same time reflect that you yourselves are men of similar passions, naturally averse to good, prone to evil, without compassion or mercy? But I can see every one of you filled with rage at so insolent a question and cleverly justifying his own conduct. "What, are we not all pious and merciful and followers of truth and justice?" My answer is that what you so boastingly say of yourselves is patently false. Your accusation of all other men whose natural inclination to evil you pretend to correct with your terrors is outrageously unjust. How impiously you reflect upon the majesty and goodness of God whom you represent as a tyrant and destroyer. How you distort human nature in supposing it to be subjected to so deplorable a fate, just as if the ordinary calamities of life were not a sufficient portion of misery for human beings. Granting that the natural corruption of man is great, which I readily allow (you yourselves are sufficient proof of it for otherwise you could not be capable of such scandalous falsities) you ought to search for a more effective remedy to heal this general disorder without introducing a worse one in its place, and to put aside those impositions which are likely to frighten only children and simple folk. On the other hand, if the disorder is incurable then cease from your vain, delusive pretenses and do not act like impudent quacks in promising men health which you are unable to give them. Be content with establishing among yourselves just and reasonable laws which provide rewards for the good and suitable punishments for the bad. Defend the cause of the downtrodden against the violence of the oppressor so that there be no complaint that justice is not executed in the earth and that there is none to deliver the weak from the hands of the strong. In sum, if men would follow the dictates of reason and live according to the laws of nature they would all mutually love one another. Everyone would then contribute his utmost to the relief of his neighbor or at least no man would injure another for that would be acting contrary to human nature. Indeed many of the evils in life arise out of the fact that men have invented laws directly contrary to those of nature and thereby create the cause for one man injuring and persecuting another. Then, too, many men easily deceive the unsuspecting by their extraordinary pretense to piety. They use religion as a cloak in order to prey upon those who are superstitious. These may aptly be compared to a thief in the night, who treacherously attacks us when we are off our guard and do not suspect any danger. Yet these are the men who continually vaunt their honesty and patriotism: "I am a Jew, or I am a Christian. You do not doubt my integrity? Rely upon me, I will not deceive you." Infamous wretches! He who pretends to be neither of these and only calls himself a man is far preferable to you. If you do not believe him you may at least stand upon your guard. But who can defend himself against you, hypocrites, who under the mask of sanctity, like a thief in the night, come in by stealth and murder us in our sleep?

There is one thing beyond many others that puzzles and surprises me. How is it that the Pharisees, living in a Christian country, enjoy so great a degree of liberty as to exercise judicial power and authority? I may safely declare that if Jesus of Nazareth, whom the Christians worship, were to preach today in Amsterdam and the Pharisees, like their forefathers, decided to scourge him for opposing and condemning their tradition and hypocrisy, they might do it with impunity. Such freedom is a matter of reproach and ought not to be tolerated in a free city which professes to protect men in the peaceable enjoyment of their liberty. Where a man is not permitted an advocate to defend his cause or a judge to punish the injuries inflicted upon him, it should not be a cause of wonder if, as a result, he takes every opportunity to defend and revenge himself.

I have here given a true account of my life. I have laid before you fairly the part that I acted on the vain stage of this world during the course of a checkered and unsettled life. Now, readers, judge impartially and render your opinion on what I have written with freedom and truth, like brave and honest men. If there is anything in my story which arouses your compassion let it teach you to pity me and to lament the miserable state of mankind in which you yourselves have an equal share. In order that it may be known who the author of this account was, let me note that while I lived as a Christian in Portugal, I was called Gabriel da Costa; but when I joined the Jewish fold (would that I never had done it!) my name was changed to Uriel.

TROUBLE IN THE SIENA GHETTO

JOSEPH DA MODENA (SEVENTEENTH CENTURY)

Because personal records of simple folk are almost unknown until modern times, this diary of a secondhand clothes dealer of the ghetto of Siena is a document of rare curiosity and significance. He jotted down his doings and feelings in Italian on the blank pages of the ledger of the business house of Jacob ben Eleazar Modena, and, although he tells us only his first name, it is probable that he belonged to the same family. Joseph did not get on well with his relatives, neighbors and competitors. The following graphic account of a squabble with his sister-in-law bares the reasons for his unsociability. From the social point of view, it portrays vividly the elements of popular democracy characteristic of community life in the ghetto.

* * *

I RECORD herewith, how, in the year 1633, Donna Stella, widow of Solomon Toscano, intended to marry Salvador, son of Isaac Gallichi. This match was treated by Donna Angela, wife of Moses Rieti. In the same year died my wife Anna, sister of Stella who died in childbed, after bearing a male child. The Donna Stella was godmother, and her father (my father-in-law) was godfather. I gave the child to nurse to my aunt Dianora, who lives over against Donna Stella. By reason of this, she took care of my son, and kept him in her house all day, for the great affection which she bore for me and for my son, her nephew, wherefore she declared many times that before she married, she would leave a hundred scudi out of her dowry on interest for my son. Besides this, I went freely into her house and into her chamber with all familiarity and liberty; she shewing me great affection and friendliness. One day, I was called by Messer Angelo Semilini, and he took me outside the ghetto, and said to me:

"You know, that your sister-in-law is in treaty to be married to Salvador Gallichi. I therefore advise you, if she has anything of yours in

95

her hands, to have it restored, because, if she comes to an understanding with Salvador, you will have great trouble to get it out of his hands."

I replied, as was true, that she had all my wife's furniture, with the brassware and copperware of my house. I, on the other hand, had some of her household goods which she had given me to look after when she was left a widow, for fear that her husband's brothers would come to make an inventory of his property and would take it away from her; wherefore she gave it to me to look after: which property was worth about twenty scudi. Moreover, I had certain pawn tickets for apparel and coats of hers, which she had lent me to use, and the said tickets were left in my hand in order that I should redeem them. All this I communicated to Messer Angelo, telling him that if she returned my property, I would return hers. But, if I thought that the match with Salvador would really come about, as he said, I would do anything to impede it, and though I did not desire to do her annoyance, after receiving my property I desired to send hers to the dead man's brothers, to prevent it from coming into the hands of the said Salvador. Whereat Messer Angelo was very content that I should act thus and hinder the match, because he hated and wished no good to Salvador, although he still spoke to him, and treated him like a friend.

Now the reason for the hatred which Messer Angelo bore for Salvador was as follows. In the year 1632 Messer Angelo had gone to Acquabona with all his household, and left no one at home. Whereat Salvador enticed Angelo, son of Donato Semilini, to enter his uncle's house by some means, while he was away, and urged Angelo to rob him of a certain sum of money. Angelo did this; he broke open a chest belonging to his uncle, and, finding there a bag containing a thousand piastri, took thereof one hundred. When Salvador was apprised of this, he threatened to play the spy, and, to prevent this, Angelo, gave him twenty piastri, in return for which Salvador promised to keep the secret. With these ill-gotten moneys, Salvador went with the wenches: whence it happened that one Saturday night at eleven o'clock he was caught in a wench's house with the money in a purse. Whereupon he was given the strappado, and the wench as well, but they both remained firm and were released without being condemned, by reason of the great bribe which his father gave.

The theft of Angelo Semilini was discovered on a certain occasion when Angelo was in conversation with a certain Abraham Cohen, husband of Fiore, a Levantine, and they were in dispute about the division of the money; and on that occasion the affair was made known. It was for this reason that Messer Angelo hated Salvador. And so Messer Angelo acted as go-between, carrying messages between the Donna Stella and myself, and always shewed himself to be on my side. He did tell me that Stella desired to give me seventy scudi in order to settle our accounts, and she commissioned Abraham Meniati to inform me thereof in the presence of the Messer Angelo. Whereupon this Abraham gave me the message, and then he informed me that Salvador would not have it, nor yet do anything else, and he summoned me before the Captain of Justice. I appeared with my attorney, Doctor Marzocchi, and the Captain of Justice made a serious charge against us, telling me that he had been informed about my affairs, how I was only occupied with stolen goods and villainies, and if I did not give up all that the woman asked, he threatened that he would have me flogged, and send me to the galleys. I answered, that he was ill-informed about my affairs, and that they were persons who wished me ill, and that the said woman had all of my worldly property, which I had given her to keep (she being my sister-in-law) in order that my brother should not squander it.

Whereat the Captain, increasing his abuse of me, forbade me to answer him on that point lest he should clap me into a dungeon, and commanded that I should give up all of the property of the woman, particularly the pawn tickets. I answered him a second time: "Master Captain, if you will not have me tell you my reasons, I cannot justify my innocence. As for the pawn tickets which she says she gave me, see, here is this box of pawn tickets she gave me which I had given her to keep no more than a fortnight ago, as I gave her other things." Whereat the Captain took the box from my hand, and said: "Since you confess that you received them from her, you must prove that you gave them to her, and that they are yours, and if you do not, I will punish you, as I said." Then the tickets were read before Stella, and she said that they were hers. The Captain then gave me a fortnight to prove that the tickets were mine, and we were thus dismissed.

Turning to my attorney, I said he should advise me in the matter, should tell me how to defend myself; for it would be difficult to prove sixteen or eighteen tickets to be mine, since the greater number of the articles specified were old household articles. He replied that it was difficult for him to defend me, since I could not prove my case, and the Captain was against me; he advised me to consult some other person besides himself. I replied, that all the Jews wished one another ill, and no one would desire to interfere. He answered that he would endeavor to settle it himself with the attorney of the opposing side, so as to prevent my bearing resentment of the Captain. His advice pleased me. I told him that I would leave it all and in every respect to him. Similarly, Stella consented to leave the matter in the hands of her attorney. Whereupon, an accommodation was made before the officials of the Mercanzia.

While they were on the point of coming to a decision, Donna Stella obtained a ban of excommunication from Rome. When this was known, there were many who would not have desired it to be proclaimed, but who, seeing my disaster within their reach, procured that it should be, amongst these being Clement and Abraham Pesar. At this time Clement was Warden; so, to demonstrate underhand that they did not wish the ban to be proclaimed, they summoned me to attend a meeting of the Council before Messer Prospero Semilini, Messer Isaac del Borgo, Messer Clement Pesaro, Messer Reuben Frosolone, Messer Samuel Nissim, Messer Isaac Gallichi, Messer Solomon Milano, father of Stella, and others of the community.

They said to me: "You know full well that Donna Stella, having no proof to shew in support of her claim against you, has procured a ban of excommunication from Rome, so that any one who has any information should be forced to reveal it. We are sure that all will tell that which they know, and you as well, in order not to fall in so grave a sin. Nevertheless, we have thought fit to call you here before these gentlemen in order to inform you of the great danger involved if your conduct should be such that the said ban be proclaimed. For in this blessed community such a thing has never happened before, and moreover (God forbid!) the whole congregation may suffer, and, as the saying goes, 'the innocent man suffers with the guilty.'" Whereupon they addressed to me a sermon composed of these and other yet better chosen words, and each one gave his opinion, to which I gave an attentive ear. Then when all had finished, I said: "I thank you all, who have had the goodness to summon me to this holy place on this account. In reply, I tell you that I do not desire aught of the property of any other person. It is true that I have in my possession some wares belonging to Donna Stella, but she has more of mine in her hands. In any case, I desire to give full satisfaction to the whole community as well as to Donna Stella, so that it should not be said that through my love any disorder arose in the community. Moreover, though I have every right on my side, one who wishes to remain a good Jew must obey Jewish law. Therefore, I am ready to submit the whole dispute to two persons, one chosen by each of us, or else to a Bet-Din appointed by the community, with respect to what she claims from me as well as to what I claim from her. In this, I do not think that anybody can oppose me." Whereupon those who wished me ill and desired that the ban should be proclaimed were dumbfounded at my reply, and all responded with one accord: "Bless you! you speak most wisely!" Then they turned to Messer Solomon Milano and said: "You can tell your daughter that Joseph here desires to abide by the Jewish law." He replied: "And I accept in the name of my daughter."

Thus we all parted, and Solomon went to tell his daughter how matters had been left in the Council. She consented to what her father had done, and gave her word to that effect in the presence of Messer Prospero, Messer Isaac del Borgo, and Messer Clement, one of the Wardens. But when Salvador knew of it, he sent word to Stella that, now the ban was arrived, she should no longer abide by the Jewish law; for, in order to avoid falling into excommunication, I would have to give up everything I had of hers, not she what she had of mine. She sent therefore to tell the Council that she was not inclined to proceed further. Whereupon the Council waited upon Solomon Milano and his daughter, and rebuked them, saying that whosoever wants to remain a good Jew must abide by Jewish law in any matter whatsoever, all the more so since her father had given his word to that effect before the whole congregation. She made answer, that in this she had nothing to do with her father, being a widow, and able to manage her affairs by herself, and that she did not wish to proceed further in the matter. They replied that, if she insisted on having the ban published, it would have reciprocal consequences, applying equally to what I had to give her as well as to what she had to give me. She answered, that nonetheless she did not wish to abide by Jewish law, since the ban was in her favor. Upon this, the entire congregation took leave of her in great indignation for having failed to do that which she had promised, and they were displeased also that the said ban should be proclaimed, because such a thing had never happened before. For these reasons they waxed resentful against her.

And thus it happened three days after, during the morning service, that Solomon Milano and Salvador Gallichi came with all the constabulary and with an order from the Governor that no one should prevent the ban from being proclaimed. Even as they were approaching they were sighted by Abraham Pesaro, who hastened into the synagogue to tell the congregation to leave, so that it might not hear the recital of the ban. And so the reading of the prayers was interrupted (the Amidah being then in the course of repetition), and the whole congregation tried to leave the synagogue. Even as they were halfway down the stairs, they were met by the constables, who made them turn back by force of blows with the flat of the sword, and locked the gate from outside. Clement Pesaro tried desperately to escape, and received many blows from the constables with the flats of their swords and the pommels of their daggers. Likewise, Solomon received many blows from them. At the same time the Bargello came up, and laid about many more with the naked sword, while others prevented people from going out by the windows. At this point, Bonaventura Gallichi, who was officiating as Hazzan that morning, took the ban of excommunication in his hand and set about reading it from the window of the synagogue, because everybody had gone out. As he stood reading it, his nephew Salvador held the black candle in his hand, and it all dripped down on the head of Bonaventura while he was reading.

Inside, there were remaining only Solomon Milano and Salvador and Bonaventura and Abraham da Bologna, and a certain Abraham the hermit, and Sforzo Nissim, and three or four more whose names I have forgotten. These were banging on the benches, while the others were outside the synagogue, and all the women were on their knees crying: "May it recoil on the head of him who is reading it and the person who has procured it!" Meanwhile, the boys were throwing cabbage stalks and stones at the said Bonaventura as he stood reading at the window. Thus on that day there was caused a great outcry and an uproar. No sooner Milano and Salvador and Bonaventura issued from the synagogue, than everyone cried after them: "On your own head," adding all manner of opprobrious insults. And everyone with one voice said of the aforementioned Stella: "It is through that shameless hussy that this disturbance has come about." In consequence of the great insults which were addressed to her by all the congregation, she did not dare to show herself either at her doors or windows: and to remedy this, she had to procure five or six injunctions from the Captain of Justice that no one should molest her, one of which was sent to me. Thus the people were quieted down.

After this, the congregation refused for some time to speak to Solomon Milano or to Salvador Gallichi or to Bonaventura Gallichi, who had read the ban. Only Prospero Semilini continued to speak to them, because Isaac Gallichi was his relative, besides having exerted himself to bring him to Siena when he failed, and sending his sons to him to study. For this reason, he made every effort in the matter, and it was to him that they had delivered the denunciations made as a result of the said ban. He excused himself by saying that he did not like to meddle in such an affair, but because he received commands from the Rabbi, he

could not do less than carry out whatsoever he was commanded. Under
his pretext, he imposed upon everybody as a point of conscience to report
to him in minute detail everything they knew about the matter, in order
not to fall into misdoing. He told the people, however, that they should
write details only of those, whether myself or any other, whom they
knew to have in their possession property belonging to Stella; but if they
knew that Stella had some of my property, or anybody else's, they should
not write about that, as he would not accept their information. Aware
that Prospero was acting partially in this matter, for the discharge of my
conscience, I went to my uncle Ephriam, and begged him to tell me
what he knew about it, since I did not wish to prejudice my soul thereby,
even though I should indubitably lose all that I had in the world. He
told me that he would study the matter, and requested me to bring
him a legal compendium entitled "Caro". When he had studied it, he
told me to banish my fears, of which he made light, since, for a variety
of reasons, he did not think that the ban was valid. Firstly, they had not
given the requisite warnings, which are usually given. Secondly, the
whole congregation was not in agreement. Thirdly, it was not heard
by the whole congregation. Fourthly, there was not even a *minyan*
(quorum) present; and even if there had been, they were all relatives
and interested persons. Moreover, he gave other reasons which I have
forgotten. I replied, imploring him not to prejudice my spiritual welfare,
to which he answered that I should rely upon him. Therefore, I did so,
and refused to make any denunciation. Three days later, all the denunciations were presented by all the men, women and boys to Messer
Prospero Semilini, and he presented them to the arbitrators whom we
had appointed according to the compromise, to whom were presented
also the pawn tickets which I had left in the hands of the Captain of
Justice. All these were returned to me with the exception of two, one
for towels and other articles, and the other for bracelets: with respect
to which they ordered me to prove within ten days that they had been
given me on account of the dowry. I summoned as witnesses Messer
Angelo Semilini and Messer Reuben Frosolone, who had valued the
said articles. Messer Reuben said that he did not remember anything at
all about it, and he refused to come to make an inspection; for he was
uncle of Salvador, and did not wish to act against his own nephew.
Madonna Fiore, widow of the late Laudadio Galletti, offered to give
evidence in my favor in this matter, because she had been present when
my property had been valued and could recognize it in all good conscience, for Solomon Milano was living at that time there in her house.

She told me, therefore, that I might summon her, and that she would testify truthfully. The reason for this was that Salvador had told her to go to empty her purse, besides which he gave her a blow. For this reason, hatred grew up between them. And so I had her summoned as witness, and Messer Angelo Semilini as well. After I had them summoned, both of them changed their minds about doing me this service, although they would have been doing what was both right and just. After my prayers, they consented to give evidence; but they had delayed so long that the time fixed by the arbitrators had passed. So, for love of the opposite party, the officials passed sentence against me, saying that the time allowed me by the award had elapsed. These two pledged together amounted to more than eighty scudi.

I have put this on record, wishing to show, that there are to be found in this world none but hypocrites and traitors. I also place on record how, in the same year that the ban was proclaimed, there died the wife of Messer Prospero Semilini; Messer Amadeo Betarbo, a young man of thirty-five years of age; Messer Aaron Emilio, a youth of eighteen, who was affianced to the daughter of the said Bonaventura Gallichi; the mother of Salvador died eight days after giving birth to a male child; a male child of my own died, aged eight months; the wife of Reuben Frosolone miscarried of a male child; and the wife of Clement Pesaro likewise miscarried of a male child; there died also Abraham Pesaro, at that time President, who sickened on the morrow following his departure from office, and died eighteen days later. Wherefore, shall I pray to God, who has left good life to me and to all Israel, to save us from traitors: Amen, and thus be His will!

MEMORIES OF AN UNHAPPY CHILDHOOD

ANONYMOUS (1668-?)

Here is the story of a simple, modest, perplexed man. The author—he records his family tree for four generations * but fails to mention his own name—was the victim of a "hot-tempered and quarrelsome" father, who placed his own ambitions above the care and education of his son. This intimate record of his childhood and youth in Central Europe during the years 1668-1685 reveals strikingly those psychological drives that made for bachelorhood (and still do) in an age when marriage among Jews was considered as essential as food and shelter. The detailed recollections of family life in seventeenth century Bohemia and of the author's survival of a plague make absorbing reading.

❊ ❊ ❊

MY father devoted himself to the study of Torah in his youth, being an only son, and he showed acumen and skill in talmudic debates which brought him recognition from prominent men and scholars. They married him to a girl of a very prominent family, Gnendel, the daughter of R. Ezekiel of Chelm, in Little Poland. The latter, my grandfather, died in Poland before the times of the terrible persecutions under Chmielnicki, and my grandmother, Nuhah, remained a widow with three sons and two little daughters. I was told that she was a good, energetic, shrewd woman, who supported her family com-

* "I can trace my family tree for only four generations. I learned from my grandfather Jacob that his father Abraham Halevi had come to Bohemia from Poland as a young man possessed of considerable scholarly attainments. He married in Kolin, Bohemia, and died soon after the birth of his son Jacob, my grandfather. As the latter was left an orphan in childhood, he did not know from which city his father had come or to what family he belonged. My grandfather married Lieble, the daughter of Kalman of Bisenz, who was the son-in-law of Eliezer Perels, the author of the book *Damesek Eliezer*, a commentary on the *Sefer ha-Kanah*, as well as other works. His son was Moses Kuskes. This whole family lived in Prague. My grandfather had many sons, but they all died early, and only my father, Abraham Halevi, and two daughters, Rebekah and Pessel, were spared."

fortably up to the time of the great uprising throughout Poland, when she fled with them to Nikolsburg, Moravia, to her brother, the famous R. Menahem Mendel Krochmal, the author of the responsa *Semah Zaddik,* then rabbi of that community and of the whole of Moravia. My mother was brought up in his house. He arranged a splendid wedding, and my father then brought her to his house. At the time he lived in Meseritsch, Moravia. My grandfather, Jacob Halevi, was then rich and prosperous. My grandmother, his wife, was very pious and charitable, and visited the synagogue every morning and evening. This was true of my mother Gnendel in an even higher degree; she was, moreover, a very intelligent woman. My father continued to study the Torah.

Three or four years after the winter wedding, the Mohammedans and Tartars swept over Moravia to destroy it, and all fled in confusion and terror to Bohemia. My grandfather, a rich man, lost nearly all his property, so that but very little of their fortune remained in his hands. My grandfather, his wife, two daughters, and my father and mother with the rest of the family remained in Bohemia. They finally came to Lichtenstadt, where my father secured a post as an elementary Hebrew teacher. After some years he returned and found his house entirely empty. My mother showed her ability in supporting the family by her own efforts, and started to manufacture brandy out of oats in a copper alembic, as was the custom in those parts. This was difficult work, but she succeeded. In the meantime, my father pursued his studies.

One day a holy man, Loeb, the Rabbi of Trebitsch, whose authority extended over Meseritsch, where my father lived, came to our town and stayed in our house. When he saw the troubles of my mother, his cousin, he had pity on her, and gave my father some gold and silver merchandise, such as rings, to get him used to trade in an honest and intelligent way. My father was successful and did a good business.

Incidentally, this brought him the acquaintance of the Count who owned the city. The Count liked him, and turned over to him the "Branntweinhaus" (distillery), in which they were working with seven great kettles, and he gave him servants to do the work and grain to prepare brandy. For this my father paid him at the end of the year a specified amount, in addition to disbursing a certain percentage of the income in taxes, as was customary. Thenceforth he became prominent. My mother bore him first a daughter who died, then three sons, my rich and prominent brother Kalman, my poor self, and a son Moses, who died during the year following his mother's death.

When my mother was at last able to rest from her exertions, she fell sick in consequence of the heat and the fumes of the brandy, and she died at the age of thirty-four. There was no one in our town or outside of it who was like her in wisdom, piety, and charity. She died on a Sabbath, May 21, 1672. I was then four years old, and my older brother seven. In the course of the next year my father married again a great lady, Freidel, the daughter of R. Meir, from Vienna. At the same time he gave his sister Pessel to his brother-in-law Samuel for a wife, so that they made an exchange. The wife of my father was herself still a young child who did not know how to bring us up in cleanliness as is necessary with little boys, nor could she properly care for us when we were sick. We have to thank God and the help of our grandmother Lieble, and her good daughters, that we grew up at all. Even so, little Moses, who was only one year old, died.

After my mother's death my father began to strive for prominence and power, for as long as my mother lived, she kept him back and reproved him in the manner that a mother reproves her son. His father, also, may God forgive him, was all his life hot-tempered and quarrelsome, and from him my father, if I may be forgiven for saying so, had partly inherited the same temperament, for he was still young and had not gone as an exile to foreign countries as I had. But he found his match, who paid him back in his own coin. For there arose against him wicked men with whom my father had quarreled for years, and who had fallen under his power through his influence with the Count. Now the Count sold his property after three years and went to war against the enemies in foreign lands. He left my father in the hands of another Count who had bought the town. This new Count was not so favorable to my father as the first had been. My father thought otherwise, and he relied on a broken reed to combat his enemies. These, however, were numerous and more cunning and deliberate, for my father at that time was hasty in all his actions, and sometimes transacted his business without taking proper counsel and consideration, and he planned great undertakings to increase his wealth and honor, but it turned out otherwise. His enemies ruined the esteem he had enjoyed in the eyes of the Count. The latter made charges against him in connection with the "Branntweinhaus" and other business matters, and put him in prison for two months. Since the first Count was far away, nothing could be done to save my father, and he had to give up half his wealth in order to be released. On this occasion his enemies wreaked their revenge on his saying, "When the ox has fallen, sharpen the knife" (Shabbat 32); and they urged the Count to expel my father, together with his old father

Jacob, from his property. The Count did so. He expelled my father in Tammuz 1675, while my grandfather fled in secret, for he owed money to many gentiles and was unable to pay them. I was seven years old at the time. My father found a temporary shelter in the town of Humpoletz, a town of wool-weavers, and he traded there for a year, while I was cut off from study and good deeds and left to my own devices. He then went to a village Wostrow, for the Count had in the meantime returned from the military expedition and bought this village, and my father followed him there.

As for myself, I was constantly going back in my studies as well as in manners and conduct. After a while my father decided to send me to Prague, which was a day's journey. My elder brother was also there; it was winter then, and I was nine years old. There, too, I did nothing, for my father did not know how to arrange matters properly, and in his endeavor to save money he placed me for a small sum in charge of a teacher who took little care of me, while I needed great attention if I were to be taught with any success. At that time my power of comprehension and my memory were weak as a result of illness. I was full of ulcers, and the meals I ate were very unwholesome, for it is the custom in Prague to eat at the midday meal peas and millet with a little butter, which proved very injurious. But nobody thought to give me medical treatment. Although my father came several times to Prague, he did not observe my need.

I gratefully remember R. Loeb Fleckeles, who gave me meals in his house and kept me for about six months for a small sum, my father paying him about six gulden a month. He wished me to be a companion to his son Simon, who was then five years old, and I helped him by taking him to school and going over his lessons with him. I was very humble at the time and ready to be a slave to everybody, and to do anything I was ordered. If my father only had left me in this house, I would have become used to good manners and learned a little more than in the village of Wostrow among the country people. My father, however, wished to save money and took me home; my older brother was there at the time also. He thought that he himself would teach us, and my brother, who was thirteen or fourteen years old, actually learned from him haggadic literature, such as Rashi and Midrashim, as well as the laws of Shehitah; but I needed a special teacher. My father started to teach me Gemara Sotah once or twice, though I had never before studied Talmud or even Mishna.

Thus a long time passed by without my learning anything, until

I became a thorn in my own eyes and even more so in the eyes of my father, because, for the lack of a mother, I was a boor, brought up in dirt without any cleanliness; and I remember that at the age of eleven I ran around barefooted and without trousers, and no one cared. My father then had many little children, for his wife bore him a son or a daughter almost every year. I am sure that if anybody had announced my death to him at that time, he would have thought this good news, for he considered me ignorant and good for nothing, so that my existence was a burden to him. My brother was a strong boy who did hard work in the slaughter-house and made himself otherwise useful, while I was oppressed by all the members of the house; everyone ordered me around. This continued for the years, 1678-1679.

In 1680 a plague broke out in Bohemia, and especially in Prague. From that city the Rabbi, Jacob Backofen (Reischer), the author of *Minhat Jacob,* came with his wife Jettel and her sister Freidel, the daughters of Rabbi Wolf ben Simon Spira; and they stayed with us in our house in the village. I still remember the great modesty of that scholar who was willing to take the trouble to teach me like a common schoolmaster. But his wife, a domineering woman, did not permit him to carry out his good intention. In the course of Tammuz I fell sick, and the symptoms of the plague became apparent. For three days and nights I had high fever, and was near to death. Then a swelling broke out behind my ear on the neck, which burned like fire, and all the members of the family became frightened. The Rabbi and his wife noticed it, and fled from our house to the house of his uncle in Wotitz.

The plague was raging in the neighborhood of our village, and the Count established a "lazaretto" (a small wooden house of two rooms) in the midst of a big forest about a mile away from his castle. If some one fell sick in one of the villages he was driven out of his house with all his belongings and forced to go into that forest. The Count had set aside an open space some yards wide all around his castle, which only those living in the castle were permitted to approach. He only kept very few people in his castle, and shut himself up there, and never left it with his people. He admitted no outsider except my father, who was clever, and with whom he liked to talk, and he wanted him to appear before him and stay with him most of the day. He had ordered my father to act in the same way, and to forbid his family to leave the house or to admit strangers. He also told him that if, God forbid, a member of his own family should fall sick, he should not conceal it, but of his own accord should leave the house and go with everything into the forest. He warned my father that if he were to find out that he had concealed such a thing he would permit the gentiles to burn the house down with all the inmates in it.

When my father now realized that he had the plague in his house, he was very much upset, and did not know what to do. To carry out the order of the Count and to go with his family into the forest would involve grave danger, for the fact would become known to the inhabitants of the villages, mostly wicked men, thieves and murderers, lying in wait for the blood and property of Jews. Even in the cities they loved to oppress and rob them in their houses; how much greater, then, was the danger of their coming to murder us in the forest. Hence, he decided to hide me in the garret, asking his father Jacob Halevi to take care of me, which he did, although he was an old man himself. He tended me so carefully that no other member of the household needed to come to the room in which I stayed. It was hoped thus to prevent the plague from attacking others. In this way he stayed with me about six days.

But one day, slanderers came to the Count and reported they had seen my grandfather with another Jew, a certain Saul Pollack, who lived in our house with his wife, go together to trade in other villages in which the plague was raging. At once the Court decreed the expulsion of both from his territory at the risk of jeopardizing their lives if they should be seen there again. Then my grandfather was compelled to leave me alone on my sickbed, for it was dangerous to hide, as they would have searched for him in all the rooms, and if I had been discovered it would have involved danger for all. Therefore, both had to leave the territory under the eyes of the Count. But God took pity on my suffering, seeing that there was no one to attend to me, and sent me full recovery, and what was particularly fortunate, the abscess did not open again when in the absence of any one to take care of me, but it went down daily by the grace of God. For there happened to come to us the brother of my father's wife, R. Samson of Kamnitz, who told my father how to prepare a plaster from the white of an egg with a little alum, about the size of a nut. Both of these had to be stirred quickly and carefully in a little kettle until they turned solid. He followed this advice. The plaster was handed to me from a distance and I put it on, although I was only a boy of twelve and sick, for I had been compelled to devise ways of how to take proper care of myself. Similarly they brought my meals to the top of the staircase, which they closed at once. I had to get up from my bed to take them. I lay there alone day and night, and at that time I saw apparitions and dreamed dreams. That I remained alive was against the laws of nature. God in his mercy gave me strength so that I improved from day to day, the fever left me, and only the place of a swelling was burning like fire, and my whole face was red.

One day, however, our gentile neighbors, who noticed my absence, began to say to one another: "See what these Jews did; one of their children evidently died of the plague, and they have concealed it. As trusty servants of the Count, we ought to go and tell him, and take our revenge of the Jews."

When this rumor reached the ears of our family, my father cleverly ordered me to dress, to fold a linen cloth around my neck, and put it on in such a way that the redness could not be seen. He urged me to be courageous, and asked me to go though the garden, over the fields, and to return along the river, passing the houses of the gentiles and the castle. If somebody were to ask me whence I came, I should answer that I was coming from school, that I had stayed with a teacher in the village of Memain two miles away, and had felt the desire to come home. I did so, and, thank God, I ran and jumped like a young deer, passed the castle and the village, and was seen by many Christians, who were thus put to shame, and their scheme failed. Many of our neighbors came to the store to tell my father: "Your son whom we thought dead has returned."

He answered them, "You are dead, but we live forever."

They almost revealed to him what had been in their minds.

My father further showed his ingenuity by telling my older brother to put a ladder to our fruit tree in the garden and ordered me to ascend the tree nearest the street of the village so that all passers-by could see that I was well. He also ordered me to be playful with the village children, to throw fruits into their faces, and to call at them and jest with them. I obeyed and laughed while my heart felt bitter. Thus it was through God's counsel that the rumors stopped. I repeated this several times, but I could not appear before them often, lest they should notice the change in my appearance, for I never used to go with a neckcloth before, and now it was already some days since I had returned from my journey. Once I saw a gentile going before me with his hand on his cheeks, for he suffered from toothache, and his face looked drawn. I jestingly remarked, "Woe unto you. I am afraid you suffer from the plague." I said this to show how healthy and merry I was, following my father's order. But he answered back, "You have the plague yourself; remove that cloth from your neck, and the swelling will be seen underneath." I was frightened and hid myself, but God made the gentiles blind and forgetful.

After a month I came down to the house and mingled with my brothers and sisters as before, participating in the common meals, and no one paid attention to it. I grew stouter and stronger after this.

In the year 1680, in the beginning of the month of Tishri, the plague stopped in Prague, but in the rest of Bohemia it spread to such an extent that people grew tired of keeping away from one another. In our village many even among the people of the castle fell sick and died. My sister Leah, who was then six years old, got the swelling characteristic of the plague, but it was not so dangerous, even though it became public, since the Count had become weary of taking precautions, and my father did not come to him. At the end of Kislev the plague stopped, but in Heshvan the plague had ranged around our neighborhood, and many Jews died from it. In some villages all the male population died out, and only a few women were left. No one was there to take charge of the dead, who remained unburied, for it was winter and the earth was as hard as marble, and there was a heavy snowfall in those parts; so the corpses were only covered with snow, and often wolves came and consumed them, and sometimes the dogs scratched the snow off the bodies. May God have pity on their souls, and may they be bound up in the bundle of life with the other righteous. In our house, thank God, no one died. Only the aforementioned Saul died from the plague two months after the Count had expelled him, so that even this turned out to our good, for in this way he did not die in our house.

In the winter of 1680-81, in the month of Kislev, a great column was seen in the sky towards the east, which was very high, and remained for a month. Some claimed that it was a natural phenomenon called "comet," which sometimes appears in a very cold winter, but the astronomers explained it in various ways, and so it happened that in this year a new great world war (the Turkish war) started, which did not end till 1698.

During this winter my father made great profits, and was successful in all his transactions with various kinds of merchandise. My own impulse led me to the resolve to go to some Jewish community to study Torah. For I was ignorant, and God had shown his great mercy to us. My father promised, but did not keep his word; I often saw guests come (with whom my father went away) and he had promised to take me with him to Moravia, but he changed his mind. This happened several times; the obstacle was that the necessary clothing for me was not ready, as no one looked upon me with kindness. My father's wife had her hands full with her own little ones.

One night before my father was to leave, I was awake the whole night sewing for myself sheepskins which are called "Pelz", and I made a kind of long gown for underwear, and something for my feet. I took secretly some shirts so that my father would not notice anything, and before daybreak I went to the place where the sleigh was prepared for my father, and stayed there. When he came, day had not yet broken, and when he noticed me he thought the house dog was there, and he wanted to kick him away. I then said, "Father, this is thy son, who is ready to serve thee on the way which I take in order to study."

There were many strangers present, business men, who had come to buy wool. They saw my good resolve, though I was very young, and urged my father to take me along; they were sure I would become a great scholar and a good man. My father answered that it was impossible to take me along, for I had no proper clothing and it was very cold. I then exhibited the results of my ingenuity, the things I had myself prepared for the journey. He finally agreed and took me along; but the cold was so severe that several times I thought I was going to die; the snow was falling and the wind blew it into our faces, and it caused my father great pain; it was literally like the sacrifice of Isaac when they (he and Abraham) were on the way, and as the Midrash tells us, Satan brought them into the water up to their throat, etc. But those who are travelling for the fulfilment of a *mizwah* suffer no harm, and we reached Herschmanik. I was left there in the house of a teacher, R. Jacob from Gaja, and he began to teach me Rashi, Midrash, other haggadic texts, and the *Sayings of the Fathers*. He noticed that I could not read properly through the fault of my first teacher, who had not instructed me well. The little I had known I had forgotten, and I was in great trouble, for the new teacher was of an irritable temper, and had neither composure nor common sense. He struck me and put me to shame, but did not make good my deficiency, and only taught me the melodies for the readings from the Torah and the Prophets and a little *Haggada* and the *Sayings of the Fathers*. I asked questions and searched in the haggadic passages, but as he often laughed at me, I stopped. This was surely a grave mistake, but the teachers are foolish, and do not realize the harm they do.

I remained with him from Adar 1, 1681 till the middle of Tammuz, boarding in his house. During the first two months, when he had to slaughter calves, he gave me good meals, the spleen and part of the liver, but when the time of slaughtering calves had passed, my meals became worse and worse, for poor though he was, he was rather fastidious, and he and his wife ate the good things themselves and gave me coarse village bread, which caused me severe headaches and stomach trouble. I was there all alone with no relative near; all the townspeople observed my appearance and questioned me; if I had told them, it might have helped a little, but I was very modest and humble and God-fearing, and I thought it would be a sin to rebel against my teacher.

In the middle of Tammuz, while the teacher was away from home, my father came in company with his brother-in-law, Samson, and stayed for some time in the town. His brother-in-law had a son Sender, who studied together with me and knew all my troubles. He told my father everything, and although I contradicted him, my father believed Sender and took me away from Herschmanik and brought me to Meseritsch, my birthplace, where all my family on my father's side lived; here my two aunts were married, and I had my meals in the house of my aunt Pessel and her husband Samuel, the brother of my stepmother. There was also a good and intelligent teacher, Mordecai from Brod. I went to minyan (became Bar-Miswah) on Sabbath Nahamu; they furnished me with new clothes, and boys of the same age who knew more than I did were jealous of me. They could follow the teacher in the study of Talmud with Tosafot, which I did not know before, and only began for the first time to study here. They were younger and went in torn clothes and rags, as was usual in those parts. Therefore they annoyed me and tried to disgrace and humiliate me, so that I became almost weary of my life. The women of the community all praised me because I was modest and treated them with respect; that was another cause of jealousy. Their parents also were jealous of my father and of me; some of them were really bad. One Aaron, the son of Berl Pollack, I am sure, is still hated by the people for his wicked deeds, which I had occasion to observe: the other, Jonathan ben Lipman ben David, a big lunatic, is now, I believe, a scholarly man. Sometimes he was friendly with me. My intentions were to devote myself exclusively to study and good deeds, but there were many obstacles; I suffered various ailments. I had boils on my whole body, and headaches. My schoolmates were wild and ill-mannered, and our teacher flattered us and showed no inclination to exert himself; what I needed was a regular tutor, but he never employed assistants, nor did he take pains himself. He taught me a little part of Kiddushin.

At the end of the summer he left the place, and the community engaged in his place the pious R. Lazar of Cracow, who was married to a pious, sensible, intelligent woman, and gifted with all good qualities. He taught us Talmud and Tosafot, she taught us the fear of God and a virtuous life. He took great pains to teach me. May he be praised and rewarded for it. Of all my teachers he alone was the one who gave me the key and taught me more than all those I had before or after, except what I studied by myself. Still the whole situation was far from satisfactory, for he too failed to employ an assistant, and sometimes he fell sick; he was also very irascible, while I suffered from headaches during the whole winter.

In the summer 1682 the old teacher returned with his wife Blümele; they had no children, and flattered the pupils and their parents. We learned with a little of Hullin and small treatises of Moed without Tosafot; moreover, I already began to study a little Talmud for myself.

Altogether I stayed in Meseritsch two years and two months. At that time many Jews from Moravia came to Meseritsch, Trebitsch, and Polna on account of the war, for the Turks came to besiege Vienna. I then returned to our house at Wostrow, and stayed there the whole winter in greater discomfort than ever. Everybody, including my older brother, ill-treated me; I was still sick and looked bad till the winter had passed.

Then, at the age of fifteen, I went to Prague, with no knowledge of life in a large community. In spite of this, I found maintenance in the house of a rich man, Moses Ginzburg, who had two little boys. They really needed a tutor better fitted than I was to guide them in study and understanding. I had never tried this before, and could only stay with them a short time. Then God sent me a happy chance, for the scholarly, acute, and pious R. Mordecai, the son-in-law of the Dayyan R. Perez of Nikolsburg, who taught me without pay, had another pupil, Sinai ben Isaiah Wagenmacher, a boy ten years of age, the only son of rich parents, fondled and spoiled, who knew better how to behave than I did. By the help of God, he acted amiably towards me. I had only to go over his studies with him. His parents were charitable people; their house was outside of the street (ghetto), on a large pleasant place; there I gained in strength and health. I lived with them about two years; I felt as if I dwelt amid roses, and never in my life did I feel as happy as in those two years.

Unfortunately no one looked after me, and I fell into bad company. They constantly talked to me about women, and led me in their evil ways. We were a misguided set of young men, of different ages, wasting our time with useless things and fooling with girls, as was their habit. I finally came to think that this is the whole aim of life, since during the entire time we never spoke of anything but of following the inclinations of the heart. The greater part of my days I spent with my young friends who lived an immoral life. Among them were some who were over twenty-three years old, and had more talmudic knowledge and better manners than I. Therefore, with the consent of my father, I joined them and followed in their footsteps, like the blind in the dark, thinking in my simplicity that the purpose of good manners was to find favor in the eyes of women, and that this is human happiness in one's youth. Even in the house where I lived, the young working men who were employed in building carriages for the noblemen were a bad sort; their ringleader was a certain Abraham Bass, who was boisterous and wild, so that I was under evil influences from all sides. I was more passionate at that time than ever again in my life. How happy should I be now if my father had then given me a wife. I would have raised a large family, no doubt, in my early life, and would now have been in a position to retire from all worldly affairs.

Now, unfortunately, I am devoid of wisdom and intelligence, without sons and spouse. I wish to retire from the affairs of this world, but I do not know whether, after all, it would not be better for me to marry; possibly I might have pious children and a capable wife who would be a help to me. I wait for an answer from God, hoping that he might notify me by a sign or a dream or a verse, of which I might think when I wake up, or which a child might answer when I ask for its lesson. May I be successful according to the wish of God. Amen.

MY JOYS AND SORROWS

GLÜCKEL OF HAMELN (1646-1724)

Glückel was a woman of immense resourcefulness and talent who composed a fascinating full-length autobiography. Born in the busy port of Hamburg two years before the close of the Thirty Years War, she spent a good part of her eventful life there as the wife of Hayyim Hameln, a successful merchant. Though engaged in her husband's business enterprises, she managed to raise and guide a dozen children. After his death, she carried on heroically; but the effort was too great, and she wed the banker Cerf Levi of Metz, only to be left the widow of a bankrupt in 1712. She died in Metz in 1724. Written for her children "upon the death of your good father, in the hope of distracting my soul from the burdens laid upon it," this memoir is unique. In its graphic account of intimate experiences, its lively sketches of character, its warm humor and frank self-revelation, it not only throws a flood of light on the period but also introduces a plucky, intelligent, independent woman whom it would have been a joy to know.

❋　❋　❋

I BEGIN this fifth book, dear children, with a heavy heart, for I mean to tell, from the beginning to end, of the sickness and death of your beloved father.

The evening of the 19th of Tebet, 1689, your father went into town to arrange certain business with a merchant. When he was close to the merchant's house, he stumbled and fell over a sharp stone, and hurt himself so badly we were all alarmed.

He came home in great agony. I chanced to be visiting my mother, and I was called back at once. I found my husband groaning by the fire, and badly frightened I asked him what had happened. He told me he had fallen, and feared there was much for me to do. He was unable to stir, and I had to empty his pockets myself. For when he set forth he had laden them with jewelry.

We did not at once, God help us! know the real nature of his injury. He had long suffered from a rupture, and in stumbling he had fallen on the ruptured spot and badly twisted his bowels.

A bed stood always ready in the lower room, but he did not wish to use it, and we had to bring him upstairs to the bedchamber. It was a bitter cold night, as though the skies would freeze together, and we remained by his side through the cold hours, doing our best for him. But we could stand it no longer, neither did it do him good to lie there in the cold, and at last he saw the harm of it, and we brought him downstairs once more.

We worried along in this way until past midnight, and still he grew no better. I saw my sorrowful fate staring me in the face, and I begged him, in Heaven's name, to let us call a doctor and attendants. Whereat he said, "I would rather die than let the world know of it." I stood before him and wept and screamed, "What talk is this?" I said, "Why shouldn't people know? It has come through no shame or sin."

But my talk proved all of no avail. He clung to the foolish fancy that it might do his children harm; people would say that the weakness was in the blood. For he never had thought of else than his children. And so we had to contend with him the livelong night, and applying every manner of poultice.

When day broke, I said to him, "Praise God the night is over, now I will send for a doctor and a rupture-cutter." But he would not listen to it, and bade me send for the Sephardi Abraham Lopez, a physician and chirurgeon barber. I had him fetched at once.

When he came and saw the injury, he said, "Have no fear. I will lay on something that will heal him forthwith. I have dealt with hundreds like him, and it has never failed me."

This was early Wednesday morning. Dr. Lopez applied his remedy, thinking it would shortly heal him. But, God have mercy! when noontime came, he said, "My cure, I see, is not enough—I will go and bring a rupture-cutter whom I know to have a clever hand." The rupture-cutter came and worked the entire day in the hope of easing the injury. But the longer he labored, the worse it became.

Thursday I brought in another rupture-cutter and two more physicians, one of them Dr. Fonseca. When I talked with him and related all the circumstances, he told me, "There is little I can say—or do. Alas, the bowels are so badly twisted he will not be able to evacuate." And what should have gone off naturally broke, God help us! through the open wound. Every aid failed him, and still he refused to have strangers about him and begged us all to keep it a secret. As for me, I knew and saw my fate before my eyes.

So Thursday passed, day and night, in bitter distress. Friday Dr. Lopez brought us a Berlin doctor, for many years physician to the Elector. He too gave him something to take and laid on a bandage, alas, to no purpose.

It was Saturday morning when my brother-in-law Joseph first learned that something was wrong with my blessed husband. He came running to our house and begged to be let into the sickroom. When my husband heard him, he said, let him enter.

As soon as Joseph saw him, *nebbich,* he knew what it meant. He struck his head against the wall and tore his hair and with bitter tears he cried aloud, "Woe unto me that I must lose a brother-in-law like him!" And he cast himself on my husband's bed, and with streaming eyes begged forgiveness for aught he had done.

My husband answered him from the bottom of his heart. "My beloved brother-in-law," he said, "I forgive you and all living men, and give me, I pray, your forgiveness too." Whereat my brother-in-law sought to calm him and bade him be patient, God would yet come to his aid. And my husband replied, he was content to be in God's hands.

As for myself, he did not tell me a half of his illness, but he kept ever at his side my son Loeb, then a lad of sixteen. When I was out of the room, he called the lad to him and told him how matters stood, and the boy wept sorely. But as soon as my husband marked I had returned, he quickly said to the boy, "Silence for the mercy of God! Your mother comes—let her not see your tears!" Even at death's door he thought of nothing but to spare me pain.

Saturday morning, after mealtime, my mother came and flung herself upon him, and kissing him between her tears, she said, "My son, must you now abandon us? Is there naught I may do for you?" Whereat he answered, "You know I have loved you like a mother—I have naught to ask or say--only comfort my poor Glüchelchen." That was the last word he spoke to her.

But who is now my comforter? To whom shall I pour out my soul? Whither shall I turn? All his life my beloved companion hearkened to my troubles, and they were many, and comforted me so that somehow they would quickly vanish. But now, alas, I am left to flounder in my woe.

Later, more doctors and rupture-cutters came, but they could do nothing. By the close of the Sabbath, no one remained but Dr. Lopez and myself.

Towards midnight Dr. Lopez sent for a chirurgeon, in the hope that the wound was fit; but he came and saw at a glance that nothing could be done, and he departed.

Whereat I said to my husband, "Dearest heart, shall I embrace you —I am unclean?" For I was then at a time I dared not touch him. And he said, "God forbid, my child—it will not be long before you take your cleansing." But, alas, it was then too late.

Upon the advice of Dr. Lopez I now summoned Feibisch Levi who knew how to be with a man in his dying hour. He arrived towards two in the morning, when I also called in our teacher, a most trustworthy man.

Feibisch Levi went at once to my husband. "Reb Hayyim," he said, "have you any last wishes to give us?" Whereat my husband answered. "None. My wife knows everything. She shall do as she has always done." And then he asked Reb Feibisch to bring him the works of the learned Rabbi Isaiah Hurwitz.

After he had read in them for about half an hour, he turned to Reb Feibisch and our teacher. "Don't you see," he said, "how near I am? Let my wife and children leave. It is high time." Whereupon Reb Feibisch thrust us by main force from the room.

Reb Feibisch now sought to engage him in further talk. He gave no answer, but began speaking to himself. They could only see his lips moving. So it was for nearly another half hour, and then Reb Feibisch said to Dr. Lopez, "Abraham my friend, lay your ear to his mouth, perchance you can hear what he is saying." Dr. Lopez did so, and after a space he heard him say, "Hear, O Israel, the Lord our God, the Lord is One!" With that, his breath ceased and he had breathed away his pure soul.

Thus he died in purity and holiness, and they saw from his end the man that he was.

What shall I write, dear children, of all our bitter grief? I had always stood so high in his eyes, and now I was abandoned with eight of my twelve forlorn children—and one of them, my daughter Esther, betrothed! May God have mercy on us and be the Father of my children, for He is the Father of the fatherless! I truly believe I shall never cease from mourning my dear friend.

Sunday, the 24th of Tebet, 5449 (January 16, 1689), he was buried with all honor. The entire community was struck with horror and grief at the sudden blow of it.

With my children gathered around me, I sat upon the ground for the seven days of mourning, and a sad sight it must have been to see me sitting thus, with my twelve fatherless children by my side.

We immediately secured our ten men for the daily prayers in the house of mourning, and we engaged scholars to "learn" Torah day and night through the whole year—be it not to my reproach! And the children diligently said *kaddish* for their departed father. And there was not a man or woman who did not come, daily, to comfort the bereaved among us.

My son Joseph was then a youngster of fourteen, a fine lad and exceedingly apt to "learn" Talmud. It liked me, therefore, to send him forth to "learn" as he should, but I hardly knew where.

At that time Isaac Polack had a teacher in his house, a solid young man from Lissa (Poland) and a mighty Talmud scholar. This teacher heard that I wished to place my son out for his studies, and proposed I should give my boy in his care. He asked not a penny for board or teaching fees until the end of two years, at which time he promised to return me my son fit to expound the Law.

I made inquiries after him, and everyone advised me to accept his offer. Whereat I drew up a contract with him, and sent my son in God's name with his teacher on to Lissa.

My son lost no time in writing me, first of his safe arrival, and then, in truth weekly, of his great content with his teacher and of how earnestly he "learned". And more of him I did not ask.

About two weeks later, my son Joseph wrote me, begging me to send on a half-year's payment for his board and teacher's fee. I was not, to be sure, obliged to do it—so he wrote me—but life had grown very dear in Lissa, so that his teacher was beset with the need of raising money, naturally a hindrance to the progress of the studies. But were his teacher relieved of these cares, he could the more rapidly advance in his learning. The teacher had other children from Hamburg—the letter continued—and their parents had all sent money, so he prayed me not to remain behind the others.

It really mattered little to me whether I paid the fees sooner or later, and I sent him the money for the half year. So all went well, and I learned from passing travelers that my son worked hard at his studies.

But when the six months were nearly over, I received a letter from

my son Joseph—it was on the eve of Sabbath as we made ready to go
to synagogue—that read as follows:

> "My dear mother, you know that I have always been a good boy
> and never done anything against your wishes. So now I hope you
> will not withhold from me your mother's love, nor let me fall
> into the hands of the gentiles.
> "For I must tell you, mother dear, that the Jewish community
> of Lissa is greatly in debt to the church powers and cannot pay
> either capital or interest. The community sees no other way out,
> save to hand the children of the German Jews over to the church
> powers by way of a pledge. And then their German parents
> may ransom them as they can.
> "The administrator of the community secretly revealed the plan
> to all the teachers with German pupils, and a Talmud student
> who is my good friend whispered it in my ears. I dare not write
> you of it myself, for my teacher watches me too closely and
> reads every one of my letters, so I have asked the young man to
> write in my stead.
> "For the love of God, mother dear, write to Tockel's son-in-law
> to give me fifty or sixty Reichsthalers that I may pay my teacher
> and that he send me home in secrecy, and I escape from their
> hands.
> "I beg you, in God's name, hasten! For if you delay I shall fall
> into the power, God forbid, of the Poles, and should that happen
> and it come to a question of ransom it will cost us tenfold. So I
> beg you, for a bit of money do not forsake your child, and let
> me not fall into hands from which it will be hard to get free."

When I read this my strength left me. I summoned my son Mordecai
and showed him the letter. He, too, was stricken with alarm. Sabbath
had just begun. At its close we decided to send my son Mordecai to Lissa
forthwith, and have him bring home my son Joseph.

Mordecai set out at once for Berlin, and thence to Frankfort on the
Oder. As he left the gate of Frankfort, my son Joseph came riding
towards him in a little Polish cart. My son Mordecai saw him, bade
him descend, and asked him by what strange hap he was riding to
Frankfort and what he meant by such a letter to his mother. And he
showed him the letter.

My son Joseph read it, and said, "What does it mean? Really, I
haven't the slightest notion. My teacher—may his name be blotted out!—
must have written it himself, and thought to pump another bit of money

out of me, as he has already squeezed all he could and pleased. He has taken all my belongings, cut the silver buttons from my coat, and made off with everything.

"When I wanted to leave him, he charged me with all manner of false debts, I had eaten like a pig, devoured his house, and despoiled him. I saw that nothing good could come of it, so I asked Tockel's son-in-law to make terms with him. He paid thirty reichsthalers and took me away, and sent me on here. Thank God I am free of that scoundrel! What is more, he taught me nothing."

My son Mordecai was only too happy to have chanced on him, and they returned at once in their coach to Hamburg. I rejoiced mightily and thereat took me an honest teacher and had my son "learn" at home.

About this time, something terrible happened in Hamburg.

There lived in Altona one Abraham Metz, whose wife was my kinswoman: Sarah the daughter of Elias Cohen. Before coming to Hamburg he had dwelt in Herford and married the daughter of Loeb Herford. Two years after marriage, his wife died, whereat he moved to Hamburg and took to himself the aforesaid Sarah.

He came a man of means, with some 3000 reichsthalers or more; but strange to Hamburg, he knew nothing of its way or manners of business. He kept losing ground steadily, and within a few years he had nearly reached the end. Thereafter he moved to Altona and became a money-changer.

One morning his wife comes to Hamburg and asks of all the houses where he was known, if he had not passed the night beneath their roof. But despite all her inquiries she found no trace of him. The woman now sank into despair. Many said she had quarreled with her husband and he had taken to flight.

So the matter stood for three years, and everyone wagged their tongues as they pleased. There were those who spoke great evil of him— God revenge his blood!—things that for the sake of a martyred saint I dare not repeat. But, alas for human frailty, our mouths often speak what our eyes have never seen.

Thus, for more than three years, our Sarah lived as a widow and sat with her fatherless children about her, suffering people to say and judge what they liked of her husband.

Then there was Aaron ben Moses, another householder in Hamburg —a money-changer too, an honest man and by no means rich, yet a decent provider of his wife and children.

Now, money-changers must run about the whole day long in search of business, and towards afternoon prayers they return home and go to synagogue. Or they have every one his *chevra* (society) where they study Talmud and then betake themselves home.

One evening the wife of Reb Aaron waited till long after dark for her husband to return, that they might sup together. But she waited in vain. Then she ran out searching among all their friends, and found no sign of him. And he, too, remained lost.

The next day a cry went up everywhere. One man said he had seen him here, and another there.

When noon came, people gathered on the Bourse and talked of nothing else. Samuel, the son of Meir Heckscher, said, "Yesterday a wench came to me, who had a little money. She asked me whether I had six or seven hundred thalers, and if so I should come home with her, where there was a well-to-do stranger who had quantities of gold and precious stones to sell. But I lacked the money and did not go with her."

When he had finished his story, a man named Lipmann, who was standing by, asked him what kind of a person the wench might be, and how she was dressed. Whereat Samuel Heckscher told him. And Reb Lipmann said, "I know who she is, and where she works. And I have no reason to think good of her master."

After this talk and more like it, everyone left the Bourse and went home.

When Reb Lipmann reached his house, he said to his wife, "What think you of this? The wench who works for the son of the keeper of the Navigators Tavern went up to Samuel Heckscher and wanted him, if he had six or seven hundred thalers about him, to go home with her. I fear me that the little fellow who is lost did as much, and it cost him his life."

Then his wife struck her head and said, "By my sins! I remember now this wench once came to me, and wanted either you or me to go off with her. You know right well the wicked head that tavern keeper's son carries on his neck. He is no one else but the murderer, and the little man, I say, was killed in his house."

An energetic soul, the wife of Reb Lipmann swore she would give herself neither rest nor peace till she brought the matter to light. But her husband answered her, "Foolish woman, even if it were true, what could be done? This is Hamburg, and we dare not breathe a syllable about it."

Several days passed. Then the Town Council was induced to send forth a crier with a drum: whoso knew aught of the missing Jew, whether he be dead or alive, let him tell what he knew and he should receive a hundred ducats reward and his name would never be said.

But no one came with anything to tell.

So time went on, and the affair was nigh forgotten, as is the way of the world. No matter how urgent or important be a thing, if it leads nowhere, it soon vanishes from the mind of man. But not so the anguish of the grass widow and her fatherless children.

Then, early of one Sabbath morning the wife of Reb Lipmann found she could not go to sleep.

Thus it was with the King of Spain who asked a learned Jew the meaning of the Hebrew words, *Hiné lo yonum ve-lo yishon shomer Yisroél.* Whereat the learned Jew gave him the plain meaning, "Behold, He that keepeth Israel shall neither slumber nor sleep." But the King said, "Nay, it means otherwise. Methinks it means 'God, the keeper of Israel, lets one neither slumber nor sleep.' For had I slept this night as it my wont, the slanders laid to the door of the Jews would have brought them to their ruin. But God who is their keeper would not let me sleep, and I rose and saw the murdered child cast into the Jew's house. Had I seen it not, it would have cost the life of all the Jews."

So, too, the wife of Reb Lipmann could not sleep. And early mornings she sat by her window, for she lived in the top story on the Alter Steinweg which leads to Altona, and everyone going to and from Altona must pass her door.

That Friday night the poor woman never slept a wink and she drove everyone mad in the house. Her husband groaned, what a life—she will drive herself crazy! But she said, there was no help for it, as long as the crime goes unavenged she could give herself no peace, for well she knew and her heart told her who had done the deed.

Meanwhile day broke, and she stood again at the window and looked in the street. There she saw the very man passing by with his wife, and a servant went with them carrying a large chest.

When the woman saw them, she began to scream, "God be with me now! And I'll have peace at last!" And she snatched her apron and her shawl and ran down from the room.

Her husband sprang from the bed and sought to withhold her. But she shook herself loose and ran after the people.

They made their way to Altona and laid their chest by the bank of the Elbe. Rebecca—that was the name of Reb Lipmann's wife—was persuaded the chest held the body of the victim.

She flew to people in Altona and begged them, for God's sake, help her, for she knew she had the murderer before her eyes. But no one wanted to hearken to her, and they said, it is easy to begin something but who knows how it will end? However, she kept on crying, Only take me to the President!

Finally, two householders went with her to the President, and told him everything. Whereat the President said to them, "Beware of what you begin. If you do not prove what you say, all you have and hold is forfeit."

But Frau Rebecca refused to be daunted, and said she would stake her very life upon it. "For the love of God," she said, "send, my lord, and fetch the man and all he has with him."

Then the President dispatched watchmen and soldiers to the Elbe. The suspects had on the instant boarded ship heading for Hamburg, about an hour away from Altona. Once they reached Hamburg, they were free, for Hamburg lay in another jurisdiction.

But the watch arrived in the nick of time, and brought the man, his wife and their chest back to the President. He ordered the chest opened. And naught was found save clothes that belonged to the man and his wife.

You can readily picture the alarm of the poor Jews. The man was questioned in every way, but he would own to nothing. On the contrary, he delivered himself of such threats that the Jews trembled with fear. For the man came of a very high family. And, finally, the Jews ran off in terror.

But Frau Rebecca never ceased saying, "Good folk, I beg you, do not despair—you will see how God shall help us!"

As she came running, all distraught, across the fields lying between Altona and Hamburg she met upon the wench who worked for the man. She knew the wench well, the same it was who had gone among the Jews to bring whosoever had six or seven hundred thalers to her master's house.

Frau Rebecca at once said to her, "Lucky for you and lucky for your master and mistress that we are met. Both of them are now imprisoned in Altona for the murder they have done. They have confessed to everything, and there lacks only your own confession, and once you have given it, the boat stands ready to carry you off to safety with your master and his wife. For all that the Jews want of you is to know that Reb Aaron be really dead, so his wife may be allowed to marry again. Apart from that we Jews want nothing from you."

Frau Rebecca kept on talking to the wench in this strain. She was a clever and glib woman, and through her chatter she won the wench over into talking herself; and pell-mell the wench told everything: how she had met Reb Aaron on the Bourse, and later Reb Lipmann and other Jews, how none, for a lucky lack of money, went with her, save the poor Reb Aaron, cursed as he was with a full purse, and how she showed him a gold chain and told him that an officer in her master's house had gold and diamonds for sale.

"So this Aaron," she continued, "went with me. But before he ever entered the house, the slaughter block was set for him. My master led him down to his chamber, and we did away with him, and buried him under the threshold."

And then she said, "Frau Rebecca, I have told you this in all confidence—you will not use it against me?" Whereat Frau Rebecca answered her, "Are you a fool? Don't you know my honest heart? I am thinking of naught but the safety of your master and mistress, that they go free from Altona. Once you come and tell our people what you have said, all will be well."

So the maidservant went with Frau Rebecca to the President's house. The President listened to the maid, and though she began to stammer and regret she had opened her mouth, still all was out, and not least the place where the victim lay buried.

Thereat the President summoned the murderer and his wife, each apart, and they both denied the deed, and said, "Everything our maid has told you is false, she lies like a strumpet."

Once again this put a bad face on things, and the President said to the Jews, "I can help you no further. If I put the man to torture on the word of his maid, and he persists in his denials, 'twould be pretty work. It is for you to seek justice now in Hamburg, and quickly as you can. Secure leave from the authorities to search the house for the body, and should you find it as the maid has said, I shall see to the rest."

The administrators ran at once and arranged to bring twenty soldiers to the spot the maid had mentioned, and began digging. They also received leave, if the body were found, to carry it to Altona for a Jewish burial. But they were likewise warned, "Take you heed, if the body be not found, you are all of you done for. You know right well what sort the Hamburg rabble are—we could never hold them back."

We one and all lay in grave danger. But Frau Rebecca was everywhere, at each man's elbow, and she kept repeating, "Do not weaken, I know in sooth the body will be found." For the maidservant had talked away her life and given her no end of proof.

Ten stout-hearted fellows and a number of seamen known to be loyal and bold were gathered together, along with certain watchmen. And they went in God's name to the murderer's house, which lay not far from the Alten Schrangen, hard by the house of the jailer.

Meanwhile a cry arose throughout the city, and a mob of working men and general rout of *canaille,* countless numbers, swarmed before the door of the murderer's house.

With one will they said to themselves, "If the Jews find the body, well and good; but if they don't, there'll not be hide or hair left of them."

But the good Lord did not keep us long in suspense. As soon as our people entered the house, they dug up the spot by the doorsill and found what they sought—at once with tears in their eyes and joy in their hearts.

They wept to find the youth of twenty-four in such a pitiable state, and rejoiced that the community was saved and justice at hand.

They summoned the entire Council, and showed them the body and the place where the maid said it would be found. The Council drew up a sworn statement of their findings and put their seal to the affidavit.

Then the body was placed on a cart and taken to Altona. Throngs of seamen and apprentices looked on, I can't tell you how many, perhaps a hundred thousand; but not one of them let slip an evil word. Wicked folk though they were and even in peaceful times forever hounding the Jews, now they were silent, and each man returned quietly to his place.

The next day our administrators took the affidavit and brought it to the President of Altona, who had the murderer and justice in his hands. And the Jews were better pleased to have the trial held in Altona.

The President again summoned the murderer and told him all that had passed. Whereat he confessed to everything. The widow received what share of the money still remained, and they sent the man back to prison for trial.

I will now resume from where I left off.

Several matches were proposed for my son Joseph, but none found favor with God save the daughter of Meir Stadthagen, who dwelt in Hamburg. We, therefore, blessed the match and celebrated the betrothals in Hamburg. The wedding was set for a year later.

When time drew near for the wedding, which was to be held in Copenhagen, I planned to journey there with my son Nathan.

Nathan was now heavily engaged in business with the rich Samuel

Oppenheimer of Vienna and his son Mendel. He held their notes to the amount of 20,000 reichsthalers, and they were on the point of falling due. But my son received neither remittances whereby the notes might be met without default, nor even a letter explaining their delay. For this reason he found himself unable to go to Copenhagen. Instead, he must keep watch for his own honor and the honor of his correspondents.

You may readily conceive our worry and heartache. I set forth alone with my son Joseph, and God knows with what anxiety and bitterness of soul. For I knew naught of how things stood with the rich Viennese.

I left Hamburg together with the bridegroom and Moses, the son of Meir Stadthagen and the son-in-law of Hayyim Cleve. And we arrived safe in Copenhagen.

There I awaited letters from my son Nathan, hoping to hear that he had received word and remittances from the wealthy Viennese. And in truth he wrote me, the good son he was, that though he had no news from Vienna I should not worry or rejoice any the less at the wedding.

Though my heart was not in it, still I left all in God's hands and dismissed my cares. We exchanged our dowries and the wedding was prepared for the following week.

From one post to another I awaited good news from my son Nathan. Praise be God, the tidings came the day before the wedding. Nathan wrote me that Mendel Oppenheimer had sent him remittances to several thousands more than we were owing him or needed, together with apologies for the delay, due to his absence from Vienna. And the wedding was celebrated in high spirits and to our mutual content.

After the festivities I was anxious to speed my way home, but I had no other traveling companion than Moses, the son of Meir Stadthagen, and he was in no haste to leave his folks. So, against my will I remained two weeks in Copenhagen. Yet despite all the honors and courtesies they bestowed on me, I longed to be home with my little ones. At length I pressed Moses Stadthagen so hard, he consented to depart. Thereupon we set forth, and praise God, arrived safe and sound in Hamburg.

I went into accounting with my son Loeb for the wares I had left in his hands, and he gave me a clean bill for everything, so I was mighty content.

DEFEAT OF SATAN

JACOB EMDEN (1697-1776)

Emden was one of the most controversial figures of his time, and the following narrative out of his full-length autobiography will introduce the reader to an issue that split Jewish communities everywhere into warring factions. It was the teaching and practices of the Sabbaitians, the followers of the picturesque false messiah, Sabbatai Zevi, who had stirred the imagination of the Jews in a period of vast upheavals. The movement had broken up into splinter factions under the leadership of extraordinary personalities like Abraham Cardozo whom Emden regarded as agents of Satan and whom he fought with satanic passion. But Emden's vehemence makes him suspect. It was not only a matter of venting spleen, but, as his unrelenting attack on Rabbi Eybeschütz reveals, there was something that weighed like a cloud upon his tormented spirit. It was not merely an opponent's job he envied, as has been suggested, but more likely the intensity of his physical and psychical ailments. Thus his autobiography is a psychological document of immense significance.

❃   ❃   ❃

BEFORE I begin the story of what befell me, I faithfully declare that I am not doing so in order to describe my name and fame; for I myself know that there is nothing worth while in me, neither Torah nor wisdom. I did not inherit greatness wherewith to preen myself. Please God that I do not write on these sheets what will reveal my deficiencies. But my people know that I have chosen humility, that ever since I have been able to think I have known my small value and defects. For this reason itself it does not matter to me and I shall inform everybody of my lowliness because I love only truth. . . .

During the period of my gestation my father suffered from melancholy because of the loss of his money. The sickness was so bad that they almost despaired of curing him had it not been for the mercies of heaven which returned him to his strength. A few days before I was born he came home from the baths at Ems. There he had taken the medicinal baths and returned to Altona after my mother of blessed memory had borne me, on the 15th of Sivan, 1697. And he circumcised me after he had already despaired of doing so and the honor of fulfilling this commandment had been entrusted to another *mohel;* and he inducted me into the Covenant with doubly great joy because he had returned to his former health and now had a son after giving up all hope. For until that time he had only had daughters; and I was the fourth child and first son and very delicate, so my parents trembled for me exceedingly, and I grew up on their knees as a plaything amid much pleasure and tenderness. My father of blessed memory, withal, hastened to put me to school after I was three years old, so that in my fifth year I was already learning the tractate *Berakot* of the Talmud. I was so devoted to my books while others of my age could not even read their prayers. But afterwards he refrained from sending my brothers who were born after me to the teacher while yet they were so small, saying that he had weakened me thereby.

When I became a little understanding I felt father's suffering, his pain and shame because of the people who wished to deprive him of his livelihood and degrade him from his honor. After this he became very sick with pleurisy on account of an excess of bile caused on account of the dispute at Altona. The doctors had already given him up but my sisters and I fasted on his account on the Monday and Thursday of one week when I was only twelve years old. When my father was appointed Rabbi of the Ashkenazic congregation at Amsterdam the time of my wanderings and exile began.

Father's household started out at the end of the winter in the year 1710, at the time of the melting of the snows, which had fallen in exceeding great plenty during that powerful and mighty winter. We were in great danger on the way. The cart in which the women and children were sitting all but broke, and fell into the water which rose vastly high. Our outcry went up aloft and if the Lord had not delivered us the waters would have carried us away. But we came alive and well to another land, Holland, which we had not known yesterday or previously; new air and new customs. How many changes we underwent until we grew accustomed to the nature of the country, particularly as the food and drink were not those to which we had been accustomed and most of all the quiet did not last long, nor did they permit my weary father to rest; for immediately there commenced quarrels and persecutions of two powerful groups. Each side strove to swallow the other alive. My

father was crushed between them, for as he could not bring them to
agreement and could not justify either of them but prevented the weaker
side from being trodden underfoot, they waged war against him and
embittered his life, thinking to bring his honor down to earth as already
described. But the Lord aided him and protected him, and at that time
the Sephardic community supported him. Nevertheless this was a time
of trouble to Jacob, and perplexity because of father's suffering. In addition, this dispute wasted much time which should have been devoted to
the study of Torah. At that point I was confirmed, but the times did not
permit me to devote myself to books, nor to acquire complete knowledge
on account of the absence of teacher and comrade, leader and director
with whom I might prosper. Nor was there any cure for this absence
of restfulness for the sins of that place led to the coming of the hypo-
critical serpent, the abominable Nehemiah Hayun who confused everybody and everything. And my righteous father of blessed memory was
compelled to engage in a heavy war, standing out against the prideful
Sephardic magnates who broke their former covenant of love with him
and became his foes, after intervening in a quarrel that was not theirs,
in order to hide the shame of their Rabbi Solomon Ayllon who was
responsible for all this. So that my father of blessed memory was compelled to remove his dwelling from thence and to wander once again in
order to find a refuge for himself and his household.

Now this is what happened. The sins of the community led to the
coming of Satan to make the world chaotic; namely the evil spirit and
poisonous serpent, the abominable hypocrite Hayun who bemused the
holy congregation of Sephardim and Ashkenazim alike. The heart of
all the people was divided into two, those who went to the right and
those who went to the left. Yet at the beginning the entire congregation
of Sephardim to a man were true to their Father in Heaven, and it was
they who awakened and roused love against which the whole wealth
of a man is esteemed with contempt, as is written in Writ. They came
to my father of blessed memory to consider the case of this hypocrite
and man of violence, to investigate his impure and worthless book;
wishing to depend primarily on the authority of my father, knowing
him to be an absolutely reliable person possessed of wisdom and
understanding.

To begin with they refused to accept their own Rabbi Solomon
Ayllon, who was already suspect in their eyes on account of a certain
unsatisfactory incident, resembling this but preceding it, in connection
with the sectarian writings of the heretic Abraham Michael Cardozo,

which had been brought to Amsterdam a year before Hayun had arrived. These writings had been written in the Spanish tongue and so were understandable to the ordinary Sephardic Jew. Reading them would be enough to make their hair stand on end by reason of the vast heresy they revealed; yet this Rabbi of the Sephardim had passed them, saying that they were good, holy and pure. But that did not help at the time since the members of the Mahamad (presiding committee of the Sephardic community) burnt them in his presence because they were written clearly in their own Spanish language. From that time forward the said teacher of falsehood was under suspicion of being affected by the filth of the false faith of Sabbatai Zevi. As is mentioned in the books *The War of the Lord* and *The Reward of the Wicked,* it was made clear that he had previously been one of the followers of that false Messiah, and although he had already departed from them and reverted to the Jewish faith, nevertheless the old weakness had remained.

Now like had found like. Therefore when this bad matter of Hayun developed they did not want to depend on him at all to begin with, not trusting him as regards this very grave and rare matter of faith. Therefore they all agreed unanimously to send to my father of blessed memory and hear his opinion and do as he counseled; for his name and fame were very widespread among them as being unique for striving to maintain and strengthen the faith. So they gave him the book of Hayun for a certain time to examine, since it had reached them only for a little while by dint of great stratagems, as is told in the two pamphlets above-mentioned. And they placed the sword in father's hands to execute justice against that enemy of the Lord who had thought to replace Judaism by his imaginary new faith; and who set out to remove Israel from the traditions of their fathers, as was finally proved in all the courts of Israel from East to West. They all thanked my father and teacher of blessed memory for being zealous on behalf of the Lord, and issuing a stern verdict against that troubler of Israel, to remove him from the boundaries of Israel. Afterwards many more of his abominations were revealed. For he did the deeds of Balaam and polluted the Holy Land; the very world cannot contain all that he has done, as has already been set out in print in sundry pamphlets and broadsheets.

Yet at that time Satan was advancing among the members of the holy congregation of Sephardim, and all but in their very sight. After they came back and took the book of abomination from my father of blessed memory, they accepted his words and accordingly undertook to drive the disgusting Hayun out of their synagogue; but then they recon-

sidered and set out to destroy all that they had built; their hearts turned
to hatred of father, they turned their backs upon him and did not wish
to hearken unto him any more about executing justice upon that man.
And after they had already done as my father of blessed memory
counseled and very shamefully thrust Hayun forth from their synagogue,
they changed their minds and admitted him to their congregation, entreating him with great honor.

The chief reason was because their said spiritual teacher, who was
bound up with Hayun, went about his dark plots. He went to the house
of each of the members of the Mahamad and fell at their feet and wept
and entreated them, saying: Despite the fact that he is a sinner and a
transgressor, still they must take pity on his honor which is their own,
seeing whither would they bear their shame and reproach in confirming
the suspicion and shameful report that he belonged to the followers of
Sabbatai Zevi, thereby increasing the rank of the Ashkenazic Rabbi over
that of the Sephardic Haham; particularly as they claimed that they had
more power and esteem than the Ashkenazim.

Ever since the community had been established, said he, the Ashkenazim had been abject and submissive before the Sephardic congregation of Amsterdam, because of the leading position of the latter with
their wealth, their pedigree and greatness; while they also had precedence
in time, since scarcely had Holland become a free kingdom on its own
than the forced-convert Sephardim fled from Spain and established themselves in Amsterdam. For the Hollanders had broken off the yoke of
the king of Spain, and all the inhabitants were liberated, and they gave
permission to men of all faiths and religions to dwell in their midst.
Hence the forced-converts of Spain had found a resting place there to
begin with, through a Jew of Emden who had brought them to Amsterdam and circumcised them and instructed them in Judaism; and only
after them had Ashkenazic Jews been attracted to settle in the town.
Hence it befitted their honor to precede them in everything, particularly
in view of the wealth of the first Sephardim who came to dwell in
Holland; for these had been great men in Spain and brought their gold
and silver with them, wealth vast indeed; and therefore they were important and honored by the government authorities.

But the Ashkenazim who had come thither were mean creatures
compared to them, since they were unimportant as regards wealth and
greatness in those days; and now what nightmare was this wherein the
lower ones were on top and the upper ones below!

The man spoke after this fashion and stole their hearts which had been whole with the Lord to begin with, by reason of his smooth foreign tongue and flattery; so that their minds turned to follow him when he said: Although the law may not be so, the time requires this so that you may protect the honor of yourselves and our chief congregation by not accepting the decision of the Ashkenazic Rabbi, but by repenting of all that you have already done. By weeping and entreaty and supplication and prostration and chicanery, by smooth words and deceitful lips he succeeded in leading them astray to destroy what they had first set about doing, to repent of the good; so they sank their feet in mire and a smooth tongue broke the well-built flight of stairs; and they agreed to do that which had never been done in Israel. By deceit and wily false conduct of the kind called politics he led them astray to withdraw and be false to their faith; he caught them in the net of error to destroy them. All this chapter and the stratagems and instruments and strange and bitter falsehoods which came about at that time have already been made known to those who are still alive and well remember this evil mishap, which is not yet as far back as fifty years. Also many works and pamphlets were written and published at the time of this grave war which lasted a full year. . . . Actually it was this incident which led me to write this book in order to proclaim the wonders and loving kindness of His blessed Name; for the new is as the old, the father reveals his truth unto his children and all that happened to the fathers befell the sons; a thing which cannot be written in full detail. Therefore I shall not deal further with this incident which occurred more than forty years ago. . . . For that which befell my father of blessed memory befell me in the case of Rabbi Jonathan Eybeschütz, an absolute parallel, so that which befell the father also befell the son.

In Summer, 1722, half a year before I left the rabbinical office at Emden there came to the town a sending of evil angels, who declared that they had been sent by the community of Minsk in Lithuania because of an ill hap that they said had befallen there. These emissaries invented this in order to mislead Israel and steal the money of the charitable, declaring that the folk of the holy congregation of Minsk were in great distress. With them they brought false documents which purported to be written by the rabbi of that community to the congregations of Israel, to make their distress known to all and sundry and beseech aid; further, that he had appointed those persons named by him in the document to go about through the length and breadth of the land and gather money everywhere to bring for those who were in peril of death. And throughout the communities of Germany it is notorious what these robbers did, how they emptied the charity chests of the poor and misled many German communities, likewise the Sephardim of London and Amsterdam. The latter in particular treated them with great honor, and generously donated for them more than ever all the honest and reputable causes had received from them since time untold. For they had banned all granting of their charity funds to German-Jewish poor, no matter who they might be. I remember that once soon after my father and teacher of blessed memory settled in Amsterdam the emissaries of the holy congregation of Lublin arrived there, worthy men and faithful to those who sent them; and father did all he could on their behalf, also recommending the Sephardic congregation to be with them in time of trouble; and by pressure and energetic intercession, since they could not send him empty away, particularly at that time when they esteemed him like a veritable angel of the Lord, they acceded and handed over to him the donation they thought fit to give the Lublin emissaries; in order that it might seem as though they gave him a gift, because they regarded him as being like a Sephardi too; but they did it that way because they did not wish to transgress against their resolution to give nothing to the Ashkenazim.

That was the strict way they kept this prohibition. But still they took a liking to these forgers and swindlers and gave them donations in plenty, disregarding their oath on this occasion. This shows that they and many of the magnates of Germany came under the curse of Jeremiah the Prophet of being misled by a people who are not worthy. At the last these men came to me at Emden. I felt that all they were doing was deceit and forgery but nevertheless I treated them in friendly fashion to begin with; particularly as one of them was a kinsman on my father's side, Reb H. Wilner, one of the scholars of the house of study of Mannheim who belonged to the sect of Rabbi Yehuda Hasid. I have no reason to be proud of the kinship. although he was a pleasant fellow, handsome and something of a scholar, and I esteemed him and liked him before the forgery became apparent.

One of the others was an exponent of practical Kabbalah and could use the Holy Names for his works. I sounded his cask and found him to be worthless, a man of blood and deceit and an ignoramus. In my opinion they certainly belonged to the followers of Sabbatai Zevi, and went about with a fellow from Minsk, who was likewise a young man of good understanding, knowing something about the insides of books, the Gemarah with commentaries and other knowledges, besides belonging to one of the proudest families of Lithuania. He had separated from the wife to whom his kinsfolk had wed him when he was still small, and dwelt in Germany. This was the fellow they took with them to bear witness to their trustworthiness and faithfulness, for he was known in Germany as an outstanding scholar about whom nothing bad was known except his separation from his wife. Maybe he had some satisfactory reason for this and did not wish to leave her a living widow, God forbid, being prepared to give her a bill of divorcement and pay what was provided in the wedding agreement; but to that she objected and did not wish to be divorced. I also liked him because I saw signs of wisdom in him; though he was still young, I said, "this little one will grow big in the course of time."

After these false emissaries had been staying with us a while in Emden I was visited by my uncle, the brother of my mother, who came from Lithuania from the town of Grodno, and whose name was Rabbi Benjamin. I had never expected to see him, but although he was at the other end of the world the Holy and Blest One made him travel and brought him to us; and when he ate at my table we began to talk of the two emissaries who were in the city at the time, and who were traveling about on account of an unfortunate incident which had happened in the congregation of Minsk. Now this uncle of mine was a simple man who spoke without ulterior motives, and when he heard this he stood gaping and could not believe his ears, saying to us, "What are you talking about? What mishap has there been at Minsk that I know nothing about? How long have I been away? The town is quite close to me and yet nothing is known about this. In our parts nothing is known of any mishap, great or small." Now the supposed mishap had already happened a year earlier according to the liars, while he had just come from there.

I therefore decided that this tale was a falsehood and a vast lie; and I brought these men to examination, and took a legal document signed by the leaders of the Minsk community which I had with me. "If you are honest men," said I to them, "I shall help you with all my power, for I am even more anxious than you to have the merit of fulfilling an injunction like the redemption of captives, as you request. But in order to put you to the test and confound the rumors circulating, I suggest that you should entrust us with the monies which you collected from the communities in Germany, Holland and England, so that we should send it to Breslau; and we shall arrange that the money should reach your Community in a safe and direct manner, to whatever worthy leader you choose. And we shall give you a properly attested quittance to deliver you from ill report and libels. Further, whatever gifts you have received for yourselves will remain your own and we shall add to them; but we shall take steps to ensure that the poor of your Community should receive the sums donated specially for them. If you agree it will be all the better for you and double merit. And in any case why should you take the responsibility of the road upon you? For this is the custom of all faithful emissaries since time immemorial in order to be clear before the Lord and before Israel."

But I could not make those deaf ears hearken or understand this straightforward matter. No matter how much I spoke, whether hard or soft, calling upon them not to refuse, it all proved in vain. For these two men were cunning as serpents to mislead everybody with seductive words and smooth tongues; and even a great friend of mine with whom one of these scapegoats was staying was trapped in the net of their deceit. From beginning to end he was a friend closer than a brother to me; but this time even he opposed me and supported the evildoers, swearing in the Synagogue that these were upright and worthy men and that I had no reason to give them a bad name. Then I knew that an ignoramus cannot be truly God-fearing, and that there was no dwelling near him, because he swore in vain after hearing the falsehoods and smooth words of the suspect. In any case most of the communal leaders of our times are fools believing all the flattering deceivers and erring with unsuitable people who stay in their houses and steal their minds and their money, thereby misleading others as well through the recommendations they give to aid such transgressors. I still grieve exceedingly for this faithful friend whose end by reason of our many sins was bitter; he lost his wealth, and what was more the very gifted wife of his youth passed away sometime after I left the place; and he took a different wife who lost him all his wealth. And in a little while he also died; and his new wife took what she could and went to another husband, and what she brought him when he married was lost because she also died; and his children were left poor orphans, alas and alack. For this my heart bleeds when I think of the goodness of their mother, may she rest in peace. And who knows whether that false oath did not destroy him and his household? Let the leaders hearken and take heed, and not trust too much in their wealth; which is enough of this matter.

Now the end of the business of the said false emissaries, who were skilled in smiting fools with the fist of flattery and of trapping men with their mouths, was that they fled from under my hands at Emden and I could not get anything out of them; but they received large donations there as well; and I had to laugh at the fools who threw away their money on unworthy people. But in any case I did not rest until I found out what the truth of the matter was. What did I do, I took their attestation from Minsk with regard to their mission to deliver people who were sentenced to be slain, and to bring money to annul this evil decree. This document was signed by the leaders of the congregation of Minsk. I sent it by post to Altona to my then faithful friend Haham Hagiz, may he rest in peace, and requested him to investigate the matter and find a Lithuanian who could identify the signatures and say whether they were true, or whether anything was known there of this mishap in the said community.

And now hearken to the wonder; for the sage of blessed memory at once found a warden from Minsk whose name was also signed on the said attestation and who had just come to Altona. Now this was a worthy and aged man who had never previously been in Germany, but had lost his possessions in his old age and so had to go wandering. He arrived there the same week as the forged letter of the swindling emissaries. The Haham summoned him to his house and showed him the document with his signature, and said, can you recognize whose signature it is? Thereupon the old man stood astounded and said, what man has dared to do such a thing, to forge a handwriting and signature and to invent an evil happening which never really existed?

When I received the answer from the Haham telling me of the wonderful happening how the Lord had sent him one of those mentioned by name in the false document, and how the Lord had brought this worthy man from the ends of the world at the right time in order to prove the falsehood and forgery, thereby showing the truth of my words, I showed this letter to my friends. But not only did it make no impression, not only did they not take back what was stolen from the poor, but on the contrary they gave them gifts and sent them honorably away.

To be sure, I at least warned those men who were going to make the rounds of the world and empty the charity coffers. I adjured them for their own sakes not to go to Altona where they would fall into a trap. But they would not listen to my counsel, relying on the success they had had until then. They thought that the Three Congregations (Hamburg, Altona and Wansbeck) were the same fools as those they had found it Emden, whose eyes could be blinded and whose hearts could be stolen by smooth words; so they went there.

But if nobody was prepared to listen to me in Emden, my net was set for them in the congregation of Altona; and what I foretold them came about. For as soon as they arrived they were arrested by order of the wardens and leaders of the community, who had them imprisoned and expended the charges of arrest and imprisonment on them; but they could not succeed in delivering the money of the poor which was in their hands, nor to make them give up what they had stolen. Still, they were driven out of there with mockery and much contumely.

As for this Reb Wolf whom they had taken with them as a false witness, he parted from them and repented and confessed without being ashamed as mentioned in my volume of *Responsa;* for he confessed his sin and recognized his transgression in the query he sent me on a matter of Torah. I shall mention the subject in brief before making an end of the things that happened to me in Emden; since it was another very worthy and pious deed which His Blessed Name brought my way while I was there. The Lord sent me a certain man who came to me to be shown his way of repentance; and he already despaired of marrying because he was already old. And as a proper means of readjustment and repentance I enjoined upon him that he must wed a wife within a year; and he did so and succeeded and merited to have children ere he died.

I did not wish to have any benefit on this account from the considerable sums of money he brought with him. Afterwards he wrote me that he had merited to have a son when I was already in Altona; and he summoned me then and I remembered the incident.

I WAS A SLAVE

ABRAHAM HERTZ (1706-1776)

Autobiographical accounts of those sold into slavery are rare. This curious record is unique in Jewish literature. Hertz's recollections naturally center about an experience which ultimately led to his conversion to Christianity, and the sincerity and candor of the narrative leave little question that the conversion was a genuine religious experience. He changed his name to John C. Leberecht, and passed his later years as the principal of a small children's school in Königsberg, Germany. "The narration," says an anonymous preface, "was taken from the deceased's own lips, and his own phrase has, as much as possible, been preserved throughout."

❊ ❊ ❊

I WAS born in 1706, according to the Christian era, at Glogau in Silesia. My father Moses Levi Hertz was a man of learning. On being circumcised on the eighth day, I was called Abraham. I was brought up in my father's house till I was eighteen years old, at which time both my father and mother died, within one month of each other. Thereupon my grandfather, and other relations, sent me to the famous Jewish university at Prague in Bohemia. Here I pursued my studies for five years, till 1728, when the Rabbi procured me a place at Nikolsburg in Moravia, as tutor of the children of Moses Cohen, a wealthy Jew, in whose family I continued three years. My term in this family having expired, I went in the same capacity to Pressburg in Hungary, and entered as tutor into the family of Jacob Rachmetz, with whom I likewise remained three years. Then, with his consent, I went to his brother in Belgrade, on the border of Turkey, and was employed in the same occupation for about six years, till the year 1739.

At this period, the city of Belgrade was ceded to the Turks. About eight thousand of the inhabitants, Christians and Jews, were made slaves; and I, with the whole family in which I lived, sharing the same fate, we were all carried to the Turkish fortress Niffa. Here I was sold to a Turk, Temershe Ali, who had already purchased another of the unhappy captives, a young man, and a Christian of the Lutheran persuasion. We were both chained together, and taken by our master to Serras in Greece.

The name of this young Christian was Neuman. The Turk, our master, required this unfortunate man to submit to a very heinous sin; but not being able to persuade him to it, he ordered him to be whipped in so cruel a manner that the poor fellow had not a sound spot left on his whole body, but was covered all over with wounds and sores; and I, his fellow slave, had to wash his wounds, the stench of which was intolerable. I therefore took great care not to come too near him in my sleep, lest I should touch him, and thereby increase the anguish of his pains.

Soon afterwards, the Turk made me his interpreter, compelling me to convey his abominable desires to Neuman. And as once, in the folly and ignorance of my heart, I advised him to submit rather than expose himself to the barbarous treatment of the Turk, he remained not only adamant in his refusal, but declared that he could by no means bear the thought of thus offending his Lord Jesus, and that he would rather die than commit a sin. He then reproved me, saying: "Are you one of God's people, of the Jews, who boast of their being a peculiar people of God, and dare you advise me to commit sin?" These words went to my very heart, nor could I, from that hour, be easy in mind, but became deeply concerned for my salvation. Add to this that my poor, wounded fellow captive continually called upon the name of Jesus, which used formerly to be odious to me as a Jew, and prayed to him so fervently, that my inmost soul was often moved at it, and I, by degree, got a hearty love for this Christian.

One day, as he was speaking to me very feelingly of Redemption, I was persuaded to acknowledge his religion to be the true one, giving him my hand upon it, and promising to embrace the Christian faith and to be baptized as soon as I should again come into a Christian country. Before very long poor Neuman died of his sufferings, still bound with his chains. Notwithstanding the barbarous treatment the deceased had suffered, there was something uncommonly striking in the aspect of his lifeless body: far from filling me with the horror the sight of a corpse is apt to excite, there appeared something so lovely and pleasing in this corpse, that I could not behold it without pleasure; nor could I ever afterwards think of him without tender sensibility or forget his image.

It was as if the form of this happy man were constantly present and hovering before my eyes.

My late friend had told me, that he was the undutiful son of a Lutheran clergyman in Saxony; that he had learned the business of a stocking-weaver, or framework-knitter; but that, disregarding the admonitions of his parents, which he since often lamented, he left them. He went into Silesia, where, being taken by the Imperial troops, he entered into the army and was sent as a soldier to Belgrade, where he was taken and made a slave by the Turks.

According to a promise I had given him, I now attempted to have his body decently buried; a business which the Christians here, as well as the Turks, were afraid to undertake. But before I could do it, the Turk, my master, hearing of the unexpected death of his slave, which happened in the night, fell into such a fury that he ordered me to receive an hundred and fifty lashes on the bare soles of my feet, on the pretext that I had killed Neuman in the night. I complained of this outrage to the cadi, a Turkish magistrate, who, upon examination, found that the deceased had died of his wounds and the barbarous usage of his master. Thus was I acquitted, and the judge obliged the merciless Temershe Ali to dispose of me to another Turk, called Hadshi Mustapha. He took me from Serras in Greece to Constantinople, and thence to a place in the neighborhood of Smyrna, where he was settled. This Turk was a very good-natured man, and showed me much kindness during the two years (till 1741) I was with him. But all his mild treatment was not sufficient to lessen the unhappiness and distress of my mind. The demise of the late Neuman and the memory of all his discourses with me, presented themselves unceasingly to my spirit. I now resolved to write to a Jew at Smyrna, requesting that I might be ransomed by my nation and delivered from slavery. This letter had the wished-for effect. I was immediately ransomed, though my new master was very reluctant to part with me, and when at length he consented to it, he had the goodness to make me a present of sixteen zechins (about seven guineas) towards my traveling expenses, and kindly entreated me to call at his house, if ever I should come again into those parts.

From Smyrna certain charitable Jews sent me to Constantinople, where they endeavored to persuade me to settle. But, such was my uneasiness that I could not think of staying there. Declining therefore every proposal, I expressed a desire to travel farther in order to visit the graves of my relations in Silesia, which is agreeable to custom among the Jews. Upon this I obtained the necessary testimonials from the Haham, the Chief Rabbi, and was forwarded, by sea, to Bender, thence, by way of Jassy, to Hungary, and next to Mohilew in Poland. But being desirous to go to Silesia, the Jews were obliged to conduct me thither. We traveled to Kamenietz through the confines of Hungary, by way of Osen and Pressburg, into Moravia, and at last to Breslau and Glogau in Silesia, where, being arrived at the graves of my parents, my conductors left me.

In consequence of what I promised the late Neuman, I was determined to go in quest of his worthy father in order to acquaint him, if he should be living, how his son had died. I traveled on foot to Saxony, where I heard that the Reverend Mr. Neuman was deceased; but learned at the same time, that his widow lived at Naumburg. I went thither, and, having found Mrs. Neuman, gave her an account of the painful, and yet happy, departure of her late son, which the good woman heard with all the emotions and tears a tender parent feels on such occasions.

KING FOR A NIGHT

PINHAS KATZENELLENBOGEN (1691-1760)

The family tradition of an ancestor who reigned as king of
Poland for a night has persisted with unbroken continuity. The
author of the account here given was the great-grandson of Saul
Wahl and the Rabbi of Anspach, Leitnik and several other communities. Historians tend to identify Saul with the prominent business agent of the Lithuanian Prince Radzivill, who had considerable
influence at court as well as the unique privilege of bearing a saber,
and was known in contemporary records as Saul Yuditch. The
event occurred in the interregnum between the reigns of Stephen
Bathori and Sigismund III which would place the event in 1586.
Pinhas accepted his father's deathbed story uncritically, he is unaware
of certain historical inaccuracies, but family and national pride rarely
differentiate between legend and history.

❋　❋　❋

MY grandfather, Rabbi Samuel Judah of Padua, had a son who
was the illustrious Saul Wahl of blessed memory. The sur-
name Wahl, according to those versed in history, was conferred upon him because he was chosen (Wahl means "choice" in the
vernacular) King of Poland by the unanimous vote of the nobles of
the country. I heard from my father and teacher of blessed memory
that this extraordinary event happened in the following manner.

Saul was beloved by the great princes of Poland and esteemed for
his remarkable ability. While he was at the peak of his influence, the
king of Poland died. It was the custom of the great nobles to assemble
for the election of a new ruler on a specified day on which it was
prescribed that a decision must be reached. When that day came, the
nobles, disagreeing among themselves, were unable to decide who should
be king. They debated until evening when it appeared that it would be
impossible to elect a new king on the day prescribed by law. In order
not to permit the day to pass without appointing a ruler and thus

transgress their own enactments, all the nobles agreed to make the illustrious Saul Wahl king for the remainder of the day and the following night, thereby conforming to the letter of the law. Immediately they crowned Saul, shouting in their own tongue "Long live our Lord, the King." They loaded him with royal honors, and he reigned all that night.

My father told me that they placed at his disposal all the documents of the royal archives, for it is the custom of every ruler to add enactments according to his wisdom. The eminent Saul Wahl inscribed on the rolls many enactments and decrees for the welfare of the Jews. I have forgotten those that my father told me of, excepting one: a decree ordering that any one who murders a Jew should suffer the death penalty just like the murderer of a prince. No ransom was to be allowed—a life for a life. This law had applied up to that time only to Christians of noble rank.

The following day the nobles agreed upon a candidate and elected a king.

Now in order that these events may be remembered by future generations, I shall record how it came about that Saul won the esteem of the nobles of Poland, particularly as his father, Samuel Judah, was Rabbi in Padua and Venice in Italy. This is the account my father gave me. In his youth while his father was still alive, Saul was seized by an irresistible urge to travel to foreign countries. He left his paternal home in Padua and journeyed from country to country, and from city to city, until he came to Brisk in Lithuania. There he married the daughter of Rabbi David Drucker and lived in straitened circumstances.

About that time it happened that Prince Radziwill, who was second in rank to the King and one of the richest nobles of the realm, desired intensely to travel abroad. It was the custom of princes to travel far and wide in order to observe the character and customs of foreign peoples. So Prince Radziwill journeyed from country to country until his purse was empty. As he did not wish to reveal his plight to the princes of the land, he was in a quandry. He was in Padua at that time, and decided at length to reveal his identity to the Rabbi and make a substantial loan so that he might continue on his way. (That is the way of the Polish nobles. They befriend wise Jews, especially rabbis, in order that they may borrow from them; as a consequence, influential Jews in those days were held in high esteem by the princes.) So Prince Radziwill visited Rabbi Samuel Judah and told him his story. The Rabbi gladly provided him with money and equipment. Whereupon the Prince said to him, "Quite apart from my financial obligation to you, how can I recompense you? How can I return good for good?" The Rabbi replied, "First, I request that you act kindly and justly toward the Jews who dwell in your power. I have another request. A son of mine named Saul lives in Brisk. The good which you desire to grant me, I beg that you grant my son." The Prince immediately took the name and address of the son so that he might carry out the Rabbi's wishes.

After he had returned safely and settled himself in his home, he immediately made inquiries about Saul and summoned him. It did not take him long to discover that Saul was a man of uncommon ability. Whereupon he granted him many favors, showering him with gifts and appointments and praising him to the skies to the other nobles. They took a great fancy to him and he prospered in their circle. It was then that the incident I have related above occurred. He was chosen king for that night, and consequently they called him—Saul Wahl. I heard this whole story from the lips of my pious and learned father.

I will digress now to give an account that came to me from another source. When Prince Radziwill left his native land to see the world, he followed the custom of taking with him a large retinue of servants. As his means diminished in the course of his travels, he gradually disposed of the servants so that when he reached Padua, not only did he lack money, but only one servant remained with him. The Prince sent him to Rabbi Judah to arrange an interview. The Rabbi inquired about the Prince's background, and the servant told him the whole story of how he had lost both servants and money. Immediately the Rabbi ordered his household to prepare a banquet in honor of the Prince, and invited him to attend as the honored guest.

He came and feasted at the table of the Rabbi. Then, in the midst of festivities, the Rabbi said to his servant, "Go to the market place and fetch me one of the captive slaves." (It was the custom then, as it still is in Turkey, for every citizen to take one slave from the market, and the owner had the right to do with him as he pleased, even to kill him if he so fancied.) The servant followed his instructions and brought a slave to the Rabbi in the presence of the guests. The Rabbi, pretending to be serious, said to the servant, "Take this slave to the proper chamber and kill him." Taking the slave away, the servant waited a while in order to give the impression that he had carried out the order. Then he returned and said, "I have done as you commanded, my lord." Thereupon the Rabbi said to him, "Return to the market and fetch another slave, bigger and comelier than the first." Again the servant appeared with a slave. "Well done", said the Rabbi, "take him and do with him as you did with the first slave." The servant put the slave in the same chamber with the first and gave them food and drink. Then he returned and told the Rabbi that he had carried out his command. Then the Rabbi repeated the performance a third, a fourth and a fifth time, the servant in each instance placing the slave with his fellows and providing him with victuals.

The Prince was bewildered by the performance. He could not restrain himself. He asked, finally, "What is the meaning of this? Why in the world do you spend your money purchasing five slaves and then killing them off for no reason?" Rabbi Judah responded enigmatically, "Aren't we Jews required to spill blood? Is not my lord aware of this?" The Prince was amazed at the explanation. He scrutinized the Rabbi's face closely. At length the Rabbi broke his silence, explaining his mystifying conduct. "I have done what you have seen," he said, "in order that you may know that the accusation against us regarding the use of blood is utterly evil and false. Our religion forbids us to spill blood. Yet, as a result of this false charge, many innocent souls have suffered and many have been martyred. Now I know, my lord, that you are a great prince and second only to the King in Poland. Why have I done all this? To show you that even though it was in my power to slay five souls without hurt or murmur or responsibility, I had no such intention. Isn't this proof that the blood accusation is false? Even if we assume that the charge were true—Heaven forbid—why should the Jews of Poland endanger their lives by killing a Christian when it would be possible for us to send them casks filled with the blood of slaves? You can see that this accusation is contrary to fact and reason, and I solemnly hope that in the future you will do all in your power to serve the glory of God by correcting the injustice. Verily, we are innocent just as I am today. For I bought those five slaves, not to slay them, but to provide your excellency with the servants your station requires; and I wish to provide for your other needs."

The Prince recognized the truth of the Rabbi's acts and the wisdom of his words, and assured him that he would guard the welfare of the Jews and protect them from this sinful slander. He would like, he continued, to reward the Rabbi's generosity. "Is there anything else I can do," he asked, "to repay you for rescuing me from my plight?" Thereupon the Rabbi told him that he had a son named Saul who lived in Brisk, as I have related above. The Prince assured him that he would interest himself in his son upon his return. The rest of the story you already know.

To return to my narrative, I heard more of Saul's history from my learned and pious father in 1733. He lay mortally ill in Fürth, a city where many physicians reside. I went there from Markbreit, and I stayed with him for three weeks. When I was alone with him, he dictated his will, which I wrote down word for word. Then, speaking almost inaudibly, he told me the following in order that I might know, he said, what happened to our noted ancestor, Saul Wahl:

"The King who was elected by the nobles the day following Saul's brief reign placed him in a high position, and he was revered as a leader among the Jews. His success went to his head, however, and he became very haughty. This brought him great misfortune. He had a daughter by the name, I believe, of Händele, a girl of rare beauty and intellect who was famous throughout Poland. Many suitors sought her hand. Among them was a brilliant young scholar, the son of a noted rabbi. (My father did not reveal his name, either because he did not know it or preferred not to mention it.) To make a long story short, the Rabbi brought his celebrated son to Brisk, and, staying as a guest at the home of one of the community elders, broached the match. But our ancestor, puffed up with pride, considered himself high and mighty and thought that his beautiful daughter was worthy of a more distinguished suitor. This match he would not even consider, thus humiliating both father and son. The whole community was outraged. They murmured against Saul Wahl. They sought to assuage the wounded feelings of the distinguished guests, and one of the most prominent citizens gave his daughter in marriage to the young scholar. But from that time our ancestor suffered the hatred of the whole community. They sought eagerly to bring about his downfall.

"An opportunity came. It happened at that time that the Queen died. Some of the men of Brisk, intent upon revenging Saul's insult, went to the nobles with whom they were in favor and spoke to them of Händele. They described her exquisite beauty and remarkable intellect, as excellences worthy of a queen. As a matter of fact, was she not a queen? Had not her father sat upon the throne? They filled the ears of the nobles with such talk, suggesting that they in turn repeat it to the King and inflame his passion. Of course, they perpetrated their evil plot most subtly, lest Saul get wind of it and frustrate them. They cautioned the nobles to act quietly so that the King might seize the girl before her father became aware of it. The nobles followed the counsel of these slanderers, secretly winning the ear of the King. He had the girl brought to the palace secretly by the royal guard.

"But God, who watches over Israel and dispenses His everlasting mercies, willed otherwise. He had mercy upon Händele and granted Saul the wisdom and power to prevent the consummation of the plot. With the help of the Almighty, he acted speedily and wisely. And whoever knew what had happened and saw the outcome wondered greatly."

DAYBOOK OF AN ADVENTURER

SIMON VON GELDERN (1720-1788)

Von Geldern was described by Heinrich Heine, upon whom this grand-uncle of his made an indelible impression, as "conspicuous by his personal beauty and imposing appearance and also by the splendor of his oriental dress which exercised, especially upon the women, a magic influence. . . . He was on the one side somewhat of a dreamer, who made propaganda for cosmopolitan and Utopian ideas, and on the other side one of those adventurers who, confiding in their individual superiority, either break down the rotten boundaries of a rotten society or else disregard them. At any rate, he was a genuine man." Certainly Heine leaned heavily upon the tales related to him by his aunts about his grand-uncle's wanderings and adventures, not to mention his own vivid imagination. Von Geldern might have become a successful banker or rabbi, but he succumbed to the lure of a life of adventure. The asceticism of his later life failed to pull him out of the world of fantasy which he had fashioned to compensate for his deep frustrations. While he is not as expansive as we should like him to be in these notebook jottings, his enigmatic personality is nevertheless stamped upon the pages. The reader will find Heine's portrait of von Geldern on pages 334-335.

❉　❉　❉

HE WHO takes these things to heart will exult and tremble, since each moment brings him nearer to the terrible bitterness of the day of great and fearful judgment, in the presence of Him before Whom he must offer his explanations and submit his record. He will rue all his sins, errors and misdeeds; he will confess them—for "he who confesses and recants, merits forgiveness"—and remove himself from all those allurements which might lead him to sin again; he will control his lust for food and drink, since they are the source of all other evil desires (God save us!); he will make the Torah his everlasting absorption, and business only his passing interest, and he will bear in mind the verse: "I always have God before me," as well as the other scriptural passages which purify thought.

Behold, I now regret all my errors, sins and misdeeds; once more I resolve—though I have often done so before—never to sin again; with tears I beg my Creator, the King of Kings, to forgive the sins, misdeeds and errors that I have committed and to accept my good resolution as if I had submitted to every punishment prescribed for every sin. I haven't the strength to impose them on myself; God knows that as a result of one of the mortifications which I did undertake, I became mortally ill, and though I am finally recovered, I am still very weak. Our prophets said: "Return the day before your death." Perhaps that day is already at hand, and I am in a strange country, far from my family and my father's house—God protect them! Therefore I write all this down, as a testament, for whatever may occur, and to recapitulate my own recollection of the forces which have driven me onward from the days of my youth until now.

My venerable father, who was the respected and renowned leader of his community, and intercessor for the province of Julich and Berg (near Holland), was Elieser, the son of my venerable grandfather, the respected and famous leader of the community, Herr Juspa, of sacred memory, of Düsseldorf. My father was called Josef von Geldern; he married my venerable mother, the chaste and pious Leah Sarah, of sacred memory, the daughter of my venerable grandfather, the intercessor Simeon Pressburg of sacred memory, who lived in Vienna, the residential city of the Emperor, and who will be known and respected among his kind for generations to come. The marriage took place in Düsseldorf. Later my parents moved to Vienna, and in Vienna I was born, for good fortune, on Tuesday, the 11th of Marheshvan, 1720. Certainly, if I were to say, "It is better not to have been born," it would not seem to have been for good fortune; but I take into consideration the words, "My beginning was small, but at the end I shall become great." My godfather was my uncle Henoch Pressburg, and the circumciser was the distinguished and renowned Mordecai Pösing of Vienna, who now lives in Pressburg.

When I was about a year old, my parents took me to Düsseldorf, and I thank them for the agony they had to suffer on my account, when I fell from the wagon and a wheel passed over me. But when they lifted me off the ground, they found me safe and unharmed. From what I have been told of this period, only trivial things happened to me.

When I was four years old, I was already studying section *Beza* of the Talmud. At the age of eight I delivered an address at the consecration of a Torah scroll which my honored father had donated to the sacred vestments of the synagogue. The scroll was worth more than 1,000 gulden. Of my teachers I remember the wise Baruch of Posen (Poland) of sacred memory, and the distinguished Elia Helm of Lemberg, as well as my kinsman, Abraham Frank, son-in-law of the Chief Rabbi of Koblenz, near Düsseldorf.

When I was ten years old I accompanied Reb Abraham to Mannheim, in order to engage in the study of the Talmud at the higher academy, under the great teacher Reb Samuel Helman. I lived there two years, after which I returned to my father's home in Düsseldorf and studied another year.

In Heshvan of 1733 I was confirmed, and my parents arranged a festive dinner on that Sabbath. Then I went to Frankfort-on-the-Main and studied for about a year at the Talmudical Academy of the great Gaon, alone among his kind, Jacob Cohen, of sacred memory. I studied Talmud with Rabbi Lasi Heller of Halberstadt. I lived in a small room, though I paid a great deal of money for it. Therefore I resolved to move away, but I did not want to embarrass my landlord by moving into other quarters, though there were many people who offered me a room free of charge. So I gave my landlord more than three groschen every week and he let me have a larger room. I took leave of my teacher, who introduced me to a traveling companion, and gave me his blessing for the journey.

Invoking the Rabbi's efforts, I hope that God, glory be to Him, will save me from every sin and protect me, so that I may serve my Creator according to His will, and if such is His design, that I may receive death for the sanctity of His great Name. Behold, I confess and repent all the wicked desires which the evil instigator planted in my heart, for they are futile and temporal, and all against my will. I turn ruefully back and tearfully seek forgiveness for the sins, the missteps and misdeeds which I committed before the King of Kings.

I arranged a banquet on the Sabbath for the young people, the students at the Academy, and on Sunday I gave a banquet for the youth of the whole city. Then, in the company of Reb Jekel Nobel, the son-in-law of the Rabbi of Rappeswir (he was still a bachelor then), I went to Darmstadt, where I stayed about two weeks at the home of the distinguished Reb Israel Wiener. Then I journeyed to Mannheim, where I found my grandmother, of sacred memory, sick in bed. She had fallen and broken a limb. She arose from the illness forever freed and released of the burden of this life, on the 19th of Elul, 1735. On the same day my venerable father came to Mannheim. At this time a great war was raging between the Kaiser and the King of France, over the kingdom of Poland. Ten thousand soldiers came out of Moscow to help the Kaiser, and the whole war treasury was in the hands of my venerable uncle, Samuel Pressburg of Vienna, who brought it to Heilbronn.

When my father heard of his arrival, he went to Heilbronn to meet him, and took me along. My uncle accompanied our whole party—my uncle Reb Yehiel Pressburg, his son Isaac Berlin and others—to Frankfort-on-the-Main and then to Düsseldorf, to see his sister, my venerable and chaste mother (peace be to her).

We arrived in Frankfort in Tebeth of 1736. The distinguished Elia Wohl wished to give me his daughter in marriage, together with a dowry of 10,000 gulden. But my father did not want it, nor did I, being too tender of years, since I was only fourteen.

When we returned to Düsseldorf, my father and my uncles, Reb Samuel and Reb Yehiel Pressburg, arranged a marriage between my sister Hannah and my cousin Loeb. I found my teacher Elia Chelm in my home, and with him I studied the sections of *Yoma* and the commentary *Sifte Cohen to Yoreh Deah*. At the same time a respected citizen of Düsseldorf wished to give me his daughter in marriage, together with a dowry of 10,000 gulden. I carried on with her very zealously, since she was a kinswoman as well, and today I remember my sins sorrowfully, and regret having squandered so much time and neglected my duties. But my mother was against it, since the girl was much over thirty.

Then I wanted to marry the daughter of my uncle Reb Mendel Düsseldorf, of sacred memory. She possessed incalculable wealth, but my parents were against it. During 1737 I was ill with the four-day fever, which held me in its grip from the Day of Atonement until the month of Nisan. That same year a miracle-worker, Reb Ephraim, came to our city and laid amulets on me. I fell into a delirium and saw ghosts and spirits until the amulets were removed. The miracle-worker fled. In the month of Nissan the fever left me, but I remained weak. May God, in the fulness of His generosity, send me full health soon, may He send health of body and health of soul, to me and to all the sufferers of Israel.

In that year my father took on a business assignment from the Elector for a period of three years. In 1739 there was a great famine, so that my father lost more than 50,000 gulden. My mother decided to go to Mannheim despite the severe winter (1740), and because of her genius for negotiation and her great wisdom, she was fortunate in her trip and brought an order from the sovereign stating that she be given more than 10,000 groschen, so that a small portion of her loss might be made good. There was great joy among us, that my mother had returned safely home. I was all the more happy when she wanted to marry me to a maiden from Mannheim, the daughter of a respected resident. The marriage was very suitable, since she was the daughter of a scholar and also because the father offered a dowry of 10,000 gulden. But because of my many sins, our joy was suddenly turned to sorrow and affliction, and from that time on we suffered blow after blow, misfortune after misfortune. One day, after my venerable mother had returned home, about a week before Passover in the year 1741, the spell of an evil eye struck the abundance of our happiness. My mother took to her bed, and on the 8th day of Iyar our crown and glory fell, and the world around was darkened. I weep that my mother was wrested away from us, my venerable and chaste mother, peace be to her. She went to her rest, leaving us behind in trouble, sorrow and misery, and from that day on our distress was great.

We still had not received what the sovereign had promised, not to speak of the other losses my father had suffered. And finally, to fill my cup of misery to overflowing, conditions became such that marriage could no longer be thought of. In 1742, my father took over another business order from the Elector. I devoted all my energies to purveying and was under a great strain. These years passed; the work that I accomplished during them is not worthy of note. Once more I confess and regret, out of the bottom of my heart, every violation of the Torah and the other misdeeds I committed, and all the evil desires to which I succumbed and felt during that period. I recant in full contrition and resolve never to sin again.

At this time I was also engaged in the sale of lottery tickets, but I made no profit at all. I used to receive letters from many distinguished people in Holland, who wanted to enter into correspondence with me. Just before the Feast of Weeks, in the year 1745, I went to Aachen where warm baths, like those in Tiberias, are to be found, in order to treat the weakness in my foot, which was the result of my illness. I can still feel a residue of the sickness, because my bad foot has not been cured, and I was then in great distress. From there I journeyed to Brabant, via Maastricht, and saw some beautiful scenery. I visited Brussels and Antwerp and from there went to Rotterdam and saw all of Holland. I stopped in Amsterdam several weeks and purchased books to the value of seventy gold pieces from my kinsman, the scholarly and wise *Dayyan* of Amsterdam, Josef, of sacred memory. At this time I also had an opportunity to get married, to a young widow with a fortune of more than 10,000 gulden. But in my misery I was well aware of my impossible predicament, and knew I could not, under my present circumstances, remain in Amsterdam any longer. Besides, a wedding would entail a great deal of expense, so I went back to Nynwegen and Cleve. Here Baer Cleve-Gomperz, a most esteemed man, offered me his daughter in marriage, but I really had neither ears for listening nor eyes for seeing, because my heart was overflowing with grief. Yet no one knew this. During all the days of my misery I found no man sincere enough and worthy of my friendship so that I might bare my secrets to him and ask him for advice.

Before the 9th of Ab I arrived in Düsseldorf, and remained there about a year. After Passover of the year 1747, my father became provoked at me and suspicious without reason. (But I was in no condition to tolerate an unjust accusation, and still less to have a hand laid on me.) The matter upset me so that I left my father's house for the second time, intending to go to my native city, Vienna, to stay with my uncle Reb Samuel Pressburg. Accordingly, I went to Deutz, then to Bonn, then to Koblenz, then to Mainz, where I found a kinsman, the distinguished Mordecai Jaffe, and stayed with him about two weeks. On the 7th of Iyar, 1747, I traveled with him and his brother-in-law, Reb Seligmann, to the fair at Frankfort. I bought a winter outfit for Mordecai and a large fur for women, and rested only two days. In the company of the venerable and chaste Frau Breindel I traveled by boat to Mildenburg, and over land to Bischisa, where we spent the Sabbath. At the expiration of the Sabbath, we started out and took the road toward Rotenburg.

I arrived in Düsseldorf, spent one night in my father's house, then traveled by coach through Rheinberg to Cleve and spent the night in the house of the worthy Reb Feiwelmann, son of Reb Benedict Nynwegen (Philip, son of Benedict Gomperz). Reb Feiwelmann's sister, Frau Simelie, lived with her brother. From there I went to Nynwegen, and did not want to disclose my disagreeable predicament to anyone except to the son of Reb Benedict Nynwegen, of sacred memory. I went to Amsterdam again, stopped at an inn, and did not want to expose my circumstances to anyone. My idea was to go to England, but I lacked money for carrying the plan through. Therefore I took a boat for Hamburg and went to Altona, to my kinsman, the distinguished Josef Cohen-Düren, to whom I told my story. He accompanied me to my kinswoman, Frau Hanna of sacred memory, the wife of the Reb Wolf Scheier. Her sister Esther, of Vienna, also my kinswoman, since they were both daughters of my uncle, Reb Samuel, was stopping with her. They understood me, were much concerned about me, and helped me, so that I was able to go to England.

I spent more than twenty days on the boat from Hamburg to London and observed the New Year of 1748 on the sea. Many dangers surrounded us. There were terrible storms, and I arrived at Gravesend after the New Year. The boat had begun to leak. I left it and went ashore. A day or two before the Day of Atonement I reached London, where I spent several weeks at the home of the respected Wolf Berlin (he had been in Petersburg). He wanted to send me to Holland, but Reb Nata London, the son-in-law of my uncle Reb Liebmann Berlin (peace be to him) was also visiting there, and said to me:

"Why devote yourself to fruitless affairs? Stay here and I will find a good connection for you."

And he did so. I moved to the home of the genteel Frau Röschen, wife of the esteemed Reb Moses Cleve-Gomperz, who was in India, to tutor her son Meir. I lived there, reading the talmudic tractate *Yoma* with the boy, and more than fifty pages of *Baba Kamma*. I was very penitent, and it was God's will to accept my repentance with favor. But I lived in sorrow the whole time, and told myself that these surroundings were not commensurate with my honor or the honor of my family. I related the whole story to Wolf Berlin. He spent more than fifty gold pieces on my behalf and transferred a series of commissions to me, so that I might have earned a good deal of money if luck had been with me. But time went fast. I was born to misery and trouble, sorrow and torment. On the 7th of Adar, 5509 (February 25, 1745), I left London for Harwich and took a boat for Helfavoedsfluid in Holland. To carry out a commission for the patrician mentioned above I left on Monday, the 1st of Tammuz (June 17, 1749), for Freising, Landeshut, Dindolfing, Landau. Wednesday, the 2nd of Tammuz, I arrived at Leidling, Passau; Thursday, the 3rd, at Oberhausen, Engelhartzell, Klosterneuberg, Linz; Friday, Krems and Ibbs; Saturday, the 5th of Tammuz (June 21, 1749), I arrived in Vienna, my native city. After the Sabbath was over I moved to the home of my uncle, Reb Samuel Pressburg. Sunday, the 6th of Tammuz, before dawn, I left the house to arrange for my baggage, which was still on board the boat, and paid for its transport and release. Though I gave several esteemed gentlemen instruction in English, I left Vienna without a heller to my name on the 11th of Heshvan, 5511 (November 10, 1750), with Reb Moses Cholschin of Modena, who lived with the Reb Abraham Sinzheim. We left by coach for Steiermark and arrived in Görz the 20th of Heshvan. On Friday, midnight, I arrived in Trieste, where Reb Amschel Marburg lived with his wife Hannah, my kinswoman. I stayed with Reb Manasseh Marburg until Friday, the 13th of Kislev, when I embarked for Venice, where I stayed with the venerable Isaac Berlin, taking my Sabbath meals for two weeks with Reb Abraham Jessurun, and left the first night of Hanukkah.

I bought provisions for the trip across the sea to Alexandria. I found a good English boat, Captain Cotton's *Sitbehind*. We left Livorno Thursday, the 16th of Shevat, 5511 (February 11, 1751). On Friday the 17th, Haham Moreno came on board, with his servant Abraham Castilia, and we sailed for Alexandria in the name of the God of Israel. We were on the water twenty-five days. On Sunday, the 10th of Adar, 5511 (March 7, 1751), I arrived safely in Alexandria, bringing letters of recommendation to Señor Blanes and Señor Salomon Cohen. The latter, however, was visiting Cairo, and I spent the night at the home of the head of the community, the Haham Kunarti, who received me very hospitably. I stayed with him until Purim, at which time his wife bore him a daughter. I wanted to leave for Damiette before Passover, but I was unable to do so because of my ailment, and I spent the holiday at his home. Since I had no money at all, I wanted to sell my clothing and buy raiment according to the custom of the land.

On Friday, the 12th of Iyar, we came to Cyprus, and left it on Monday. On the Sabbath day, Haham Nissim quit the boat, and on Wednesday, the 24th of Iyar (May 19th), we reached Acre, where I spent the night at the home of a non-Jew, a French merchant named Monsieur Martin Blanc à Acre.

On Friday, the 27th of Iyar, I went to Meron to visit the graves of our worthies of old, of Rabbi Simon ben Yohai, his son Elieser and Isaac Luria, and the sepulchres of Johanan Ha-Sandelar, Shammai and Hillel, and that of the daughter-in-law of Shammai. On Monday I returned to Safed and received a gift from the community, in the form of wine and meat—the best of the land. I lived in the house of the Haham Isaac Sagura. On Sunday, the 25th of Tammuz (July 18th), I became very ill and was at the door of death, but the Eternal, praise be to His Name, in the abundance of His grace and compassion, sent recovery to me from Heaven. But I remained weak. God grant full recovery to me and to all the ailing of Israel. Amen!

On Wednesday, the 8th of Marcheshvan, I left Safed in the company of Aaron, the horse-trader, intending to return almost at once. On Friday, the 10th, just before sundown, we reached Zidon. Thursday, the 22nd, at supper time, I set out on a French boat for Damiette, which I reached on Thursday, the day before the first of Kislev. The following Thursday, the 7th of Kislev, I left Damiette and, with God's help, reached Bulak safely on Thursday, the 14th. I rested there one hour and then traveled in peace, with two donkeys, to Cairo. With God's help my departure and my arrival were unmarked by sin. I stopped with a poor man, Reb Israel, who came from Brest-Litovsk. I was ill, and the doctor put me on a diet of chicken and rice.

On Wednesday, the 16th of Tammuz, I arrived safely in Rosetta, where I lived at the home of a wealthy and influential man, Reb Moses Sakim. Then, with two mules, I set out in good company for Alexandria. Thursday, the fast day, turned into a day of rejoicing. I arrived in Alexandria for the second time, and put up in the home of the wise Reb Isaac Kunarti-Provencal.

On the 15th of Ab, I received a letter from Loppard, from Reb Liebman Jost Berlin, may he rest in peace, containing a message from my father and my brother Reb Juspa, bringing me the good tidings that my sister Yente had married the worthy Reb Liebermann of Bonn.

5513 (1753): Friday, the 25th of Tummuz, the boat set sail very early and I had to undertake its pursuit in a small boat. My life was in danger, but God saved me. From Friday until Monday I was seasick. On Tuesday, the day before the first of Ab, we arrived in Cyprus, where I visited the English consul, with whom I stayed three days. On Friday, the 2d of Ab, the captain set sail without giving me notice, and I was left in Cyprus without my belongings.

5514 (1754): A terrible storm has been raging all this time—Monday, Tuesday, Wednesday and Thursday. I could neither eat nor drink. Only on Friday, the 7th of Adar, did I recover, with God's help, and the sea grew quiet. Yet I was uncomfortable all the time. On the holy Sabbath, however, I had quite recovered. We saw Rhodes that day. On the 9th and 10th of Adar, a dreadful storm raged again. Only on Tuesday, the 11th of Adar, did the fury of the sea subside, and we saw Rhodes again, as we had on the Sabbath. May God send us fortunate winds! Amen!

On Tuesday evening, the 11th of Adar, clouds darkened the sky; there was a terrible storm and heavy rain. During that night we passed Rhodes and on Wednesday we passed Capo Stanzio (Chios). The following night and Thursday we spent in a dreadful storm, in a haven in an unpopulated part of the Calabrian coast. Thursday night and Friday

I read the *Megillah* (Book of Esther) and observed Purim. Before dawn, on the holy Sabbath, we quit our haven and on Sunday, the 16th, we passed Capo Samos, where we met a French boat under Captain Chiraud. Reb Moses del Medigo was a passenger on the boat. On Sunday night we passed through the Straits of Chios; on the 17th we reached the island of Duracco. But we had to turn back to the harbor of Voghera, because of the great storm which arose. There we met Captain André's boat from Ragusa, which had left Alexandria fourteen days before us. On Tuesday, the 18th of Adar, we were still in port. I had a fight with a Turk, who almost killed me. Wednesday, the 19th, was again stormy and rainy, as was Thursday. The wind subsided on Friday, and we left port that night, in completely calm weather. Saturday afternoon such a terrible storm arose that we were forced to anchor in the open sea. It stormed so during the whole night that we lost our anchor. Praise be to the Lord, who saved us from this danger. Sunday, the 23rd of Adar, the storm and rain continued. On Monday, the 24th, I set off in a small boat and arrived safely in Ismir (Smyrna).

5515 (1755): Sunday, the 27th of Tishri, I left Semlin on the way to Pancsova and Weisskirchen, to see a widow. On the 28th, I left for Merschetz, to see Reb Moses. On Thursday, the first of Heshvan, I left for Temesvar, to Reb Meir Amigo. On Sunday, the 11th, I arrived in Bodin (Ofen) at Reb Shemaya Pressburg's, where I met my kinswoman Chaya and remained for the marriage of her daughter.

5516 (1756): On Wednesday, the 5th of Tishri, I left Nancy for Luneville and Phalsbourg. On Wednesday, the first day of the Feast of Tabernacles mid-week, I left Rosheim for Oberrehnheim. I went to visit the Rabbi of Niederrehnheim, Josef Steinhard. He had married the venerable Kröndel, the widow of Yehiel Pressburg, my esteemed uncle, of sacred memory. And behold, my sins confused my thoughts. Though I held to my intention of spending the winter in the northern countries, going as far as Denmark and Königsberg, I was so oppressed by the vanity of the world, that I was unable to make a decision. May God, praise to his Name, grant me support. I was forced to spend almost three weeks in Berlin, during which time the entire community was at the Frankfort fair. During this period I quarreled with Reb Hirsch Präger, the silk manufacturer. On Tuesday, the 21st, I was summoned to the prime minister, Prince Heinrich von Podewill. I spent some time with him and presented him with my coins. On Friday, the 24th, I visited his daughter, Madame de Marschall, and I shall never forget the graciousness with which she received me. I also talked with the Margrave Karl

von Ausbach and saw his palace. On Tuesday, the 28th, I went to Potsdam. The next day I went through Sans Souci, the palace of the King,
and talked with a son of the Prince of Prussia. An officer invited me to
visit Prince Heinrich in the evening, but I did not know whether he
meant it seriously or not. I went to the synagogue of Potsdam on Thursday, and talked with Reb Simeon Alik, who graced the position of
cantor. He had once been a teacher in the home of my venerable father.
On Monday, the 5th of Nisan, I went to take my leave of Madame
Marschall. She told me to visit the Princess Amalia, though my baggage
was already gone. While I waited in her court, one of her ladies came to
tell me she had gone to the Queen.

I arrived safely in Breslau on Friday, the 9th of Nisan, at the home
of my kinswoman, Hannah Spitz. On Sunday I had a quarrel with Reb
Abraham ben Eleasar and his son, who had slandered me to the police
inspector. I went to see the Minister, to whom I had been recommended
by the esteemed Reb Daniel Halfon, and the Governor. But the police
inspector had denounced me and I did not want to start a tedious suit.
On Saturday, the 8th of Iyar, I had a quarrel with Reb Jakob Neufeld,
the teacher at Reb Löw Wertheim's and son-in-law of Reb Saul Kemp-
ner, and with the brothers Wolf and Moses Zirels, who hurled the vilest
insults at me but did not beat me. All this baseless hatred, however,
arose from their envy of me, because of the praise and the commendation
with which I am received. I had always dreaded this. On Monday, the
first of Tammuz, I left Vienna by stagecoach and arrived in Larbach on
Friday, the 5th of Tammuz. I was forced to spend the Sabbath there and
received much consideration from the Count of Auersperg and Baron
Roset. I went through the castle of the Count of Lamberg and made the
acquaintance of a certain Captain Brown, an Irishman, captain of a
regiment. Before dawn on Sunday, the 7th of Tammuz, I left for Trieste
again. Near the village of Pilanje, I met Baron Roset and his wife. They
and other travelers urged me to break my journey, since robbers were
in the vicinity. Praise be to God that I stopped there, because just at this
time three traveling merchants were gruesomely murdered. On the evening of the same day I came uninjured to Trieste, for the second time,
and stopped with the esteemed Reb Manasseh Marburg.

Tuesday evening, the 15th of Tammuz, I arrived safely in Venice,
and though I had letters of recommendation to Mordecai Padua, Abraham Cracovia and Isaac Delama, I was forced to live in very poor quarters, in the house of an inn keeper. On Tuesday, the 29th of Tammuz, I
arrived in Padua, a large city, but full of fools and of poverty. Here I

lived in a miserable house, whose mistress was very surly. Dr. Cantarini, the treasurer of the Palestinian Charities, was not at home, but away at a health resort. Dr. Fortis was quite unfriendly. Friday I arrived safely in Verona, with recommendations to Senor Virlingo and Dr. Navarro. On Monday, the 6th of Ab, they gave me fare and recommendation to the rabbi of Mantua and to Dr. Cazes. In Venice I was cheated by a scholar named Jekuthiel, who gave me an *En Jacob* for a *Zohar,* the *Tikkunim* included, *Hesed Abraham* and a Gemara *Berakoth.* I lost more than six florins thereby. All the rabbis in Italy are either Sabbatians or cheats. I found fasting on the 9th of Ab very difficult. On the 10th I was in Guastalla, on the 12th in Reggio, on the 13th in Modena. Tuesday, the 14th, I was in Bologna, where I met a woman from Zirndorf, in Germany. On the 15th, Signor Sulami and Signor Sanguinetti arrived from Modena with a sick girl. The same evening I set out for Florence by sedan-chair.

I had to leave Livorno because it was not easy to find a safe boat, since there was war between England and France. Jewish merchants frequently sent out boats, on which I could have traveled practically free of charge. Yet I was afraid I would have to spend the winter in Livorno. May God soon send me suitable surcease for my needs. I haven't the patience to be docile any longer, and to listen to a daily lecture from my dear Swedish captain, who, like a Polish scholar, believes himself to be the most cultured man in the world. In addition to his other attributes, he is also deaf. . . .

VICTORY FOR JUSTICE

BER BIRKENTHAL (1723-1805)

Wine not only gladdened the heart of man, but constituted an old and honorable trade among Jews since biblical times. Ber was a successful wine merchant, blessed with intelligence and great energy. His business took him to all parts of Eastern Europe, and as a consequence he developed a more worldly outlook than most of his coreligionists in Poland. Recorded in his memoirs are day-to-day business experiences, sketches of persons humble and great as well as events of historical importance in which he was involved. For Ber was a leader of communal affairs, serving as President of the Provincial Jewish Assembly which was dissolved in his time and taking an active role in the Frankist Disputation in Lemberg in 1759. Toward the end of his long life, he wrote, in addition to his memoirs, a book on Jewish sectarian movements.

❋ ❋ ❋

I WILL now tell how my knowledge of the Polish tongue proved of great advantage to the children of Israel, and how the esteemed Chief Rabbi and President of the Rabbinical Court of the holy community of Lemberg heard of me.

It happened that the respected and wealthy Reb Aaron died in 1753 in the town of Komarno, which is in the neighborhood of Lemberg, and willed his fortune to his sons. But his son-in-law, Reb Samuel, the son of Reb Jacob, the son of Reb Fischel, who lived in Kalusz, a small town in Eastern Galicia, appeared before the court and presented a deed in which the deceased father settled upon his daughter half of the amount willed to the sons. The deed, attested to by trustworthy witnesses and properly sealed, stated that the late Reb Aaron had promised him 40,000 gulden.

The case was brought before the great Rabbinical Court of Lemberg and the Provinces and the eminent jurist, Rabbi Hayyim Cohen Zedek Rapaport, heard the case. Reb Samuel presented the deed and placed it on the examination table of the court so that the rabbis might test the genuineness of the seal and thoroughly investigate the claim. The heirs of the deceased presented a counter claim against their brother-in-law, charging that the deed was a forgery. Their late father, they declared, could not have made a deed for so large a sum because the total value of his property was less than 40,000 gulden and because their father's whole fortune, even during his lifetime, probably was never so large.

The judges, presided over by the esteemed Rabbi Rapaport, requested that they be furnished with corroborative letters signed by all persons who had acted as witnesses. When these letters were presented, the judges scrutinized them and compared the signatures with those on the deed, written at Komarno, and found that they did not differ in any detail. The claim of the dependents the heirs, was therefore without proof and the deed was found valid.

The arguments of the defendants, however, were considered sincere and weighty. In order to prevent injustice and to pacify the defendants, the judge and the members of the court ruled that the plaintiff, Reb Samuel, should take a solemn oath and should swear publicly as to the truth and justice of his claim by the oath of the Torah; in addition, his wife was ordered to be present in the synagogue to listen to the oath and to verify it with the response "Amen." After these instructions had been carried out, the defendants were to pay the whole sum mentioned in the deed out of the choicest property left by their father. This verdict was signed and sealed by the presiding judge and given to Reb Samuel.

Reb Samuel's wife, however, refused to be present in the synagogue in order to listen to and corroborate the oath, for she felt that such action would wrong her brothers. Her husband was thus obliged to arbitrate and to accept a compromise settlement. Both parties chose two judges each and the President of the Rabbinical Court of Lemberg was selected by both parties to be the fifth judge or what is known in Latin as the "superarbiter." All of them appeared before their chosen judges and declared that they were acting voluntarily and they would agree to whatever decision was made and abide by it. They signed and sealed the declaration, and, in accordance with established custom, withdrew their claims and handed over the documents to the court. The judges agreed upon the following verdict: the heirs must desist from their demand on oath of the Torah, and they should give to Reb Samuel, in exchange for the deed, 10,000 gulden. The first verdict was declared null and void.

When Reb Samuel reported the whole affair to his father, Reb Jacob, who lived in Kalusz, he made the verdict the beginning instead of the end of a story by slandering the President of the court. He said that the

Rabbi had accepted a bribe of forty ducats from him for the first verdict and for the second verdict his brother-in-law had paid him ten ducats. Reb Jacob was incensed because his son had lost 30,000 gulden through the bribery of the President of the court.

Soon afterwards there arrived in Kalusz, Cieszkowski, Chief Steward of the estates of Prince Czartoryski, the Regent of the province of Red Ruthenia and Governor of the district of Lemberg. Red Jacob laid before the Steward a serious charge against the President of the court. He accused him of perverting justice by accepting bribes from both parties concerned. Reb Jacob explained to the Steward the Rabbi had first given a verdict in accordance with Jewish law, whereby his son was to receive 40,000 gulden, and that the Rabbi had accepted a bribe of forty ducats. Later he had given another verdict whereby his son received only 10,000 gulden; the Rabbi had accepted a bribe of ten ducats from the defendants. "Has it ever happened," he declared, "that a Rabbi and President of a court committed so great a wrong and that on his account my son should lose the huge sum of 30,000 gulden?" He strengthened his accusation by heaping more slanders against both the Rabbi and the court until the Steward became very angry and declared that such a travesty of justice was unheard-of in all of the courts of the world.

He immediately summoned the Rabbi's grandson, Rabbi Judah Loeb, who, although a young man, was President of the talmudic Academy of Lemberg. After pouring abuse on his grandfather, he said excitedly: "Has it ever happened anywhere that in one lawsuit two contradictory verdicts should be given?

"After accepting a bribe of forty ducats from one side, your grandfather took ten ducats from the other side to make his first decision null and void. Neither God nor man can tolerate such a wrong, and you may tell your grandfather this: Until now I have been his friend. Since he was made a rabbi I trusted everything he said and did. I presented him to the Prince, the Voyevoda, and I succeeded in obtaining for him a letter of appointment. I have used whatever influence I commanded to keep him in his position for twenty years. Charges were made against him by several Jews, yet I regarded them as groundless calumnies cooked up by his envious enemies. I kept him in his position because I considered him an elderly man of upright character, respected and loved by his fellow-Jews. But now that his real worthlessness has come to light, I realize that he has had committed many injustices while he was in office and that all the charges made against him are true. I see no other alternative for him therefore but to quit Lemberg before I arrive there, if he wishes to escape the severe punishment which I shall be compelled to inflict upon him. Do not regard my warning as an idle threat. Since you are his grandson, write to him immediately and say that should I find him in Lemberg, he will regret it because I will judge him as befits a rabbi who perverts justice."

It happened at that very time that a Jew from Skole, Rabbi Jacob, the son of Rabbi Loeb Klimster, appeared before the Steward to request his seal to confirm a verdict passed by the President of the Jewish court of Lemberg against another Jew of Skole. When he observed with what contempt the Steward spoke of the President of the court of Lemberg, he decided not to present the verdict lest the nobleman tear it up in his rage. As he left, he advised the Rabbi of Kalusz not to stay any longer with the Steward. "If you wish to write a letter," he said, "and send it to your venerable grandfather, I will wait until the letter is written and deliver it to him directly." The Rabbi wrote a letter in which he told his grandfather that the Steward was incensed because it was alleged that he had taken bribes from the two parties to a suit and had given two contradictory verdicts in one case.

When Rabbi Jacob arrived in Lemberg, he immediately delivered the letter to the President of the Court. Visibly perturbed, this venerable Rabbi said, "If I could only find some one who writes Polish well, then I would be able to explain the whole affair to the Steward. He would understand that I surely did what was right in this case, and how greatly I really benefited the son of the man who now denounces me." Rabbi Jacob came to his aid. "I know a man," he said, "who is a Jew and writes an incomparable Polish. All the nobles are surprised by the excellence of his prose and praise him for his fluency in the Polish tongue. Only it is a pity that I cannot bring him here, for he is engaged all day selling wine in his shop and cannot leave his business for even an hour. I refer to young Ber, the brother of the well-known Rabbi Aryeh Loeb of Bolechow." The Rabbi answered: "I myself know Polish but not sufficiently well so that when a gentile writes for me he never expresses precisely what I want to say. The only course left for me is to write what I want to say in Polish on a fresh sheet of paper, and if you will be good enough to take it to Ber and request him to rewrite the substance of it, then I will examine both copies and send to the Steward the one which pleases me better." The Rabbi sent immediately for Rabbi Isaac, the *shtadlan* (public Advocate) of the Council of Four Lands in Poland (governing body of the Jews) and ordered him to copy from his minutes both verdicts, that is to say, the first sentence passed in accordance with Jewish law, which prescribed that if the plaintiff took the oath he would receive 40,000 gulden, and the second based upon the decision of the judges chosen by both parties to the effect that he should receive 10,000 gulden if he did not take an oath. The Rabbi then finished the letter and gave it to Rabbi Jacob who, after he had said his afternoon prayers, brought it to me, before dark and requested me on behalf of the Rabbi, to read it and write it anew. He gave me several sheets of fine, heavy foolscap paper on which to rewrite the better, relying on my thorough knowledge of the Polish tongue. After reading the whole document I understood that the Rabbi had a perfectly good case and that the accusations of his detractor were the insensate calumnies of an ignoramus who had no conception of legal procedure.

In the middle of the night I took my pen and composed a letter in scholarly Polish, such as is used in legal affairs, stating the Rabbi's case. I explained precisely how two verdicts came to be rendered, and because they were written in a style unintelligible in the Polish tongue I rewrote the two verdicts. Then I placed the three documents in an envelope and wrote upon it all the titles of the Steward. In the morning Rabbi Jacob came to get the letter for the Rabbi who, after reading it through, said to his wife, "Blessed be the Lord whose loving-kindness has not left me. I trust to the compassion of Heaven that when the Steward sees this letter he will surely acknowledge that my action in this case was just and that those who libel me are liars, ignorant of legal procedure." An expert Jewish horseman was fetched at once. The Rabbi wrapped the letter together with the copies of the verdicts in one envelope and gave it to the messenger. It was placed into the Steward's hands in the town of Brzezan (in Eastern Galicia); after reading it, he quickly understood that the Rabbi's decisions were just and that the charges of his defamers were malicious lies and repudiations of God and His holy law.

PIONEER IN SWEDEN

ARON ISAK (1730-1817)

Something of the strength and individuality of Isak is reflected in an oil portrait of him which is reproduced as a frontispiece of his autobiography. His father, a wealthy merchant, was the only Jew in Treuenbrietzen (a small city in the Duchy of Mecklenburg) who had the right of residence. Beginning his career as a peddler, Aron succumbed to a strong inclination to become an artist. He taught himself the craft of seal-engraving and enjoyed a modest success until the Seven Years War, when he turned to trade. Learning from Swedish soldiers that there were no practitioners of his craft in Sweden, during the period that followed, he resolved, even though he knew that Jews had no right of residence there, to make a place for himself and his people. His sobriety and persistence won the favor of the king, and he thereby became the founder of the Jewish community of Stockholm. He composed his autobiography at the age of 71, when he recalled with satisfaction the eventful life that had made him the most respected burgher and elder of an established community. Among his descendants is Sven Heden, the great Swedish explorer.

* * *

WHEN the Seven Years War broke out in 1756, I was the father of four children, and the cost of living was high. I had tried to make my way in the world like an honorable man. When the enemy Prussians seized Mecklenburg, I did a brisk business with them, selling mostly fancy goods. The following year the Swedes entered Mecklenburg as friends. They gave me a lot of work and I sold them huge quantities of fancy goods. Indeed, within a short time I earned 500 reichsthalers, which I used to purchase more of the same stock at the fair in Frankfort-on-the-Oder. That is how I suddenly became a fancy goods dealer, a trade that was much more profitable than seal-engraving. So I packed my tools away in a trunk, and as a prosperous merchant I bought a house and garden. Within five years I had a fortune of several thousand reichsthalers and a fine establishment filled with good furniture and beautiful silverware.

At the end of the war it was difficult to sell fancy goods to the officers. I consequently thought of going into another business. I invested a few thousand reichsthalers in dry goods which the farmers needed, and choosing four lads who used to sell to the army for me, I sent them to the country in pairs in order to sell the goods to the farmers and at the ducal castles. They were to return every three or four weeks. The sales, however, were slim, bringing little profit for me or my salesmen. Yet I held out for about two years. Then two of the men vanished with considerable merchandise and cash collections amounting to more than 1,000 reichsthalers. I was also cheated out of a large sum by a business associate in Bützow. At the same time my sister was married in Malchin. My brother had promised the groom a dowry of a 1,000 reichsthalers and asked me to make it good. My brother Moses, who had married well, contributed 200 thaler, my brother Mordecai 100 thaler, and I took care of the rest. I arranged the wedding, made a gift of furniture, and attended with my wife. Altogether my expenses exceeded 500 thaler.

Well, my affairs were not in good shape. Fortunately, I was not indebted to anybody. I was a free man. Then I recalled that the Swedish officers had given me a good deal of seal-engraving to do and had suggested that I should go to Sweden, as there was no practitioner of my craft in the entire realm. Conditions took a bad turn in the whole of Mecklenburg. A plague spread among the cattle herds, killing them off like flies. Milk was scarce. Of 500 cows in Bützow barely thirty survived. My whole household, my wife and five children, the manservant and maid, were afflicted with dysentery and were confined to bed for three months. You can readily understand that under these circumstances business was at a standstill and everyone sustained losses. One had to seek a new occupation if disaster were to be averted.

I decided to take a trip to Schwerin before departing for Sweden, for the court-medalist, Herr Abraham Pach, who was the most expert diamond-cutter and seal-engraver in Germany, lived there. I had worked with him in his brother Lipmann's workshop. During the reign of the former duke he had been court-medalist and had an annual stipend of 500 reichsthalers. However, when the duke died the mint was closed and he was dismissed. Then this Abraham had himself appointed court-medalist without salary; he earned a mite—barely 100 reichsthalers a year—from the waste of the mint. On the eve of his marriage his capital amounted to 1,000 reichsthalers, and he received 1,500 reichsthalers as a dowry. But I knew that he had already used up his money.

We took a stroll. I felt towards him like a brother. When I inquired about the state of his affairs, he complained bitterly.

"It serves you right," I observed. "It is incredible that an artist of your talent should remain in Mecklenburg where you can't make a living. Come to Sweden with me. We shall be the only practitioners of our craft there, and we shall have more work than we can handle. Why, you admitted that you haven't earned ten reichsthalers in ten weeks!"

I impressed upon him that I knew the fancy goods business, but he was hesitant.

"I have never been away from home," he replied. "How can I leave my wife and children? Besides, how can we succeed when Jews are not permitted to live there? You say that because there are no craftsmen of our kind in Sweden, it will be possible to secure the right of residence. Very well, then. Suppose you make the trip. I will share the traveling expenses with you, and as soon as you secure permission to live and work there, I will join you."

I replied, "Brother, I agree. Keep this a secret. Tell it to nobody, not even your wife."

He likewise asked me not to mention our plan, even to my brother.

"Brother," I continued, "I will give you my answer tomorrow."

Then I went to the house of my brother Abraham, who was the richest Jew in Schwerin and was said to be worth 100,000 thalers. He knew nothing of my difficult circumstances. I owned some serviceable silver worth about 200 thalers, and on the next morning I sold it to him. After lunch I returned to Herr Abraham and said, "I accept your proposition. But we must put it into writing and have it notarized."

He agreed wholeheartedly. As we did not want any one to learn of our plan, we were at a loss as to where we could have the agreement drawn up.

At length Herr Abraham said, "I have a very good friend who works at the grinding-mill less than a quarter of a mile outside the city where we will not easily be seen. I also know a notary who will accompany us."

We returned to his house and drank coffee.

"I must go out for a while," he said. "Please stay here in the company of my wife. I'll be back soon and we shall take a stroll by the City Gate."

He left and arranged with the notary to go to an inn outside the Gate, order a bottle of wine and await us. He returned home, we left together, met the notary, paid for the wine, and walked further. We found a room where we enjoyed privacy and wrote down our agreement in the form of a contract, taking a sacred oath to observe it faithfully. It could be broken only by mutual agreement; all profits, whether from work or trade, were to be shared equally.

Hours passed; it was evening. I wanted to go to my brother's house; but Herr Abraham had arranged, without my knowledge, that his wife prepare a special dinner and insisted that I join him and a group of friends. To be sure, the dinner was excellent, the wine superb, and the evening gay. It was eleven o'clock before I could tear myself away.

When I reached hime I found that the table was set. My sister-in-law grumbled.

"We delayed supper and waited for you so long," she scolded, "that the children fell asleep. They refused to eat without their Uncle Aron and went to bed hungry."

My brother chimed in, "Of course, he could hardly be spared from his beloved card game!"

Well, the wine had gone to my head. I retorted, "Where is the maid? I want to go to sleep. I visit you so seldom and now you fuss as though you want to get rid of me. Very well, I'll leave tomorrow."

She begged me to have a bite, explaining that she had meant no harm. I replied that I did not wish to eat. As there was no maid in the house, I took one of the three lamps on the table, said good night, and went towards my room. My sister-in-law followed closely.

"I never would have believed," she said meekly, "that you could become so enraged."

But her grumbling impelled me to increase her aggravation. "I certainly will not visit you again. Good night, dear sister-in-law," were my last words. But I knew in my heart that I was quite tipsy.

The next morning when I came downstairs, pipe in mouth, she was there to greet me. Immediately she asked whether I was still in bad humor.

"What do you mean? Are you as angry as you were last night? Heavens, I have been good to you always and you must believe that I really was not angry last night."

Thus I apologized and kissed her hand. She kissed mine and said, "You are indeed my dear brother-in-law."

Then she asked me whether I wanted my coffee as usual, for I always arose earlier than they did. I said that I would wait for the whole family. Finally my brother joined us and coffee was served.

As we were drinking, he addressed me as follows: "Tell me, brother, why didn't you eat with us last night? You are always as welcome here as you were at home in Treuenbrietzen. Perhaps you need something? We have never quarreled. Must you leave today?"

I replied that I must depart. He paid me for the silver, and after posting the money to Bützow I took leave of my good friends and journeyed home.

As soon as I reached home, I said to my wife, "You know that about a fortnight ago I received a letter from Count Janke of Stralsund (in Swedish Pomerania), asking me to visit there. He and his brother, the Lieutenant-Colonel, have been decorated, and I have been recommended to engrave their coat-of-arms on their medals. As you know, I promised to be there in three weeks, and since a fair will be held the following week, I will leave on Sunday. I will be the only engraver there, so that I may be detained for several months."

Not knowing what I was up to, she readily consented. I gave her 120 reichsthalers and left her and my five children.

I arrived safely with my tools in Stralsund, and went immediately to Count Janke. He and his brother gave me stones to engrave. Then I reported to Count Fredrik Çarl Sinclair, the Governor, and to Count Anders von Höpkin, the Commandant. Work was abundant. I sent the orders requiring delicate craftsmanship to Herr Abraham in Schwerin, requesting that he take special pains as I was depending upon these folks to recommend me to the King of Sweden. I was flooded with work —already more than 200 reichsthalers—from all the élite. I was much esteemed by Count Höpkin, who recommended me to his brother, the Imperial Councillor, and to the Governor-General Karl Sparre. In fact, he made it a point of speaking of me in all his circles in Stralsund with the result that the whole government gave me letters of approbation to the king. When Herr Abraham's engravings arrived and were delivered, everyone was amazed by their exquisite craftsmanship. And whatever I desired was freely and respectfully given.

In the meantime one of the Stralsunders must have written to Schwerin reporting that the aristocracy held me in high esteem and the government had granted me a passport to journey to Sweden. My brother heard the news, but nobody knew of my agreement with Abraham Pach. My brother immediately wrote to my wife urging her not to allow me to go to Sweden. At the same time he sent me an insolent letter to Stralsund, accusing me of abandoning my wife and children.

"It is unthinkable that you are in such miserable circumstances. You have done many stupid things in your life, but this beats them all. To think of going to a country where a Jew has never lived, which does not welcome Jews, and whose language you do not know! You must be mad. Think twice about the step you are taking. I have often warned you not to put your confidence in bad people, but you would never listen. Now take my advice. Return home. There is a large Jewish community there, and I never heard of anyone who went away and left a wife and children to fend for themselves. I will give you whatever help you require."

However, I had made my decision and refused to be deterred. I made no reply to my brother's letter. A few days before my departure, my eldest daughter came to Stralsund with a piteous letter from my wife pleading that I should not sail. My daughter was more precious to me than anything.

"Dear father," she pleaded tearfully, "if you leave us now, we will never see you again."

I was aware that this had unfortunately happened in other instances. Nevertheless, I explained the state of my affairs to her and how this was an opportunity to make my fortune again. Then I gave her some gifts and set her mind at peace. The next day she went home on the mail-coach.

I had made a reservation on a packet-boat and paid my passage to Ystadt. All the Stralsund Jews came and reproached me and urged me not to sail. But I never was a poltroon. I always stuck to my decisions. As I went down to the bridge to embark, the householders, including some of the women, accompanied me. They continued to discourage me even when I was on the ship. The women lamented as though I were leaving for America. But I was determined to carry out my plan. When they saw that the anchor was about to be lifted, they left the ship, shouting and waving their blessings as long as the ship was in sight.

We sailed from Stralsund at three o'clock in the afternoon and arrived in Ystadt at eleven o'clock the next morning. The captain of the ship found lodgings for me at the home of a modest couple. The man, a native of Germany, spoke German fluently. I intended to remain in Ystadt for a month in order to acquire a smattering of the language and to see what sort of relations might be established with the people. As I had my tools with me, I might also find work. My host advised me to report my presence and my plans to the burgomaster. So I did. The burgomaster spoke a little German, and I showed him my passport and fourteen letters of recommendation to the King. He proved his cordiality by ordering a signet from me. I did not receive a great deal of work, but I netted a good profit from the sale of pearls and jewels. When there was no work, my host tried to teach me Swedish. The words came difficult to my tongue.

Four weeks passed and I was about to continue onward with my journey. My host warned me that it would be disadvantageous to travel in Sweden without a knowledge of the language. He suggested that I first spend a month in Malmö, a port on the southwestern tip of Sweden. He said it was a lovely city where I could undoubtedly secure work and at the same time learn more of the language. He gave me a letter to a good friend, an organ-builder who had traveled widely in Germany and spoke German. Furthermore, he had his apprentice accompany me as a guide and helper.

I followed his advice and all turned out well. I reached Malmö safely. My host, an upright and wealthy man, provided me with beautiful lodgings. Then I went to the burgomaster. I presented my passport and letters of recommendation and related my desires. He knew no German and I knew no Swedish; but he signed my passport, returned it to me, and only said, "Good." I bowed politely in appreciation and bid him adieu.

On my way home I encountered a Jew who had been converted to Christianity. Shaking my hand, he said, "How do you do, Herr Aron!" I was puzzled. I asked him where we had met.

"When I was an itinerant Talmud student, I once spent a week end in Bützow accompanied by a fellow-student. That was about four years ago and I was then called Abraham Brody, but I have since joined the Church and my name is B——. I recall that I had arrived in Bützow on Thursday and spent the Sabbath with Rabbi David who lived near the castle. On Sunday I followed the custom of the Talmud students, making the round of the homes in order to gather some money for living and travel expenses. I also went to your home, knocked at the door, and entered. Nobody was in sight. I noticed a pair of black silk stockings on a chair, and as I was desperately in need of them I quickly concealed them under my cloak and left. Outside the door I met your wife. I greeted her and asked for a contribution to enable me to continue with my journey. She gave me four shillings and some bread and butter. My companion and I traveled on but we were unable to find suitable employment. Finally I came to this city, found happiness and married. Now, dear Herr Aron, I should like to repay you for the stockings. I am now a grain merchant and I should be pleased to have you accept the hospitality of my spacious house. Please don't think that on account of my conversion I am not to be trusted; on the contrary, my heart is filled with joy whenever I meet a Jew."

I thanked him for his offer of hospitality, and explained that my stay in Malmö would be brief for I had to attend to some legal matters in Stockholm; also that my portmanteau was already at my quarters. But he was so persistent (he pleaded too that his wife had never seen any other Jew) that I could not shake him off. I accompanied him to his house. It was large and beautiful, and his wife was genteel. They had an infant about a month old.

The way he had won his wife makes an odd tale. This B—— appeared one day at the church in the German colony in Malmö and informed the pastor that he wished to be converted. The pastor taught him the elements of Christianity and took him into his own home. He was a noble old man, and as he had neither wife nor child, a niece served as his housekeeper. B—— became intimate with the girl and she found herself in a family way. Her sister, who was the wife of a prominent Malmö merchant, told her to get rid of B—— and seek an upright man, else she would have nothing more to do with her. But the girl insisted that since B—— had deprived her of her honor, he must restore it. Meanwhile the good, old pastor died, quite unaware of the affair. During his illness B—— took good care of him. While the pastor was considered a man of means, no money was found among his possessions. Then B—— married the girl and led a merry existence. He bought a big house and told tall tales. He bought a share in a trading company, paid little attention to business, and entertained lavishly. With his money, it was easy come, easy go. This is the gist of the story that my host told me.

Having spent a month in Malmö quite profitably—I did especially well in trading pearls and jewelry—I thought of continuing my journey. When B—— heard that I was going, he hastened to me and said, "Dear friend, if you remain here another week, I will accompany you to Stockholm. I have 6,000 thaler in the bank, and I will gladly lend it to you at five per cent. interest. I am very well known in Stockholm and can help you with legal matters by recommending you to my friend Duke Karl. You will prosper in trading pearls and jewelry. Besides, you will require two horses and it will be more economical if both of us use them."

I let him talk me into it only because my knowledge of the language was so meager. His wife begged me to speak to him about his impetuousness. She had thought that all Jews were like that until she saw how calm I was.

We journeyed to Kristianstadt, where I spent a month. On the way

B—— behaved himself, but in the city he came home tipsy every night with a bunch of drunkards. I warned him that he would either have to change his ways or seek other quarters. This had some effect on him, but I made up my mind to get rid of him as soon as we arrived in Stockholm. He tried to get me to go to Gothenburg. He said it was a large city where much business could be gotten, and proposed that he would hawk for a third of the income. But he was a toper and a brawler. I was not personally concerned, but such company embarrassed me exceedingly where I had taken lodgings. Finally we left Kristianstadt. I did not want to be delayed by any more stopovers. I gave him no indication of what my real object in Stockholm was.

We arrived in Stockholm at nine o'clock in the morning on a hot day in July, 1774. For two hours he left me alone on the street where I was waiting in the carriage. Passers-by stared at me. When he returned, I asked him where he had been all that time.

"Lodgings cannot be found here as quickly as in other cities," he replied. "Of course there are places that can be rented, but a stranger is in great danger."

Assuring me that he would have definite word in half an hour, he left me again. Then a brewer who lived nearby and who understood German passed by the carriage and heard the driver grumble about waiting and threatening to dump the portmanteaux. The brewer noticed that I had been waiting there a long time and inquired if anything was wrong. I told him that my companion had said he would return in half an hour from his search for lodgings, but that he was an hour late.

"There are plenty of vacant rooms here," he commented genially. "There is no reason for keeping the horses and porter while you wait, you are being charged for this time."

I paid the driver a sum suggested by the brewer so that he would wait until my companion returned. At two o'clock, I was still standing there. I was incensed. At that time the brewer reappeared and asked whether my companion had succeeded in locating quarters. He offered to direct me to suitable quarters in the neighborhood, at the home of a man who spoke German fluently. I thanked him and he accompanied me to the house of an upright man, where I rented two rooms.

Late in the afternoon B—— turned up, indignant and drunk. Why, he had searched the whole city for me and thought that I had already been murdered. Even on the journey he had filled my head with tales about the dangers that beset a stranger in Stockholm. His favorite warning was that one risked one's life if one merely ventured to drink a glass of brandy or a bottle of wine. It was his purpose to inspire me with fear so that I would be sure to keep him with me.

I arose early as usual the next morning, and smoked my pipe. My host was already up. I told him that I had a letter to the Lord Mayor and would like to present it to him. This fine man offered to take me to the Mayor's residence at ten o'clock. I asked him not to say anything of this to B——, of whose bad habits I disapproved. At the appointed time he accompanied me to the Lord Mayor's residence, directed me to the proper hall, and told an attendant that I wished an audience with His Excellency, for whom I had a letter. Of course I had taken along my passport and all my letters.

The room was full of people. An hour passed before I was called.

I entered holding the letters in my hand, and stammered in Swedish, "Your Excellency, I regret that I am unable to speak Swedish."

"You are a Hebrew," he began without hesitation. "You may speak German. I spent five years as a volunteer cadet in the service of the King of Prussia."

I quickly told him my wish and showed him my letters of recommendation from the government officials and notables of Stralsund.

"Dear friend," he commented, "this is an extremely difficult matter. A Jew has never lived in Sweden. My good friends have recommended you very highly, but it is not in my power to grant your wish. I will gladly give you whatever aid I can. Suppose you return in a few days and I shall let you know what you may expect. I must ask you in the meanwhile not to trade in gold or silver, for if anyone complains I will not be able to help you. But you may do as much seal-engraving as you can secure."

He asked me to leave all my documents with him and to set his own coat-of-arms in carnelian stone. He was most gracious with his time, permitting me to tell him about Abraham Pach and my brother Marcus.

On my way home I met B——. He was angry.

"You won't get out of Stockholm alive," he ranted. "You are taking too many chances in running about the city so freely."

I did not want to be in his company, as he might insist upon breaking my promise not to trade. I simply said that I would not lock myself in my room. After all, no one would murder me on the streets.

I immediately sent the Lord Mayor's coat-of-arms to Abraham Pach at Schwerin. I also write to my brother Mordecai, suggesting that he join me as soon as possible via Wismar, whence ships frequently sailed to Stockholm in three days. A few days later I saw the Lord Mayor again.

This time I brought my Mecklenburg certificate of residence. I pointed out that I had lived in Bützow for nineteen years and showed him a certificate from the local university attesting to my good character and reputation. He advised me to consult a German-speaking attorney whom he recommended, and sketched the contents of the application for the right of residence that should be drawn up. I was to bring the application to him and he promised to deliver it to the King in person.

I followed his advice and engaged the attorney. He asked me to return in two days and he would have the application ready. During this time I visited several councillors to whom I had letters of recommendation. All of them said that they would help me.

When the document was completed I took it to the Lord Mayor and asked him to forgive me for putting him to so much trouble.

"You may come as often as you like," he said, "and if I have the time I shall be glad to talk with you. I enjoy conversing in German. Come to see me again in a few days."

When I returned he was most gracious. He reported that he had given my application to the King and was glad to inform me that the King was not averse to aiding me to secure the right of residence. He promised to have more definite word in eight days.

Two days later Duke Karl sent a lackey to my house to escort me to the palace. As he already knew that I could not speak Swedish, there was a courtier present to act as interpreter. He asked whether I was the man who had petitioned for the King's aid in order to engage in seal-engraving and stone-cutting. Duke Karl looked on as the interpreter told me that the Duke wished his coat-of-arms (he held an impression of it in his hand) cut in precious stones. We agreed upon a price of forty ducats. I could not help feeling that the Duke was acting for the King, who wanted to see a specimen of our work. I immediately sent the impression to Abraham Pach and wrote a letter stressing the importance of doing his best. It was a sample for His Majesty and our fate hung thereon.

One morning my host hailed me. "My dear Herr Aron," he remarked, "I threw that low rascal out of my house during your absence. He has already taken his portmanteau. His impudence and insults drove my wife to tears. Of course you may remain here as long as you wish, but I cannot tolerate that scoundrel. He deserved a sound drubbing, but I restrained myself because I didn't want to aggravate you."

I told the good man that I still had some business accounts to settle so that I could not let him go. This was the truth. I remained over night, and on the morrow B—— met me outside the house. He said that he had taken other quarters in the neighborhood, with better rooms and more light for my work. I went with him and found that the owner of the house was a modest widow. I moved in and set up my workshop.

I had lived there hardly a week when this hostess complained that B—— was a mean wretch and that he gave her no peace. She said that she would be delighted to have me remain, but he must go. Well, that was the last straw: I settled our accounts and told him that if he wanted me to handle any of his business he could visit me, but I could not live in the same house. He took about 100 reichsthalers, which was due him, and never turned up again. He carried on in the city until his money gave out and then returned home.

The very same day that I broke off with B—— (it was September 2, 1774), my brother Mordecai arrived on the Wismar ship. We accepted the hospitality of one of the Queen's footmen, who was a fellow-townsman from Mecklenburg. Then I took my brother to the Lord Mayor in order that he might learn of his arrival. He was pleased.

"I must tell you that the King has sent your application and recommendations to the Council, where a decision will be reached. You may give this information to your attorney. He will know what to do."

My attorney accompanied me to the Council, where he inquired whether the petition that I had given to the King had been acted upon. They requested that we return in a month for the decision.

When we reappeared at the end of the month, they again refused to act on the petition and asked that we come again in two weeks. My attorney now told me that he would not accompany me again, but inasmuch as I knew where to go I should go alone. I was to let him know of the decision when it was made. A month must have passed before the Council acted. Their decision was laconic:

"We cannot permit you to practice your religion in this country, much less to engage in business."

It was signed by Karl Sparre.

I was shocked. I went directly to the Lord Mayor. "You promised to aid me," I complained, "and now see the sort of decision you approved."

"Let me explain," he replied. "In my capacity of president of the tribunals I must affix my signature to all decrees and decisions. However, you need not let the matter rest there. You must ask your attorney to appeal the Council's decision."

We followed his advice, but another month passed before we received the very same decision. I complained again to the Lord Mayor, declaring that if he simply signed whatever action the Council took, I had better

save his time and my money and return home. He laughed, and told me
that I was much too impatient, that I must again make an appeal before
the magistrates.

I consulted my attorney. When I mentioned the suggestion of the
Lord Mayor, he was skeptical. He thought that the magistrates would
act just as the members of the Council had done. I went to see all the
councillors who had promised to help me. They pointed out that the
Lord Mayor, who was president of the judges, could do much, but that
their own hands were tied. However, they repeated that they would be
glad to help when the appeal came before them. Their friendlinss
heartened me. A week later I again went before the magistrates. I waited
two hours. Finally one of them took down my name and address and
said that they would send for me at the proper time. I returned home. I
was much esteemed by all these notables. They lavished praise on my
work and I got a reputation as the greatest artist in the world.

I saw a good deal of the jewellers, especially those gallant gentlemen,
Herr Suter and Herr Wilhelmson. They were my good friends and knew
how great was my desire to remain here. At long last I was summoned
to the town hall by the magistrates. One of them, by the name of Flodin,
a gentleman and a scholar, came forward and spoke to me in German.

"My dear Herr Aron," he said, "you have petitioned the King for the
right to live here. All of us have seen your recommendations. You have
been praised as a man of character as well as an expert craftsman, and
we know that these testimonials are justified. The King himself wishes
you to remain, especially since there is no other such craftsman in the
realm. But your adherence to the Jewish religion is an insurmountable
obstacle. Let me show you what the statutes say in this regard." He
translated freely into German from an old tome: " 'If a Jew comes to our
shores on a ship that requires repairs, the said ship shall have precedence
over all others in order that the Jew may leave the realm. If a Jew
becomes ill while his ship is in port, a physician shall be sent to cure him
that he may quickly leave the realm. A Jew may neither buy nor sell in
the realm.' Such is our law and our franchise."

"So this is your franchise!" I replied. "O how miserable a franchise!
How contrary to human life!"

He replied quietly but firmly, "A Jew has not lived in our kingdom
since the beginning of time. Nevertheless we have decided, because it is
the King's wish, to make it possible for you to remain here. You cannot
do so as a Jew, since that is contrary to our laws; but if you embrace
Christianity, you may have your citizenship immediately, together with

exemption from all taxes for a period of ten years. Such an offer has never been made to anyone else. Think it over and let us have your decision within a week."

I replied without hesitation, "My dear man, I do not need to think it over. I would not change my religion for all the gold in the world. I did not come here to trade in religion. How could I deny a faith through which I hope to gain salvation?"

He listened very patiently and remarked, "We are ignorant of the Jewish religion and its doctrine of salvation."

"I am not a learned man," I continued, "and certainly this is not the place to expound religious doctrine. This much, however, I can tell you: the fundamental principle of Judaism is to fear God and to love one's neighbors. I intend to hold this sacred as long as I live."

"We hold the same beliefs," he responded, "but man cannot attain salvation without the Savior whom Jews call the Messiah."

I repeated that that was not the place for a religious disputation, and in any case no good end could be served. The upshot was that I would be informed of their decision. I bowed and went my way.

A few days later I met Councillor Flodin on the street. He asked me to visit his home, which was nearby, and examine an exquisite carnelian that he would like to have cut into a seal. I accompanied him to his house and agreed to make the seal. Then I asked him whether he would help me to remain in the country. He told me that neither he nor all the magistrates could grant my petition. Only the King could make it possible, if he wished to exercise his authority. He was inclined to think, however, that the King would not be in favor of granting me these rights since there was no precedent for this act. He was sure that I would have the decision of the magistrates by the end of the week.

Again I received the same answer, again the signature of Karl Sparre! My hopes were crushed. I hurried to the Lord Mayor.

"Well," he inquired cheerfully, "what is the good news?"

"There is only bad news. Here is the decision to which you affixed your signature. You know well its contents. Is this the last word?"

"Yes," he replied, "that is the final decision from the Town Hall."

"Your Excellency might have told me long ago that I might as well return home," I replied, expressing my disappointment, "and I could have saved a large sum of money."

He said that I surely had had no experience in legal proceedings. "If you wish to take issue with me, why don't you institute a suit?"

I bowed humbly, asked his forgiveness, and requested him to tell me when I should leave.

"No, no," he protested, "you misunderstand me. I am quite serious. You must make a legal protest against my decision to the King. Ask your attorney to draw it up and take it to Johan von Heland, the Secretary of State, who will present it to the King. I will do all that I can to help."

My attorney drew up a brief and I took it to von Heland. He was at home in the German language. I handed him the brief, requesting that he bring it to the King's attention. He read it from beginning to end. When he had finished, he cried angrily, "Who in the world do you think you are? How dare you bring this sort of protest against the Lord Mayor? Would you like to be horsewhipped? You had better leave the country at once or I'll drive you out. What stupid arrogance! Out! Out!"

I shook with fear. "Gracious Sir!" I explained, "the Lord Mayor himself asked me to do this." He stood motionless for a while, summed up my appearance, and exclaimed, "Hear him now! A liar to boot!" I repeated anxiously that the Lord Mayor had instructed me to make the protest. "I cannot accept your word alone," he said finally, "I shall call on him this afternoon. Meanwhile I will keep this document, and you may return in the morning."

As I left I suddenly realized that I had blundered. I had given my word to the Lord Mayor that I would not divulge our understanding, and now the cat was out of the bag. I ran to his office as fast as my legs could carry me. Still panting, I exclaimed, "Your Excellency sent me to a horrible person!" "What happened?" he asked with concern. "What did he do to you?" "He read the protest and told me that I should be whipped for bringing an action against you, that I should leave the city or he would throw me out. He was so angry that I expected him to thrash me then and there. I was so terrified that I told him you had sent me. I hardly knew what I was saying. He kept the document and said that he would speak to you this afternoon." The Lord Mayor assured me that I had acted properly, and I went home relieved and overjoyed that he was not angry with me.

The Secretary of State was most cordial when I saw him again the following morning. He told me that he had had a satisfactory conversation about me with the Lord Mayor. The protest, however, required some revision. He volunteered to attend to this and suggested that I return the following day to sign the new document. After I had done this, he asked whether I had spoken to the councillors. I told him that I had seen some of them. He suggested that I intensify my efforts. "Tomorrow the

King will hold council in Ulrichsdal and four councillors [he named them] will be present. If you know any of them, go to see them immediately and ask their assistance." He added that he would be away for four or five days but would be glad to see me upon his return.

It so happened that two of these councillors were among those to whom I had letters of recommendation. I had seen them often and won their favor. I went to them once more, and to the other two as well, and told them the story. All of them promised to do everything in their power and assured me that I need have no fears about the outcome.

At the appointed time I again went to see Secretary of State Heland. As I entered his office, he congratulated me. He told me that my request had been granted and I would find the papers at the Lord Mayor's. I thanked him more than a thousand times and said that I hoped I would have the privilege of repaying this great obligation. Then I hurried to the Lord Mayor's. He instructed me to go to the Chancery at the royal castle and ask for the royal secretary, von Sieverts. Off I went to the castle. The secretary gave me the privilege papers and I paid the required fee.

When I visited the Lord Mayor with the intention of expressing my deep appreciation, he spoke to me abruptly. "I've done the Devil's work and prefer not to hear of it. If you must thank some one, thank the King. But be sure to go to the Town Hall tomorrow with your attorney and have the papers officially recorded."

The councillor there requested that I leave the papers and return for them in a week. I hesitated to let them out of my hands, but as my attorney assured me, in German, that there was no reason for worrying about their return, I left them. The papers were certified in Ulrichsdal on May 2, 1775. They granted me, my brother Mordecai, and Herr Abraham Pach the right of residence with our wives and children provided we paid the regular levies.

A week later I returned to the councillor and received my papers. I wrote forthwith to Herr Pach asking him to join me, and to my wife, whom I told to sell the house and garden and to bring the children.

A KABBALIST IN PARIS

HAYYIM DAVID AZULAI (1726-1807)

Azulai's diary bears witness to the cosmopolitan character of
the numerous itinerant rabbi-scholars who appeared in the capitals
of Europe and America in the eighteenth century. They were
lionized by learned men and aristocratic ladies whose journals
contain many colorful references to their picturesque dress and
esoteric wisdom. Ezra Stiles, the first president of Yale, recorded
the topics of learned conversation with Rabbi Hayyim Isaac Karrigal
and even wrote a memoir of his life. Azulai was born in Jerusalem,
traveled considerably in behalf of the Hebron Rabbinical Seminary
and was the premier bibliophile of his generation. Despite his devotion to kabbalistic lore and practices, these jottings of his observations
and experiences in Paris on the eve of the Revolution reveal keen
intelligence and a vivid personality. The time is December, 1777.

❊   ❊   ❊

THIS city, the capital of France, is of great size, it is said to be
fifteen miles round. Its streets and squares are wide enough for
two coaches to pass each other with ease, even though foot pas-
sengers are walking along the sides of the roads. The city is served by
its river, the Seine, over which there is a great bridge, long and wide,
called the "Pont Neuf," that is to say, the "New Bridge." All day long,
and all through the night, without ceasing, pedestrians are wending their
way over it. Here stands the clock "la Samaritaine," which is surrounded
by water. There is a saying that never in the twenty-four hours is there
an instant without a white horse, a monk and a prostitute at this spot.
The city is of great beauty and everything is to be found in it, but all at
a very high price, except prostitution, which is very cheap and openly
displayed; there are said to be thirty thousand public prostitutes inscribed
on the registers, without counting the thousands who are not public and
offered to all comers. There are academies in great numbers, and every
kind of manufacture is carried on. The Jews enjoy tranquillity, there are

many Germans, many Portuguese from Bordeaux and Bayonne, and many who hail from Avignon. People pray together every Saturday, but there is no fixed community, birds of passage for the most part resorting hither for trading purposes. The synagogues are without "privilege," and exist only by a miracle.

On Tuesday evening M. Israel Bernal de Valabrègue came. He enjoys a salary from the King, twelve hundred livres a year, and the title of the King's Interpreter, because he pretends to know all the Oriental languages. He thinks he is a rabbi, a casuist, a poet, and versed in the sciences: he knows the kabbalistic names. He boasts that all the world writes letters to him. He came to see me three evenings in succession. The first time he sang his own praises as a scientist, the second time as having journeyed to Amsterdam; the third on account of the ladies who correspond with him, he says, and the academies which consult him. One evening his boasting of himself was to the tune of making a mock of M. Mordecai Ravel; the latter has roundly insulted him and lavished praise on him too. But enough.

In the course of the day M. Fabre came to visit me, a learned Christian of the Academy of Science. He plied me with questions about science and kabbalist practices, which I answered.

On Friday I paid a visit to him and stayed with him a couple of hours. He showed me a book in French in which were written the names of the angels, their features, and their letters, as well as consultations in regard to dreams by means of adjurations, all in the French language. This Christian gave me a cordial welcome; I went to him in the company of M. Mordecai Venture, a grammarian and linguist, who took a great deal of trouble on my behalf. May God reward him!

The evening before I had gone to dine at the house of the eminent David Naquet. There were present the *parnassim* (administrators) of the synagogue and a certain number of private individuals. It was a great affair. Much honor was paid to me. Then we dined with M. Venture and M. Mordecai Ashkenazi, of the town of Hâvre-de-Grace in France. The master of the house treated me with much distinction, as did also his worthy wife. On Saturday we went to the synagogue. There was singing in honor of the confraternity "Gemilot Hasadim" just founded. My name was placed at the head, and they brought me the honor of opening the ark and of carrying the sefer-Torah (Scroll). Much oil was offered to the synagogue in my honor. I took lunch with M. David Naquet. M. Elie Perpignan, brother of the mistress of the house, and his wife, were fellow guests. Great disputes between this couple had ended in a quarrel, and I had been asked at Bordeaux to make peace. After our meal we went to the synagogue and I preached on morality and the praise of the brotherhood "G. H.," after which they made me an offering without being asked to do so. May God reward them for it!

On Sunday, the 28th of Kislev, came M. Elie Perpignan and his wife. I gave her a "Shema Israel" to swallow, according to the formula of R. Menahem Azariah, because it was feared she contemplated being converted, and I invited them to make peace once and for all.

After that came MM. Mardochée Ashkenazi and David Naquet, and I visited a rich German Jew who told me he would come to see me in order to give me an offering.

On Sunday night MM. Abraham Vidal and Moses Perpignan came and gave an offering for Hebron with many tokens of respect. I thank God that I have a great name and am held a hundred times higher in esteem than I deserve. It is useless my telling them that I am an ignorant man; they think that is all modesty. My renown has even spread among Christian savants, who question the Jews about me—it is extraordinary! When I speak to them they hold my words more precious than pearls. These, indeed, are the wonders of Him who "raiseth the poor out of the dust and lifteth up the beggar from the dunghill to set them up among princes." But what rare goodness have I met with from the man of Avignon! Wherever they are to be found, even if it is only one, I have reaped honors and profit. Thus it has been in the seven cities of France where I have come across them and they have been my guiding light; they live in the Four Communities, Nimes, Montpellier, Pézénas, Narbonne, Bordeaux, Paris. To them I owe every care for my comfort and much honor; their persons and their money have been at my service, and they have never ceased to cherish and respect me—it is extraordinary! "And David blesses them," them and their houses. May God repay them, and may their reward be riches and honor, a long life and worthy posterity; may God deliver them from all evil and may the virtue of the Holy Land protect them and their descendants so that they may be prosperous and flourishing, with abundance of all things! Amen!

That evening there came to me the very wealthy M. Peixotto to discuss with me the question of his wife and induce me to get her to accept the act of repudiation. He undertook to give a thousand "crowns" for Hebron if I would move in the matter. I answered: "If you wish to make peace, I will interest myself in your affair with a good grace, for everyone knows that your wife is a virtuous woman; lay down what conditions you will, I will strive to obtain them. But as to a separation, that would be sacrilege." I added that the Law forbids him to repudiate his virtuous wife as long as she is a mother and his first wife. I have told him, moreover, many other things of this kind. A man even offered me four "louis d'or" to countersign a decision written by a celebrated rabbi concerning the marriage of Israel Vidal to his second wife, and I replied that though the decision may be just in principle in the eyes of the people, it was a sacrilege, and that I would not see the decision and still less would I countersign it. May God help me, for the glory of His name, and may all our actions be done in the sight of Heaven, that I may act according to His will! Amen!

On Rosh-Hodesh Tebet I went to see Monsieur Fabre, the Christian savant mentioned before. He showed me an abridgement of the Kabbalah in French, which began with the name of seventy-two letters, by whose help Moses was said to have brought about the plagues of Egypt and which confounded these things with the constellations. I told him: "You must know that that is a branch of the practical Kabbalah, the ten plagues have not been the work of this name; moreover, it has nothing to do with the constellations." This Christian paid me great honor, and had us served with chocolate and "pain d'Espagne." Snow was falling; he took us in a coach to the "Bibliothèque." But as it was the end of the civil year, none of the conservators were there, and we came back again. I went with M. Mordecai Venture to Elie Perpignan. To his wife I addressed remonstrances of a general nature, and, on her husband's arrival, I got him to concede that he would give her all that was necessary for their expenses, so that she might be the mistress. In short, I strove to do all that was in my power to make peace between them.

On Thursday evening I was speaking in praise of the science, when a young Portuguese, Jacob Laguna, got up to speak in a contrary sense; he told me he knew he was not orthodox. I was much pained, and afterwards made inquiries about him. I was told extraordinary things; my informants said definitely they had had it from himself, from his own mouth, that he had studied the books of Voltaire and believed in nothing, etc. What is more, a man of standing told me that here in Paris, at the table of the master of the house, he did not drink wine prepared by gentiles, but that he would go forthwith and drink with him in a Christian "auberge," and had done so many times. In truth, I was much troubled about him for many reasons. If this is all true, may God bring him back to the way of perfection. Amen!

In the daytime, we went to pay a visit to M. Peixotto. It was a considerable distance to go, for as we wrote above, this is a very large city, said to have nine hundred and fifty streets, five thousand coaches, and more than a million inhabitants; they say a day is not long enough to go round all the town on foot, if one wants to go everywhere. And at the end of it all he was not at home. In the evening, I went with Hananel de Milhaud and his son in a coach to visit M. Liefmann Calmer. He is a German Jew who in his youth was in the service of the rich Suasso de la Haye in Holland; then he entered commerce and has elevated himself to the position of Baron of Picquigny, that is to say, lord of the town of Picquigny (which he has bought from the heirs of its lord for the sum of a million and a half francs) and "vidame of Amiens," that is to say, he is a "defender" of the "church," for that is what the lord of Picquigny must be. He has a great privilege from the Government. In fact, the late King Louis XV had a mistress whom he had served, and she procured him this elevation. We went to see him; he gave us a cordial welcome and an offering of two "louis." I recommended to him, and to his son also, M. Benjamin Abraham of Bordeaux, because he is related to him, and grows poorer and poorer. They said they would send him an offering.

On Friday we went with the Christian, M. Fabre, to the "Bibliothéque" of manuscripts, and such is the consideration in which he is held, although it was not the day for it to be open, he received the necessary authority, and it was opened for us. There are thousands of manuscripts there dealing with all the sciences. I saw a Bible on parchment which was written in 1061 of the ordinary reckoning, about seven hundred and seventeen years old now, and which seems quite new, hundreds of our (i.e., Hebrew) books in manuscript, among them David Kimchi on the Psalms, with additions to the edition (on Psalm II, verse 12, we noticed nearly a whole column demi-folio), many works on natural science, on philosophy, on mathematics, on the calendar, the ancient Kabbalah, the works of R. Joseph ibn Caspi, and of Isaac Israeli, who composed the *Yesod Olam* for Rabbi Asher; many copies of *Semak* and of other printed works, the *Shibbole ha-Leket* (1st part), and the *Sefer Yereim* complete (and it contains 464 precepts and the author says he has followed in his reckoning of the precepts the order of Rab Jehudái Gaon, the author of the *Halakhot Gedolot,* except that he has sometimes put two precepts together into one), and the notes of Rabbi Isaiah the Elder on the Pentateuch (in these he sometimes criticises Rashi).

I took my three Sabbath repasts in the house of the rich David Naquet, where I was a much honored guest; on Friday evening and on the day itself M. Abraham Vidal and M. Mordecai Venture partook of these meals.

On Sunday I went to see the decision (about Vidal), but read the question only. I saw that the facts were not correctly stated, so it is possible the decision may differ . . . treats him as a man who has been deceived but with overabundance of epithets; probably the copyist's contribution . . . to make a big sum of money out of it . . . I was promised a certain sum if I would countersign, but I avoided "what is ugly and what looks like it," and may God bring them to penitence! Enough.

Monday. I took chocolate with Solomon Ravel. Then I went, with David Naquet, to Jacob Goldschmidt, a rich and eminent Ashkenazi. It was a miserable day; the snow was falling, the distance was great, and we could not find a coach. When we got there he behaved as all the Ashkenazim do, they are full of doubts and arguments; the end of it was he gave us twelve francs. After that we went to M. Jacob Péreire, who had been twice to see me, he is a notable held in great consideration. I found at his house a letter from my son, written with modesty and respect, etc.

The evening before, Tuesday, the Marquis de Thomé, a Christian savant, came to see me with great demonstrations of respect, as well as another Christian of mark and an "Italian abbé." They stayed nearly two hours, and I answered their questions. At the end the Marquis asked me to bless him. I blessed him, as well as the other Christian—it is strange!

Next morning M. Fabre sent a fine coach for us to go to Versailles. We went there with M. Venture. . . . I put on a handsome coat, and went to the sign of the "Cheval Rouge" in the "rue du Vieux-Versailles" at Versailles, where M. Fabre was in the house of a relation of his, a lady. We had a cordial reception and drank chocolate.

Then we went to Court. The Christian entered and we followed. We came first into a beautiful room, adorned with numerous gilded columns arranged in two rows and supporting great candlesticks. This is the gallery, and courtiers were standing about. We went through numerous royal apartments to reach the Council Chamber. At the upper end there is a canopy royally gilt and painted. There the King sits on his throne, while the courtiers take their places lower down the room. We next went through into the inner apartments, and stopped at the further end of the chief room. After a little while some great lords began to pass us, and among them the King's brother, "Monsieur le Comte de Provence", called "Monsieur" and nothing more, and his younger brother, "Monsieur le Comte d'Artois". They stayed beside me nearly five minutes. Then it was the King who passed, accompanied by great lords, and I pronounced the benediction for the King. He was dressed in red, wearing the "ordre d'azur", on which were arms. Hardly had he passed, when a lord came to say to M. Fabre, who was by my side, that the King was asking from what country I was ambassador. He answered him that I was not an ambassador, but that I came from Egypt out of "curiosity" to see what I could. Then we took our leave, saluted by all the company. Some of the "ladies" who were passing even made a curtsey to us, as their manner is.

We returned to the house of M. Fabre's relation, where great honor was done to me. He gave me a cup with its dish, in "porcelain", which "Madame la Comtesse d'Artois" had presented to M. Fabre's relation; the cup bore the arms of King Louis. He gave me also at the same time a little chest for taking papers, such as a newspaper; this box was made of crystal and the shape of a coat-of-mail. The mistress of the house asked me what I should like to eat. I replied, some eggs cooked by my servant. They laid the table, we sat down, and I ate some bread with two boiled eggs. I then recited grace and afternoon prayer.

We took our places in the coach again; everything was covered with snow. The Christian told me there was a collection here of great animals, but that on account of the snow they were shut up under cover, and could not be seen. The "garden" is twenty-one miles round, but in winter, when there is snow, nothing is to be seen. We got back without more ado. The Christian wanted to pay for the coach. It is wonderful to see with what kindly feelings of regard God had filled him for me. I give Him thanks and homage. . . . The relative of this M. Fabre and her daughter asked me to give them my blessing; I went a little nearer to them and did bless them, but would not place my hand on their heads —it is extraordinary! Praised be God, who has elevated me, unworthy as I am of so many favors, lacking everything, in such wise; it is His mercy which has been granted to me; may He be forever blessed and exalted!

In the evening, the eve of Thursday, the Marquis de Thomé came, with the Marquise de Croix. She took a seat near me and asked me to pray for her. Then she told me that she was studying the Bible, and that she saw angels and spirits who talked with her, but that, when they were evil, she repulsed them. She made offering of a "louis" for Hebron, and mentioned the Baal-Shem of London. She told me that a Jew had given her a book of kabbalistic lore, and other matters she imparted to me, too. How strange it all is! As for myself, I answered her with such remarks as were suitable to her. Then she informed me that she was a lady held in much consideration and that at Avignon she had saved many Jews from the hands of the Inquisitor, that she was the daughter of a Marquis and her husband was a Marquis—so many tales of this Christian lady. But how many Christians have been led away by the man called Baal-Shem who, in his pride and presumption, has revealed the practices of the Kabbalah and the adjurations to so many nobles and ladies out of vanity. I have been plied with many questions about him, which I have answered.

On the morrow I went to the "Bibliothèque" and copied a part of the *Notes* of Rabbi Isaiah on the Pentateuch. I went over the whole building; it holds many rooms filled with manuscripts in all languages dealing with all the sciences and all the religions. Among the Chinese manuscripts there is a book, with a beautiful, upright clear handwriting. There are said to be nearly fifty-thousand manuscript volumes here. The "Bibliothèque" of printed books I have not, however, seen this time, but I did see all over it twenty-two years ago: it is marvelous and worthy of a King. This "Bibliothèque" of Paris is said to be the largest and most remarkable in the world.

On Friday I went to collect some of the offerings written down below for the Yeshiba "Keneset Israel" of Hebron.

On the Sabbath—the day itself and the evening of the day before—I was at the house of M. David Naquet, where I was received with much honor; M. Abraham and M. Venture shared our meals. May God reward them!

On Sunday we departed in peace from Paris, accompanied, until we reached the outskirts of Paris, by M. Solomon Ravel, M. David Naquet and M. Hananel, who made the start with us in our coach.

A TRIP WITH ISRAEL BAALSHEM

MEIR MARGOLIS (?-1790)

The extraordinary figure of Israel Baalshem Tob, the founder of Hasidism, is obscured in legends that parallel in many ways the gospels of the New Testament. His opinions were recorded by a host of disciples but his life was transfigured into miraculous performances by the naiveté and mysticism of the masses. The following brief reminiscence, not entirely untouched by legendry, is a unique portrait by a contemporary. Meir is said to have been a pupil of the Baalshem. He was rabbi of the community of Lemberg, the center of Poland then ruled by Austria-Hungary, and the author of a number of works dealing with ethics and mysticism.

❊   ❊   ❊

ONCE Israel Baalshem Tob was journeying to the holy city of Brody by way of Horodenka, and he stopped in front of my house and sent for me to come out. He said, "Meir, come, join me on the wagon and accompany me to Brody." I took my bag with prayer shawl, phylacteries and long coat and made the trip. When we reached the city, he took quarters at an inn in the manner of the merchants. There he was visited only by two honorable men, one who was rich and a second who was not. They spent a good deal of time with him and brought him peace.

Now, I noticed that the Baalshem Tob did not carry a cent, and I was worried. Why didn't I take some money from my house? I thought. Then I heard him say to the wagoner, "Make ready for travel." I went and informed those two men that the Baalshem Tob was leaving. They came. Finding that his departure was delayed, they said, "We are going to the Beth Hamidrash. Do you let us know when he is ready to leave and we shall come."

And so it was. I let them know and they came.

Now, during the first visit the rich man had given the Baalshem

190

Tob a gold ducat. But when they returned to bid him adieu, the Baalshem Tob returned the ducat to this man, saying, "Take the money and give half of it to the members of the *Klaus*.* (The members were much beloved by Baalshem Tob. He said that the Shekinah—the Presence of God—rested upon the Klaus.) And divide the other half among the poor." Then we left the city.

When I saw him squander the gold ducat, my heart melted within me, for I knew he was without a penny. I inquired: "Why did you do it? Does it add to your stature to be without a penny for living expenses?" He simply answered, "O faithful guardian, know that so long as the blessed Lord lives we have nothing to worry about."

And so it was. When we arrived in Radwill, the people came to him to be healed. The same happened everywhere until in the end his home did not lack the wherewithal to live.

* Hasidic conclave for prayer and discussion.

MY STRUGGLE WITH AMAZONS

SOLOMON MAIMON (1754-1800)

Maimon's self-portrait was characterized by George Eliot as "that wonderful piece of Autobiography." He is, indeed, the autobiographer *par excellence*. Born into the medieval climate of Lithuanian rural culture, he fought his way to the enlightened circle of the *Judengasse* of Berlin, which was then dominated by the personality of Moses Mendelssohn. He was soon recognized as one of the keenest minds among the Berlin intellectuals—Immanuel Kant paid him high tribute—but he never completely succeeded in divesting himself of the impress of his early background. Maimon is an extraordinary example of the "marginal mind," in which two streams of culture were in constant conflict. So utterly frank and revealing is the narrative of his life—even the following chapter hardly suggests how fascinating it is—that the book has always had, and probably will have, a warm circle of fans.

❋ ❋ ❋

IN my youth I was very lively, and had in my nature a good deal that was agreeable. In my passions I was violent and impatient. Till about my eleventh year, as I had the benefit of a very strict education and was kept from all contact with women, I never traced any special inclination towards the fair sex. But an incident produced a great change in this respect.

A poor but very pretty girl about my own age was taken into our house as a servant. She charmed me uncommonly. Desires began to stir in me, which till this time I had never known. But in accordance with the strict rabbinical morals, I was obliged to keep on my guard against looking on the girl with attentive gaze, and still more against speaking with her, so that I was able only now and then to throw her a stolen glance.

It happened once, however, that the women of the house were going to bathe, which by the usage of the country they are accustomed to do two or three times a week. By chance my instinct drove me without reflection towards the place where they bathed; and there I suddenly perceived this beautiful girl, as she stepped out of the steam bath and plunged into the river flowing by. At that sight I fell into a sort of rapture. After my feelings had calmed down again, being mindful of the strict talmudic laws, I wished to flee. But I could not; I remained standing, as if rooted to the spot. As I dreaded, however, lest I might be surprised here, I was obliged to return with a heavy heart. From that time I became restless, was sometimes beside myself; and this state continued till my marriage.

Our neighbor, the arendator, had two sons and three daughters. The eldest daughter, Deborah, was already married. The second, Pessel, was about my age; the peasantry of the place professed to find even a certain resemblance in our features, and therefore, in accordance with all the laws of probability, conjectured that there would be a match between us. We formed also a mutual affection. But by ill luck the youngest daughter, Rachel, had to fall into a cellar and dislocate one of her legs. She herself, indeed, completely recovered, but the leg remained somewhat crooked. The arendator then started a hunt after me; he was absolutely determined to have me for a son-in-law. My father was quite agreeable, but he wished to have for his daughter-in-law the straight-legged Pessel rather than Rachel of the crooked leg. The arendator, however, declared that this was impracticable, inasmuch as he had fixed on a rich husband for the elder, while the youngest was destined for me; and as my father was unable to give me anything, he was willing to provide for her richly out of his own fortune. Besides a considerable sum which he agreed to give as a dowry, he was willing in addition to make me a joint-heir of his fortune, and to provide me with all necessaries the whole of my life. Moreover, he promised to pay my father a fixed sum immediately after the betrothal, and not only to leave him undisturbed in his rights, but also to try and promote his domestic happiness in every possible way. The feuds between the two families were to cease from this time, and a league of friendship was to unite them for the future into one family.

Had my father lent an ear to these representations, he would without doubt have established the fortune of his house, and I should have lived with a spouse, who, it is true, had a crooked leg, but (as I found out some time afterwards when I was a tutor in her family) was in other respects an amiable woman. I should thus have been freed from all cares in the midst of good fortune, and I should have been able to apply myself without hindrance to my studies. But unhappily my father rejected this proposal with scorn. He was absolutely determined to have Pessel for his daughter-in-law; and since this, as already mentioned, was impracticable, the feuds between the two families broke out afresh. But as the arendator was rich, and my father was a poor man, the latter was necessarily always the loser.

Some time afterwards another matrimonial proposal for me turned up. Mr. L. of Schmilowitz, a learned and at the same time a rich man, who had an only daughter, was so enchanted with my fame that he chose me for his son-in-law without having seen me. He began by entering into correspondence with my father on the subject, and left it to him to prescribe the conditions of the union. My father answered his letter in lofty style, made up of Biblical verses and passages from the Talmud, in which he expressed the conditions briefly by means of the following verses from the Canticles, "The thousand gulden are for thee, O Solomon, and the two hundred for those who keep his fruits.* " Consent was given to everything.

My father accordingly made a journey to Schmilowitz, saw his future daughter-in-law, and had the marriage-contract drawn in accordance with the terms agreed upon. Two hundred gulden were paid to him on the spot. With this, however, he was not content, but insisted that in his letter he had been obliged to limit himself to two hundred gulden merely for the sake of the beautiful verse which he did not wish to spoil; but he would not enter into the transaction at all unless he received for himself twice two hundred gulden (fifty thalers in Polish money). They had, therefore, to pay him two hundred gulden more, and to hand over to him the so-called little presents for me, namely, a cap of black velvet trimmed with gold lace, a Bible bound in green velvet with silver clasps, etc. With these things he came home full of joy, gave me the presents, and told me that I was to prepare myself for a disputation to be held on my marriage day, which would be in two months' time.

Already my mother had begun to bake the cakes she was expected to take with her to the wedding, and to prepare all sorts of preserves. I began also to think about the disputation I was to hold, when suddenly the mournful news arrived that my bride had died of smallpox. My father could easily reconcile himself to this loss, because he thought to himself that he had made fifty thalers by his son in an honorable way,

---

* Evidently VIII, 12, rendered in the Authorized Version, "Thou, O Solomon, must have a thousand (pieces of silver), and those that keep the fruit thereof two hundred." Maimon translates apparently from memory, "Die tausend Gulden sind für dich, Salomo, und die Zwiehundert für die, die seine Früchte bewahren." In this rendering of this, the pronoun "his" must be understood in its old English latitude as either neuter or masculine.

and that now he could get fifty thalers for him again. I, too, who had never seen my bride, could not particularly mourn her loss. I thought to myself, "The cap and the silver-clasped Bible are already mine, and a bride will also not be awanting long, while my disputation can serve me again." My mother alone was inconsolable about this loss. Cakes and preserves are of a perishable nature and will not keep long. The labor which my mother had expended was therefore rendered fruitless by this fatal accident; and to this must be added, that she could find no place to keep the delicious cakes from my secret attacks.

Meanwhile the domestic circumstances of my father became every day worse. He saw himself, therefore, compelled to make a journey to the town of Nesvij, and apply for a position as teacher there, whither I also had to follow him. Here he opened under favorable conditions a school of his own, in which he employed me as assistant.

A widow, celebrated for her superior talents, as well as for her Xanthippe-like character, kept a public house at the extremity of one of the suburbs. She had a daughter who yielded to her in none of the above-mentioned qualities, and who was indispensable to her in the management of the house. Madam Rissia (this was the widow's name), excited by my constantly increasing reputation as a talmudic scholar, fixed on me as a husband for her daughter Sarah. Her family represented to her the impossibility of carrying out this plan; first, my father's pride and the demands which he would therefore make and which she could never satisfy; then my fame, which had already excited the attention of the most prominent and wealthy people of the town; and finally, the moderate character of her own fortune, which was far from sufficient to carry out such a proposal. All these representations, however, were of no avail with her. She had once for all taken it into her head to have me for a son-in-law, cost her what it might; and, she thought, the devil would needs be in it, if she could not get the young man.

She sent a proposal to my father, let him have no rest the whole time he was in the town, discussed the matter with him herself on various occasions, and promised to satisfy all his demands. My father, however, sought to gain time for deliberation, and to put off the decision for a while. But the time came when we were to return home. My father went with me to the widow's house, which was the last on our road, in order to wait for a conveyance which started from that place. Madam Rissia made use of the opportunity, began to caress me, introduced my bride, and asked me how I was pleased with her. At last she pressed for a decisive answer from my father. He was still holding back, however, and sought in every possible way to represent the difficulties connected with the subject.

While they were thus treating with one another, suddenly there burst into the room the chief rabbi, the preacher, and the elders of the place, with many of the most respectable people. This sudden appearance was brought about without any magic in the following way. These gentlemen had been invited to a circumcision at the house of a prominent man in this very suburb. Madam Rissia, who knew this very well, sent her son at once to the house with an invitation to the whole company to come, immediately after rising from table, to a betrothal at her house. They came therefore half tipsy, and as they believed nothing was wanting but to write out and subscribe the contract, they sat down to table, set my father in the midst, and the chief rabbi began to dictate the contract to the scribe of the community.

My father assured them that on the main point nothing had yet been decided, and that still less had the preliminary articles been settled. The chief rabbi fell into a passion at this, for he supposed that it was only a quibble, and that his sacred person and the whole honorable company were being made sport of. He turned therefore to the company, and said with a haughty air, "Who is this Rabbi Joshua, who makes himself of so much consequence?" My father replied, "The Rabbi is here superfluous. I am, 'tis true, a common man; but I believe no man can dispute my right to care for the welfare of my son, and to place his future happiness on a firm footing."

The chief rabbi was greatly offended with the ambiguity of the expression, "The Rabbi is here superfluous." He saw clearly that he had no right to lay down the law to my father in the matter, and that it was rash of Madam Rissia to invite a company to a betrothal before the parties were agreed on the preliminary articles. He began therefore to strike a lower tone. He represented to my father the advantages of this match, the high ancestry of the bride (her grandfather, father, and uncle having been learned men and chief rabbis), her personal attractions, and the willingness and ability of Madam Rissia to satisfy all his demands.

My father, who in fact had nothing to say against all this, was compelled to yield. The marriage contract was made out, and in it Madam Rissia made over to her daughter her public-house with all its belongings as a bridal portion, and came under an obligation also to board and clothe the newly-married couple for six years. Besides I received as a present a complete edition of the Talmud with its commentaries, together worth two or three hundred thalers, and a number of other gifts. My father came under no obligation at all, and in addition received fifty thalers in cash. Very wisely he had refused to accept a note for this sum; it had to be paid to him before the betrothal.

After all this had been arranged, there was a capital entertainment, and the brandy bottle was vigorously plied. The very next day my father and I went home. My mother-in-law promised to send after us as soon as possible the so-called little presents and the articles of clothing for me, which in the haste she had not been able to get ready. Many weeks, however, passed without our hearing or seeing anything of these. My father was perplexed about this; and as the character of my mother-in-law had long been suspicious to him, he could think nothing else than that this intriguing woman was seeking some subterfuge to escape from her burdensome contract. He resolved therefore to repay like with like.

The following circumstances strengthened him in this resolve. A rich arendator who used to bring spirits to Nesvij for sale, and to lodge in our house on his journey through Mohilna, likewise cast his eye upon me. He had an only daughter, for whom he had decided on me as a husband. He knew, however, what difficulties he would have to overcome, if he were to treat of the subject directly with my father. He chose, therefore, an indirect way. His plan was to make my father his debtor; and as his critical circumstances would make it impossible for him to clear off the debt, he expected to force him, as it were, to consent to this union with the view of wiping out the debt by means of the amount stipulated for the son. He offered my father some barrels of spirits on credit, and the offer was accepted with delight.

As the date of payment approached, Hersch Dukor (this was the name of the arendator) came and reminded my father. The latter assured him that at the moment he was not in a position to clear off the debt, and begged him to have patience with him for some time yet. "Herr Joshua," said the arendator, "I will speak with you quite frankly on this matter. Your circumstances are growing daily worse; and if no fortunate accident occurs, I do not see any possibility of your being able to clear off your debt. The best thing for us both, therefore, is this. You have a son, and I have a daughter who is the sole heiress of all my property. Let us enter into an alliance. By this means not only will your debt be wiped out, but a sum to be fixed by yourself will be paid in addition, and I shall exert myself to improve your circumstances."

No one could be more joyous over this proposal than my father. Immediately a contract was closed, in which the bride's dowry, as well as the required presents, was decided in accordance with my father's suggestion. The bill for the debt, which amounted to fifty thalers in Polish money, was returned to my father, and torn on the spot, while fifty thalers in addition were paid to him.

Thereupon my new father-in-law went on to Nesvij to collect some debts there. Unfortunately he had to lodge at my former mother-in-law's. She, being a great prattler, told him of her own accord about the good match which her daughter had made. "The father of the bridegroom," said she, "is himself a great scholar, and the bridegroom is a young man of eleven years, who has scarcely his equal."

"I also," replied the arendator, "have, thank God, made a good choice for my daughter. You have perhaps heard of the celebrated scholar, Rabbi Joshua, in Mohilna, and of his young son, Solomon. He is my daughter's bridegroom."

Scarcely had these words been spoken, when she cried out, "That is a confounded lie. Solomon is my daughter's bridegroom; and here, sir, is the marriage contract."

The arendator then showed her his contract too; and they fell into a dispute, the result of which was that Madam Rissia had my father summoned before the court to give a categorical explanation. My father, however, did not put in an appearance, although she had him summoned twice.

Meanwhile my mother died, and was brought to Nesvij for burial. My mother-in-law obtained from the court an attachment on the dead body, by which its interment was interdicted till the termination of the suit. My father, therefore, saw himself compelled to appear in court; my mother-in-law endeavored to satisfy all his demands in accordance with her promise, clothed me from head to toe, and even paid my father for my board from the date of the betrothal to the marriage. My mother also was now buried, and we returned home again.

My second father-in-law came too, and called upon my father for the ratification of his contract. He, however, pointed out that it was null and void, as it contravened a previous contract, and had been made by him merely in the supposition that my mother-in-law had no intention of fulfilling hers. The arendator seemed to give an ear to these representations and reconcile himself to his loss; but in reality he was thinking of some means to get me into his hands. Accordingly he rose by night, yoked his horses, took me in silence from the table on which I was sleeping, packed me with all despatch into his carriage, and made off with his booty out of the gate. But as this could not be accomplished without some noise, the people in the house awoke, discovered the theft, pursued the kidnaper, and snatched me out of his hand. To me the whole incident appeared at the time like a dream.

In this way my father was released from his debt, and got fifty thalers besides as a gratuity; but I was immediately afterwards carried off by my legal mother-in-law, and made the husband of my legal bride. I must, of course, confess that this transaction of my father's cannot be justified from a moral viewpoint. Only his great need at the time can in some measure serve as an excuse.

On the first evening of my marriage my father was not present. As he told me at my departure that he had still to settle some articles on my account, and therefore I was to wait for his arrival, I refused, in spite of all the efforts that were made, to appear that evening. Nevertheless the marriage festivities went on. We waited the next day for my father, but still he did not come. They then threatened to bring a party of soldiers to drag me to the marriage ceremony; but I gave them for an answer that, if this were done, it would help them little, for the ceremony would not be lawful except as a voluntary act. At last, to the joy of all interested, my father arrived towards evening, the articles referred to were amended, and the marriage ceremony was performed.

Here I must mention a little anecdote. I had read in a Hebrew book of an approved plan for a husband to secure lordship over his better half for life. He was to tread on her foot at the marriage ceremony; and if both hit on the stratagem, the first to succeed would retain the upper hand. Accordingly, when my bride and I were placed side by side at the ceremony, this trick occurred to me, and I said to myself, "Now you must not let the opportunity pass of securing for your whole lifetime lordship over your wife." I was just going to tread on her foot, but a certain *Je ne sais quoi,* whether fear, shame, or love, held me back. While I was in this irresolute state, all at once I felt the slipper of my wife on my foot with such an impression that I should almost have screamed aloud if I had not been checked by shame. I took this for a bad omen and thought to myself, "Providence has destined you to be the slave of your wife; you must not try to slip out of her fetters." From my faint-heartedness and the heroic mettle of my wife, the reader may easily conceive why this prophecy had to be actually realized.

I stood, however, not only under the slipper of my wife, but—what was very much worse—under the lash of my mother-in-law. Nothing of all that she had promised was fulfilled. Her house, which she had settled on her daughter as a dowry, was burdened with debt. Of the six years' board which she had promised me I enjoyed scarcely half a year's, and this amid constant brawls and squabbles. She even, trusting to my youth and want of spirit, ventured now and then to lay hands on me, but this I repaid not infrequently with compound interest. Scarcely a meal passed during which we did not fling at each other's heads bowls, plates, spoons, and similar articles.

Once I came home from the academy quite famished. As my mother-in-law and wife were occupied with the business of the public house, I went myself into the room where the milk was kept; and as I found a dish of curds and cream, I fell upon it, and began to eat. My mother-in-law came as I was thus occupied, and screamed in rage, "You are not going to devour the milk with the cream!" The more cream the better, thought I, and went on eating, without disturbing myself by her cry. She wrested the dish forcibly from my hands, beat me with her fists, and let me feel all her ill will. Exasperated by such treatment, I pushed her from me, seized the dish, and smashed it on her head. That was a sight! The curds ran down all over her. She seized in rage a piece of wood, and if I had not cleared out in all haste, she would certainly have beat me to death.

Scenes like this occurred very often. At such skirmishes of course my wife had to remain neutral, and whichever party gained the upper hand, it came home to her very closely. "Oh!" she often complained, "if only the one or the other of you had a little more patience!"

Tired of ceaseless open war, I once hit upon a stratagem which had a good effect for a short time at least. I rose about midnight, took a large vessel of earthenware, crept with it under my mother-in-law's bed, and began to speak aloud into the vessel after the following fashion— "O Rissia, Rissia, you ungodly woman, why do you treat my beloved son so ill? If you do not mend your ways, your end is near, and you will be damned to all eternity." Then I crept out again, and began to pinch her cruelly, and after a while I slipped silently back into bed.

The following morning she got up in consternation and told my wife that my mother had appeared to her in a dream and had threatened and pinched her on my account. In confirmation she showed the blue marks on her arm. When I came from the synagogue, I did not find my mother-in-law at home but found my wife in tears. I asked the reason, but she would tell me nothing. My mother-in-law returned with dejected look, and eyes red with weeping. She had gone, as I afterwards learned, to the Jewish place of burial, thrown herself on my mother's grave, and begged for forgiveness of her fault. She then had the burial place measured, and ordered a wax-light as long as its circumference, for burning in the synagogue. She also fasted the whole day, and towards me showed herself extremely amiable.

I knew of course what was the cause of all this, but acted as if I did not observe it, and rejoiced in secret over the success of my stratagem. In this manner I had peace for some time, but unfortunately it did not last long. The whole was soon forgotten again, and on the slightest occasion the dance went on as before. In short, I was soon afterwards obliged to leave the house altogether and accept a position as a private tutor. Only on the great feast days I used to come home.

In my fourteenth year I had my eldest son, David. At my marriage I was only eleven years old, and owing to the retired life common among our people in those regions, as well as the want of mutual intercourse between the two sexes, I had no idea of the essential duties of marriage, but looked on a pretty girl as on any other work of nature or art, somewhat as on the pretty medicine box that I stole. It was therefore natural that for a considerable time after marriage I could not have any thought about the fulfillment of its duties. I used to approach my wife with trembling as a mysterious object. It was therefore supposed that I had been bewitched at the time of the wedding; and under this supposition I was brought to a witch to be cured. She performed all sorts of operations, which of course had a good effect, although indirectly through the help of the imagination.

My life in Poland from my marriage to my emigration, which period embraces the springtime of my existence, was a series of miseries with a want of all means for the promotion of culture; and, necessarily connected with that, an aimless application of my powers, in the description of which the pen drops from my hands, and the painful memories of which I try to stifle.

Once Prince Radzivil, one of the greatest Polish magnates, sent for a respectable Jewish barber, who, suspecting nothing but that he was wanted for some surgical operation, brought his instruments with him and appeared before the Prince.

"Have you brought your instruments with you?" he was asked.

"Yes, Serene Highness," he replied.

"Then," said the Prince, "give me a lancet, and I will open one of your veins."

The poor barber had to submit. The Prince seized the lancet; and as he did not know how to go about the operation, and besides his hand trembled as a result of his hard drinking, of course he wounded the barber in a pitiable manner. But his courtiers smiled their applause, and praised his great skill in surgery.

He went one day into a church, and being so drunk that he did not know where he was, he stood against the altar and acted like a beast. All who were present became horrified. Next morning when he was sober, the clergy brought to his mind the misdeed he had committed the day before. "Eh!" said the Prince, "we will soon make that good." Thereupon he issued a command to the Jews of the place, to provide at their own expense fifty stone of wax for burning in the church. The poor Jews were therefore obliged to bring a sin offering for the desecration of a Christian Church by an orthodox Catholic Christian.

He once took it into his head to drive on the wall round the town. But as the wall was too narrow for a coach with six horses—and he never drove in any other—his hussars were obliged, with much labor and peril of their lives, to carry the coach with their hands till he had driven round the town in this way.

Once he drove with the whole pomp of his court to a synagogue and, without any one to this day knowing the reason, committed the greatest havoc: he smashed windows and stoves, broke all the vessels, threw on the ground the copies of the Holy Scriptures kept in the ark, and so forth. A learned, pious Jew, who was present, ventured to lift one of these copies from the ground, and had the honor of being struck with a musket-ball by His Serene Highness' own hand. From here the train went to a second synagogue, where the same performance was repeated, and from there they proceeded to the Jewish burial place, where the buildings were demolished and the monuments cast into the fire.

Can it be conceived that a Prince could show himself so malicious towards his own poor subjects, whom he was in a position to punish legally whenever they really did anything wrong? Yet this is what happened here.

On one occasion he took it into his head to make a trip to Mohilna, a hamlet belonging to him, which lay four short miles from his palace. This had to be done with his usual suite and all the pomp of his court. On the morning of the appointed day the train went forth. First marched the army in order according to its usual regimental divisions—infantry, artillery, cavalry, and so on. Then followed his bodyguard, Strelitzi, consisting of volunteers from the poor nobility. After them came his kitchen-wagons, in which Hungarian wine had not been forgotten. These were followed by the music of his janissaries, and other bands. Then came his coach, and last of all his satraps. I give them this name, because I can compare this train with no other than that of Darius in the war against Alexander. Towards evening His Serene Highness arrived at our public house in the suburb of the town which was His Serene Highness' residence, Nesvij. I cannot say that he arrived in his own high person, for the Hungarian wine had robbed him of all consciousness, in which alone, of course, personality rests. He was carried into the house and thrown with all his clothes, booted and spurred, on to my mother-in-law's dirty bed, without giving it a supply of clean linen.

As usual, I had taken to flight. My amazons, however, I mean my mother-in-law and my wife, trusted to their heroic mettle and remained at home alone. Riot went on the whole night. In the very room where His Serene Highness slept, wood was chopped, cooking and baking were done. It was well known that when His Serene Highness slept, nothing could waken his high person except perhaps the trumpets of the Judgment Day. The next morning, when he wakened and looked around, he scarcely knew whether to trust his eyes when he found himself in a wretched public house, thrown on to a dirty bed swarming with bugs. His valets, pages, and Negroes waited on his commands. He asked how he had come there and was answered that His Serene Highness had yesterday commenced a journey to Mohilna, but had halted here to take rest, that his whole train had meanwhile gone on, and had undoubtedly arrived in Mohilna by this time.

The journey to Mohilna was for the present given up, and the whole train ordered back. They returned accordingly to the Palace in the usual order and pomp. But the Prince was pleased to hold a great banquet in our public house. All the foreign gentlemen who happened to be in the palace at the time were invited. The service used on the occasion was of gold, and it is impossible adequately to realize the contrast which reigned here in one house, between Asiatic splendor and Lappish poverty. In a miserable public house, whose walls were black as coal with smoke and soot, whose rafters were supported by undressed round stems of trees, whose windows consisted of some fragments of broken panes of bad glass and small strips of pine covered with paper,— in this house sat princes on dirty benches at a still dirtier table and had the choicest dishes and the finest wines served to them on gold plate.

Before the banquet the Prince took a stroll with the other gentlemen in front of the house and by chance observed my wife. She was then in the bloom of her youth; and although I am now separated from her, still I must do her the justice to allow that—leaving, of course, out of account all that taste and art contribute to the heightening of a person's charms, inasmuch as these had had no influence on her—she was a beauty of the first rank. It was therefore natural that she should please the Prince. He turned to his companions and said, "Really a pretty young woman! Only she ought to get a white chemise." This was a common signal with him and meant as much as the throwing of a handkerchief by the Grand Sultan. When these gentlemen heard it, they became solicitous for the honor of my wife and gave her a hint to clear out as fast as possible. She took the hint, slipped silently out, and was soon over the hills and far away.

After the banquet His Serene Highness proceeded again with the other gentlemen into town amid trumpets, kettledrums, and the music of his janissaries. Then the usual order of the day was followed; that is, a carousal was carried on the whole afternoon and evening, and then the party went to a pleasure house at the entrance to the Prince's zoological garden, where fireworks were set off at great expense, but usually with accidents. As every goblet was drained, cannons were fired; but the poor cannoneers, who knew better how to handle the plough than the cannon, were not seldom injured. "Vivat Kschondsie Radzivil," that is, "Long live Prince Radzivil," shouted the guests. The palm in this bacchanalian sport was of course awarded to the Prince; and those who awarded it were loaded by him with presents, not in perishable corn or golden snuffboxes or anything of that sort, but in real estate with many hundred peasants. At the close a concert was given, during which His Serene Highness fell gently asleep and was carried to the castle.

The expenses of such extravagance were of course extorted from the poor tenantry. If this was not sufficient, debts were contracted and estates sold to wipe them out. Not even the twelve golden statues in life-size—whether they represented the twelve apostles or the twelve giants, I do not know—nor the golden table which had been made for himself, were spared on such emergencies. And thus the noble estates of this great prince were diminished, his treasures which had accumulated during many generations were exhausted, and his tenants . . . But I must break off.

The Prince died not long ago without heirs. His brother's sons inherited the estates.

The place where I first occupied the position of family tutor was at the distance of a league from my residence. The family was that of a miserable farmer in a still more miserable village, and my salary was five thalers in Polish money. The poverty, ignorance, and rudeness in the manner of life which prevailed in this house were indescribable. The farmer himself was a man of about fifty years, the whole of whose face was overgrown with hair, ending in a dirty, thick beard as black as pitch. His language was a sort of muttering, intelligible only to the boors with whom he held intercourse daily. Not only was he ignorant of Hebrew, but he could not speak of a word of Yiddish; his only language was Russian, the common patois of the peasantry. His wife and children were of the same stamp. Moreover, the apartment in which they lived was a hovel of smoke, black as coal inside and out, without a chimney, but with merely a small opening in the roof for the exit of the smoke, an opening which was carefully closed as soon as the fire was allowed to go out, so that the heat might not escape.

The windows were narrow strips of pine laid crosswise over each other, and covered with paper. This apartment served at once for sitting, drinking, eating, study, and sleep. Think of this room intensely heated, and the smoke, as is generally the case in winter, driven back by wind and rain till the whole place is filled with it to suffocation. Here hung a foul washing and other dirty bits of clothing on poles laid across the room in order to kill the vermin with the smoke. There hang sausages to dry, while their fat keeps constantly trickling down on the heads of people below. Yonder stand tubs with sour cabbage and red beets, which form the principal food of the Lithuanians. In a corner the water is kept for daily use, with the dirty water alongside. In the room the bread is kneaded, cooking and baking are done, the cow is milked, and all sorts of operations are carried on.

In this magnificent dwelling the peasants sit on the bare ground: you dare not sit higher if you do not wish to be suffocated with the smoke. Here they guzzle their whisky and make an uproar, while the people of the house sit in a corner. I usually took my place behind the stove with my dirty halfnaked pupils, and expounded to them out of an old tattered Bible from Hebrew into Russian Yiddish. All this together made such a splendid group as deserved to be sketched only by a Hogarth, and to be sung only by a Butler.

It may be easily imagined how pitiable my condition must have been. Whisky had to form my sole comfort; it made me forget all my misery. This was increased by the fact that a regiment of Russians, who were rioting at that time with every conceivable cruelty on the estates of Prince Radzivil, was stationed in the village and its neighborhood. The house was constantly full of drunken Russians, who committed all sorts of excesses, hewed to pieces tables and benches, threw glasses and bottles into the faces of the people of the house, and so on. To give merely one example, a Russian, who was stationed in this house as guard, and whose charge it was to secure the house against all violence, came home once drunk, and demanded something to eat. A dish of millet with butter was placed before him cooked. He shoved the dish away, and shouted an order for more butter. A whole small tub of butter was brought, when he shouted again an order for another dish. This was brought immediately, whereupon he threw all the butter into it, and called for spirits. A whole bottle was brought, and he poured it likewise into the dish. Thereafter milk, pepper, salt, and tobacco, in large quantities had to be brought to him, the whole being put in, and the mixture devoured. After he had taken some spoonfuls, he began to strike about him, pulled the host by the beard, struck him in the face with his fist, so that the blood flowed out of his mouth, poured some of his glorious broth down his throat, and went on in this riotous manner till he became so drunk that he could no longer support himself and fell to the ground.

Such scenes were at that time very common everywhere in Poland. If a Russian army passed a place, they took with them a *prowodnik,* or guide, to the next place. But instead of seeking to be supplied by the mayor or the village magistrate, they used to seize the first person whom they met on the road. He might be young or old, male or female, healthy or sick; it mattered nothing to them; for they knew the road well enough from special charts, and only sought an opportunity for outrage. If it happened that the person seized did not know the way at all, and did not show them the right road, they did not allow themselves to be sent astray on this account; they selected the road all right, but they cudgeled the poor *prowodnik* till he was half-dead, for not knowing the way!

I was once seized as a *prowodnik* myself. I did not indeed know the way, but luckily I hit upon it by chance. Fortunately, therefore, I reached the proper place, and the only violence I suffered, besides a good many blows and kicks from the Russian soldiers, was the threat that, if I ever led them astray, I should certainly be flayed alive—a threat which they might be trusted with carrying into execution.

The other places which I filled as tutor were more or less similar to this. An incident of psychological interest, which happened to another person and of which I was simply eyewitness, must be mentioned here.

A tutor in the next village, who was a somnambulist, rose one night from his bed and went to the village churchyard with a volume of the Jewish ceremonial laws in his hand. After remaining some time there he returned to his bed. In the morning he rose up, without remembering the least of what had happened during the night, and went to the chest where his copy of the ceremonial laws was usually kept, in order to take out the first part, *Orach Hayyim* or the *Way of Life*, which he was accustomed to read every morning. The code consists of four parts, each of which was bound separately, and all the four had certainly been locked up in the chest. He was therefore astonished to find only three of the parts, *Yoreh Deah* or the *Teacher of Wisdom*, being wanting. As he knew about his sleepwalking, he searched everywhere, till at last he came to the churchyard, where he found the *Yoreh Deah* lying open at the chapter, *Hilkhoth Abheloth* or the *Laws of Mourning*. He took this for a bad omen and came home much disquieted. On being asked the cause of his disquietude, he related the incident which had occurred, finishing with the remark, "Ah! God knows how my poor mother is!" He begged of his master the loan of a horse and permission to ride to the nearest town, where his mother lived, in order to inquire after her welfare. As he had to pass the place where I was tutor, and I saw him riding in great excitement without being willing to dismount even for a little while, I asked him the cause of his excitement. He related to me the above-mentioned incident.

I was astonished, not so much about the particular circumstances of this incident as about somnambulism in general, of which till then I had known nothing. My friend, on the other hand, assured me that somnambulism was a common occurrence with him, and that it meant nothing, but that the circumstance of the *Hilkhoth Abheloth* made him forebode some misfortune. Thereupon he rode off, arrived at his mother's house, and found her seated at her frame for needlework. She asked him the reason for his coming, when he replied that he had come merely to pay her a visit, as he had not seen her for a long time. After he had rested for a good while, he rode back; but his disquietude was by no means wholly removed, and the thought of the *Hilkhoth Abheloth* he could not get out of his head. The third day after, a fire broke out in the town where his mother lived, and the poor woman perished in the flames. Scarcely had the son heard of the conflagration, when he began to lament that his mother had so miserably perished. He rode off in all haste to the town, and found what he had foreboded.

WEDDED TO THE MUSE

MENDELE MOCHER SEFORIM (1836-1917)

Writing under the pseudonym Mendele the Bookseller, Sholom
Jacob Abramowitz was pre-eminent in Yiddish and Hebrew Letters
of the nineteenth century. Mendele was a born writer with a gift
for easy flowing narrative and an imaginative grasp of plot and incident. He loved life and nature, but hated the social system which
degraded his people. His novels depict with warm sympathy and a
strong dash of satire the butcher, the baker and the candlestick
maker of the ghetto and pale of Tzarist Russia; with due reservation
he may be considered the Dickens of the nineteenth century Jewish
literature. He also wrote a library of books designed to enlighten and
enhearten the oppressed masses. This account of how he wedded the
Muse reveals as much of his character as of his personal history.

* * *

MY birthplace was Kapuli, a tiny country town in the Sutsk
District of the Minsk Governmental region, which God had
forgotten to supply with property and wealth and to which He
has distributed neither commerce nor trade; instead He had given it the
glories of Nature, magnificent forests and the splendor of Life, with
valleys and delightful fields all around. The day of my birth was not
recorded in any document, for in former times that was something which
our people did not bother about, particularly the small townsfolk. But
I was told that I was born in 1836, and my family fixed my birthday
as December 20th. Hayyim Moses, my father of blessed memory, was
held in high respect in our town and the neighborhood, on account of
his extensive scholarship, his large-heartedness, and his knowledge of the
way of the world. Half of his life was devoted to the Lord, that is, to
study by himself and with others gratuitously; and half to himself,
to his own requirements and those of the community to which he devoted
himself. The Lord had given my father a good tongue with which he

would at times deliver sermons, and he had a good and fluent style in our holy language. His sermons and letters are still preserved among the few people left who honored and esteemed him. He was particularly fond of me, choosing me of all his children in order to educate me in a fashion which was then entirely new to our parts. When I was six years old and already knew how to read, he engaged an excellent teacher to teach me Scripture and make me familiar with both Holy Writ and its Aramaic renderings, the Targumim. This teacher, Joseph Hareubenei (further details of whom can be found in Binstock's biography of me) used to engage in his duties faithfully for about twelve hours a day; so that within three years I knew the entire twenty-four books of the Bible by heart and had the Lord's Torah within my very bowels.

While I still delighted in the sweet words of those who saw God and my soul itself visioned forth the Almighty, my teacher led me to the marches of the Talmud, that primeval giant and veritable Og, King of Bashan, among all the literatures of the world. When I came there I was like a person arriving for the first time at a great fair and market, astonished and wondering at the sight of so many kinds of goods and wares and all the many strange and desirable things, and half-dazed at hearing the tumult and noise and shouting from every corner and quarter. There they are, buyers and sellers, agents and merchants, hasting about with much hullabaloo, possessed with the desire of and longing for trafficking, dashing urgent and breathless, one with his pitcher and the other with his barrel, each man thrusting his brother out of the way, these asking questions of those and those shouting answers to these, winking and blinking their eyes, shuffling their feet, chaffering and conferring, weighing and measuring, to the sound of a mighty noise in the camp. By virtue of the power of visualization that is implanted within me I gave shape to all things and form to all that entered the gate of this Talmud. The "former Tannaite" who appeared and reappeared in the arguments, and "the one who said so-and-so", seemed to me a mighty man, meticulous, pernickety and swift to anger, with flaming face; the first, close and middle of the discussion were women all jealous of one another, each pounding at the other, one declaring this and that and the other dissenting, nay indeed, spitefully arguing, with nothing easygoing between them. Then there were the nubile female, the barren woman and the maiden who had been seduced; the deaf and dumb, the idiot and the miner; the man or woman with an issue; the two holding the shawl; the ox that gored the cow; the vicious and the innocent ox; all of these stood as clear as though they were alive in my imagination, each one in its special form and its own strange shape. To be sure, I knew the language of all of these as soon as I met them, for from my childhood I had been familiar with the Aramaic of the Targumim; but much of their actual conversation was beyond me. All this, however, was the case only at the beginning, when first I entered the gate of the Talmud. In the course of time I grew accustomed to it and loved it at heart. I would lodge in the deeps of the Law with the flocks of my comrades, seeing signs and wonders in castles that flew in the air and mountains hanging by a hair, and wonders even greater than these in the field of Sharp and Peppery Debate. I loved to stroll at my ease in the wondrous orchard of the Agada. That orchard is no carefully designed garden with fence and gates and trees set out in orderly rows each according to its own kind, matching one another, growing absolutely level, nature being bound with the bands of a cunning artificer; no, it is like the boundless and endless wildwood, unfenced and unordered, with its plants all one great medley. Flowers innumerable you will find there, all kinds of strange plants growing in profusion like the wild flowers of the field. Yet the lily is the Lily of Sharon, the rose is the rose of the valleys set about with greenery and grass and herbage of all kinds in thousands and myriads. There is a wealth of color before you, a tapestry lovely to see. Imagination wanders free and far in such a garden, and achieves great things. Sometimes it even reaches to the skies and brings down the mighty chariot of God; and sometimes it raises the earth to the heavens, so that angels and mortals do kiss.

At the age of eleven I left my teacher's class. And at the time the following was my manner of study: following the morning prayers my father and teacher taught me a passage of the Mishna at the House of Study, and for the rest of the day I sat there and studied my own. When I returned home in the evening and my father was disengaged from most of his activities he would explain and clarify for me a leaf of Gemara with all the commentaries. If he had many other matters engaging him in the evenings he would rise before dawn, awaken me from my sleep, and we would go off together to our House of Study to engage in the study of Torah there. Truth to tell, it was very hard for a little boy who wanted to go on sleeping, particularly in winter; but once I was actually up and doing and went off to my day's work, I was pleased at heart; while as for my remuneration, the compensations of getting up and studying before dawn were plentiful indeed. There was an absolute silence in all the streets of the town, which was still sunk deep in slumber; and the moon and stars in their set places in the sky wakened my imagination and I listened, listening hard. Then in vision I could see the Man Gabriel crowing like a cock and announcing the hours of night in the highest heavens. Hosts of angels would speedily follow, and open their mouths in pleasant song. In yet a little while the gates of Paradise will swing noisily open for the God of Glory to enter. When the sons of God see the coming of my God and King in all holiness, they are silent and stand trembling each in his troop and each beside his banner, never a wing quivering, not one opening his mouth to whisper. And then suddenly the Lord thunders with a mighty thundering, and the Most High bursts forth in bitter weeping. It is for His desolate Temple that He weeps by night, for Jerusalem the forsaken that was once the city of His glory; for His people, the beloved sons of Zion, wandering wide amid the gentiles and for the humiliated Shehinah, that Divine Presence which goes wandering with them in their exile, and which suffers in their sufferings. His eyes, His eyes do weep—and that is the dew on the ground and the drops of night upon my curls. . . . And at the voice of God the saints of the world do quiver, and bitterly they weep with the angels of peace. And with all these imaginings within me I rouse myself to study with all my heart and soul. Sweetly I chant as I study, moving my argumentative thumb. My soul desired for the Lord's Torah knowledge of all the suggestive hints of the Talmud, that furrowed my forehead and took all my attention.

This method of study had a double effect on me; on the one hand it sharpened my intelligence with regard to analysis and acute hypotheses and gave my scholarship a fine edge, so that I examined and tested everything in order to arrive at the plain truth; and on the other hand it awakened my emotions and my imagination with very exalted vision, preparing me for the influence of fine writing and its holy spirit. In those days I knew nothing save the four ells of Law, nothing apart from the Talmud. I had neither seen nor heard of profane books, and as yet knew nothing about literature, theatre or any artistic activity, for my birthplace was a lonely nest in a forgotten corner where no strange feet passed. And in my innocence, like a chick within its egg, I thought that I saw the whole world before my eyes, and that beyond Kapuli's horizon lay nothing but a desolate wilderness, the place of the "Mountains of Darkness" and Sambatyon River, with all kinds of strange and weird creatures. The earthen houses of my town seemed like beautiful palaces to me, while the synagogue and the close did not have their like upon earth, seeing that here Wisdom had builded her house and the towns-folk were the choicest and wisest of mortal kind; particularly those with long beards and fine appearance. For in those days it was my belief that where there was age there was Torah and wisdom. If anybody was blessed by the Lord with a cow or a goat he seemed to me as wealthy as Korah had been in his own times, and blest with a fat portion here upon earth. The trumpet, even the hurdy-gurdy which found its way to us in some mysterious fashion, and the simple musical instruments heard at local weddings, made up the totality of orchestras and there were none besides them. And happy the trumpeter who could win people's heart and soul by the blast of his trumpet.

I knew the Scriptures, but had not yet attempted to write myself. But when the spirit of the Lord began to move within me I did not pour it forth in verse and fine writing, but stayed solitary and silent, the waves of my emotions coursing and racing; while my soul wept in secret at my heart's belief that this must be the work of Satan, that my evil inclination was moving me to waste my time with evil thoughts and diverting me from the study of Torah; and in order to save myself from this I found no method better than prayer and entreaty to the God of the winds and spirits. There were days when I would suddenly awaken with a sense of energy, telling myself, "Let my soul bless the Lord." And I would promptly be praying. To such prayers I gave up my spirit, and they brought me the pleasures and delights of Eden; and I was satisfied. Then afterwards, if that abominable one came my way I dragged him to forests, to hills and mountains afar, where I spent my time thinking and gazing at the plenitude and magnificence of Nature which, in the course of time, put heart into me with her radiance and glory. I was drawn to her by the cables of love and delighted in her as the bridegroom finds joy in his bride. Day by day I went out to the fields to visit my beloved and take my delight in this most gracious and charming of all that exists. I sought my love in the deeps of the forests and in the shady groves, in green pastures and beside the still waters; and she let all her goodness pass before me, playing before me everywhere. I pursued her leaping upon the hills, clinging to the trees and seated among the sheepfields listening to the bleating of the flocks. The nightingale sang me its songs and the voice of the turtledove was heard in the choir of the winged singers. All of them sang me their best, love songs to my divine beauty, daughter of God who fashions all things. And the love which was then like a bursting flame in my heart was a love of the spirit, not of the flesh, a holy love which bears no corporeal form, a secret hidden love of all that is good, beautiful and exalted, that makes a man rejoice while garbing him in humility and training him to be upright and faithful, loving all creatures and raising him above all happenings. The secret of this love and this outpouring of the soul in prayer and entreaty is known to all poets and men of spirit. They are the musical notes of the Almighty, the signs which the God of Song has set in the heart of his chosen ones. . . .

I remained quietly in my nest thus until I was thirteen years old, thinking that I would stay in my birthplace until the end of my days. But things did not come about as I imagined them. My father suddenly died at the age of forty-one, leaving his wife and children destitute. On account of my poverty I was exiled from my birthplace and went wandering to the Yeshiboth (Rabbinical Colleges) of the towns of Lithuania, near and far. I shall not relate here all that happened to me there, for the happenings were very numerous and I propose to devote a special book to them as a memorial to the Children of Israel regarding the Yeshiboth in those days. Here I merely wish to say that I lived according to the way of the Torah, the suffering life of a disciple of the wise with the "eating days" (eating each day's meals with a different kindhearted householder if the student was lucky, and going without food if he was unlucky) down to the last detail. At the Slutsk Yeshiba I studied with the renowned Rabbi Abraham Baruch in the first class, from which I passed up to the top class and became one of the pupils of the Head of the Yeshiba, the keen and tried Rabbi Michel Mass. Afterwards I fixed my place of study in the House of Study of the wealthy Reb Yonah, and sought Torah from the great Rabbi Abremele. In Vilna I studied with the far-famed Rabbi Reb Senderel at the Rum Mealeh (Lofty Height) Yeshiba and also in the House of Study of the Vilna Gaon Rabbi Elijah of blessed memory. There I meditated on the Lord's Torah by day and night, studying at my post all night long. I came to Vilna at the advice of my kinsman the honored and wealthy Nahum Hayyim Broida, who promised to be a father to me and supply all my requirements. My stay there did not last long, however, and I returned to my birthplace.

At about that time my mother married a man who held the lease of a mill at Melniki about ten miles away from Kapulie; and my mother went to his home together with her smaller children, leaving me forsaken in the town without any support. Suffering at heart and abased in spirit I felt sick of life. For I was a boy, my experience of life very brief and my troubles very great indeed. While I was in this gloomy state my stepfather summoned me to him; and in order not to eat the bread of idleness I taught his children for a few hours a day. My stepfather's house was surrounded by forests, vast ancient woods inhabited by all the forest animals; at night the wolves would howl there for their food and from time to time bears would make their home there. Within its deeps the birds would nest, and give voice from its boughs. The wild goose and every kind of waterfowl were to be found there, sounding their cries from the marshes and swamps. And a great river curled and twined its way between the trees all the way down to the mill, where it dashed down a slope and in so doing thunderously turned the clattering wheels; and the noise of the mill and the crashing of the waters together made one's ears ring.

It was in this lonely and forsaken dwelling that my muse, my first love, appeared to me again, after having forsaken me while I went from Yeshiba to Yeshiba with the puny students; I had no longer hoped to see her again. She appeared to me in all glory and her gracious lips persuaded me to follow her into the woods; there she made a covenant between me and the trees of the field and the birds of heaven and the creeping things of earth, and taught me to understand their tongue and to consider their manners of living. My soul thirsted for these friends, who told me ancient tales and much that was adoing in their world, and the glory of God who fashioned them and His great goodness toward them. I in turn told them of what was in my heart; for the first time I took pen in hand to pour forth my soul, singing them a new Hallelujah that I had written down. The river clapped its hands in applause and all the trees of the fields responded in chorus.

I still have these first poems with me in manuscript but they will never be published, as they are unripe and taste like crab-apples, but, wonderful to relate, no sooner did I begin to sing and devote the first fruits of my pen to the praises of the Lord, than my Satan arrived; that angel of jest and mockery who now rules over me in the guise of Mendele Mocher Seforim, and he incited me to mock at mankind and twitch aside the mysterious masks they wore. And I wrote a drama in rhymes after the fashion of *Praise to the Upright* of Rabbi Moses Hayyim Luzzatto, though I did not know what a drama was and had never read any books of the kind. This work too was childish and full of innumerable errors. This mocking childish Satan of mine babbled a lot of nonsense and gave birth to its first words without knowledge. And if I sometimes mock at my Satan and laugh at him on account of my youthful effusions, he mocks at me and firmly responds: Haven't you learnt yet that the Ancient of Days has never passed anything absolutely perfect out of His hands, and that all He created in His world calls for shaping and reworking? That is the evolution which is a Law of the world and all that is therein, and which applies here too; as you ought to know.

This period of rest did not last long. It seems that Heaven had decreed ere I left my mother's womb that I must be a writer among my people, a nation impoverished and weak; so the Lord wished me to learn something about the ways of my people and consider their behavior; and therefore He said to my soul, wander O bird through my world, misfortunate amid the misfortunate and Jew among Jews shalt thou be upon earth. So the wind raised me and flung me up and down the ladder of life, up and down, up and down; and the Angel of the Lord thrust me ever on. He lowered me down to those of my brethren dwelt at the lowest of levels, at the very bottom, to live their life of suffering with them and feel all their pains; and of the distresses of their souls I received a double portion. At times he elevated me to the very peak of our life where I came and went among our calm and settled wealthy, who rule the House of Israel, in order that I might know their works and see their sitting and their standing, their walking and their lying down, and their dealings—to see all this without being delighted in their goodness. From the time that God took me out of the house of my step-father a new chapter began in the book of my life; a chapter of wanderings, vicissitudes and countless troubles, followed by other chapters of my life all woven together in a tapestry that covers the whole life of the House of Israel, which will be told in separate stories and will serve as a memorial in the history and literature of our people. And the few of them hinted at in Bienstock's biography of me can be taken from there.

I wish to turn over those pages and disregard the happenings of those years of my life in order to describe how I became a writer in Israel and the aim I set before me, for the sake of which I prepared my heart and pen; also the books and essays I have written.

Hebrew literature was something precious and rare in my youth; there were no books or journals published at regular intervals of days, weeks, months or years as at present, to rouse the sons of Judah and set the love of our holy tongue in their hearts. In the absence of any awakener or competition between writers there were few to write, and the daughters of song were abased. When I was at Kamenetz-Podolsk, at the home of my honored and wealthy father-in-law, and later, after I had divorced my wife and become a teacher at the government school (which the Russian Government introduced here and there for Jews as an experimental measuretrans), I devoted myself to study in order to acquire by dint of toil all the knowledge that I lacked; and if anyone had suggested to me that I would ever become a writer among my people, I would have reckoned that he was joking. In my simplicity I thought writers all belonged to some higher sphere; and who was I to come thither?

Chance alone made an author of me, and it happened all of a sudden. One winter night, a dark, cloudy, misty and stormy night, I sat alone in my room, my soul dripping away veritably in unhappiness. In order to drive this away from me by doing some work, I took pen in hand to write a reply to a certain teacher. And all at once I found I had covered both sides of a large sheet with my ideas on education. Next morning I copied a few remarks from this sheet for my correspondent, throwing the sheet itself aside into a corner as something unimportant. It lay there in its corner for a long time till it fell into other hands, and then shifted from place to place in the house, while I had long forgotten about it.

Then one day the postman brought me a packet from abroad. I opened it in surprise, anxious to know who was writing to me from a foreign country where I had no acquaintance; it was No. 31 of the journal *Ha-Maggid*, first year of issue. The lines of the leading article seemed to contain familiar things; its title was *A Letter on Education* in large square Hebrew characters. I turned over the first page in astonishment, and found my name at the end. Further, a note after the essay praised it highly, and ended with a request to those suitably gifted to translate it into other languages. For several minutes I was astonished and all but stupefied; and the letter of the late A. L. Silbermann, editor of *Ha-Maggid*, written in the highest terms and asking me to continue to write for him and enter into relations with him and his journal, only added to my astonishment and wonder. Naturally I soon found out what had happened; my friend M. Levin, secretary of the noble Ginsburg (Baron Ginsburg) had come across the sheet in question at my house, and had liked it so much that he had secretly sent it to the poet Abraham Ber Gottlober for his opinion on it; and in this way it had reached the editor of *Ha-Maggid* and had seen the light. The hands of those two sages planted this first essay of mine in Hebrew literature in those days; and it had proved the foundation stone of all I have done there since.

I then began to examine the state of Hebrew literature in our country, its habits and customs and what was going on in it. I sought worthwhile things, knowledge and intelligence, good taste and beauty; but very little of all these did I find. At that time the literature was a field that lay waste, a garden forsaken in the winter; there was no yield of plants, there were no sweet blossoms; the leaves had withered and the trees had let their leaves fall; here and there could be seen a straggling aftergrowth, but the state of desolation was the thing most noticeable. And the writers? Those keepers of the vineyard were engaged in their eternal rest, calm, quiet and secure, playing like innocent children and babbling nonsense; in their rest they hallowed one another's names and everybody was satisfied.

Indeed, at that particular time somebody had expressed this thought: "There were many days for the writers of Israel, days of peace and contentedness, days of light and goodness, of ineffectuality on the part of the critics, when man's understanding lay concealed and did not disturb and upset their rest or steal their honor and glory from them. Every book and its sanctity were twin; the name of the writer and of his work were as father and son together." He, however, was referring to the distant past and in his simplicity found all this to be highly satisfactory; whereas I found that his remarks suited our own days and our own contemporary Jewish writers, and was highly dissatisfied. For times when men's understanding remains concealed are not good days of light. And a literature in which the critics are ineffectual and every book and its sanctity are twin, is a park without owners; calves graze there and destroy what is planted; swine chew whatever there is and little foxes damage its rows of plants. And if people come into such a vineyard and destroy as much as they like wantonly and then fill their baskets as well, the feeling is that there is no harm done; for license reigns and anarchy, and ye shall know that ye are in the midst of Israel, there are none to see, there are no witnesses, judge and justice are equally absent except for the Lord your God, and therefore my people need never more be ashamed. . . .

All these things I saw and took to heart, and the fruit of my thoughts was my book: *Mishpat Shalom* (A Peaceful Judgment) printed at Vilna in 1860. This book, which passes strictures on the author of *Minim Veugav* (Musical Instruments and Harp) in particular and aims at a number of other authors as well, was like an arrow suddenly shot into the calm and peaceful camp of the writers, who were resting at their posts. To them I seemed like a cruel, hardhearted man come to disturb their rest, to steal their honor and glory; and there was a great outcry in their congregation. There were quarrels and writers' conflicts in the columns of the journals *Ha-Melitz* and *Ha-Carmel,* which were just beginning to appear at that time. But I went on with the good work and from time to time shot my barbed essays among them, finding many holding with me in my conflict. Whether I judged well or always hit the target is something for others to judge; but I knew that I had caused things to move in our literature. Fresh young critics followed me in judging the works of the writers; many of the latter profited and improved their ways; and the discussion between the writers was a living spirit in the literature, the force of which attracted many new readers.

In my eyes the three aims of the writers ought to be: to teach our people good taste and understanding; to bring the daily life of their world and their actions into the sphere of literature in order to make the public fonder of the latter; to instruct and prove beneficial. I wished with all my heart that our poets and writers should not look up to the lofty heavens, nor take as their themes subjects such as the daughters of Lot or the wife of Potiphar and the like trifles which have long come to an end. It is no use questing after life among the dead. Instead let them walk the earth, watch the life of the people and all that is being done in their homes and communities, and offer it to the eyes of the public. Let them try to improve the taste of the latter by writing in good fashion in accordance with the principles of beauty and logic; further, let them instruct their readers in wisdom and knowledge, so that they may gain understanding.

I then thought things over and said to myself: I examine the ways of our people and wish to provide them with tales from Jewish sources in the holy tongue; yet most of them do not know this language and speak only Jewish-German (Yiddish); and what is the use of all the writer's toil and all his fine ideas if he does not benefit his people? This question, for whom do I toil? would not let me rest and put me into great perplexity. For at that time Yiddish was an empty vessel, containing nothing good but only a lot of nonsense written by stuttering fools, nameless folk; and these things were read by the womenfolk and poor folk without any understanding. As for other people, even if they did not know any other language or literature, they felt ashamed to read such stuff for fear other people got to know about it. If anybody did pick up a Yiddish pamphlet and begin reading it, he would laugh at himself, saying, fancy me casually reading a "woman's book". These silly, lightheaded women, how this makes me laugh! While as for our own writers and stylists who wished to increase the influence and prestige of Hebrew and felt no contact with the ordinary people, they proudly looked down on Yiddish and held it in very low esteem. And if one in a town and two in a country occasionally remembered this accursed one and wrote a few lines, they did so secretly and covered themselves over with their works, so that their immodesty might not be revealed nor their good name be lost. How great then was my perplexity when I realized that if I entered this arena I would find my good name replaced by reproach. But my desire to be of use overcame my sense of honor; I told myself, whate'er befall I shall take pity on Yiddish, that unloved and unpetted daughter, for it is time to do things for our people. Certain of my friends also joined me, and together we decided to induce the owner of Hemelitz to issue a periodical in the vernacular of our people. May God remember in his favor that he came to aid his people with the journal *Kol Mevasser* (The Proclaiming Voice) and did much good. And the spirit rested upon me and I wrote *Zemiroth Israel* (Hymns of Israel) for the Sabbath Eve, Sabbath Day and Out-going of Sabbath, translated into verse and well explained, so that each individual Jew may know how much is to be gained, how lovely they are, a very wonder of God. (Jitomir 1875.) What induced me to translate the hymns was that I saw the translation of prayers for Jewish women in the *Korban Minha* (Gift Offering) Prayerbook and found them to be tasteless, badly expressed, abominable and unsatisfactory. I therefore decided that something must be done for our sisters the daughters of Israel and the plain folk in our midst, who should be supplied with a pure gift in clear language, seeing that they have souls like the rest of us and long to view the sweetness of the Lord; and we have no right to deprive them of this and let their souls do without that goodness, knowledge and wise counsel, keeping true wisdom only for the few chosen. If our forefathers translated the Torah into the common language, and our rabbis, may they rest in peace, appointed special translators so that the ordinary people might understand the living words of God, why should not we too instruct them, providing wisdom and counsel to the seed of the Holy People in the language they understand; and why should we not feel for our daughters and all the multitudes of Israel and give them an opportunity of enjoying the great gifts and wealth concealed in our prayers and faith, instead of leaving them to walk the ways of darkness, going astray with void things and silly tales, while we merely turn our eyes to the few? Are not all the congregation holy, and is not the Lord among them? I began this holy work with the Sabbath Hymns as a specimen; then I translated the Psalms into rhymed verse and still have the manuscript. Then I prepared the work, *A Chapter of Song* (a long hymn of praise which gives the biblical verse that expresses the praises of each kind of creature in the Universe for the Lord) translated into Yiddish rhymed verse with an introduction written in the holy tongue and a commentary *Tub Taam* (Good Taste) which explains each utterance of those who praise, in accordance with natural history and the words of our sages of blessed memory. Let the righteous see and rejoice, and those who honor our rabbis of blessed memory find the key I have given them, wherewith to enter this locked garden; and let them rejoice to see how great were the works of our sages, and how deep indeed were their thoughts.

HOW I WROTE MY SONGS

ELIAKUM ZUNSER (1840-1913)

Zunser was the first popular troubadour of the Russian ghetto. His numerous ballads and lyrics embody the vicissitudes of the old world culture that has almost vanished. Fortunately he recorded his experiences toward the end of his long career, telling of "the times in which I first saw the light, in which I passed my early childhood, and which have moulded my development." Zunzer is a frank, spontaneous, natural autobiographer, as the following lively pages indicate. In 1889 he came to America, where his fame had preceded him, and he continued to compose popular folk melodies and give concerts.

❋ ❋ ❋

ON THE first day of Elul in the year 5613 (1853), after long wanderings, I came to the city of Bobruisk, in the Province of Minsk. As might have been expected, I found no embroiderer there with whom I might work and thus earn my bread. For several days I wandered through the streets of Bobruisk, seeking I know not what. And, to be sure, I found it, in the image of the hazzan, Reb Joel I. Humener (famous in those days), who used to come to Bobruisk annually to chant the services during the holy days. If I cannot work at an embroiderer's, why not earn something as a chorist? thought I, and off I went to Reb Joel Humener. He tested me and found that I had a good voice and a fine ear. He engaged me as a singer at a salary of two rubles (what a fortune!) for all the holy days. He provided me with board at the house of the president of the synagogue, including permission to sleep regularly on a bench in the synagogue.

At that time I composed my song *The Light,* and immediately afterwards a second song, *Reb Tahanun.* This latter song had immense popular success. It was sung everywhere.

We spent a holiday evening very enjoyably in the house of the president of the synagogue, and later in the synagogue. *Reb Tahanun* was sung by the choir, and all the hassidim were delighted with me—the young composer. The joy all around affected me but little; nor could the honors shown me that evening comfort me much. Like a dark cloud, the question "What will become of me after the holidays?" was continually before me.

After the holidays the hazzan gave me two rubles, and told me to go. Whither? The world is large enough, and Jews, bless the Lord, are plentiful. What matters it, then, where a Jew goes?

It had become very cold, however, and I had nothing but my light summer clothes. Since I had plenty of money—two rubles—I went to the market and bought a fur coat. Readers with delicate nerves might be seriously shocked at the words "fur coat"; but let me hasten to reassure them a coat was called a "fur coat" solely because it had a fur collar. There were also in those days "fur coats" which did not have even a fur collar, but a "future-collar", that is, a collar which might some day, with the help of a kind Providence, hope to be covered with some cat or fox fur.

A few days later, as I was proudly parading the streets of Bobruisk in my "fur", I met a farmer who lived four versts' distance from the city. He was seeking a Hebrew tutor for his children. I offered myself for the position, and we readily came to an understanding. My salary was to be twenty-five rubles for the term (six months), with the privilege of sleeping on the warm oven. (The Russian "oven" is a house fixture, built as an extension of one of the walls, allowing the top to be used as a bed.)

It is generally admitted the world over that a Jew eats that he may live; whereas, it is the opposite with the Christian—he lives that he may eat. My new employer devised a novel theory of his own, to wit: neither to eat nor live, but just to "pass away" the few years of our earthly existence. And for mere "passing away" purposes, a bit of bread, baked from oats and barley, with a little *groipen,* to which a few drops of oil were added, was quite ample. Throughout the week not a morsel of meat came into the house, and the week days were "passed away" with this bread-of-misery and with the "soup" in which even the Jewish impressors could not find one groip.

For the Sabbath, however, the farmer would bring from town a sheep's head, and I would often refresh myself with a bone. The same oil with which the hard foods were softened was also used for lighting the house. And before such light I would sit for six hours daily and talk myself hoarse in teaching my "scholars", who mentally were not a whit superior to the children of the village peasants. After this exhausting labor, even such foods tasted royally to me.

Meanwhile, my clothes were wearing down rapidly. Because zero weather was quite frequent, I almost fell ill of exposure. I asked of my employer some part of my salary so that I might clothe myself somewhat decently. At first he gave me empty excuses, but towards the Feast of Passover, he informed me that he would employ me for another term and then he would give me all the money I would want. As I had no choice, I remained with him. All this time I was clad in rags, and my shoes were torn. At the end of Passover, I wrote my song *The Eye,* in which I sang of my own misery.

At Shabuoth he again put me off with some excuse, and, after the holiday, when I began to demand my money, he hit upon a "clever scheme". He went to Bobruisk, approached the leaders of the commune, and offered, if well-paid, to give them a "nefesh" (soul). He received twenty-five rubles, and took along with him an impressor and two Cossacks, who were to bring me to the *isborschik.*

Not knowing my danger, I had sought my bunk and went to sleep. Suddenly I felt a heavy hand fall upon my young body and shake me violently. I awoke and opened my eyes. Three strange men stood before me. One of them held a lantern, which he placed close to my eyes.

"What do you want?" I asked.

"Nothing, sonny—get up," the impressor answered.

"Get up? Why?"

"You'll have to go with us to town."

"Why? What business have I in town?"

"Well, you'll see! Dress yourself, boy, and be quick."

"I don't want to. I won't go!"

A blow in the face dazed me. I was wrapped in my torn clothes, thrown into a wagon, and brought to Bobruisk.

There I was locked up in the barracks.

In order to get rid of the "hidden Jews" (that is, the Jews who were not regularly entered on the public records), Czar Nicholas I issued an ukase which permitted every "hidden Jew" to be sent off as a soldier; a "hidden man" was one who had no passport, and obviously a man whose birth was not recorded could get no passport. This gave anyone the right to seize any young man or boy who had no passport and hand him over to the community as a soldier in lieu of some member of his own or some other family.

For the communal leaders of those dark days, who constantly

sought to thrive on Jewish misery, this ukase opened a new traffic. Each
Jewish commune sent out its impressors on all roads and highways;
they hid in village inns and watched for prey. Into their hands fell
all unfortunate Jewish youths who could not show passports. Nor could
all who had passports escape them. Passports were often torn before
the very eyes of the victims, who were seized as "hidden" ones.

Those who were seized were bound like sheep, brought to town and
locked up in the barracks. There they would be kept for weeks until
the recruiting (*priom*) would begin. The authorities were not over-
scrupulous with these unfortunates. Were they weak, sick, or defective?
No matter—they were taken, dressed in military clothes, and packed off
to serve the Czar. These "bodies" were sent in place of men whose
families could pay a satisfactory price; the deputies and the *isborschik*
divided the money. Many private individuals took part in this traffic.
They would seize young children and sell them to the community
"bosses". Those times were known among the Russian Jews as the
dreaded days of the "impressment" (*Piomanes*). Hundreds of "sales of
Josephs" occurred daily. The lesser rabbis of the smaller towns gave
supine assent to such outrages, with the argument that it was "more
pious" to protect the children of their own towns. The more important
wept in silence at these open outrages, but they dared not protest for
three reasons. First, these proceedings were in accordance with the
Czar's ukase; secondly, they feared the *isborschik* and the deputies at
whose pleasure they held their positions; and thirdly, they feared denunciation to the government officials. The result of such denunciation
would inevitably have been exile to Siberia. These were times when men
devoured men openly and with the consent of the government.

And so at the age of fourteen, I was one of the victims.

I stayed in the barracks for five long weeks. The community was
waiting for the recruiting; and as for chances of redemption, it seemed,
I had none. How could I? Whence could help come to me? Through
what miracle? Can poor sheep bound in the slaughter house hope to
escape the slaughterer? Legally or illegally, I would remain a soldier.
I would have many years to serve among the cantonists. I would be sent
to some peasant in a village many thousands of miles away, perhaps to
faraway Siberia, there to tend swine, chop wood, make clumsy peasant
shoes, and for every trifling offense suffer cruel beating. Should I emerge
safe from this dreadful ordeal, the real Gehenna, with all its horrors,
would only have just begun—the "elder" soldier, the Russian barracks,
the drills, the marches under a load of three hundred pounds—the lash,

the beatings, and other "diversions" of this sort. More than all else, the thought of my unhappy, widowed mother, helpless and miserable, tormented me. For twenty-one dark years she lived with her husband, and when an evil chance deprived her of her supporter, she was left with two orphans. With them she could share only her sorrows—for joys she never had. Her sole comfort were the two orphans, and now she is robbed of both. "A cruel beast hath devoured them!" Nay, no wild beasts of the forest were these, but human beings with hearts of wolves!

Such thoughts occupied me the entire time that I spent in the barracks together with other Jewish victims. Those thoughts stirred my emotions and then, in the barracks, I wrote my poem of 108 stanzas, *The Piomanes*. The theme for the poem I took from the prophet Haggai.

Haggai came to the priests and inquired of them: "Does a man or a garment become holy when this man or this garment touches the holy meat of the sacrifice?"

"No, he does not become holy," the priests replied.

"And does a man or a garment become unclean when either of them comes into contact with the unclean?" the prophet further inquired.

"Yes, verily, they become unclean," answered the priests.

"Such is the entire people," Haggai sorrowfully exclaimed. "No good, clean or holy thing adheres to them; only unholy things cling to them. That is, while living among strange nations, they do not learn good deeds or fine customs; from them they learn only the bad, the impure."

The horrible ukase of the impressment was a severe test for the Jews of that generation, and many stood that test poorly. In thus seizing and bartering their own brothers into conversion and suffering, they revealed to the world a bad element among them. Alas, that this bad element should have gained so strong an ascendancy!

The above is, in brief, the burden of my song, *Tried at the Bar of Justice and Convicted*. I wrote this not with my own blood alone, but with the blood of all my unhappy peoples. Not alone my sorrows resound through my verse, but the despairing wail of all Israel.

And how heartrending was the sight within the barracks! Eighty miserable, pale, emaciated, hungry, half-naked little beings, lying on the floor on a pile of dirty straw! The greater part were small children, who had been snatched from their mothers by tyrannical hands, and who could not realize the great misfortune awaiting them. Even here in the barracks, not comprehending the dark fate awaiting them, they laughed, frolicked, and played with one another; the older ones, regarding them, forgot their own sorrows and shed bitter tears. Twice daily the iron doors opened, and the hideous lackey of the community bosses entered and brought some loaves of bread and a few pots of soup, too dirty even for dogs. If any one dared to complain or make a request, he was seized by the hair and thrust to the wall with such a violence that his young bones cracked.

"I want to go back to my mother," some child broke out with a sob.

"You'll see her, indeed, in the other world! Only be patient!" the Jewish Antiochus replied with a leer.

"Let me go home! I want to go back home!" wailed another little one.

"Wait a few more days!" roars the human tiger. "You will then have a large home! It extends from Bobruisk to Archangel!"

Night is coming on. All lie on the floor and say their prayers; others, the older ones, recite the Psalms by heart, and thus lull themselves to sleep. A flock of sheep awaiting slaughter! They lie on each other in the dirty straw. Misfortune and misery have united these strangers into one body. Here and there a heavy sigh breaks forth from the breast of some older one. The very young ones sleep peacefully, a serene smile on their wan features. Of what are they dreaming? Very likely they are dreaming that they are slumbering on their mother's lap, and she is stroking their pretty curls.

Among the eighty who were in the barracks with me, there were some who possessed good voices for singing. From among them I selected a choir of ten and drilled them in my song, *The Piomanes*. Several times each day we used to sing it, and when the sad strain of the music would resound through the barracks, tears would steel into every eye and not a heart remained unmoved. Even our hideous jailers wept with us, those men with hearts of stone and nerves of iron, who watched us day and night.

The month of Ab passed, and finally came the night preceding the day on which we were to be led to slaughter—to the recruiting.

But help was nearer than any of us suspected. On Purim of 1855 (that is, about a half year before I was seized and locked up in the barracks at Bobruisk), Emperor Nicholas I suddenly died. Alexander II ascended the Russian throne, and the treaty of Paris was signed. The Crimean War was at an end. One of the very first edicts issued by Alexander the II was for the release of the *poimaniks*.

At about one o'clock in the morning, while we were all asleep in the barracks, we were awakened by a great commotion in the street. The noise came nearer and nearer, and soon we heard vigorous knocks on the iron doors and shutters.

"Get up, children! A deliverance! You are free!" some one shouted.

"An ukase from the Czar to release you!" shouted another.

"Praise God, children! Say 'Hallel!'" several voices called out together.

This news sounded to us like the blast of the Great Shofar which will awaken the dead on the day of Resurrection. With a cry of joy we sprang up from our wretched straw heaps, washed and fell to saying *Hallel*. I was the hazzan, and my choir accompanied me. After *Hallel,* we all joined hands and danced a Jewish Karehod (folk dance). I wrote my song *The Deliverance* (Die Yeshuah), and arranged a beautiful melody for it.

It was decided to release us from the barracks at ten o'clock in the morning. The rich Reb Isaac Rabinovitz of Bobruisk donated forty rubles to the synagogue for the privilege of opening the door of the barracks. Long before the appointed hour a great crowd of men and women, young and old, had gathered about the doors of the barracks and waited impatiently for the moment when the doors would open and we would emerge—free. Each and every one praised and blessed the good Emperor Alexander II, who had issued this edict and who had also revoked many of the cruel edicts of his father.

The happy moment came. With the benediction, "Blessed be He who releaseth them that are bound," the rich Reb Isaac Rabinovitz unlocked the door and the crowd surged into the barracks. The town hazzan recited a prayer of blessing for the Emperor, and sang the 45th Psalm. ("I waited patiently for the Lord; He inclined unto me and heard my cry", etc.)

Then my choir and myself were placed upon a large table, and we sang my song, "Placed before the Bar of Justice and Convicted." Many of the people wept. The song also had another effect; the people became so enraged at the community bosses that they were ready to tear them to pieces. But they had already gone into hiding.

Upon the request of some well-known citizens, I sang two additional songs, *The Deliverance* and *Better to Take than to Give,* which described my employer, the farmer, who sold me to the community for twenty-five rubles instead of paying me my hard-earned salary. This song evoked a storm of indignation. Many were ready to proceed to that village and wreck dire vengeance upon him, but Reb Isaac Rabinowitz quieted them and promised to deal with that monster himself. Then the door was opened, and the eighty of us came forth singing from the barracks. Reb Rabinowitz took me to his home in his carriage.

In this rich man's home, I too became somewhat of a personage. I decked myself out in fine clothes, and had in addition a capital of one hundred rubles in cash. My wealth, like my misery, came to me in an unusual manner. To begin with, Reb Rabinowitz sent for the farmer at whose house I slaved with my three scholars. Slapping him soundly across the face several times, he ordered him to pay not only the fifty rubles he owed me for the two terms but also the twenty-five rubles he had received from the community for my "body". This excellent gentleman pleaded that he was poor and could not pay, but this did him little good. My benefactor sent several Cossacks after him, and they seized all that they could find in his house. A few days later the farmer came with the seventy-five rubles and redeemed his chattels. Thus, I suddenly became a wealthy man.

At that time I believed myself to be almost a Rothschild. I had from time to time also received, in addition, some small sums of money from the guests who would visit my host and for whom I would sing the three songs I had composed in the barracks.

When I was first seized as a *poimanik,* the news of my capture had reached a Vilna woman who happened to be in Bobruisk at that time. She immediately wrote of it to my mother in Vilna. One morning, when I had been living at my host's house for some time, the servant informed me that a strange couple—a Jewish man and a woman— wished to see me, and that they were waiting outside. My joy was indeed great when I came out into the street and there to confront my mother and my uncle Abraham-Leb. With a cry of joy my mother threw herself upon me, weeping, and for a long time clasped me in her arms. Just as soon as she had received the letter from Vilna telling her of my capture, she had obtained a passport for me from the Vilna community and walked fifty Russian miles to Bobruisk to free me. My good uncle Abraham-Leb would not hear of letting her walk this long distance alone; he therefore accompanied her the entire way. We spent eight days at my host's house and then left Bobruisk.

I returned to my mother's home in Vilna, and the very first to greet me was again Old Poverty, who still reigned there as a gaunt, grim monarch. It became once more evident that I had no one to provide for me, that I must myself earn my daily bread. The only way to do this was to seek work again at some embroiderer's; but this I could not do in Vilna, for my contract with my first master-embroiderer still hung over me like the sword of Damocles. I had no choice but to leave my mother; I therefore started off to seek work in Kovno, fourteen Russian miles from Vilna.

In Kovno I went to work at an embroiderer's, but at night I used to study at the *Musor-stubel* of Reb Israel Salanter in Yatke-Gass.

Young as I was during the liberal era of Emperor Alexander II, the changes stirred me greatly. Seeing how the Jewish people blossomed forth like a beautiful flower and spread its tender leaves in the sunshine of enlightenment, and with a truly youthful ardor, I wrote my song *Die Blume* (The Flower), in Yiddish and in Hebrew, with the words beginning "Neglected, on the Mother of Highways, lies a beauteous rose."

In that song I represented the Emperor Alexander II as an angel who found in the dust a flower which had been torn from the garden of Zion; and beholding how all trample her under foot, he mercifully rescues her, revives her with living waters, and places her in his garden, among his other flowers.

During the time I spent in Kovno, I wrote many other songs in addition to this one, such as *The Clock, The Inn, The Ferry, Summer and Winter, The Farmer and the City Man*. They were sung everywhere. All Kovno spoke of the young embroiderer, who composed such pleasing songs, and almost every evening I was invited to some social gathering. Crowds of people would assemble around the house in which I sang my songs, and would listen until they learned them by heart. Very soon I discovered that the singing of my songs yielded me better returns than my embroidery, from which I could never hope to have more than three rubles a week. So I decided to abandon that trade.

I will not sing my own praises, and I will not say that my success as the people's bard came solely from the excellence of the songs themselves. Of that only the people must be the judge. But it is certain that I owe my success to the circumstance that at that time I was the only Jewish bard in Russia. That is, I was the first one who composed songs together with appropriate melodies. There lived at that time in Galicia Velvil Zbarser (Ehrenkranz) and Beril Broder; but their songs had not reached Russia, least of all, Lithuania. Russia had as yet not a single railway, and intercourse with Galicia was almost nil. Michael Gordon, too, had written some Yiddish songs, but he lived in Poltava. and Poltava was then to all purposes as distant from Lithuania as

America is from Europe today. In those days the Russian Jews had no songs outside of my own. It is therefore to this fact that my success was largely due.

I spent one year in Kovno, and so great was my success that I could well get along without doing any manual labor.

I returned to Vilna where my songs had made my name known, and I began to officiate as a *badhan* (jester) at weddings. This was in 1861. In that year I published my first volume, *Shirim Hadashim* (New Songs). That same year the building of a railway from St. Petersburg to Warsaw via Vilna was begun, and for the occasion I wrote *Die Eisenbahn* (The Railway). Sixteen years later in Minsk I wrote another song with the same title.

At the outset my new profession yielded me a very small income. I can adduce two reasons for this. First, only the poor invited me to weddings, and my compensation was naturally small; secondly, the recital of my songs necessitated instrumental accompaniment. The musicians who furnished the accompaniment took away the greater share of my earnings. If they did not succeed in getting a very comfortable share on the spot at the wedding they frequently attacked me in the street on my way home, and forcibly took away the money. But later my fortunes improved. The rich begin to invite me to their weddings, and then I was well-paid. Each band of musicians in those days had its own *badhan;* and the rich families used to engage only those musicians who engaged me.

Before my songs had become known, Moses Warshaver alone shone like a bright star among the *badhanim*. He used to be invited to the weddings of the wealthy, and therefore easily earned both glory and money. With my advent in the same profession, I became a serious competitor. He tried to suppress me by various means, but without success until he conceived a plan by which he trapped me.

Through some friends of his he induced me to enter into partnership with him. I let myself be persuaded, and signed a contract with him. Just what was in the contract I did not exactly know. I discovered only later that he had inserted a clause in the contract stipulating that I was to be in his employ for a term of three years at eight gulden a week. Of course I immediately left him. This was exactly what he wished me to do. He at once sued me for breach of contract, declaring that all the money I should be ordered to pay as fine he would present to the wounded soldiers. (This was during the Polish Rebellion). Then began the most troublesome time of my early years. If I would attend a wedding, Moses Warshaver would be sure to come with the police and take me away. This reached such a stage that people ceased to invite me to weddings because the joy of the occasion was sure to be disturbed by the descent of Moses Warshaver with an escort of police. Thus I remained without means of livelihood; what little I did earn went to my lawyer. Each day I was dragged like a criminal to the police, and daily my troubles increased.

It is curious how help often comes to us in life at the very time when need and despair are greatest, and when we have long abandoned all hope. At the time when I struggled in Moses Warshaver's iron grip and had not the least prospect to escape from his clutches, something happened which led me from slavery to freedom.

Some time before this the Polish Rebellion had broken out, and Count Mouravieff became Governor-General of the four provinces of Vilna, Kovno, Grodno, and Minsk. He resided at Vilna, and from there all orders and ukases dealing with the Polish Rebellion went forth. The war with the Poles began, and blood flowed freely.

I was so young then that I could not judge which side was right in the bloody controversy. My childish instincts inclined me to the side of the stronger. I sympathized with Russia, and inspired by that sympathy, I composed a song entitled *The Polish Rebellion*. I sang this song at the Jewish weddings to which I was invited, and my audiences enjoyed it greatly.

Now it came to pass that I sang this song at a "rich" wedding in Vilna at which a Russian colonel was a guest. He requested that my song be translated to him into Russian, and when the translation was given him, he found it worthy of being presented to the Governor-General, Count Mouravieff. This song greatly pleased the Governor-General, and in recognition he sent me a gift of twenty-five rubles through the colonel. Later, when the wealthy Reb Judah Apatov of Vilna came to visit the Governor-General, with whom he was on terms of friendship, Count Mouravieff praised me to him.

Immediately afterwards an opportunity came which made me acquainted with Reb Judah Apatov, of blessed memory, whose great influence made him a very powerful personage in Vilna. He invited me to the wedding of his daughter to Reb Abrehmele Parness. My songs and my sermon pleased him so much that he engaged me into friendly conversation. I disclosed my sad condition to him, and told him of the bitter persecutions I had to endure from Moses Warshaver because of a false contract. Reb Judah Apatov promised to help me; and he kept his word. A short time later the contract was declared worthless and Moses Warshaver was obliged to leave Vilna.

I now began to breathe freely and to earn comfortable returns. But, day by day, the time set for my wedding was fast approaching. My father-in-law thought it necessary to introduce me to the Rabbi of Kaidanov, and he took me to spend one Sabbath at the Rabbi's. He probably wanted to show the Zaddik what a "find" he had been blessed with for a son-in-law. The impression which the Rabbi of Kaidanov made upon me I described in my humorous song, *The Rabbi's Little Key.* From this song, my father-in-law became only too fully aware of the "treasure" he had gotten, and did not bring me to his Zaddik any more. Two months after my marriage I again returned to Vilna.

At this time I set to work seriously to compose songs. Of the songs that I composed during this period the following attracted most attention: *The Ruble, The Iron Safe, Childbirth,* and *Yekele Bass.*

As a result, my name became widely known, and I was called to weddings in Grodno, Warsaw, Dinanburg, Vitebsk, Kovno, Minsk, and ever further. The Libavo-Romayn Railway had just been built, and it was possible for me to attend weddings in distant places, and hence my earnings increased considerably. I must note here that the melodies to my first songs had never quite satisfied me, because I had drawn mainly upon the motifs of the hazzanim in the Vilna synagogues, and they were by no means musical. During my childhood the hazzan in the Vilna synagogues was Ortschig the Hazzan. He was indeed a brother of the famous hazzan of the Slutzk, known as the Fiedele Hazzan. But he had not the latter's talent. Before becoming hazzan, Ortschig had been a military drummer. Since I had no better source to choose from, I adapted his melodies to my songs; hence my first songs lacked sufficient melody. Later my songs became much more melodious. For this I owe gratitude to the great hazzan, Reb Waserzweig, or Reb Hayyim Lomzer, who became the hazzan of Vilna. He was a good composer, and his book, *Shir Mikdash* (Holy Song), enjoyed a great success among those who loved Jewish music. It was under this new influence that the melodies to my later songs were written.

LOVE FOUND A WAY

EZEKIEL KOTICK (1847-1921)

The engrossing fascination of Kotick's two stout volumes of *Memoirs* is due not only to his fine gift of storytelling but above all to the exotic life of the Jewish villages and ghettos of Eastern Europe in the second half of the nineteenth century, that he describes. He wandered most of his life without purpose "like a fish in water", as he says. But he kept his eyes and ears open so that the swarming humanity of which he was a part takes on robust flesh and blood in these remarkable recollections. He gives us fascinating glimpses of all the typical characters—matchmakers, wagoners, musicians, panhandlers, cemetery wardens, synagogue habitués and the like—of a world that is now virtually non-existent. The tragedy, the gaiety, and the tenderness of that world are vividly illustrated in the following tale of the vicissitudes of his marriage. It shows how Hasidism, which began as a protest against the rigors of the talmudic Judaism in the eighteenth century and afforded an escape for the masses during a time of great insecurity, degenerated into a system of rabbi-worship. Communities and families, as this account indicates, were split into warring factions, the *hasidim* (literally "the pious," the adherents) versus *mithnagedim* (the opponents). But the poetic side of Hasidism, arising out of its doctrine of worship through joyousness and a return to Nature, should not be overlooked. You will find an account of that aspect of the movement in Martin Buber's memoir on pages 514-522.

❋ ❋ ❋

IN 1865 my father decided that it was high time for me to marry. I was then seventeen years old, and he was afraid that I would be considered an old bachelor and looked upon as a public disgrace. Accordingly the marriage was set for August. It was to take place at our house because the bride was an orphan. My father ordered white socks, slippers and a satin caftan for my wedding clothes. He refused to hire the musicians from the town of Kobrin because Todrus the Bard, was not a convinced hasid. He preferred the musicians from Brisk because their fiddler and bard were hasidim.

I, on the other hand, declined to make a spectacle of myself at my own wedding by wearing socks and slippers, and wished to have Shebsel's band. In the end I won out. I was to be married in boots, and Shebsel's entourage arrived the day before the wedding.

On that day, too, the bride and her party arrived. They stopped at my uncle's house, where the marriage ceremony was to be performed. It was the custom that on the wedding day women and girls would gather at the bride's quarters at noon and stage a preliminary dance that lasted for several hours. At twilight the men folk would give a similar send-off to the bridegroom, who climaxed the event with a speech, then treated his guests to honeycake with jam, and liquor. Afterwards he was led with music through the streets to the ceremonial veiling of the bride, and thence to the synagogue for the marriage ritual. After the wedding, the principals and guests repaired to the bridal quarters for supper and all-night festivities.

If the wedding took place on a Friday, the couple was paraded home from the synagogue, and the guests left for the services. Only a small party returned to celebrate. Sabbath morning relatives and intimate friends came for the bridegroom and led him to the synagogue, where he was called upon to read from the Holy Scroll. In the evening there was the usual supper and hoopla.

My father, who was a strict hasid, did not think it advisable to introduce me to my bride before marriage. When she arrived, everybody in town went to see her except me. They brought back glowing reports of her beauty. Naturally I felt curious, and resolved to see her for myself. With my trusted friend, Arieh-Leib, I made off secretly to my uncle's home. Indeed she was beautiful! Though I felt shy in her presence, I managed to wish her "good luck". I wanted to prolong the pleasure of her company, but Arieh-Leib said I must not stay; it was forbidden. Wearily I left for my "station"—grandfather's home.

Under the wedding canopy my bride stepped on my foot. I thought it was accidental. Immediately after the ceremony, her relatives whisked her away towards the house so that she might be the first to enter it. This was done in accordance with the then current belief that the one of a newly-wedded couple who first stepped into their home would dominate the other for the rest of their conjugal life. But my friend, Arieh-Leib, was not to be outsmarted. He led us over a shortcut so that

I might get there first. That started a race. I was encumbered by the traditional white gown I was wearing over my satin caftan, and a coat on top. To make running easier for me, Judah-Leib, the tailor, rolled up my overcoat, and the white gown showed, much to my embarrassment.

When we arrived, the bridal party was already perched on the balcony. Sensing failure, Arieh-Leib decreed that the bride must step down, and enter the house with me shoulder to shoulder. She did, and members on both sides were watching carefully that we keep in step while crossing the threshold. In the process, voices kept up a continuous din:

"Keep in line! Keep in line!"

They might have been drilling soldiers.

In my heart I laughed at the whole procedure, and deliberately allowed her to enter first. Let her have the pleasure. This incensed Arieh-Leib, who ordered us to my grandfather's house. If she again attempted to run ahead of me, he threatened to have us do it all over again even if it took us a whole night. They led the way with music. When we reached the house, her group felt tired and disinclined to wrangle with Arieh-Leib. Nevertheless, they watched our feet, and this time we entered the house together.

The "golden" wedding soup was brought over from uncle's to grandfather's house. The musicians, too, were divided between the two domiciles. Sabbath eve descended upon us. Candles were lighted and blessed. The guests departed for the synagogue. We remained home for the prayer.

Grandfather was at odds with father because he refused to have hasidim at the wedding. So they agreed between them to set aside Friday night, Saturday morning and evening for hasidim only. They made merry, and discussed topics of special interest to their kind. I listened to their confabulations. They did not know me for the opponent that I was, nor suspect that I regarded their ways as strange. Throughout the week we made parties for different sections of the town population, according to a long-standing custom.

On the eve of the New Year my father was going to Slonim for a visit with the Rabbi. After the wedding he treated me as a grownup He did not tell me what or what not to do. I usually divined from his eyes what to do or say. He took it for granted now that I was a married man, that I would join him in the visit to the Rabbi. Newly married hasidic young men usually followed that custom. He thought that since he was going, I would grasp at the opportunity and say,

"Father, I want to go along!" My silence therefore wounded his heart, and he went off alone.

My father felt ill at ease before the Rabbi. The venerable man knew I had been married. Once he had prophesied that I would up to be a handsome hasid. Now my father came to him without me! The situation for him was difficult indeed.

I made up my mind to talk things over with him, and deliver him and me from our common torment. I could stand my ground in argument. He should know that I never was, nor ever could be a hasid. Let him get used to the idea.

That, I soon learned, was not an easy task. My father was a man with an angelic temperament who had brought me up with his eyes, his glances, and mere hints. How could I hurt such a father by proving to him that his ideas were fallacious? To die was much easier. Yet I looked for an opportunity, and prayed for courage.

Unfortunately, my wife was also a fanatical hasid. She was reared in Karlin, at the home of her brother-in-law, an ardent hasid himself. She was fond of relating how Rabbi Aaron, that town's spiritual leader, visited them and how she served him boiled fish especially prepared for him (Pinsker Jews were famous for their fish cooking). As the Rabbi ate, and he was no small eater, he smacked his lips and confessed he had never tasted anything like it.

"Who cooked it?" he wanted to know.

They told him it had been cooked by a young orphan girl who could do everything well. Thereupon he blessed her and predicted that she would one day marry a great hasid. You can imagine my wife's predicament when she found her husband was no hasid at all, and declined to pay the Rabbi homage.

She played a great part in my family's life. They loved her for her beauty, her efficiency, and her tact. My father hoped she would convert me to Hasidism.

On the Sabbath and holidays my wife and I were dinner guests at my grandfather's. On the way we met and joined father, who was on his way home from the prolonged services. With her he talked about Hasidism; for me he had only stinging remarks.

In his desire to have her sway me, my good father went any length to humiliate me, and at the same time he praised her to the skies. He did not understand that such tactics were bound to create friction between us. It would appear that he was determined to wreck my married life if he could not succeed in making me a disciple of his rabbi.

On the Festival of the Joy of the Torah we dined at grandfather's as usual. Leaving at about one o'clock, we saw father leading a number of hasidim home for lunch. Yankel Essigmacher and Shebsel, the scribe, had collected the foodstuff from all the available ovens in town for the occasion.

As they caught sight of us, we crossed over to the other side of the road. Yankel was drunk and bent on insulting me. He yelled at me: "For what does a man desert his father and his mother. . ." and again: "'Hund-Tate' dog-father), 'Hund-Mame' (dog-mother), may a devil enter the soul of your wife!" and so on till we reached home.

I demanded of my father why he allowed Yankel to abuse me in public. Here Yankel broke in apologetically:

"What? When did I abuse you? I merely explained to him a portion of the Pentateuch in the style of the Desser heretic. . ." (He meant the commentary written by Moses Mendelssohn, who was called Rabbi Moishe Desser.) He also added slyly that he said, "Und (and) -Tate" and "Und-Mame."

Then and there I decided to make an end to all this. I would get drunk and start a discussion. In drunkenness one sometimes finds strength.

On the evening of the Festival, following a long-standing custom, the preacher arranged a feast in his home for the town's married young men at public expense. He served roast duck, fruit, wine and liquor. Everyone enjoyed it hugely.

The preacher's son and son-in-law arranged similar dinners at their own homes in honor of the students. I decided to go there and be among my own friends in defiance of my father and his hasidic clique. That day was one of the best in my life. We were twelve in all—the town's prize students. We danced, kissed and sang, and felt a warm comradeship. Later in the evening we joined our elders.

I remember seizing Shmerel, the father of a friend. I was a strong fellow, and the man nearly choked in my embrace. It took the combined efforts of several people to pry him loose from my arms. Then I fell asleep, and was carried off into another room. About one in the morning Moses Aaron, the preacher's son, woke me up and sent me home.

At home the hasidic revelers were still in high gear. Yankel was drunk as Lot. He immediately got hold of me and shouted:

"Hatzkele, you've come from Moses Aaron? May evil spirit seize his father!"

Impulsively I rejoined: "A curse on your rabbi's father!"

Were it not for the presence of my grandfather the enraged hasidim would have pounced upon me and beaten me within an inch of my life. As it was, they gnashed their teeth in silence.

When I went to my room, I found my wife on the bed, crying bitterly. She sobbed that I had ruined the hasidim's fun. It was terrible! Moses Leizer's son had cursed the father of the rabbi! Woe to one's ears for hearing such a thing!

I took her out for some air. We walked along a side street that led to the Polish church. On the way she cried with renewed passion. I could not endure her sobs.

"I love you, Hatzkel," she moaned through her tears, "only now I wish I were dead and not your wife. Don't think I want a divorce, God forbid! But if you could find it in your heart to curse the father of Yankel's rabbi, I am afraid to live under the same roof."

She started weeping all over again. I said nothing, but her whimpering sent shivers through me. Returning home, we heard the men leaving. They seemed to mutter something about "our misfortune", and failed to sing their way home as they were wont to do. My outburst apparently had disrupted their festive mood.

As I was going to my room, my father stopped me. He asked me to take a seat, and directed my wife to the bedroom.

"What is the matter with you, Hatzkel? What possessed you?" he asked in a quiet, trembling voice.

His face frightened me. It was deathly pale; his eyes were bloodshot. I had never seen him so agitated. It was not anger. Anger was not in his nature. It was rather a feeling of profound sorrow. It was the sorrow he showed when a child died, when his sister passed away. Yet not even then was he so moved.

I had an impulse to kiss him, to ask him to forgive me. I was ready to sacrifice my life for him, and wished that somebody would drive a spear through me if that would spare him further agony. I truly loved my father. I have idealized and worshipped him to this very day. I knew what my rebelliousness cost him. He was not to blame.

I confess that whenever I am about to do something wrong, the vision of my father quickly dissipates that urge. Unfortunately, his vision does not come to my mind too often.

I would gladly have given him every drop of my blood. But what to do with my soul? How could I believe in something which I did not believe? Why should I want to destroy my father and my wife whom I both dearly loved?

"Why do you keep quiet?" he finally demanded. "Why don't you speak up? Once and for all I want you to tell me everything that is in your heart. It is all my fault. I should have spoken with you more about Hasidism. I didn't because I thought you needed but few words. Only now I realize my mistake. I should have guided you from the beginning."

It was past midnight. The shutters were closed. Only a single candle light was burning. I spoke for a long time. Whenever his lips moved, I quickly silenced him by telling him what he was going to say. I was in a frenzy. My father sat motionless, listening to me intently without interrupting. When I had finished, morning was already upon us. The clock on the wall struck seven.

I was like a new man to him. He wondered how it had happened. He thought it was sufficient to study under Isaac Asher, without acquiring different ideas in the process. He had an idea that I would naturally become an active hasid, not a tenacious opponent. The glaring error of judgment made him feel faint, and he fell on the bed sighing.

My heart was breaking as I left his room, and tears ran down my face. I composed myself before entering my own room. Opening the door, I realized that my wife had not slept a wink, and had been crying all night. The pillows were drenched with her tears. At the sight of me she became hysterical. Father and mother hurried to our room in great alarm. Father took in the scene with one glance and left.

I did not know how to soothe her. The die was cast. For eighteen months I had accomplished nothing. I explained to my father that I wanted to resume my studies. Father loved my wife as his own, and would certainly take care of her. I was eager to prepare myself for the rabbinate. Upon ordination it would not be difficult for me to find a congregation. In my time the grandchildren of the Wolozhin Rabbi played a prominent part in Jewish life. Any principal of the talmudic seminaries would gladly recommend me to a desirable community. My beautiful young spouse would yet be a rabbi's wife!

My mind was set, even though her crying nearly drove me mad. With the thought that she would eventually calm herself, I reluctantly left for the synagogue. That night's experience imbedded itself permanently in my consciousness.

Friday night, Simche, my cousin, invited me to debate the hasidim at his home. I accepted the challenge. About thirty, with Mr. Orele at their head, were present. Their aim was to win me over to their way of thinking. They regarded me as a spirited, energetic young man. If they could succeed in converting me, they felt I would help them to transform the newly married men into fervent hasidim. They were also afraid of me. If I remained their opponent, they knew it would be the end of Hasidism among the youth of Kamenietz, which they wanted to avoid at any cost.

I won the debate. I answered all their questions; they dodged mine. "The Rabbi will answer that," Simche said repeatedly.

I countered: "What need have I to follow Hasidism? This blind faith in a rabbi does not appeal to me. I shall adhere to my own way of thinking, and be spared the doubts."

"What is wrong with asking questions?" interposed Simche.

"Traveling to the Rabbi for the answer," I replied.

"I'll give you fifty rubles for expenses," persisted Simche. "Ride over to Karlin and see Rabbi Aaron. He will settle everything to your satisfaction."

He religiously pledged the money the moment I was ready to leave for the rabbinic audience. That ended the debate, and my triumph was assured. From then on they showed me great deference, and regarded me as a precocious fellow.

Sabbath morning I said my prayers among the hasidim in their own little chapel, and on weekdays at the new synagogue. After the services I held forth on Hasidism. My victory over the hasidim was widely known, and as time went on, more and more young men flocked to hear my discourses. I was invited to speak at the old synagogue, and for the next few decades not a single young man in Kamenietz was converted. That town has been unhasidic to this very day.

However, I made a mistake in arguing with my father. I hoped he would reconcile himself to my dissenting conviction. Instead, he started to plague me with biting allusions, and to turn my wife against me. He appeared unconcerned over the possible consequences to my married life.

As things were going from bad to worse, I decided to go to Wolozhin and resume my studies for the rabbinate. That would put an end to the friction. The truth was I did not want to leave my beloved wife. I was married only a few months. On the other hand, to continue under those circumstances was impossible.

I wanted to secure a passport. I also wanted a visa, although it was then not necessary for traveling. But no visa could be issued to me without my father's consent. Yet I felt confident that Jacob, the tax-collector, would give it to me. Indeed, he promised that he would. Secretly, however, he sent word to my father, which made me see the folly of exaggerated self-confidence.

"Hatzkel, why do you need a passport?" my father inquired.

"To travel to Wolozhin," I replied, looking at my toes.

Suddenly his patience snapped, and in the presence of my wife, he struck me twice in the face. "Only a few months after marriage," he screamed, beside himself, "and you are planning to desert your wife! Do you want to be a hermit?"

At that moment he was perhaps not so much concerned about my wife as he was intent on antagonizing her against me. He went on at the top of his voice:

"Do you want to desert your orphan-wife? Whoever heard of such a thing? It's criminal! What right have you to plan such a thing without first consulting me? If not your father, why not talk it over with your wife? You are pious, you say. Well, then, don't you know it is written in the Torah that you should stay at home with your wife at least one year even in time of war! So you want to go off to study? I don't believe you want it that much. You could study at home, too, you know. There must be something else. Maybe you don't love your wife any more?" he wound up with a quizzical grin.

His words incensed me. He knew how much I loved my wife, and how gladly I would have given my life for her. He didn't have to pour salt on my wounds. He went on abusing me in her presence and picturing me as the worst possible person in the world.

As usual, my wife reacted with a deluge of tears. Father, who really loved her and could not bear to see her in anguish, kept on raking the fire. Finally, when she became hysterical, he stopped in his tracks, frightened. He immediately sent for Yashke, the healer. Pandemonium broke loose in the house. The family put her to bed. At that moment I realized how cruel my father could be to those who opposed him.

At that time they caught Isaac Beer, an employee of my father, who had been looting his safe with a passkey for God knows how long. Yet the discovery left my father unperturbed. He did not say an unkind word to the thief.

"Tell me, Isaac Beer, did you steal at least with restraint?" And he merely paid him off.

When Isaac Beer whined that he was left without means to support his family and that he had no money for the fare home, which was at Brusk, my father handed him a hundred rubles and wished him luck as if the fellow were a saint, not a crook.

But upon sober deliberation, I could not blame him too much. I concluded it was easier for one to turn hasid than for a hasid to change into an opponent. An ordinary opponent was simply a religious, law-abiding Jew; a hasid believed that God, heaven and paradise were created exclusively for his pleasure. As intensely as hasidim loved their cult, just so intensely they hated disagreements. Moreover, father feared that I might win over my four younger brothers. In this he was right; they took sides with me.

Unfortunately, my wife was on his side, and he sought to fight me through her. Had she not been so lovely, he probably would have gritted his teeth and resigned himself to the situation. But he knew how much I loved her. In that sense she constituted a power for him against me. My intention to leave her and home therefore disturbed him. If I stayed, I might yet, with her aid, be converted. If I didn't, all was lost.

As always in such conflicts between father and son, he gained nothing by his tactics. Instead of my bending under his efforts, I became increasingly obstinate. He failed to comprehend that I would not change my conviction just as he would not yield his. It was not in my nature to falsify, deceive, lie, or pretend. Others, dressed as hasidim, haunted the Rabbi for the sake of a wife, a father, a father-in-law. On the sly they cheated, and even smoked cigars on the Sabbath. I could not be guilty of such duplicity.

The day on which I wanted to procure a visa was the saddest in my life. My wife became bedridden. My father did everything to restore her to health. She refused to speak with me. Her condition affected me badly. My father refused to permit me into her presence. The whole family puttered around her; everybody assisted in one way or another; I alone did nothing!

When she recovered, her attitude changed. She seemed to be sorry for me, to sympathize with my groping. I explained to her that my father had no right to persecute me. He would never make a hasid out of me so long as my heart was not in it. "He insults me in your presence, and humiliates me. No my darling, I would do anything except believe in what I can't. . . . About my going to Wolozhin and leaving you alone," I continued, "you know that my heart belongs to you. I want to go away because our capital is small, and there is not a business here which I could consider with a sense of security. One thing is left: to attain ordination. If not for my father, I might have been a rabbi by now. But I am still young, only eighteen, and it isn't too late. You will be taken care of here in my absence. In four or five years, if God wills it, you will be the beautiful wife of a rabbi."

Fundamentally a practical woman, my wife agreed with me at once. Never for a moment did she doubt my loyalty and devotion. Sensing that we had reached an understanding, my father ceased to torment me.

LIFE OF A HUMORIST

SHOLEM ALEICHEM (1859-1916)

No writer has won greater esteem and popularity among the masses of his people than Sholom Rabinovitch, who adopted as his *nom de plume* the time-honored greeting "Peace be with you". The son of a hasidic squire in a small Russian village, his strong imagination drank in both the beauty and the degradation of the common folk, and it is easy to understand why the gently humorous manner in which he treated their foibles and sentiments endeared him and his numerous writings. He found, like Emerson, that something always sings in the mud and scum of things, and he laughed infectiously when he recorded the music. "To see the comic side of everything and everyone was almost second nature with me." It is a pity that he never composed *The Story of Sholem Aleichem's Life Written by Himself* * which he planned, but we may be grateful for this blithe thumbnail self-portrait.

❊ ❊ ❊

IN THE little town of Voronko, no larger than an olive, a little distance away from the city of Pereyaslav (where I was born in 1859), I spent the golden years of my life, the first lovely, innocent days of my childhood. In this little Voronko, my father was one of the pillars

---

* "You ask me to give you a few notes for my biography," wrote the author to his friend, V. H. Ravnitski, noted critic. "I am afraid my biography may be superfluous. Isn't it a bit too early? That is point one. Secondly, I myself should very much like to write the story of my life—a whole book of it. (I actually started to write this book in Italy, entitling it, *The Story of Sholem Aleichem's Life Written by Himself*. Sholem Aleichem's note, 1913.) And thirdly, I am—I hope you may be spared the same—very, very busy—actually with literature. Ever since I started to write, never have I been so productive and fruitful as now. Good or bad, but I do write a lot. And, as you know well enough, I can write sitting on a pinhead, on the blade of a knife. The trouble is that the times are bad; the clouds have been gathering over our people. It's hard to laugh, and if a laugh burst through, there is a note of bitterness in it. . . . And then my correspondence with our elite—the Jews and the gentiles—takes a good slice of my time. And here a good hour of my time has been stolen for you—thief that you are!—in order to let you have a few memoirs. Perhaps they'll be useful in your work. May God help you!"

of the town, the "squire," the chief trustee of all societies—he was "Reb Nahum Vevik's." And we, Reb Nahum Vevik's children, were also of some account. Every Sabbath night the whole town would attend the *melaveh malka* (hasidic communal feast to speed the departing Sabbath Queen) at our house; on every holiday the townspeople would pay their respects to us; all news was brought to our house and carried away from our house; a glassful of wine was drunk at our table; at our house stories were told about hasidic rabbis, and politics were discussed—all at our house. And we, Reb Nahum Vevik's children, were considered of great importance—we were guided in the straight path, given into the tutorship of the best teacher, Reb Zorah, and we really were God-fearing and pious.

To this day I remember the taste of the tears we shed at our teacher's homilies. Every day our teacher, Reb Zorah, would have a new homily for us, and afterwards at prayer time we would beat our breasts, crying "We have trespassed!" in repentance of our sins; for side by side with our piety, we were preys to temptation and were great transgressors; we were liars and gluttons; we disobeyed father, cheated at prayer, stole money from the charity box . . . and what of the strange thoughts and desires! Afterwards, came the teacher with his homilies, and we would weep again. We would again shed copious tears; we again prayed devotedly, without cheating, and beat our breasts crying "We have trespassed," weeping, weeping and repenting.

From very childhood my flaming imagination was remarkably developed. Houses seemed to be transformed into cities; courtyards into empires, trees into people, girls into princesses, rich men's sons into princes. Haystacks became warriors, thorns and thistles were Philistines, Edom and Moab, and upon them I would make battle.

To see the comic side of everything and everyone was almost second nature with me. Quite unwittingly I would imitate people and their actions, beginning with the teacher and his wife, including all my comrades and their parents, down to Baruch Baer, the drunkard, and Oniska, the bowlegged watchman. I got plenty of blows for my aping. In school I was the "constant nuisance"—the comic. Everyone would laugh himself sick, except myself. However, when my mother got wind of my pranks, she started to wean me out of them.

There was only one equal to me in mimicking, "acting," "dressing up," and singing pretty songs. This was Meyer'l, the Rabbi's son, or Meyer'l Medvedeff, afterwards the famous singer. He showed signs of talent when he was still running about barefoot, singing pretty songs for a penny, sometimes for half an apple. The two of us used to play *Robbers,* a drama of our own composition. Medvedeff was the robber, I a pauper Jew. The rest of our comrades were the trees of the forest—the "supers." I, the pauper, would kneel in front of the robber pleading, "What do you want of me? I am only a poor, poor Jew, a pauper! Mercy on my wife and little children!" And he, the robber, with a kitchen knife in hand, would stand over me, singing a song to the effect that he must, he absolutely must, slaughter all Jews. . . .

As spoiled and naughty as we were, compassion for all living creatures was so strong in me that I felt pangs of suffering at the sight of a sick horse; a lame dog would bring tears into my eyes. Even cats—the lowest of the low—aroused tenderness in me, to say nothing of poor sick children.

Remarkably enough, Reb Zorah was responsible for my first urge to write. It was due to his extraordinarily beautiful calligraphy. For a nice "hand" father would present us with a penny (the first "royalty"); and in order to cultivate a nice "hand," I fashioned a notebook and in beautiful characters wrote an entire composition on the Bible and Hebrew grammar. When I showed it to father, he was much amazed at my "creation," and for a long time carried it in his pocket to show everyone how beautifully his son wrote (I must have been ten years old), how well he knew the Bible, and how great was his knowledge of grammar. On this occasion a neighbor of ours, a hasid with a goatee, Reb Isaac by name, whose prayers sounded like the squeal of a kitten, commented, "Grammar-yammer—the real thing is the hand—a golden hand!" (My first "critic.")

In those days I was drawn into the world of the spirit and of dreams. I was drawn to singing and to the world of music; and after bar mizwah I secretly tried playing the fiddle—and got a good dose of it from father.

Then we lost everything; we moved from Voronko back to Pereyaslav. There we were for the first time dressed up in "modern" suits with slit coattails. And after mother died of the cholera, father placed us in a government school, where I distinguished myself. There, at the age of fifteen, I read my first modern book, *Robinson Crusoe,* and at once composed a Robinson Crusoe of my own, entitled *The Jewish Robinson Crusoe.* I showed it to father, who in turn showed it to his customers (at that time we kept a wayside inn), and everyone thought it marvelous!

From that time on, father started to treat me like a precious object. He took me out of stepmother's power, would not permit her to punish

246 MEMOIRS OF MY PEOPLE

me, forbade me to mind the babies, crush raisins (we kept a wine-cellar called "South Shore"), polish the customers' boots, prepare the samovar, run errands or perform similar tasks which in those days used to be mine.

In that epoch, between the ages of seventeen and twenty-one, wanting to become a government rabbi, I started studying seriously. I therefore read a good deal, and wrote even more. I wrote . . . everything that I had read in books: songs, poems, novels, dramas without end, and "articles" about everything under the sun. I used to send my "works" to all the Jewish and non-Jewish editors (I wrote both in Hebrew and Russian), and the editors must have blessed me for providing them with fuel for their stoves. The *Ha-Melitz* alone printed a couple of my "articles," adding a footnote in tiny type: "Sfatcha itcha (thy tongue is with thee) . . . Shlah dvoreyha veklibdanum (Send thy words, and we shall honor them)." Thereupon I started writing Hebrew articles by the ton; I sent wagonloads of articles—but why they were not honored, I do not know.

In those days (1883) there appeared a Yiddish periodical, the first periodical in that language—the *Folksblatt* of Alexander Zederbaum— and since the gentiles would not print my "novels" nor my "dramas," and since the Hebrew "articles" were also languishing unhonored, I tried my hand at writing in the spoken tongue—the tongue of Mendele Mocher Seforim, whose books at that time first came to my notice. And picture my amazement when the *Folksblatt* grabbed it up, and Zederbaum, the editor himself, in his own hand, wrote me a letter requesting me (do you understand—*requesting* me!) to write more. From that time on, I started writing articles in the *Folksblatt,* and the more I gave, the more was demanded of me. Moreover, there appeared one Mordecai Spector, of the *Folksblatt* staff, who never ceased to egg me on to write—and hasn't ceased doing so until this very day. Yet in those days, this was merely a pastime for me, until the affair with a certain penknife which created an upheaval in my writing and in my entire life.

That epoch was for me one of commerce, money, the Bourse, stocks and bonds, and similar things that have nothing to do with literature. I had, as the saying goes, scaled the ladder. I handled thousands and tens of thousands, and it is possible that I might have chosen quite a different path—in the opinion and aspirations of some, the "strait" path. One day, some important business affairs took me to the great city of Kiev. There, during the day, I wore myself out, but when at night I lay down on the bed, I could not fall asleep. Then I rose, sat down at the desk and started to write. I did not really write—rather, I poured out on paper some of the memories of my childhood and gave them the name of the *Penknife*. This I sent to the editor and promptly forgot about it.

And there came a day when I picked up the *Voshod* and suddenly in a literary survey of all kinds of trash by "Criticus" (S. M. Dubnow), I found my *Penknife*. My heart beating furiously, I read his warm lines. He praised the story and prophesied that the author of the *Penknife*, who gave promise of talent, might some day give more good things to our impoverished Yiddish literature.

With tears of joy and gratitude I reread the words by the benevolent "Criticus," and then swore that I would continue writing in the same vein. Until this very day, I see those kind, warm words before my eyes, and sometimes after finishing a new story, I ask myself, "What would 'Criticus' say to this?" Afterwards I lost my money, but I was left with courage, and I have been clutching the pen in my hand with all my might. Do I owe "Criticus" thanks, or otherwise? That is not for me to judge. My writing-sickness has become so bad that I no longer belong either to myself nor to my family, but rather to our literature and to that greater family, called the public.

MEMORIES OF CHILDHOOD

AHAD HA'AM (1856-1926)

Under the pseudonym Ahad Ha'am, "One of the people," Asher Ginzberg won preeminence as an advocate of modern Hebrew nationalism. Vigorously opposed to Herzlian political Zionism, he employed his wide culture (he was in private life a tea merchant) and mastery of the Hebrew tongue to promote self-understanding and advocate a cultural renaissance. During the latter part of his life, he withdrew from literary activity and made his home in Tel Aviv in Palestine where he was regarded with high veneration. The combination of humility and intellectual forthrightness which characterized his later life are noticeable in this chapter of his youth. While he rejected the external expression of his inherited Judaism, the warm and vital core of it remained with him always.

❊ ❊ ❊

I RECEIVED the beginnings of my education from hasidim on the knees of which I was born and within which I spent my early years. My father was one of the chief Sadagore hasidim in the town where I was born, and naturally educated me along similar lines. I used to pray with him in the chapel of the Sadagore hasidim, and learnt to honor the wonder-rabbi of Sadagore, Reb Abraham Jacob, son of Rabbi Israel of Ruzhin. My leisure time, when I was not at school, was spent in the class where I read hasidic books and any others that might be there.

At the beginning of Autumn, 1868, when I was twelve years old, my father took me with him on his visit to the Rabbi for the Tabernacles festival; for he desired that the Rabbi should bless me before my bar mizwah (confirmation) and should put his hand in mine, besides telling me some worthwhile things. We spent the whole of the festival at Sadagore in the company of the Rabbi and his children. One evening (as far as I remember the eve of the Festival of Drawing the Water, which hasidim have revived after it had fallen into desuetude following the destruction of the Temple in Jerusalem) there was no feast at the house of the Rabbi, so father went to the feast of the children and took me with him. We came to the succah (booth), which was full of people. One old man, a Galician, stood beside the table and diverted the children (namely, the Rabbi's eldest son and his better-known brother-in-law) with his gross stories which were full of coarse language. The stories were so gross that even I, a child of twelve, understood practically everything. All those present laughed to their heart's content. Suddenly one of the children closed his eyes tight with great fervor and exclaimed, "Where's Yoshke" (a famous cantor and Sadagore hasid who had also come for the festival). When they found Yoshke he said to him: "Sing 'Let the Rock command His Loving-kindness'." The cantor began to sing and the young "saint" listened with closed eyes to the song, his fervor increasing meanwhile until he seized the saltcellar, which stood not far from me, and began to beat time with it on the table, while the salt shot far and wide across the entire succah; and so it went on until the cantor had finished his song. This scene, particularly the sudden transition from dirty stories to such fervor, made a very bad impression on me; and that impression made a great breach in my Hasidism.

When I arrived at Sadagore my father and I went to "give peace" (a hasidic expression for calling on the Rabbi, who at such times stood at the door of his study with outstretched hand, while all the new guests came and shook hands with him). When father's turn came we both approached the Rabbi and shook his hand like all the other guests; and because my father was one of the important hasidim the Rabbi spoke to him for a few minutes. Many years later, when I was already "outside the camp," certain of the hasidim who had been present on that occasion swore that after I had shaken hands with the Rabbi he had wiped his hand on his girdle.

I could relate a great deal of the days we spent at the Rabbi's, but that is not my purpose here. The outcome of it all was that I left my Hasidism behind me at Sadagore and returned home a complete mitnaged (opponent). I had already begun to study the Talmud and Scriptures and medieval Hebrew literature; and when I returned from Sadagore my devotion to all of these increased and I began to be particular about commandments with which hasidim do not usually concern themselves (such as praying precisely at the duly appointed time). My father, a shrewd man, a scholar and also somewhat advanced, greatly regretted this change which had come about in my manner of life and would bring home the lions of the company of hasidim, in the hope that they might bring me back to the right path. But he did not succeed.

That was the first and last time that I saw a famous saint. He himself, it is true, made a deep impression upon me, both on account of his remarkable appearance, his behavior and his manner of speech; but that did not suffice to close the breach made in my hasidic faith by the behavior of his children and the whole assembly of his hasidim there. Little by little the entire bundle fell apart, as they say in Hebrew. Although I continued to live in that hasidic environment for many years to come, I separated from them and there was no link between us. They went about their own business, while I devoted myself to my studies with all my heart and paid no attention to them.

From my early boyhood, when we still lived in the town and I was about ten or eleven, I had grown accustomed to being examined in my studies. For matchmakers already abounded who took the provision for my future upon themselves and proposed all kinds of matches for me, after my name and fame had spread abroad through the entire district as an infant prodigy. Since there were no *yeshiboth* (higher schools for the study of talmudic literature) in our parts and it was not the custom thereabouts, as it was in Lithuania, for the wealthy folk to choose bridegrooms for their daughters from the yeshibah lads, cases like mine were in great demand. When there were boys in different places for whom great futures were foretold on the strength of their studies, the wealthy folk would compete with each other to get them as sons-in-law. I was one of the boys whose name and fame as a desirable bridegroom went ahead of him. The rich folk who wished to make a match would send "understanding" scholars to our town in order to examine me in my studies in order to learn whether the rumors as to my prodigious attainments were true or not.

As a result strangers came to the school where I studied almost every week, folk I had never seen before, in order to examine my knowledge of Talmud and the great rabbinical authorities. During the final years before I actually became a bridegroom there were two competitors. One was a wealthy man, but an ignoramus, while the other belonged to a pedigreed family into which I did actually marry. The girl in question had been orphaned of her father, the Rabbi of Zhitomir, who died while still a young man. Naturally she had no dowry. The former was famous in our parts at that time as a very wealthy man who was prepared to give his daughter quite a considerable dowry. My father wished to do everything as was most fitting and proper, and resolved that I must be questioned as to which I preferred. The matter was entrusted to my then teacher; he was told to talk to me and did so. I was very perplexed and did not know what to answer. At bottom I preferred the match with the wealthy man, for I feared the excessive sanctity and Hasidism which characterized the pedigreed family. But I was ashamed to admit this openly to my teacher, and instead of a direct answer I reminded him of a saying in the Talmud, "Let a man sell all he possesses and so on," without finishing the quotation, for I thought my teacher would understand what I was driving at. I had wished to indicate that the sages of the Talmud had not thought it of vital importance to marry the daughters of scholars, since one version of the proverb beginning as above ends "and marry the daughter of a scholar," while another, which commenced in precisely the same way, ends, "and buy shoes for his feet." My teacher, however, did not grasp this but thought simply that I was referring to the former of the two sayings. In this way my fate was determined, and before very long my father went to the place of residence of the head of the pedigreed family and arranged the match. The bride was not there, for she was staying with her maternal grandfather some distance away. However, the wife of the head of the family produced her own daughter, who was indeed a pretty girl, and said to him, "Do you see this daughter of mine? I assure you that the bride is no worse than she is." That was sufficient evidence for my father to arrange the match.

But it was about the examinations that I started this section, and I want to finish about them too.

Apart from the examiners who visited my school from time to time, it was the custom of father to examine me himself every Sabbath, after arising from his noonday sleep. In accordance with his system of education he would always end his examination by slapping my face whether I deserved it or not. The same moment my mother would open the door of her room and would say to him: "Hitting him again! May the thunder hit you!" That was the almost invariable end of the examinations, after which I would be free to go out and play with my friends until the time of the afternoon prayers.

Naturally, that was when we still lived in the town, before moving to the village; for in the latter I had no friends and did not take part in any children's games.

While referring to my father's educational system, I should mention another incident. It was the habit in our house that when sitting down to a meal at table each one would bring a book to read between courses. My father himself usually brought the *Midrash Rabbah,* while I would choose various books from father's library. Once father came to see what my book was. After inspecting it, he said to me, "Do you know that the author wrote this book when he was eighteen?" "I know," I answered. "As for you," my father went on, "when you're eighteen years old you won't even be able to understand what he's written in it." This annoyed me exceedingly for I had understood everything perfectly well, despite all its finespun dialectic, although I was no more than eleven at the time. But that was one of the foundations of education according to my father; to lower me in my own eyes. Though I do not know what the purpose was in doing so.

As already mentioned, I married, or rather was married off, before my seventeenth birthday. My wife belonged to a very good hasidic family indeed. On her father's side she was the granddaughter of the then famous Wonder-Rabbi Jacob Israel of Tcherkossi. The latter was then very old and could not come to the wedding which was conducted at Ovrutch in the Wolhynia Government. Some time later the family demanded that my wife and I should go to Tcherkossi in order to be seen by the Old Man. I finally agreed for politeness' sake. At the end of the summer in the same year or the one following—I do not quite remember which—we went there. On account of his age the "Saint" could not take his place at the head of the public table on the Sabbath day, as was the custom. So his place was taken for the purpose by one or other of his many grandsons who used to visit him at frequent intervals. For the Sabbath when we were there, there came one such grandson who was afterwards a "Saint" in his own right; and when I arrived, I went to visit him as well. Among the other things of which we spoke we talked of the day when we would return home. I said that I would be leaving on the Tuesday, to which he replied that in that case he would leave earlier because he wished to go on the Sunday. For some reason or other, which I do not know, I told him: "No, I shall be leaving here first." He laughed, and we made no further reference to the matter.

This happened in the middle of the week. On Friday he went to the bathhouse and a nail ran into his leg and wounded him. The doctor ordered him to stay in bed. And so that Sabbath there was nobody to sit at the head of the table. Thereupon the choice fell upon me to replace the "Saint"; with the result that I was suddenly transformed into a "Saint" conducting the table for his believers, at a time when deep in my heart hasidim was considered a very defective system and institution.

Though this was already practically common knowledge among the hasidim, they nevertheless did not refrain from grabbing what was left on the plate just as they did with the Rabbi himself when he was there (for it is believed that the Rabbi's holy touch imparts some special virtue to the food). On the Tuesday when as I arranged I was to leave, I paid a visit to the grandson with whom I had spoken and who had injured his leg, in order to bid him farewell. I found him still lying in bed. In this way my prophecy was fulfilled and I went first, thus becoming an unintentional wonder-worker.

BEFORE THIRTY

HAYYIM NAHMAN BIALIK (1873-1934)

Bialik was a distinguished Hebrew poet, and in recognition of his attainments an annual "Bialik Prize for Hebrew Literature" has been established in Palestine. His versatility was quite remarkable, for in addition to verse he wrote stories, essays, criticism; he edited anthologies, managed a publishing house, spoke in behalf of his cherished causes and acted as spiritual guide to writers, pioneers and educators. The impulse to creative activity was intensified by the agony of his early life, which he so revealingly recounts in the following fragments out of his posthumous works. (Despite slight overlapping, they interconnect and round off each other.) Here he reminisces less cautiously than in his more formal autobiography, *Aftergrowth,* and thus allows us a few steps closer to the inner spirit of the man.

※　※　※

YOU ask me to do you the trifling favor of writing the chapter headings of my life, but I stand and find it very hard indeed. I think to myself: before asking me to write the chapter headings of my life's history, first ask me whether I have any "history" at all? Upon your life: my dear, if there is any man in the world who has no "history," I am that man. My history is so simple, and so resembles the histories of all men like me, that there is nothing to learn from it and willy-nilly it requires no study.

A brief introduction: in the events of my life do not look for order, evolution or connection, cause or effect. There is nothing of that kind or similar to it. I am a passive man by nature, "feminine" in the sense of being subject to influences, and never participated actively in those things that exerted a creative effect upon me. All my powers are sustained, like those of any plant, from what is set prepared round me and nearby, without taking anything of their own; and all the vicissitudes of my life are only in the nature of separate broken notes played by a variety of musical instruments, each being played independently without thought of the rest; and if by chance all those nevertheless combine into one complete tune it is a true heavenly miracle.

Just think: I was born in a village and grew up there until I was six years old. The glory of Nature, the lovely world, fields and forests and all the rest. And in the midst of this lovely world, where my heart and I all but choked, there already sat an usher nipping me in the neck and giving me the command: "Listen, you little bastard, do you see this yoke and two pails?—Call it Aleph!" And then all of a sudden there I was in town, Hebrew classes, thrashings, a muckheap, an inn (my father kept an inn and studied Mishna while serving). Then a year later I am out of the town again.

And once again there are fields, forests, a river and all the rest. . . . And at the same time my heder (Hebrew class) is gloomy as the shadow of death, and the teachers are thoroughly abominable and disgusting, or not thoroughly abominable and disgusting, as the case may be.

And then all of a sudden I am an orphan aged seven and am transferred to the house of an old man of over seventy. My childhood was seething within me, but he threw the ice of his old age over my infancy. My movements, my face, my sitting and my standing were an abomination for him. I showed him my childish actions; and he would respond by producing the *Shebet Musar* (Rod of Reproof) and the *Reshith Hokmah* (Beginning of Wisdom). Then once again the heder and teachers, teachers and heder. The man weds (this was one of my first lessons in Gemara at the age of seven), he who brings a divorce from overseas. Teacher, what's overseas? And what's a divorce? You little ignoramus! A divorce is a divorce. When a woman bears seed (I do not remember which I first began to study—Pentateuch or Talmud); there was the *Or Ha-Hayyim* (The Light of Life, a mystical commentary on the Pentateuch held in high favor by the hasidim), the laws of every oddment and trifle.

And then all of a sudden I found myself in the heder of a strange and lazy teacher with a fondness for legend. We used to study at twilight when the flocks were returning home, for he slept all day long. He taught us Agada (the non-legal portion of the talmudic literature) and Bible, and my heart was attracted to both, and skipped and danced like a lamb on a verdant pasture. And my grandfather had a bookcase full of yellow-leaved old books, large and small, of every kind, and I read them and read them, at first only half understanding, but finally understanding everything. And everything was to be found there: Agada (Legend),

Halakah (Law), Ethics, Kabbalah, Research. There I found how one merits the Holy Spirit.

And in the heart lay hidden some Holy of Holies, something hidden and concealed, all kinds of yearnings the nature of which I do not know but which give me no rest. In my neighborhood I got the reputation of a fine young rascal. I am unique in my suburb as regards both rascality and sharp-mindedness. And so all of a sudden I find people to act as "fathers" to me; uncles and cousins, relations and neighbors, all prepared to teach me how to behave as is fitting for an orphan. One cousin, a big lad, hauls me off without anybody's knowledge to the lavatory, lets down my breeches, turns back my shirt, beats me and laughs, beats me and goes on laughing. I am ashamed to tell anybody about this shameful thing, so come out feeling as though I were full of filth; and in my state of nervous excitement I take open revenge upon old men for the shame done me in private. Sometimes I hid in an attic or in some secret corner, sat daydreaming and staring out of my hiding-place at the outer world, daydreaming all the time. Seen through a crack, the world is much nicer. And sometimes I begin weeping in secret for an hour or two hours; a weeping the taste of which is difficult for me to explain or transmit to you.

Between one teacher and another I was sent to a village and remained there about a year. And once more, and in between whiles, I enter another heder. The teacher was a complicated young fellow, a sort of mixture of Hasidism with a spark of the Enlightenment. Rabbi Meir Leibush Heilprin, the "Malbim," was the end of all wisdom for him, while Hartwig Wessely's *Songs of Glory* was the ultimate peak of poesy; and both of them together were no more than a sandal for the feet of some starched and pressed Hasidism that also had a fine delicate fragrance of scholarship about it, very slightly spiced with it as it were. He knew a little about grammar, bookkeeping, algebra; he could play the violin and chess as well. He was well-versed in the *Or Ha-Hayyim* (a kabbalistic commentary on the Pentateuch by Rabbi Hayyim ibn Atar, and almost a vade mecum for many hasidim and Jewish mystical thinkers) and in ibn Ezra's biblical commentaries. The *Biur* ("Interpretation" or commentary on the Bible prepared by Mendelssohn and his disciples) was not so dangerous; it might be kept on the bottom shelf of the bookcase for reference in case of need. It must be held to the merit of Isaac Bär Levinson that he had written the *Efes Damim* (a book refuting the Blood Libel), and so on and so forth. This teacher opened my heart a little with his talk of hasidim and of the disciples of the sages; he taught us with genuine enjoyment. But in the last resort his zeal spoilt things and he turned very disapproving eyes on my one companion and myself because meanwhile we had advanced considerably in Talmud and he knew less than us.

I was born in the village of Radi (Volhynia Government). In this village I received my first impressions of the world and Nature. It was a place of forests and vast plains. Quiet low white peasant houses lay there in amplitude, lost in a sea of green during the summer and in a sea of snow during the winter. Through the windows of our house I could every day see the magnificent forest standing facing me in its black loftiness, mighty, mysterious and full of hidden things, standing there silent and beckoning, come and search me out!

In summer noons and evenings I would set out, usually alone but sometimes with a little gang of children my own age, to this shady wood and would pass through and through it, leaving my companions for some hidden corner where I would sit alone, meditating silently, with some vast "hidden" one whose breathing I could hear behind me but whose name I did not know.

The rustle of leaves, a light cloud, a strip of sky, the melancholy note of a cuckoo at the top of a tree, the shadow of a plant falling across its own branches, a tiny pool concealed in the deeps of the forest, simple and modest forest flowers, the croaking of frogs, splashes of light falling between the branches to spangle the ground—these were the letters which combined to create my childhood universe, bringing me vague dumb feelings and thoughts the nature and meaning of which I did not know. The world surrounding me and standing over me was not explained to me but remained as sealed as ever, sealed yet calling to my heart. While as for what was explained to me out of the prayerbook—it did not attract me nor did I wish to know it.

And the sunsets? I remember one twilight. A broad plain spread out to the ends of earth. It was all swathed in lush fresh herbage and embroidered with wild blossoms of every kind; white, yellow, blue and pink. The plain and the fringes of the firmament and the whole vast space of the universe were all of them at that hour one sea of radiance, one awesome glorious crimson sea of radiance wherever my eyes might rest. The skies were red, the plain was red, the wild blossoms grew red. And I, together with two little girls dressed in white, stood among the grasses picking "birds' milk"; and the white juice of their cups squirted onto our fingers. Then suddenly I lifted my eyes to the ends of heaven—

and there was the vast light decked with flame hanging great and radiant between the lips of the firmament and the earth, and a sea of fire coursing from thence across the world.

"Yonder! Yonder!" I cried in wonder to my two little companions, and began dashing towards where the sun was, dragging my two pale little friends after me. It seemed to me that nothing more than a small stretch of country lay between me and it; and that finally I must reach it.

Then there is another summer sight which my heart preserves from those days. I understand that it is impossible for such a vision really to have existed, yet my heart and I knew that we actually saw it and very concretely; nor has my heart ever doubted the fact. It is a moonlit night. I stand alone outside the gate of our courtyard; there is a wood to right of me and a plain to left. Over my head is sky and again sky, and in front of me is a small sloping hill covered with dewy green grass, glistening with its myriad tiny drops, gently and quietly in the moonlight. The little hill sloped all the way aloft till it ended where there was a small white house on its top. Everything drowses, sliding into unconsciousness and congealing under a faint dusting of pale bluish light. And suddenly there are two files of child-dwarves, clear of face and black of garb, crossing the hill, proceeding towards the forest. And there was a kind of unutterably sweet song, a silent, interior song, flowing voicelessly from the heart, which came from them to my heart. To my heart. For it was not with my ears I heard their song but with my heart. They passed their way without observing me; but I gazed after them till they had passed out of sight. I remember that when I entered the house the power of speech had left me. I caught at my mother's apron and wished to say "Mamma!" but could not. The word mamma stuck in my throat and is there to this day. (See my poem *Night Dwarves*.)

When I began to grow up and became a heretic and began to disbelieve such things, I invented all kinds of explanations for the vision; at some time or other I must have had some kind of very vivid dream of this kind, and it had stuck in my memory; or else I must assuredly have heard some tale of the kind when I was a child, and it had remained fixed in my imagination. Maybe that is the explanation, and indeed it almost certainly is so; yet all the same that vision will never cease to seem to me a real thing which I saw with my waking eyes in every detail. I can even remember the sight of the fence of our courtyard at the time, the sight of the post next to the gateway, the sight of the little house and its roof on top of the hill and the sight of the byre facing it there. From the roof of the house to the roof of the byre was stretched a rope on which a white shirt hung drying.

All in all, at that time my heart and head were an overflowing treasury of imaginings and dreams both clear and incomprehensible, such as the mouth cannot tell nor the ear hear; but I never told my mother and father what was in my heart. Some kind of silence was enforced upon my heart and everything concealed itself and grew dumb therein, writhing and striving to come out and find expression but unable to do so.

Any kind of stain on the wall, flyspecks on the lamp, beads of moisture on glass, the images of the household utensils in the mirror— all of these were the raw material for my imagination. In particular I used to shape forms for myself and create whole universes during rainy days from the stains of damp on the inner walls of our house. I would gaze and lose myself within those green pale sunken patches, would combine them with each other so that they became mountains and valleys, strange animals and all manner of creatures. . . . All in absolute silence. I would raise my eyes to the world, wonder—and remain silent.

Many more memories of this kind remain from this period of my childhood but even now I feel that despite all the explanations it is absolutely impossible to give you the flavor of those visions. Such things derive from the heart and even the person experiencing them within him as on the day when they were first received; and only at a few rare happy moments will they gleam within him, flashing like lightning just as they had been and with their own original flavor—and in the same instant they grow dim and faint; and they are no longer there.

When I was five or six years old my father moved to Zhitomir. (In the ms. there is another version of this incident: "When I was five or six I left the village with my father's household for Zhitomir in order to dwell there. I remember that when we left the boundaries of the village and the forest, and the trees grew fewer and gradually thinner and poorer, our cow which was tied by the horns behind the cart with a long rope kept on turning her head from time to time as far as the rope would permit her, towards the village behind her, and lowed loud and long, moooooo!") There father built a house outside the town, near a broad sandy track on the flanks of a forest; and there he opened an inn, for selling food and liquor to the peasants passing that way on market days from the villages near the town. Father used to sit behind the bar, reading a book studying a passage of Mishna and incidentally filling a glass for a peasant. I was sent to the Hebrew class; first to a beginners' class and later to a mixed one. It was a place of hills and valleys, with springs rising between the hills, bubbling their song along as they dashed down to the River Titirev.

These were good times for me, particularly the free days, those of the twilights, the Sabbath eves, the Sabbaths themselves, the festivals, the times between terms. The hills led me away, and the valleys hid me in their shade. On this side of the river were lofty rounded hills of clay and sand, spreading with bare flanks like vast monsters that have taken the skin of their bones, so that the piles of living flesh on these flanks gleam red and pink. Beyond the River Titirev there gazed at me a nut wood which called at me. One lofty tree standing above its fellows with what seemed like head and shoulders would peer at me through the twilight like a robber at arms, planting a sweet dread in my heart. I knew that it was a tree and not a robber, yet all the same I enjoyed being afraid of it. . . . Then there was the bathing in the river, and the little sandy islands in its midst where the naked children would do battle like the savages in the South Sea Islands. And ever so many things more.

The teacher who taught me my letters was a rough bear. The fare which he set before his pupils consisted of curses, blows and beating. Yet I got plenty that was precious out of him. I remember holy and dread moments and holy and sweet moments. It suddenly became dark at noon and there was gloom everywhere. It was very dark outside and twice as dark in the heder. There was a storm coming. The fear of God fell upon the teacher and upon us, his little pupils. We all let fall our Pentateuchs and rose frightened from the benches. The teacher also stood up and gave an order with his eyes. We stood ready. . . . Lightning flashed. And forty mouths suddenly recited the blessing at the top of their voices. The heavens began to thunder and growl from the depths of their belly, and suddenly there came a crash and a reduplicated crash. The heavens split and the earth was cleft in twain; and the children cried out: *Blessed art Thou, O Lord, Whose might and power fill the universe.* And the thunder grew louder and crumbled away and rolled afar, and the children became partners of it and of all the works of creation, in voice, in heart and in fear. . . . While as for the teacher, upon your soul, he was a fine fellow just then; for he was our shield and guardian.

While as for the Thirty-third day of the Omer! And the walks through the forest! These, however, had nothing to do with the teacher, but came direct from the Holy and Blest One. The Thirty-third day of the Omer was His and the forest was His, and the wild apples and wild nuts and "Kol Nidre!" pears were all His; and so were the birds' nests and the wild grapes, together with the Fridays and the Sabbaths; and we just picked it all up where it lay for the taking! Oh, how sweet was one hour of that irresponsible freedom!

There was a big branchy, shady berry tree just opposite the entrance to my father's place at the wayside, with a hollow trunk within which there was a beehive and honey. And every evening we would warily help ourselves to a little of the honey. While behind our house there was a curly birch with long hair standing and dripping with resin in the springtime: and we would catch it in some broken dish and drink it; and the resin was very sweet and clear indeed. Oh friend, friend! Why must a man grow up?

The "mixed" teacher was a pleasant fellow with a good deal of nobility about him, pure of eye and a poet by nature. He and his son were talented and could draw beautiful pictures for the *mizrah* (stylized representation of the Wailing Wall in Jerusalem which were hung on the eastern walls of living rooms in memory of the verse in Psalms "If I forget Thee O Jerusalem, let my right hand forget its cunning"), the plan of the Tabernacle and its vessels, the Candelabrum, all kinds of queer outlandish creatures. The teacher's son used to cut out the shapes from paper with a pair of scissors and would paste them on the window-panes so that folk outside might enjoy them as well. His tiny house with the little booth beside it stood on the slope of the hill leaning over as though about to fall at any moment into the abyss yawning below. . . . And there down in the valley bed, there was a spring flowing and darting and chattering and helping us to chant the Psalms which our teacher taught us in summer under the open sky or under the foliage that covered the booth. In this heder I first began to understand the things I was repeating, and the teacher was very fond of me and loved me. I remember that when I once asked him a knotty point which arose in my mind out of Rashi's commentary, he was as pleased with me as though he had discovered a great treasure, for the point was one that had struck one of the other ancient commentators (at the time I was seven years old). He praised me to my face and showed me to my fellow pupils as a prodigy, though they were much older than I.

This teacher would interpret the simpler Sabbath hymns to us, and at his order we would learn them by heart.

Before two years had passed in this delightful little suburb my father died of poverty and need after a prolonged illness which consumed our household as might the moth. My mother remained a desolate widow with three small children on her hands.

Days of darkness and gloomy oppression came upon us. That period has realized itself in my imagination in the form of a vision which, like that of the dwarves, I actually saw with my eyes, and which will never vanish from my sight. It is a wintry twilight. Outside everything is gloom and darkness, and a furious raging snowstorm. But in the house it is doubly gloomy, doubly dark, with desolation too heavy to bear in all the corners. The two rooms of the tavern stand poor, mournful and empty; and this emptiness seems to have doubled their size. There is far too much space about them. . . . All that day not a single peasant had come there. My mother sat behind the little kegs of spirits, which were empty, her hands on her heart, silent but shaking her head. My little sister and brother sat barefoot on a bench, silent as well. On the floor of the house were little hollows filled with mud and dirty water; I sat kneeling near the stove, shivering and goose-fleshed with cold, my eyes fixed on the stove and the bits of wet wood on which the fire was just beginning to take hold, quivering and starting with weak little tongues that timidly licked at the ragged bark all around. We were all hungry and all half-dazed with cold. The tongues of fire did their best, twist, lick, take on all kinds of colors, yellow, white, red, blue. . . . Tiny snakes. . . . Bits of wood seethe and snap and burst, snap, snap. And everytime there would exude from the crack an ugly drop of green dirt which would spurt and squirt furiously into the fire. I am cold, it is dark, I am hungry. I try to make myself still smaller at the mouth of the stove in the hope that I may feel warmer. Suddenly a tiny, very thin woman, as broad and tall as my finger, appeared from the well of the stove against which I was crouching, came out of there dressed in filthy garments, with a filthy three-pointed kerchief round her head. She went walking along the wall until she entered the mouth of the stove and seated herself on the end of the piece of wood sticking out from there. Suddenly she catches hold of the two ends of the cotton shawl, worn and tattered, which is round my neck and begins dragging, dragging, dragging me down into the stove. . . . I was all but choked. "Mother!" I wished to cry, but the power of speech had departed from me.

My mother could not maintain all her orphans, so brought me to the home of my father's father at the other end of the same town. And here began the second chapter of my life, a chapter of orphaned and foolish education—education that sundered body and soul.

My grandfather was comfortably off and very old, well over seventy, and for the past fifty years had bade adieu to the foolishness of the world and its affairs, remaining closed in his house and engaging solely in Torah for its own sake. By nature he was stern, ascetic and no easy taskmaster, and like most old people had forgotten the spirit and needs of childhood; he disapproved of childhood and its happiness. He felt the burden of looking after me in his old age as something too heavy to bear but which could not be avoided; as at best a commandment which demanded fulfillment at something other than its proper season but which he had of necessity to fulfil according to all the rules and regulations of the codes even though he might not wish to do so. So the old man educated me after *his* fashion, giving me a training in the Fear of God according to the *Reshith Hokmah* and *Shobet Musar* and *Sefer Hasidim*. All my self-reliant movements of behavior were abominable to him. Everything had to be done according to the book and fashioned according to the taste of the ancients, even the clothes I wore; and they were cut after his own.

My grandfather placed me in the usual schools. My first teachers were bears who performed the work of the Lord with fist and strap. Since I was an orphan, hot-tempered and a scamp, I naturally came in for more beatings and blows than all the rest. Incidentally, uncles and cousins took a hand in the good work of teaching me how to behave, together with kinsfolk and neighbors. Many of my aunts and uncles were jealous of me because my talents and knowledge were greater than those of their own children; and they always endeavored to make the old man disapprove of me for all he was worth.

"Just have a look what Isaac Yosi (my father's name) has left behind him," they would say to the old man whenever they saw me entering or leaving his house. "Today that grandson of yours smashed a window at so-and-so's house. That jewel of yours swore at so and so today." And many more such silly charges, whether false or true. Sometimes they would gather together at my grandfather's house to take counsel as to what was to be done with the ruffian. And the end of the discussion would be a thrashing. I would be thrashed by them all jointly. One would let down my breeches, another lift me over his knees, one held me by the legs, another by the arms and another would do the thrashing, proper. Sometimes they would shame me in public at the House of Study and make me bitterly angry and empty filth on my spirit. Such hours of shame degraded me and made me feel contemptible. Hatred and vengeance would heat my soul and sear my little heart. I'll pay them out when I grow up; that was what I was always thinking.

And sure enough this teaching yielded fruit. I became excitable, bad-tempered and malicious and used to work off my hot spirits with all kinds of mischief, in which I achieved for more than the normal run of scamps; and my orphan state served to draw all eyes upon me so that I became notorious throughout the neighborhood, notorious and famous simultaneously.

And my grandfather, who had become a widower, now married a new grandmother, who was excitable and noisy and shouted a great deal when angry, and good-hearted and talkative when in a good mood. When things were all right she would sit knitting socks and telling me fine tales of the good old times and all the marvels performed by her ancestor the Baal Shem Tob, from whom she claimed to be descended, "may his merits protect us. Amen." And I would hang my eyes on her lips, prick my ears up, open my mouth wide, and listen with vast devotion and swallow it all. Listen and swallow. . . .

In my grandfather's house there was a bookcase full of all kinds of outlandish books covering every range of Jewish literature. Legend, law, homilies, ethics, wonder tales and hasidic legends, Kabbalah and a few early research studies and so on and so forth. When I was finished with my studies at the heder I would start looking at these volumes, passing from easy to difficult. The wish to read took possession of me from childhood and every book that came my way, no matter what it might be, I held fast to until I had some detailed or vague idea of its contents. This reading possessed my heart and brain and turned me into a daydreamer. Fragments of ancient ideas and slivers of thought and imaginings with many useless things went coursing in a muddle through my mind; and out of them I would fashion myself all kinds of queer universes.

Somehow or other books of the Enlightenment came my way. Deuce knows where they came to me from but they came. Gradually these books began to attract me and divert me from Torah and from faith. They came my way at a time when my piety and hasidic spirit had risen within me to their absolute peak. And by that time I was already awaiting the Holy Spirit on the basis of Rabbi Hayyim Vital's book *Shaar Ha-Kedusha* (the Gates of Holiness), which teaches how the Holy Spirit can be attained. I hallowed and purified myself with Torah, prayer, immersions and holy concentrations of thought and so on and so forth; and there the secular literature was all of a sudden. . . .

When I was thirteen years old I left the schools to study. Absolutely by myself, far apart from the *dayan* (judge, the title of an assistant rabbi in a large town, who would remain in the House of Study until midday) there was not a soul to be found there. Those who dwelt in the suburb were mostly those middle-class people so common of late, who had nothing that interested them in their world except business and money. The dayan, who was a worthy and straightforward man, joined me of his own free will and like comrades we studied Gemara and rabbinical authorities several hours a day. Before a year had passed I had reached the point where I could instruct regarding that which is prohibited and that which is permissible. For even before that my chief studies had been Gemara and Authorities; and when the dayan was not at home I would decide ritual questions in his place.

For the rest of the day I would read much in secular books and write poems on the things I was thinking of. The desire to write had been in me from childhood and I remember that even when I was small and did not yet know how to write my letters properly I used to spoil any amount of paper writing down the conversation of the children and the tales I heard them tell at heder.

After many misadventures which it is difficult for me to touch upon now, I made the journey to Wolozhin at the age of fifteen on the strength of rumors current among the boys in town that at Wolozhin, together with the Talmud, they also taught either openly or secretly the seven wisdoms and the seventy tongues; and that there was barely more than a single step from Wolozhin to Berlin itself. In brief, however, I learned at Wolozhin neither the seven wisdoms nor the seventy tongues, but only how to read Russian. In place of this, however, I devoted myself for the last few months to the study of the Talmud and made great progress. "It can't be anything else but that you are the descendant of a Litvak," said the head of the yeshiba to me during the examination three months after I had come. "This is the first time that I find a boy from Volhynia who knows Talmud as you do." I had almost despaired of the Enlightenment, and the diadem of the rabbinate once more began to gleam before me; were it not that "all those who have come thither do not return."

Day by day my first enthusiasm for the Talmud declined. I would stand at my lectern for hours on end, my mouth repeating "Abaya says" but my heart in quite different words. During the early days of spring I would vanish from the yeshibah and dash as though crazy through the entries and the alleys of the town, my spirit beating frantically like a captive bird.

Those were the days when the first essays of Ahad Ha'am had begun to appear. The best and most enlightened of the Wolozhin lads formed a single group and took oath to devote their lives and abilities to work for their nation. The idea underlying the society they formed was really fine. They argued thus: The Wolozhin yeshibah is the center of the best forces and a refuge for the best talents, which must ultimately be scattered afresh through the Jewish people, to enter into it and take the lead, some as rabbis, some as doctors and scholars, some as presidents and as leaders of the community and some as writers in Israel. For this reason we ought to establish a permanent "nursery garden" of lovers of Zion among the Wolozhin lads and these would afterwards turn everybody into lovers of Zion, and the like. The society was founded and consisted of the best and finest and most disinterested of the yeshibah. Before a member was accepted he was examined sevenfold from every side, and only those were chosen who showed reason for hoping that they would be a blessing to the community in future. I, too, as a future writer (which was already my reputation) was one of those accepted. In a little while two tendencies began to mark themselves in this society: that of Ahad Ha'am and that of Yabetz. I was one of the former. The very name of Ahad Ha'am brought a sort of sacred affection to my heart. Until Ahad Ha'am, I had loved but had not honored the new Hebrew literature, but that sense of honor suddenly started within me immediately after I had read his first essays. The day I read an essay by Ahad Ha'am was a festival for me. Every word which came forth from his pen seemed to be directed to the very center of my heart and to express the quintessence of my thought. My heart prophesied to me that with him a new lustrum was coming in our literary world. At this very time I wrote my first literary attempt at the request of the fellow members of the Society. It was entitled *On the Idea of the Yishub* and was printed in *Ha-Melitz*. This essay was to have served as a sort of manifesto of our society and an expression of its views. I neither knew nor remember the value of this essay, but do remember that it was written in the spirit of both Ahad Ha'am and Yabetz. But at that time there was a new spirit abroad in the yeshibah and its pillars grew weak. Everybody saw that its time had come and its end was approaching. So I told myself, let me get away from here in good time to some other place where I can study in my own fashion. And at the advice and with the assistance of a few of my companions and confidants I went to Odessa in order to prepare myself for Berlin. This departure was made without the knowledge of my grandfather and family.

Wild and dumb, speechless and without manners, I came to Odessa and suffered there for about six months without anybody taking notice of me. An Odessa rabbi who took me into his house found me lessons to a value of twelve rubles a month and a German teacher (an agriculturist) who translated Schiller and Lessing for me into Russian. My pupils did not understand a word of Yiddish and I understood Russian only with difficulty; and now you may imagine the sort of things I taught and learnt. Whenever the time for my lesson came I would have liked to die. Shame, contempt, spiritual suffering. Never have I suffered so painfully as in those lessons. But thank the Lord, the lessons came to an end of themselves within a month. My teacher married and I was left without anything. In Odessa I began to read a little classical Russian literature such as Gogol and Dostoyevsky, and my eyes were opened to a new world. Nevertheless I was careful not to devote myself to Russian too much. I was to get most of my knowledge in Germany, so why waste time to no purpose on Russian.

Meanwhile, however, everything had come to a finish. There was nothing to eat, the Wolozhin yeshibah had been closed and I received a letter from my grandfather (through Wolozhin, sent on by my companions who had remained there) that he was about to die. And my friends wrote me from Zhitomir: "Return home. If your grandfather learns that you are in Odessa it will hasten his end." I wandered like a lost sheep through the streets of Odessa and decided to return home; and let my end be as that of all other Jewish lads.

I forgot to tell you that in Odessa a small collection of my poems came into the hands of the famous writer, Moses L. Lilienblum who chose one of them (*To the Bird*) for publication in a miscellany to be known as *Ha-Pardes;* and he sent it to Ahad Ha'am, who sent me on to Ravnitsky. The latter accepted the poem for *Ha-Pardes,* paid a little attention to me and did something to make me feel at home; but he too could not help me. I would come and visit him at his house on occasion, and the two of us would sit and remain silent together.

I finished off like the other young men in Israel. At the age of eighteen I came under the bridal canopy and from the bridal canopy to commerce; and full stop.

All the time after Odessa, both before and after my wedding, I devoted myself to reading and read much Russian. Afterwards, when I engaged in the forest trade, I spent a number of years alone in the woods. A couple of years ago I lost the little money I had and became a teacher. Now I am thirty years old.

Thus for the open part of my history; but the secret part—which in my opinion constitutes the essential history of every man—that remains deep in the heart and is not talked about.

Finally I shall tell you one thing: all the events of my life are no more than separate fragmentary notes of different instruments each playing for itself, which have all come together to the same place by chance. And if they nevertheless all combine to make some sort of tune it is nothing other than a miracle.

And something else: all my powers have drawn and been maintained, like any wild plant, from what is ready, from what is close at hand and what falls upon it from heaven. And if they are not a barren tree, it is nothing but the bounty of God.

Alone, alone, in a dark corner I grow all my life. I bore and buried seven dreams a day and no man knew I spread my hands like a fearful mother over the tender and modest blossoms of my heart concealing them from the mocking eyes of the gross crowd round about who scorned and laughed at all things wherein my spirit lived.

And when I returned from Odessa to my family, desperate and defeated, the same people received me with secret vengeance and open mockery. "Ha, ha, ha, Hayyim Nahman," one of my uncles slapped on the shoulder, "You've come back to us at last." As much as to say, "and now you'll be one of us."

My instinct of self-preservation taught me to conceal my holy of holies in the deepest places of the heart, and on the surface I became like one of them. My content, soft and tender, since my creation became surrounded with a hard shell on which anybody trying to injure it would break its teeth. In this way it was preserved from their polluting breath, from the gaze of their evil eyes and the fumbling dirty hands of those among whom I lived.

CHILDHOOD IN LITHUANIA

REBECCA HIMBER BERG (1878-   )

The author of this memoir was sixty when she began to compose. She is a born storyteller, and her experiences as a child in Lithuania, as a mother struggling for survival in the squalor of the London ghetto, as the wife of a mechanic of the Seaboard Airline Railroad in Portsmouth, Virginia, and finally as the happy matriarch of three children of high intellectual attainments, is rich material for her pen. "It was in these circumstances—highly favorable to a review of her whole life—," writes her son in a letter, "that she decided to write her memoirs. I think my praise of a small sketch (for my diversion and at my insistence, of an episode which she had described to me with great spirit and fine humor) had a good deal to do with the larger undertaking, despite her insistence that she was writing her autobiography entirely for the benefit of her children—so that they might understand her and her times. In brief, I suspect that she always had literary aspirations—and talent." Mrs. Berg rarely misses a class in English for foreigners—the memoirs are written in Yiddish—where she is reported to be the star pupil.

❋ ❋ ❋

PROPERLY, I ought to begin this account by telling when I was born. But—I am ashamed to admit it—I do not know. You see, I was only a Jewish girl, and in my day and time, in the place where I was born, female births were not recorded.

With a boy it was different. The Jewish community and the Russian Government collaborated in observing his birthdays. The Jewish community had to know when he would be thirteen, so that he could then be confirmed in the faith of his fathers; while the Russian Government wanted to know when he was twenty-one, and a year or two later would not do at all—because they wanted him for the army. But a girl! It was enough if one reckoned that she was born some time before the "big fire," and after that one could begin checking off the places where she

269

had lived—at Sarah Rifke's one year; at Yankel Hirsh's five years; at Sarah Nachman's three years—and if one happened to miss a place or two, what did it matter? Could it hurt a girl to be a few years younger?

Therefore I must begin my autobiography, and count my years as pleases me. I was born more than sixty years ago, and the world into which I was born was—then as now—bad for the Jews. My birthplace was Yanesok, in Lithuania.

My father was a poor man, a petty merchant. He had a reputation as a scholar, which meant that he spent most of his time in the synagogue when he should have been earning a living. I was the youngest child of many, and therefore I know nothing of my parents when they were young. An older sister of mine once told me that they were formerly well off, but when I remember them they were desperately poor, and for the rest of their lives they remained so.

My mother was, I think, an interesting woman. In those days she was slightly in ill-repute as a modern. She spoke a number of languages quite well—German, Russian, Polish, Lithuanian, Latvian—and she was well-read, but in her day, especially in the villages, it was better for a woman if she concealed her knowledge. When I began to grow up she told me something of her past. She was born in Jacobstadt, which is a town in Courland, near the German border. Her mother died in childbirth, and she was reared by a stepmother. Her father was a dayan, which is to say he used to assist the rabbi in judgments involving Jews, and these judgments were accepted as legally binding by the Russian law courts. He was a shrewd man in drawing truth from reluctant witnesses, and a fair man in rendering decisions. His second wife, my mother's stepmother, ran a tavern that was patronized by both Jews and gentiles. Jacobstadt at that time was a fine and handsome town, and a large military garrison was stationed there. My mother's beauty attracted a number of young officers to the place, and they used to chat with her and pay her many compliments. On that account her father was in great haste to get her married off, and married off she was when she was only fourteen.

Each year, as the custom was, my mother used to give birth to a child, but by the time I was grown, there were few of them left. Some had immigrated, far overseas, and some had died, and my mother was old and sick with grief over them before her time.

At the time I begin my story, I was the only child left at home. A married sister, many years older than myself, lived elsewhere in the village. So that my mother and I were drawn closely together, and she would sit and talk to me for hours, not as to a child, but as if she had found in me a good friend, who could understand her, in whom she could confide. And I did in fact understand her, and the words she used to speak to me are still engraved in my heart. I remember even the German and Russian songs she used to sing for me, in a low voice, because it was forbidden a woman to sing aloud. But even when she sang under her breath, it was sweet and sorrowful, as if a lost soul was weeping that could not find its place of peace. Tears would come to her eyes, and then I would throw my arms around her and say: "Mother, you will see. When I get married I will take you with me, against everybody in the world."

And my mother would kiss me and laugh bitterly. Now I understand her bitter laughter. Time serves no one's convenience.

As a child I suppose I was as other children. I played, I cried. Life was bitter around me and I knew nothing about it. Therefore I prefer to begin my story with the time when I began to notice and to understand things. Five years at Gershon Kremer's, a year at Sarah Rifke's— I must have been about fourteen years old, and we were living at Yankel Hirsh's.

Yankel Hirsh was a shoemaker, but he had done well for himself in this world. He owned a house with nine rooms, and also a wife, eight children, and a cow. The milk from the cow was sold in the village, and six of the nine rooms were rented out to tenants. In one of the rooms we used to live. It was regarded as the best room because one of the walls was built adjoining the back of a huge oven, and it was warm in winter. And in summer as well.

In the second room lived a melamed, a Hebrew teacher. He was an undersized Jew, with a fat little belly that seemed to stick out almost to a point, a pockmarked face, and two tiny eyes, like splinters. In the center of his face a nose was planted, but you saw no more than the tip of it, for his face was puffed up around it like a cake that had risen too high in the oven. He carried a whip with him constantly, as a policeman over here carries a club. He had no children of his own—may it never be said of a Jew—so he used to give vent to his temper on the poor children, his pupils. Every few minutes you could hear through the walls the stifled sobbing of a child. They were whipped double for crying aloud.

In a third room lived a widow with three children. She used to make her living selling meat, which she made kosher at home, and then peddled from door to door. She was my father's customer, my father being, you might say, in the meat business.

After the evening prayer, whenever the spirit moved him, my father would rush around to the market, and if there were a few peasants still around, he would buy up their produce—at a cheap rate because it was usually their last. Sometimes it was a sack of corn, sometimes a bundle of flax. In the course of a month or so he would have a wagon load. And then he would hire a horse and wagon, and drive with the load over the border to Latvia.

In those days Jews used to have to pay a heavy tax on kosher meat. But my father would trade his load for meat, and smuggle the meat home—fisnogis, which is calves' feet for jelly, to be distributed among neighbors, and a side of calf for the widow. But one had to be careful as with a theft. If a Jew were caught with as much as one contraband calf's foot, he would be fined three rubles, and the calf's foot would be taken away from him. A fine business! To pay three rubles when the whole value of the fisnogis was no more than a few kopecks. It was a terrific risk. But my father was a bold man in such matters.

Once, however, he was nearly caught. The neighbors said afterwards that only because Reb Velvel, my father, was such a pious man did God save him from the hands of the gentiles. It happened in this manner:

In every town the Czar stationed a Jewish official, a dershednik, whose business it was to collect the tax, and you can well imagine what sort of a Jew that would be. It was an important post for a Jew in Russia; like here a policeman, but one had also to be like a policeman —a villain, a murderer—to rise so high. One had to be able to tear the flesh from living human beings. And such a one there was among us, a renegade, whom the government had covered with medals. He had the keenest nose to smell out an innocent fisnogis, or maybe it would be a liver, or a side of goat meat. And when Baer Shepps, for that was his kosher name, was to be seen running through the streets in circles like a poisoned rat, then it was known that he had detected somewhere some contraband. And soon, for a fact, there was Baer Shepps coming out of a house with a sack of smuggled veal over his shoulder, and behind him, like a lamb being led to slaughter, the poor Jew who had been caught.

Unhappy Jew. Full well he knew what was in store for him. One did not escape lightly from Baer Shepps' hands. An hour later Baer Shepps would visit the home again, and this time emerge with pillows and a pair of copper candlesticks, in lieu of the fine. For when in his whole life did the little Jew, "the arch criminal," possess three rubles? His whole wealth lay in those same copper candlesticks and the pillows which Baer was now carrying off in triumph. How many nights had his wife sat up with the children, picking the feathers for the pillows! The mother would say to the little ones: "Children, if you finish all the feathers tonight, there will be a *beigel* for each one of you in the morning." And when the children would hear: "A beigel for breakfast!" then their tiny fingers would fly until they would drop asleep from sheer weariness, and it would be impossible to distinguish the sleeping children from the basket of feathers.

In just such houses would Baer Shepps seek out his prey. And it happened at one time that my father smuggled in a load of meat—a whole half-dozen calves' feet, a lung and liver, and a side of meat for the widow. And Baer Shepps somehow got wind of it.

My father had left the pack with the smuggled goods close to a window, and had gone off to the synagogue to give thanks. And I, as it happened, found no vacant chair, and so I spread a white cloth over the bundle, and seating myself upon it, I began to knit a shawl for a neighbor. Because this was to be the very first money I had ever earned, I was happy, and I hummed to myself as I worked. The bundles of wool were on the floor nearby, and my mother was busy unraveling them for me. Just then two women rushed in with faces pale as death, and scarcely able to talk for fright.

"Grandmother," they cried. "God be with you! Baer Shepps is coming!"

My mother trembled with fear, and I sat paralyzed, unable to move. And the smuggled goods were under me. Hastily my mother and the women piled a few things around me, partly concealing the bundle, and I sat with beating heart and resumed my knitting. In marched Baer Shepps like a grenadier, and began to throw things around in his search. He looked under the bed, under the table, in all the corners, everywhere but the right place. Afterwards he went outside to search in the woodshed, and when he returned his eyes were blazing like those of a wild beast in the forest. This time he noticed me, as if the first time. He threw several piercing glances in my direction, but he did not disturb the bundle on which I sat. Finally, he approached and picked up a German book that lay near me. He turned a few pages, and then he pinched my cheek.

"Do you know," he said, "you are a pretty girl. And you read

German? Does that idiot, your father, who has his back bent all day long over a Gemara—does he permit it?"

I did not answer.

"Do you know what," he said. "One kiss from you, and your father could bring in all the stinking calves' feet he pleased."

With this he stroked my hair, pinched my cheek again, made a few obscene Russian gestures, spat on the floor, and left.

No sooner was he gone than all the neighbors came rushing in, and they fairly wept with joy. The widow danced like a little girl. And all agreed that we had been saved by a miracle. God had made Baer Shepps blind at just this particular time, and we prayed that he might remain so forever.

Two rooms of the house in which we lived were occupied by Yankel Hirsh and his wife and eight children. There was really only one room, partitioned off with rude boards into a sleeping chamber and a workshop. In the rear compartment, which held the oven, stood a huge sleeping bench, which served during the day as a dining table and workbench, and at night returned to its original purpose. It was large enough to hold all eight children, packed in a row across the width. And if one child wetted itself during its sleep, the others would dry it.

Yankel Hirsh, our landlord, the shoemaker, was a tall thin Jew, with a bad stomach, who went about continually belching. His first wife had died, leaving him with two children. The second Mrs. Hirsh was a short, fat woman, everlastingly big with child. She had already delivered six children into the world, and was, of course, on her way to the seventh.

I have never made up my mind whether the women in those days were heroines or animals. When the time came to give birth to a child, an old woman was called in, a midwife. She made small ceremony about the affair. The prospective mother was ordered to lie down in bed, and soon after there was a cry of pain and the wailing of a child. Mazeltov! And the very next day you could see the mother sitting up in bed, supping of a huge bowl of groats, and looking smugly innocent of the whole business, as if not she were intended. Nor was there much trouble taken with the new arrival. An old dress would be torn into strips and bound tightly around the baby's body, hindering all movement. It would then be placed into its cradle, and one of the other children, hardly much older, would be assigned the task of rocking it, and of tending to it thereafter. And if the newborn child cried excessively, the mother would take a little bread and sugar, chew it into a pap, and stick it into the infant's mouth. And all would be peaceful again. As for the other children, they wallowed about undisturbed on the floor, smeared with dirt, and with other things as well. Children were cheap in those days. Therefore people could afford to have them often.

And now, into Yankel Hirsh's already crowded establishment, a father brought another darling, his ten-year old son, to learn the cobbler's trade. The boy pleased Hirsh, and a contract was made for three years, for which the father had to pay only ten rubles. Before he left, the father called his son aside, and said to him sternly:

"Listen well, Meishke! From this day, and for time and time to come, this is your new home. Obey your master and your mistress."

And he went away with a light heart. With the help of God, and only ten rubles, he had provided for his son's future, and also rid himself of one of his burdens. It had not been easy to raise ten rubles, but now that it was done, he was pleased. Yankel Hirsh was well thought of as a master. He was hot-tempered, but he kept a good table, and most important of all, he set the apprentice immediately to work learning the trade.

Room was made for Meishke, the apprentice, on the bench where the eight children slept. Close by, hanging by four ropes from the ceiling, was a wooden box that served as the cradle for the youngest child. When the child cried during the night, it was Meishke's job to rouse himself and begin rocking. The job never bothered Meishke. He used to sleep with one hand resting on the cradle. And if the baby so much as whimpered, the boy's hand would automatically begin rocking, without his waking from sleep. Apparently he had had practice at home.

His mistress was, therefore, highly pleased with him. Every morning she gave him a glass of tea with milk, and stroked his hair. And Meishke for a glass of tea and a kind word was willing to go through fire and water. He loved his mistress more than he did his own mother, and followed her about like a faithful dog. When he was through with his own work, he would run to help his mistress.

Once, when he was helping her milk the cows, he noticed that the pails were partly filled with water. He said nothing until she began milking, and then suddenly he began to laugh immoderately. "See, mistress," he said, choking with laughter, "you have forgotten to pour out the water."

His mistress smiled. "I'll tell you, child. You must not question what older people do. Pure milk is unhealthy; it leads to constipation. Therefore we have to add water."

Meishke was satisfied with the explanation. He was a simple-minded child. Nevertheless, he was an apt apprentice, who learned the trade quickly, and soon was doing the work of a full-grown man. Even his master, who was enabled thereby to sleep through most of the day, had to acknowledge himself pleased.

At five in the morning Meishke would rise, and he and the master's oldest son, a boy of eleven, would work at the bench, while the mistress cooked breakfast, and the master scratched himself. Soon the pungent odor of roast herring would fill the room. Over the herring the mistress would pour boiling water, and in a moment a rich steaming herring soup was ready. . . . The herring was for the master; the soup for the apprentice, and for the children. In addition, a large pot of potatoes would be prepared for the whole household. And the master would call out: "Children, wake up! The potatoes will grow cold!"

The children would scramble out of bed, wet and bedraggled in their night clothes, and crowd around the table. The chickens, kept in a coop under the oven, would begin to cackle, the rooster to crow. The cow, in the yard outside, would low. And the neighbors, as if attracted by the noise, would begin to stream into the kitchen for their hot water, which the mistress prepared for all the tenants.

And the children would grab the scalding potatoes with the corners of their nightclothes and seating themselves on the floor, they would begin to eat breakfast, all together. The peelings would be fed to the chickens. The cat, too, would draw close and rub itself purring against the legs of the children. The cat, the chickens, the children, all partners. A lively world!

Breakfast over, Meishke and the master's son would return to their work. And as he tapped with his hammer, Meishke sang. His eyes were still heavy with sleep, his hair thick with feathers, but he sang light-heartedly. He liked it here. Home had never been so good.

But a tragedy was due which was to mar all of Meishke's childish happiness, and to sour the remaining days of his youth and apprentice-ship. It happened on an occasion of great joy—when the sister of his mistress was, with the help of God, finally married.

Our landlady's sister was no longer young—past thirty, and to make matters worse, she had no great dowry. Moreover, she had to take care of her old blind mother. She had, therefore, been long given up as hopeless. But, as the old women used to say, even before a girl is born, the name of her betrothed is called out in heaven. True as gold! For heaven assuredly had a hand in the betrothal of Rosa-Leah, the sister.

Among us Jews, in the old country, Purim was quite a holiday. No small matter, indeed, to have gotten rid of Haman, the evil one. It certainly called for a schnapps or two. True, Haman had given birth to a breed worse than himself—in place of the one Haman there were now thousands! But a Jew lives in hope. The God of Israel had permitter him to suffer so long on this earth; he would permit him to suffer a little longer. Accordingly on Purim he drank until he was merry, and then ran joyfully to the synagogue, where he beat his hands and stamped on the floor, and each beat was a blow to Haman dead and buried these thousands of years. Returning home he was joyful. He had reckoned for once with his enemy!

At Yankel Hirsh's it was the custom to invite many of the towns-people to a Purim celebration. Chia Feige, his wife, would make *teiglich*, syrup cakes, and the men would eat the teiglich and play cards with sticky fingers. At one of these celebrations a stranger appeared, an elderly man who came in the company of his brother, a townsman. All marveled to look at him. So old a man, with so well combed a beard, and such a clean white shirt, like a banker. It was observed that every few minutes this elderly Jew would turn to steal a glance at the landlady's sister, who was busy serving the guests. And sure enough, the very next day, the marriage broker of the town paid a visit.

Chia Fegie saw him, and wondered. She called him aside. "What have you good to tell me!"

And the marriage broker answered: "Such good as I could wish upon all Jews. I have a husband for your sister."

And he went on to explain: "You observed, did you not, a fine, well-dressed Jew at the celebration, with a neatly combed beard?"

"I saw him," Chia Feige said, "and I wondered. Why should so old a man dress up like a youth to his wedding."

"Wait! Wait! He is not so old. Not even past sixty. I assure you. And wealthy. I could wish to have twelve daughters of my own if I thought I could find for them such fine bridegrooms. And he wants to marry your sister. Just so! Without a dowry. Could you believe such a thing! Would you dare to hope for better!"

Naturally, Chia Feige was not content with this. She asked questions.

"He had a wife," the marriage broker answered. "She died last year. He has, it is true, four daughters, all married, but he has—may it never be said of a Jew—no son. He owns his own house, left to him by a grandfather, and he has made improvements—a new straw roof, and a barn where he keeps his own cow. In his youth he was a tailor, one of the best, but now he has given up working in the city. But he still does work for the peasants in the country, and they pay him well, even better than he was paid in the city. True, the peasants have no money to pay him with, but they bring him sacks of flour, beans, barley, eggs, and sometimes even a chicken. His house is stocked from top to bottom with good things to eat, so what does he want with money? And who said there is no money? There is even money. His own brother told me that when the man's wife died, there was found under her pillow a ruble and twenty kopecks. But he would not touch a penny of it. Gave it to the old men to say prayers for her soul, you understand me. Money has no value for him. And if his wife should still need a few groschen, for a bath, let us suppose—why, she can take in washing, and earn enough for a bath, and other luxuries besides. You understand me? A man in the prime of his life—not yet seventy. And generous. His daughters fight to have him with them, but he wants to marry again. Why not? God has helped him, his first wife is dead. Why shouldn't he marry again? And he has no son—God forbid it should remain so. And this fine Jew has seen your sister, and—would you believe me?— he is enamored of her. He says a mother-in-law who is blind is better than one who sees everything. Ha! ha! A lively youth! I tell you, it is a stroke of good fortune such as comes only once in a lifetime!"

And Chia Feige had to agree. She kindled with enthusiasm. In short, the wedding was arranged, and all mothers with elderly daughters were genuinely envious. The wedding was such as no one had dreamed of. Apparently, the marriage broker had not lied. The bridegroom sent in geese, chickens, eggs, flour—enough to feed the village. Chia Feige prepared her famous syrup cakes, and permitted the children afterwards to lick up the syrup in the pans, so that they went around all day with smeared faces.

And the day after the wedding was still a holiday. Chia Feiga still wore her white apron, and wasted half the day receiving the congratulations of her neighbors and extolling the virtues of the bridegroom. And Yankel Hirsh slept.

In the afternoon, a man came in to inquire for his shoes which he had left to be patched. He was in a hurry. In a few hours he was going away on a journey. No one could find his shoes. The house was topsy-

turvy from the wedding feast. The shoes had been crammed away somewhere in a corner, and no one could remember where. They had to
wake up the master. Yankel Hirsh swore, and hunted everywhere for
the shoes, and when he found them at last and saw that they were not
mended, he turned white with rage. His own son, who was in his way,
received such a slap that two teeth were loosened. But with Meishke
he went about the business more deliberately. He grabbed the boy by
the collar and began to beat him over the head with one of the shoes,
until the blood flowed as from a slaughtered animal. In addition, he
kicked him brutally and with method, and at last threw him out of the
house.

He himself then sat down to the bench, and went to work repairing
the shoes that had caused all the trouble. And as he worked he grumbled
to himself, "Such an ingrate. I cram him with the best food . . . the
lazy brat."

Meanwhile my mother and I had happened into the house, and had
witnessed the whole scene, but we were paralyzed with fear. Now, however, we ran out into the street, and found Meishke trembling in front
of the door, half dead with pain and fright. We took him into our room,
and washed his wounds. We put cobwebs over the open cuts to check
the flow of blood, and afterwards bound up his head with a white
cloth. And we gave him bread and butter and tea. He munched the
bread apathetically, and watered the tea with his tears.

When he had somewhat recovered I said to him: "Go straight home
to your father and tell him how cruelly you have been treated."

The child dragged himself home, and hardly ten minutes had
passed when we saw him returning with his father. The man had a
look on his face that boded ill for someone. Now, I thought, there will
be a real scene. Even Yankel Hirsh, who was no coward, turned pale.

Without a word, the father brushed past us, straight into the room
of Shmuel, the Hebrew teacher. When he came out he was carrying
the whip that Shmuel used on his pupils. And then, as the shohet grasps
the chicken he is about to slaughter, he took hold of his son, Meishke,
placed him across the bench, and began to whip him until the boy
quivered with pain like an epileptic. And with every stroke of the whip,
the father yelled:

"Take that, you bandit, and that! Now you will know how to obey
your master. I work myself to the bone to get the ten rubles for your
apprenticeship. I try to make a bit of a man out of you. And this is my

reward. Remember this in the future, you worthless rascal. You are not to come back to me! Remember that!"

And before he left he asked Hirsh's pardon. "Do not hold it against us, Red Hirsh. If it happens again you have my permission to break every bone in his body."

With these words he left, without even another glance at his child. Hirsh said and did nothing. But my mother and I, innocent cause of the child's further misfortune, took Meishke into our room again, and began to stroke his hair and to soothe him. Meishke no longer wept. He seemed to feel and hear nothing.

The next morning he was back to his place at the bench, at work patching up a pair of old shoes. But he no longer sang. It was not the same Meishke. Overnight he had matured, had grown old.

And this was the same Meishke who in later years was hunted by the Czar's police, and who was known in our village as Meishke, the revolutionist.

MY ROAD TO HASIDISM

MARTIN BUBER (1878-   )

The literary quality of this personal history is characteristic of
Buber's manifold writings. Whether he is interpreting ancient Scripture, unveiling the spirit of folklore, fashioning the concept of nationalism or probing the recesses of the human spirit, his artistry is
warmed by an impassioned vision. It is for this reason that he has
inspired several generations of thinkers and scholars who regard him
as the paladin of contemporary Jewish thought. This autobiographical
excursion indicates dramatically how Buber brought into harmony
two divergent veins of culture—the mystical heritage of Israel and
the tradition of the West. He has combined them in practical life
too, for he taught Religion and Ethics at the University of Frankfurt
until 1933, and for the past several years has been a member of the
faculty of the Hebrew University in Palestine.

❋   ❋   ❋

IN MY childhood (I left Vienna, where I was born, for Galicia at
an early age, and grew up in my grandparents' home), I spent the
summers on an estate in Bukowina. Occasionally my father took
me to the neighboring town of Sadagora. Sadagora is the seat of a
dynasty of zaddikim (zaddik: a just man, a perfect man), that is, of
hasidic rabbis. The initiates talk of miracle-rabbis and consider themselves well-informed. But they are like all initiates—informed only in
the realm of external superficialities. The legendary ancestral greatness
has waned in the descendants of the zaddikim. They try to retain their
power by utilizing all kinds of petty magic, but their manipulations do
not dim the hereditary glow on their foreheads, nor distort their innate
grandeur. Their involuntary nobility is more telling than all their deliberate activity. Certainly, the soaring faith of the first hasidim is lacking
in present-day communities. The supreme devotion of the early believers
no longer exists, attended by adoration of the zaddik as the perfect man,

in whom immortality has found mortal incarnation. Our contemporaries are rather disposed to look on the zaddik principally as a mediator, through whose intercession they hope to find gratification of their mundane desires. And yet their baser inclinations are deflected; they shudder with fear when the rebbe stands in silent prayer, or, at the third Sabbath meal, holds magic discourse on the secrets of the Torah. Even these degenerates, in the unknown depths of their souls, retain Eleasar's luminous dictum: that the world was created for the sake of the perfect man, for it is said: "And God saw the light, and it was good," but good means only the perfect one (Yoma 38b).

This knowledge I acquired in my childhood, in the dirty little town of Sadagora, from the benighted hasidim. My perceptions were those of a child—not through ideas, but through pictures and emotions. I learned that the world is for the perfect man, and the perfect man is none other than the real savior. These days the zaddik is generally entreated in regard to essentially earthy needs, but is he not still, despite this, what he was once thought and held to be: the savior of the spirit, the teacher of the cosmic, the guide to the divine spark? His power is misinterpreted by the believers, he himself misuses it, but does it not remain, at bottom, the legitimate power of the abundantly overflowing soul over the soul-impoverished? Does it not contain the germ of a future order? Somewhere, in a childlike fashion, these questions dawned in me. And I was able to make comparisons. I compared the zaddik, on the one hand, with the district chief, whose power rested on habitual coercion; on the other hand, with the Rabbi, who was a righteous and God-fearing man, but the employee of a worship-directorate. Here was something incomparable; here—humbled, but uninjured—was the living germ of humanity, true community and true guidance. Something primeval and eternal was in it; something lost, yearned for, returning.

The ornate palace of the Rabbi repelled me. The hasidic house of prayer and its ecstatic congregation were strange to me. But when I watched the Rabbi stride through the rows of supplicants, I understood what a leader was; when I saw the hasidim dance with the Torah, I knew what a community was. Out of this grew the perception that common veneration and common joy are the foundations of real human communion.

During my adolescence this early perception began to slip into the unconscious. I spent my summers elsewhere and was finally on the verge of forgetting the hasidic impressions of my childhood. But after several years I returned to a newly-acquired estate of my father's, near Czortkow, which was the seat of a collateral line of the same dynasty of zaddikim. Even today the traditional memory of the great Rizhiner dominates Sadagora. He was called the great Rizhiner because he fled from the town of Ruzhyn, near Berditschev, when the Russian government suspected him of claiming kingship over the Jews. After much wandering, he settled in Sadagora. The immediate memory of his son David Moshe was alive in Czortkow. Unfortunately, I learned little about him then. My impressions this time were indistinct and fugitive. This may have been due to the fact that in the interim I had been seized by the mental ferment which frequently characterizes the decisive years of youth, awakening the creative functions of the intellect, but bringing to an end the natural vision and perception of childhood. I was intellectually estranged from the hasidim, deprived of a naive communion with their being. Because of my thinking processes, I believed myself removed from their world. I confess that I looked on them no differently from Graetz: I looked down on them from the heights of a rational man. I saw nothing of their life, even when I was directly before it, because I wanted to see nothing.

Nevertheless, though I paid no attention, I first heard, at this time, the name which I later identified with superb revelation—the name of Besht. It is made up of the initial letters of the words Baal Shem Tob (Master of the good name, therefore master of the spiritual forces). The name refers to Rabbi Israel ben Eliezer, the founder of Hasidism. One of the dairy farms of my father's estate was called after Tlust, the market town nearby. The Baal Shem had once been a poor teacher in Tlust. (The town became famous during the War, in Russian army dispatches, for it was fought over a long time.) According to legend, it was here, on the night he completed his thirty-third year, that the Baal Shem had the dream which announced that his time had come.

But during my visit, I was remote not only from Hasidism; all Judaism was strange to me.

Until my fourteenth year, I lived with my grandfather, the midrashic scholar. Salomon Buber's world was the Midrash; he lived in it with a wonderful calm of soul and intensity of labor. He issued text after text derived from the Midrash, that incomparable compilation, overabundantly rich in lore, proverb and magnificent metphor. In it, split into a thousand fragments, lies hidden a second Bible, the Bible of Exile. Without ever having acquired the philological training of the western world, my grandfather labored over the scripts with the thoroughness of a modern scholar, but he possessed, in addition, the mastery of the talmudist. The talmudist has at his command, for every sentence, and every phrase, every possible reference in his literature, not as stuff retained in the memory, but as an organic part of his whole person. The intellectual passion which is evidenced in his stream of work grew out of the untouchable, unerring childishness of an untainted soul combined with an essentially Jewish being. When he spoke Hebrew, as he always did to foreign guests, it sounded like the speech of a sovereign returned from banishment. He did not think about Judaism; he had it in him.

So long as I lived in his home, I was well-rooted, though some queries and doubts disturbed me. On my departure, the turbulence of the period assailed me. Until I was twenty, and to a lesser degree even afterward, my spirit was in constant and multiple flux. Tension and release followed one another, determined by manifold influences, forever assuming new forms, but remaining without a pivot and without cumulative substance. I really lived in the *Olam Ha-Tohu*, the world of confusion, the mythical limbo of lost souls. I experienced mobile spiritual fulfillment, but neither Judaism, nor humanity, nor the presence of the divine was in it.

Zionism provided the first impetus for my release. I can only suggest here what it meant to me: revival of coherence, equilibrium and replacement in the community. No one needs the salvation of a racial bond so much as the youth gripped in spiritual search, and flung by his intellect into the ether. A Jewish youth needs it more than any. The others are protected by thousands of years of inherited unity with a native soil and by traditional national sentiments. The Jew, even if he has a newly-acquired, natural feeling for and a cultural understanding of German natural art and customs, is nevertheless immediately threatened by it and abandoned to it insofar as he does not find his way to his own group. The most dazzling accumulation of intellectual wealth and the most wanton pseudo-productivity (only the well-rooted person can be genuinely productive), are not enough to compensate the unrooted person for his lack of the sacred insignia of humanity, of placement, of communion and unity.

That Zionism influenced me and allowed me to re-appraise Judaism was, as I said, only the first step. National confession alone does not change the Jew; he may remain as impoverished spiritually—if not quite as unsupported—with it as without. For some people, however, national confession is not sufficient unto itself, but a soaring upward. It is not a haven, but a passage to the open sea. Such people are led to transformation, and so it happened with me.

I became acquainted with Judaism before I actually comprehended it. My second step, after considerable groping, was therefore the will to cognizance. By cognizance I do not mean a storing up of anthropological, historical and social data, though these may be important. I mean the immediate recognition, the eye-to-eye recognition, of national character in its creative documentation.

That is how I came to Hasidism.

Hebrew, which was part of my boyhood background, had been neglected in the world of confusion. Now I acquired it anew. I began to take hold of it in its essence, which cannot be transmitted to any other language, least of all to an occidental language. And I read, again and again driven off by crude, awkward, unformed content, but gradually overcoming the unfamiliarity, unveiling the substance, contemplating and essence with growing devotion. One day I came on a booklet, the *Zevaat Ribesh,* the testament of Rabbi Israel Baal Shem, and these words shone before me: "He apprehended the character of ardor in its entirety. He rose from his sleep in a passion, for he was sanctified, he had become a different person, according to the characteristics of the Holy One, blessed be He, when He created the world." It was then that I, suddenly overwhelmed, experienced the hasidic soul. Something indigenously Jewish rose in me, blossoming, in the darkness of exile, to a new conscious expression. I perceived the very resemblance of man to God, as deed, as an act of becoming, as a duty. This indigenously Jewish concept was also indigenously human; it was the content of human religiosity. Judaism as religiosity, as piety, rose in me at that moment. My childhood experience, the memory of the zaddik and his followers, reawoke in me, and lighted my way. I comprehended the idea of the perfect man. And I perceived my responsibility in proclaiming it to the world.

Now came the time for study. At the age of twenty-six, I withdrew from party activity for five years. I refrained from writing and lecturing. I lived in solitude. With great effort, I gathered together what I could of the scattered literature—some of it has disappeared entirely—and sank into it, discovering one secret domain after another.

My first published work came about in a strange way. Among all the books, anthologies of the sayings of zaddikim and collections of legends about their lives, there was one volume which was peculiar and different from the others. Therefore it was the most nationally characteristic of all. It was the *Sippure Maasiyoth,* stories by Rabbi Nahman of Brazlaw, a grandson of the Baal Shem. Nahman had told these tales to his pupils. After Nahman's death, one of the pupils had written them down and published them, in an obviously distorted form. In part, they were pure fairy tales, on the oriental model, in part they were creations of a singular art, symbolic, sometimes vaguely allegorical, woven out of the calm of mystical experience and the gossamer of constructive fantasy. They were not teachable, but they possessed an instructive trait in common. Rabbi Nahman himself called them the garments of his teachings. A comprehensive commentary had been provided by the pupil. But the content was distorted by all kinds of utilitarian and vulgarly rationalistic interpolations; the form was ruined by a confusion of line and opaqueness of color, which—as one could see from certain surprising passages—had been pure to begin with.

Almost involuntarily I began to translate. I began with a few of the stories. I thought of children as my readers. When I finished, I found that what lay before me was more wretched than I had supposed; it was in no way comparable to the similar tales found in the *A Thousand and One Nights*. When I saw my pieces in print, I was utterly disheartened. This could not go on. In translation the distortions were more apparent and the organic form even less distinct. The purity was not even sustained, let alone enhanced. The stories would have to be told out of my own being, just as the painter absorbs the lines of his model in himself and creates the picture out of the formative memory. Modestly and clumsily, I began with the *Tale of the Bull and the Ram;* with added assurance and freedom, I went over to the *Tale of the Wise and the Simple,* then to *About the Son of the King and the Son of the Maid. The Tale of the Rabbi and His Son* was the first one which was born of itself, in my own writing. In the two final stories, *The Tale of the Master of Prayer,* and *The Seven Beggars,* and in the pieces I reconstructed anew, I experienced a sense of union with the spirit of Nahman. I had found real fidelity, more adequately than his immediate disciples. I had conceived and carried out the task of serving as a belated messenger to the kingdom of a strange language.

I felt my innate bond with hasidic truth even more strongly in my second book, *The Legend of the Baal Shem,* which sought to reconstruct the inner events in the life of the master through a selection of traditional sayings. These I drew from popular literature and from the spoken word. A short time after writing the first of the Nahman tales, I had begun to translate for the second book as well. And here, too, I was met by disappointment. The stories I encountered were, for the most part, recorded in a crude and clumsy form, and they failed to acquire winged words in translation. Once again, with increasing independence, I arrived at an individual form. But the more independent I became, the more profound grew my fidelity. Therefore, despite the fact that the greater part of the book consists of my own treatment of traditional motifs, I may honestly maintain that I bear within me the blood and the spirit of those who created the motifs. Through blood and spirit they were re-created in me.

Later, several years after the completion of both books, I evolved a different form of artistic fidelity to popular hasidic tales. But this does not fall within the scope of these memoranda, which tell of my way to Hasidism.

However, a humorous but significant experience I had in 1910 or 1911 does belong here. It also occurred in Bukowina, in Czernowitz, the capital, which is not far from Sadagora.

After a lecture I had given there (it was the third of my *Three Lectures on Judaism*), I went to a café with several members of the organization which had arranged the evening. I always liked to follow a formal speech, which does not permit contradiction, with an informal chat in a small group. Here conflicting views, objections and questions are brought out, and personal influences may be brought into play.

We were in the midst of a moral-philosophical discussion, when a well-built, prosperous-looking, middle-aged Jew approached our table and greeted me. My obviously cool reply brought from him a reproachful: "Doctor, don't you recognize me?" When I was forced to confess that I did not, he introduced himself as M., the brother of one of the farmers on my father's former estate. I invited him to join us. After inquiring after his personal life, I resumed the discussion with my companions. M. listened to the talk, which had taken a turn for the abstract, very intently. It was clear that he did not understand a word of it, but the devotion with which he listened was like that of believers who do not need to know the meaning of the words of a litany, since the combination of sounds gives them all the benefits they need and is more sententious than content. After a while, I asked him whether he wanted to talk to me. I would be glad, I said, to go off with him to discuss his affairs. M. said energetically that he did not. The talk resumed, and with it, M.'s attention. After another half hour had passed, I asked him again whether there was anything I could do for him. No, no, there was nothing, he assured me. The discussion came to an end, and we arose. It was late, but as frequently happens after such an hour of give-and-take, I was not tired. I felt even more refreshed than before, and decided to take a walk. At this moment M. approached me with an unspeakably shy air. "Doctor," he said, "I would like to ask you something." I told the students to wait, and sat down with him. He was silent. "Please go ahead," I said, "I will give you any information I can." "Doctor," he said, "I have a daughter." He stopped, then he continued. "And I also have a young man for my daughter." Again a pause. "He is a lawyer. He passed his examinations with honor." M. was silent again, for a longer time. I looked at him encouragingly. I assumed that he wanted me to do something for his prospective son-in-law. "Doctor," he said, "is he a good person?" I was overwhelmed, but I felt that I must not deny him a reply. "Well, Mr. M.," I explained, "after what you have told me, one may easily assume that he is diligent and capable." But he persisted: "Doctor," he asked, "has he got a good head?" "That is harder to say," I replied, "but he could not have accomplished what he did with industry alone. He must have something inside his head." Again M. was silent; then he put one more question, obviously the last. "Doctor," he said, "should he become a barrister or a solicitor?" "In that I can give no advice," I answered. "I don't know the young man and even if I did, I would hardly be able to make a suggestion on such a point." Now M.'s face assumed an expression of almost dejected resignation, half-plaintive, half-understanding. He spoke in a tone which was an indescribable fusion of grief and humility. "Doctor, you don't want to tell me, but I thank you just the same for what you have told me."

Though this amusing, meaningful incident seems to have nothing to do with Hasidism, it nevertheless gave me new insight. As a child, I had received an impression of the zaddik, and through all the surrounding pollutions of reality, I had sensed the pure idea—the idea of a real leader of a real community. In the interim between youth and manhood, there blossomed out of this perception of hasidic teaching the concept of the perfect man, the realization of God in this world. Now, in an amusing incident, I perceived the function of leadership incarnate in my own person, through my own experience. I, who was not a zaddik, not a man secured in God, but one endangered before God, a man ever wrestling anew with the light of God and ever newly offending before God's abyss—I had the inner experience of a zaddik, I had been asked about trivialities and I had replied in trivialities. The true zaddik is asked about revelation and replies with revelation. But I had experienced the fundamental conduct of his soul before the world; I knew his responsibility.

Every person has an infinite sphere of responsibility—responsibility before the infinite. He moves, he talks, he observes, and every movement, every word, very glance stirs waves in world events. How strong and how far-reaching they are he cannot know. Every man affects the fate of the world through his whole being and all his acts, to a degree unknown both to him and to others. Such unreality as we can perceive is only a tiny segment of the inconceivable, manifold, invisible influence of all on all. Every human act is a vessel of infinite responsibility. But there are some people in whom this infinite responsibility exists perpetually, in a special, unusually active form. I am not referring to rulers and statesmen, who wield power over the external destiny of large commonwealths. The sphere of their influence may be delimited, but in order to be effective, they turn from individual, enormously-menaced existences, which look on them with a thousand questions, to the abstract, which appears unseeing. I refer to those who hold their ground against the thousandfold querying glance of individual lives, who give faithful response to the trembling lips of every questioning creature that comes to ask an opinion. I mean the zaddikim, the real zaddik. He is the person who continually compounds the depths of responsibility with the lead of his words. He speaks, and knows that what he says is fate. He does not decide the destiny of countries and nations, but always and again the petty and the great paths of individual, finite and yet boundless lives. People come to him, and each one demands his verdict, his help. Though the needs they bring to him are corporal, in his discernment there is nothing corporal which does not undergo transfiguration; there is nothing material which cannot transcend into spirit. This is what he does for them all: he elevates their needs before gratifying them. So he becomes the savior in spirit, the teacher of the cosmic, the guide to the divine spark. Around him, around the perfect man and the real savior, the world revolves. It weighs against him, forever and ever.

SOURCES AND LITERATURE

There is no intention of providing here a full bibliography of Jewish autobiographical literature. Rather, the aim is to indicate the scope of the field and offer examples that will aid those who may desire to plough the field further. The following divisions give, (I) collections of literature that include autobiographical excerpts, (II) articles and books that treat of the subject interpretatively and bibliographically, and (III) sources of the selections in this book together with relevant autobiographical literature. It should be added that while periodical literature has been utilized in the preparation of this work, the items are so copious, especially during the last seventy-five years, that a description of all the references would require a little book; consequently only some of the most vital of these memoirs are included in the notes under III.

I

Anonymous ("Editors" unnamed), *Youth Amidst the Ruins,* published by Hashomer Hatzair Organization, New York, 1941. Excerpts from diaries of European pioneers-in-training during the Blitz years 1939-1940.

Appel, Judah, Editor, *Betokh Reshith ha-Tehiah,* Tel Aviv, 1936. Memoirs of members of the Hovevi Zion movement in Tsarist Russia.

Bach, Hans, Editor, *Jüdische Memoiren aus drei Jahrhunderten,* Berlin, 1936. Excerpts from the memoirs and diaries of thirteen German Jews.

Basuk, Moses, Editor, *Sefer he-Haluz,* Jerusalem, 1941. An anthology of the writings and recollections of members of the Haluz movement.

Ben Zwi, Isaac, Hashin, A., and Zerubbabel, Editors, *Yizkor, Zum Andenken fun die fallene Wachter un Arbeiter in Erez Yisrael,* New York, 1916.

————, Editor, *Kobez ha-Shomer,* Tel Aviv, 1937. Reminiscences and letters of the Shomer organization in Palestine.

Bernfeld, Simon, *Sefer ha-Demaoth,* Berlin, 1923-1926, 3 vols. Exclusively martyriological excerpts.

Broides, Isaac, Editor, *Vilna ha-Zionith we-Asakneha,* Tel Aviv, 1930. Some memoirs of Vilna Zionists, 1881-1924.

Citron, S. L., Editor, *Sefer Zikkaron,* Vilna, 1925. Friends' recollections of a remarkable woman, Esther Rubenstein.

Dinabourg, Ben-Zion, Editor, *Toledoth Yisrael,* Tel Aviv, 1926-31, vols. V, VI (each 2 parts). Occasional brief excerpts.

Eisenstein, J. D., Editor, *Ozar Masaoth,* New York, 1926. 24 texts of Jewish travelers from the 9th to the 18th centuries, a large part of which has been Englished in E. N. Adler's *Jewish Travellers,* London and New York, 1931.

Gaon, Moses David, *Yehude ha-Mizrah be-Erez Yisrael,* Jerusalem, 1928, 2 vols. Short excerpts in vol. I.

Goitein, S. D. F., Editor, *Von den Juden Jemens,* Berlin, 1934. Several interesting fragments.

Habas, Berahah, Editor, *Aliyath ha-Noar,* Jerusalem, 1941. Memoirs of youth settlers and pioneers in Palestine.

Höxter, Julius, *Quellenbuch zur jüdischen Geschichte und Literatur,* Frankfort a.M., 1922-1930, 5 vols. A one-volume abridged version in English, translated by Moses Jung, London, 1938. A number of excerpts.

Kahana, Abraham, Editor, *Sifruth ha-Historia ha-Yisraelith,* Warsaw, 1922-1923, 2 vols. Excerpts presented as historical sources.

Katzenelson-Rubashow, Rachel, Editor, *The Plough Woman,* New York, 1932. English translation from the Hebrew by Maurice Samuel. Reminiscences of pioneer women in Palestine.

Marcus, Jacob R., Editor, *The Jew in the Medieval World* (315-1791), Cincinnati, 1938. Brief excerpts as historical sources.

Schwarz, Leo W., Editor, *A Golden Treasury of Jewish Literature,* New York, 1937. Some modern literary autobiographies.

Sokolow, Nahum, Editor, *Sefer Zikkaron,* Warsaw, 1889. Brief memoirs of Hebrew writers, pp. 117-194.

Winter, J. and Wünsche, A., Editors, *Die jüdische Literatur seit Abschluss des Canons,* Trier, 1896, 3 vols. Some excerpts in vol. III.

II

Baron, Salo Wittmayer, "Biography," pp. 324-348, and supplement, pp. 214-218 in *Bibliography of Jewish Social Studies,* 1938-39, New York, 1941. Lists autobiographies published during 1938-1939.

Grunwald, Max, "Memoirenliteratur" in the *Jüdisches Lexicon,* vol. IV, pp. 71-82. Especially valuable for modern European items.

Letteris, Meir Halevi, *Zikkaron ba-Sefer,* Vienna, 1868. Opens his memoirs with a brief discussion of general and Jewish autobiography.

Marx, Alexander, "Glimpses of the Life of an Italian Rabbi of the First Half of the Sixteenth Century (David Ibn Yahya)," in *Hebrew Union College Annual,* vol. I, pp. 605-639, Cincinnati, 1924.

Roth, Cecil, Editor, "Biography," pp. 114-156 in *Magna Bibliotheca Anglo-Judaica,* London, 1937. A number of English-Jewish memoirs.

———, "The Memoirs of a Sienese Jew" in the *Hebrew Union College Annual,* vol. V, pp. 353-402. Illuminating comment and bibliography.

Schechter, Frank, "An Unfamiliar Aspect of Anglo-Jewish History" in *Publications of the American-Jewish Historical Society,* vol. XXV, pp. 63-74, Phila., 1917.

Schechter, Solomon, "A Jewish Boswell" in *Studies in Judaism,* First series, Phila., 1915, pp. 142-146.

Spiegel, Shalom, *Hebrew Reborn,* New York, 1930. Considerable reference to modern Hebrew autobiographical literature, with valuable bibliography.

Waxman, Meyer, *A History of Jewish Literature from the Close of the Bible to Our Own Days*, New York, 1932-1941, 4 vols. Discussion of memoir literature in vol. II, pp. 506-516; vol. IV, pp. 842-866, 1044-1047.

Zinberg, Israel, *Die Geschichte fun der Literatur bei Yiden*, Vilna, 1929-1935, 6 vols., 8 pts. Occasional discussion of memoirs.

FAMILY ALBUM: The manscript of Ahimaaz' memoirs—he modestly calls it *Sepher Yuhasin*—was discovered by Adolph Neubauer in the Cathedral Library of Toledo in 1895, after being buried more than 800 years, and reproduced in his *Anecdota Oxoniensia*, vol. II, pp. 111-132 (Oxford, 1895). The present translation by Leo W. Schwarz is abridged and the order of the original somewhat rearranged. Kahana has edited the text, with notes in *Sifruth ha-Historia ha-Yisraelith*, vol. I, pp. 113-140 (Warsaw, 1922), and M. Salzmann has edited a critical edition with a rather literal translation in *The Chronicle of Ahimaaz* (New York, 1924). There is also a brief self-portrait of the famous physician Sabbatai ben Abraham Donnolo (913-982), a relative of Shephatiah ben Amittai, in the Preface to his commentary on *Sefer Yezira*, p. 123 ff. (Warsaw edition). Another personality in the 9th century of whom we have a bit of autobiography is Eldad the Danite. See the English version in L. W. Schwarz' *The Jewish Caravan* (New York, 1935), pp. 193-196, and the critical edition of D. H. Müller, *Die Recensionen und Versionen des Eldad Had-dani* (Vienna, 1892). For the contemporary Arabic account of Ibn Yaaqub, a Jewish ambassador to the court of Otto the Great, see G. Jacob, *Ein Arabischer Berichterstatter aus dem 10. Jahrhundert* (Berlin, 1896).

LOGBOOK OF A PHYSICIAN: Five of these excerpts are from the personal correspondence of Maimonides, collected in A. Lichtenberg's *Kobez Teshuboth ha-Rambam* (Leipzig, 1859). The first jotting is quoted by a 16th century writer, Eliezer Askari, from an old manuscript in his *Sefer Haredim* (Sedilikow, 1836). It fittingly opens the account, despite the doubt that has been cast upon its authenticity (v. Simon Eppenstein, "Moses ben Maimon, ein Lebens- und Charakterbild" in *Moses Ben Maimon, Sein Leben, Seine Werke und Sein Einfluss*, edited by J. Guttmann, vol. II, p. 24, Leipzig, 1914). The account under "1172" is excerpted from the noteworthy *Epistle to Yemen*. The whole letter has been rendered freely from a Hebrew translation of the original Arabic, by Sabato Morais, in *The Jewish Quarterly Review*, vol. XXV, no. 4, pp. 330-369 (April, 1935). See also in the same issue, published in commemoration of the 800th anniversary of the birth of M., "Texts By And About Maimonides" by Alexander Marx, which contains the text from another manuscript of the absorbing letter to Samuel ibn Tibbon, included here under '1199' and reprinted from *Maimonides* by Yellin and Abrahams, pp. 202-203 (Phila., 1903), a handy, delightful biography. An illuminating comparative study could be made of M. and the auto-biographies of his Islamic contemporaries. Consult, e.g., Heinrich Frick, *Ghazālis Selbstbiographie* (Leipzig, 1926); the first considerable auto-biographic Arabic work of the military leader, Usāma ibn Munqidh (1095-1188) in *Souvenirs historiques*, edited by H. Derenbourg (Paris, 1895); and the travel-journal of the poet Ibn Jubyr of Valencia (1145-1217) in *Ibn Gúbayr, Viaggio*, edited by C. Schiaparelli (Rome, 1906). There are also autobiographic passages in the poetry of Judah Halevi (c. 1085-1140) and in the *Tuhḳemoni* of Judah Alharizi (1170-1230) par-ticularly the travel-diaries in "Gates" 35 (pp. 289-296) and 45 (pp. 348-369) in the edition of A. Kaminka (Warsaw, 1899) which may be compared with the literary reminiscences of the Arabic editor Yāqūt in his *Geographical and Literary Dictionary*, edited by C. Barbier de Meynard (Paris, 1861).

EVERY MAN HIS OWN MESSIAH: Slightly abridged from "Ozar Eden Ganuz" published in A. Jellinek's *Bet ha-Midrash*, vol. III, pp. xl-xlii (Leipzig, 1855), translated by I. M. Lask. The paragraph relating to the attempted conversion of the Pope is from part of the ms. of "Sefer Eduth" which was reproduced in the *Monatschrift für Geschichte und Wissenschaft des Judentums*, vol. XXXVI, p. 558 (Krotoschin, 1887). The memoir of A.'s pupil is reprinted from G. Sholem's *Major Trends in Jewish Mysticism*, pp. 145-150 (Jerusalem, 1941) where the life and thought of A. are brilliantly elaborated. The following was composed by an otherwise unknown Abraham ben Samuel whom scholars such as Jacob Reifman and Israel Davidson have identified with A. The char-acter of the writer and his individual approach have a great deal in com-mon with that of our subject, and the following translation of what is a spiritual autobiography of a high order is therefore appended here:

> To what avenger of blood shall I cry
> When my eyes are the hands that have shed my blood?
> I have tested the hearts of haters amany
> None can hate me as hates me my heart.
> Many were wounds of foes and their blows.
> None did smite and wound like my soul.
> Wanton misleaders led me to do ill.
> Nothing hath led me astray like mine eyes.
> From fire unto fire I went wandering wide.
> Flame burnt me not like my scorching desires.
> In nets and in traps I was snared, I was caught.
> Never a trap snared me like my soul.
> Scorpion and serpent have stung me and bitten.
> My flesh has been bitten more deep by my teeth.
> Princes gave chase, they pursued me for naught.
> None gave chase as chase gave me my feet.
> Yea my pains grew too mighty, too heavy for me.
> No pain so great as my obduracy.
> Aye, my grief and my sufferings at heart are increased.
> My sins even more, even more.

To whom and of whom can I make my wail
When all my destroyers come forth out of me?
Therefore I know nothing so good as to shelter in Thy hidden mercies.
Make Thy mercies plain unto those who cannot even moan
O God, O King seated on Thy Mercy Throne.

Incidentally, A.'s contemporary, Nahmanides, has recorded his experience at the religious disputation at Barcelona in 1263 in his *Sefer Vikuah ha-Ramban;* v. J. D. Eisenstein's *Ozar Vikuhim,* pp. 86-94 (New York, 1926) which contains extant texts of the most important Jewish-Christian disputations.

BY THE WATERS OF THE TAGUS; Abridged from Asheri's testament in Israel Abrahams' *Hebrew Ethical Wills,* vol. II, pp. 163-200, a testamentary collection that contains occasional autobiographical excursions. Five vivid accounts of the suffering during the Crusades by contemporaries are available in *Hebräische Berichte über die Judenverfolgungen während der Kreuzzüge,* edited by A. Neubauer and M. Stern (Berlin, 1892).

CASTILIAN VIGNETTE: From the Preface of the author's *T'sedah la-Derekh we-Zavdin le-Orha,* translated by Leo W. Schwarz. The text used is that of Kahana, *op. cit.,* vol. II, p. 33 ff. For the brief experiences of Esthori Pharhi, see the preface of *Caftor wa-Pherah,* p. 1 ff. in Edelman edition (Berlin, 1852). Incidentally, until modern times the preface was widely utilized as the literary form in Hebrew literature for autobiography. Mr. Abraham Yaari of the Library of the Hebrew University of Palestine has prepared a bibliography of about 200 examples, which is in manuscript awaiting publication. One of the best sources for memoirs in later Hebrew literature is *Kiryath Sepher* (Jerusalem, 1923—), a quarterly bibliographical review issued by the Library of the Hebrew University.

ADVENTURE IN THE HOLY LAND: A copy of the Florentine manuscript of Meshullam's letter was made by D. Kapsal and A. Berliner and sent to A. M. Luncz who published it in *Yerushalayim,* vol. I, pp. 166-219 (Vienna, 1882). It is reproduced, somewhat massaged, in Eisenstein's *Ozar Masaoth,* pp. 86-106 (New York, 1926) which was used as the text for the translation of E. Adler, *op. cit.,* pp. 156-208. The above-mentioned books contain the texts as well as references to other pilgrims in the Holy land from medieval times to the 18th century. V. also the valuable descriptive bibliography by Luncz, "Sifruth Yisrael be-Madah Erez Yisrael" in *Yerushalayim,* vol. XI-XII, pp. 1-50 (1916), and vol. XIII, pp. 18-40 (1919). An interesting parallel of an Arab historian-traveler will be found in the autobiography of Abdar-Rahman ibn Khaldun (1332-1406) edited in *Prolégomènes* by MacGuckin de Slane (Paris, 1863-68).

TWILIGHT OF SPANISH GLORY: This self-portrait has been pieced together from passages in the Prefaces to A.'s commentaries on the books of Joshua, Kings and Deuteronomy, and translated by Leo W. Schwarz from the texts in Kahana, *op. cit.*, pp. 59-64. V. the autobiographical poem of A.'s son Judah, "Telunah al ha-Zeman" in his *Vikuah al ha-Ahabah*, pp. 6-11 (Lyck, 1871). The expulsion of Jews from Spain is writ large in contemporary records: v. the account of Abraham ben Solomon of Torrutiel who brought up to date the *Sefer ha-Kabbalah* of Abraham ibn Daud and who was a lad of ten when the catastrophe occurred (in Kahana, *op. cit.*, vol. I, pp. 202-205). Among the distinguished refugees was Abraham Zacuto, historian and court astronomer to Emanuel I of Portugal, who frequently alluded to his experiences in his *Sefer Yuhasin* (v. e.g., pp. 57a, 222a-223a, 228a in Freimann edition, Frankfurt a. M., 1924) and the Preface to his astronomical work, *Der Almanach perpetuum des Abraham Zacuto,* edited by B. Cohn, with Hebrew and German texts (Strasburg, 1918). Rabbi Elijah Capsali recorded the tales of the refugees in Candia, thus presenting a vivid eyewitness account in his historical work. V. Moses Lattes, *Likkutim Shonim me-Sefer debei Eliyahu* (Padua, 1870). Similar accounts may be found in the Ibn Vergas' *Shebet Yehuda,* Gedaliah ibn Yahiah's *Shelsheleth ha-Kabbalah,* Joseph Ha-Cohen's *Emek ha-Bakha,* and Joseph ibn Yahia's *Torah Or* (Bologna, 1537-38). There are also tales by refugees in A. Marx' "The Expulsion of the Jews from Spain" in *The Jewish Quarterly Review,* Old Series, vol. XX (1908), pp. 240-271, and addenda in the New Series, vol. II (1911-12), pp. 257-258; also Jacob Moses Toledano, "Mi-Kitbe Yad" in *Hebrew Union College Annual,* vol. V (1928), pp. 403-409. A good account of the decades immediately following the expulsion can be found in S. P. Rabinowitz' *Mosaei Golah* (Warsaw, 1894).

THE ROAD TO ROME: Only a facsimile of the original ms. of the Diary remains in the Bodleian Library in Oxford. It was published by Neubauer, *op. cit.,* vol. II, pp. 133-223 and abridged in Eisenstein, *op. cit.,* from which E. Adler made an English version, *op. cit.,* pp. 251-328. The excerpt here included is the first part of the story, and it is rounded out in the following Molko selection. A handy edition of the original edited by A. Kahana was published in Warsaw, 1922. For a description of R. by Abraham Farissol, a contemporary, v. Kahana, *op. cit.,* vol. II, p. 55 ff.

POPE, EMPEROR, AND THE INQUISITION: from J. Ha-Cohen's *Dibre ha-Yamim le-Malke Sarpath ule-Malke Beth Ottoman Ha-Tugar,* vol. II pp. 91, 94-96 (Amsterdam, 1733), translated by L. W. Schwarz. V. also for additions to the omitted visions *Hayath Kaneh* (17th cent.?). Of the extraordinary circle of mystics in Palestine during this period, M. Probably met Joseph Karo who mentions him in his curious spiritual diary, *Maggid Mesharim* (in which a voice speaking in the first person, quite parallel to Socrates' *daimon,* acts as his mentor). V. also the autobiography of Hayyim Vital, the disciple and successor to Isaac Luria, *Shibhe R. Hayyim Vital* (named also *Sefer ha-Hezyonoth*) which was published from the autograph ms. by a descendant (Jerusalem, 1866).

THE STORY OF MY IMPRISONMENT: The selection is an abridged version of *Megillat Ebah* ("Ebah" comprises the first letters of the opening words of Lamentations, "How doth the city sit solitary!"), translated by I. M. Lask. A text based upon an old ms. in Kahana, *op. cit.,* vol. II, pp. 277-290. David Gans, a contemporary (1541-1613), of Prague chronicled important events in his history, *Zemah David.* There are a goodly number of autobiographical writings of this time, occasioned particularly by the brutalities of the Chmielnicki massacres: *Yaven Mezula* (a phrase from Psalms 69:3, "I am sunk *in deep mire . . .*") by Nathan Nata ben Moses Hanover, in Kahana, *op. cit.,* vol. II, pp. 298-318; the great talmudic scholar Sabbatai Cohen who fled from Vilna to Moravia wrote, in addition to elegaic poems, *Megillat Efah.* V. the Wiener edition of *Shebet Yehuda,* pp. 134-139 (Hanover, 1885). Of the same circle was Aaron Kaidanover who fled to Fürth and tells his story in the Preface to *Birkat ha-Zebah,* edited by his son-in-law Nahum (Amsterdam, 1669). Experiences of those living in Central Europe during the 15th and 16th centuries are recorded in the following: a Hebrew diary edited by M. Ginsburger, *Die Memoiren des Ascher Levy aus Reichshofen im Elsass (1598-1635),* (Berlin, 1913); the diary of the great *shtadlan,* Josselman of Rosheim, edited by Kracauer in *Revue des études juives,* vol. XVI, pp. 85-101; Judah Loeb of Prague described the capture of the city by the Swedes in 1648 in his *Milhama ba-Shalom:* v. Hebrew text and Latin translation by J. C. Wagenseil in *Exercitationes Sex Varii Argumenti,* pp. 103-159 (Altdorf, 1687); another fascinating figure was Joseph Solomon Delmedigo (1591-1657), physician, scholar and traveler whose personality may be glimpsed in the Prefaces to a number of his works by Samuel bar Judah Leib, v. Kahana, *op. cit.,* vol. II, p. 165 ff. Of incomparable interest is a batch of letters written by Jews in Prague on the afternoon of Friday, November 22, 1619, to relatives and friends in Vienna and impounded by the Imperial forces. They were discovered in the Imperial Archives in recent years and published by A. Landau and B. Wachstein in *Jüdische Privatbriefe aus dem Jahre 1619* (Vienna, 1911).

LIFE IN LOMBARDY: The selection is from M.'s *Haye Yehuda,* edited by A. Kahana, p. 13 ff. (Kiev, 1911) and translated by I. M. Lask. Additional personal glimpses can be found in his letters: L. Blau, *Leo Modena's Briefe und Schriftstücke* (Budapest, 1905-06). The earthquake referred to by M. is described in the first part, "Kol Elohim," of *Meor Enayim,* pp. 6-22 (Vilna, 1864) and partly translated by the Editor in the Introduction. The memoir of M.'s grandson, Isaac Ha-Levi, "Medabber Tahpukot," edited by L. Blau in *Ha-zofeh me-Erez ha-Ger,* II-III Budapest, 1912); Joseph ibn Yahia, *op. cit.,* and David ibn Yahia in A.

Marx' *"Glimpses of the Life of an Italian Rabbi . . ."* (listed above under II). In addition to the document from which "Trouble in the Siena Ghetto" is excerpted, there are a number of Italian memoirs of the following centuries: an earthquake in Livorno in 1743 is recorded by a Yedidiah ben Nahman Michael Nahmani in "Megillath Yedidiah mi-Liborno," edited by Isaac Rivkind from a ms. in the Mortimer Schiff Collection of the Jewish Theological Seminary, *Reshumoth*, V, p. 405 ff. (Tel Aviv, 1927); there are flashes of self-revelation in the letters of M. H. Luzzatto; a diary of a medical student in Rome, one Judah Gonzago (the Editor was unsuccessful in his attempts to locate this ms.), is described and quoted from by A. Berliner, "Aus den Memoiren eines römischen Ghetto-jünglings" in *Jahrbuch für jüdische Geschichte und Literatur*, vol. VII, pp. 110-132 (1904); also S. D. Luzzatto's which exists in Italian and German translations, the original having been lost. (*Autobiografia di S. D. Luzzatto* (Padua, 1878), and some recollections of his childhood were published serially between 1858 and 1862 in the earliest Hebrew weekly, *Ha-Maggid* (Lyck).

MY DOUBLE LIFE AND EXCOMMUNICATION: The Latin original may be found in *Uriel Acosta's Selbstbiographie, lateinisch und deutsch* (Leipzig, 1847). The present translation is a revision of the rare Limborch version, *The Remarkable Life of Uriel Acosta* (London, 1740). V. Gebhardt's *Die Schriften des Uriel da Costa . . .* (Amsterdam, 1922); I. Sonne, "Da Costa Studies" in *The Jewish Quarterly Review*, vol. XXII, pp. 247-293. For the picturesque contemporary, Rabbi Manasseh ben Israel, v. the prefatory memoir of *De Termino Vitae*, translated into English by T. Pocock (London, 1709). Manasseh was acquainted with Joseph Delmedigo (v. note on Heller). The luminary of those times, Spinoza, gives occasional personal glimpses in his letters, A. Wolf, *The Correspondence of Spinoza* (London, 1928) and in the first part of the unfinished essay, *On the Improvement of the Understanding*.

TROUBLE IN THE SIENA GHETTO: Pp. 391-399, "The Memoirs of a Siennese Jew (1625-1633)" edited with an admirable Preface and Notes by Cecil Roth in *The Hebrew Union College Annual*, vol. V (Cincinnati, 1928). For other Italian memoirs v. note on Modena.

MEMORIES OF AN UNHAPPY CHILDHOOD: The ms. together with an English version which is used here, slightly revised, was published by Alexander Marx, "A Seventeenth-Century Autobiography," in *The Jewish Quarterly Review*, New Series, vol. VIII, pp. 276-283 (1917-1918).

MY JOYS AND SORROWS: This selection comprises three passages: pp. 146-153, 180-194, 197-208, out of the fifth book of Marvin Lowenthal's *The Memoirs of Glückel of Hameln* (New York, 1932), translated from the original Judeo-German. There are also a number of German and Hebrew versions. Of G.'s notable descendants, two autobiographers, Simon de Geldern and Heinrich Heine, are included in this volume.

DEFEAT OF SATAN: The extraordinary full-length autobiography of E. in which he includes a biography of his illustrious father was published by D. Kahana, *Megillat Sefer* (Warsaw, 1896), the part included here p. 54 ff. A stimulating psychological study of E. has been made in M. J. Cohen's *Jacob Emden: A Man of Controversy* (Phila., 1937). Among contemporaries who crossed swords with E. v. Preface to E. Landau's *Noda bi-Yehudah* (Prague, 1811), and the apologia of J. Eybeschütz *Luhot Eduth* (Altona, 1855); A. Cardoso's autobiography from a ms. in the E. N. Adler collection was published by C. Bernheimer in *The Jewish Quarterly Review*, vol. XVIII, pp. 112-127 (1927-28).

I WAS A SLAVE: From an undated booklet, probably printed in England soon after H.'s death, entitled *An Authentic Narrative of the Life and Conversion of J. C. Lebrecht, a Jew, who died in the Faith of the Son of God, November 13, 1776, at Königsberg in Prussia.* Autobiographies of converts are extensive in and after the 18th century; a reading of the literature is a fascinating excursion into psychology and indicates that the tendency to regard converts as charlatans is unjust. E.g., v. P. Cassel's *Aus guten Stunden* (Berlin, 1874), A. Capadoce, *Conversion du docteur Capadoce, Israélite portugais* (Paris, 1848); *Conversion de Marie-Alphonse Ratisbonne* edited by T. R. de Bussières (Lille, 1894); a Rabbi who became a Protestant minister, C. Freshman's *Autobiography* (Toronto, 1868); of the 3 autobiographical vols. of E. A. Steiner, v. *From Alien to Citizen: the Story of my Life in America* (New York, 1914); R. F. Schwob's *Moi. Juif* (Paris, 1928); two Jews who became converts and returned to the Jewish faith, D. Harnsohn's *Zichroines fun a Baal Teshuvah*, 2 vols. (Jerusalem, 1934), and S. Freuder's *My Return to Judaism* (New York, 1922); and a Catholic convert to Judaism, A. Pallière's *The Unknown Sanctuary*, translated from the French by Mrs. Stephen S. Wise (New York, 1928); the wife of the eminent Catholic philosopher, R. Maritain's *We Have Been Friends Together* (New York, 1942). An extraordinary amount of material has been assembled in the works of S. L. Citron, *Meshumadim* (Warsaw, 1921) and *Me-Ahare ha-Pargod*, 2 vols. (Vilna, 1923).

KING FOR A NIGHT: All the family documents relevant to Saul Wahl were published in H. Edelman's Gedulat Shaul (London, 1854). The translation of the selection by Leo W. Schwarz is from pp. 1-6, based upon a unique ms. in the Bodleian Library, Oxford. For biographical data on K. v. *Shem ha-Gedolim he-Hadosh*, pp. 114-115 (3rd ed. Warsaw, 1882). An historical appraisal in G. Karpeles, *Jewish Literature and Other Essays*, pp. 272-292 (Phila., 1895).

DAYBOOK OF AN ADVENTURER: This travel-diary, together with a documentary study of the Von Geldern family, was first published in D. Kaufmann's *Aus Heinrich Heines Ahnensaal*, pp. 283-296 (Breslau, 1896) and edited in German by H. Rubin in *Archiv für jüdische Familien-*

forschung, vol. I, pp. 18-22, 33-42 (Vienna, 1913) from which the present translation was made by Libby Benedict. The continuation of the diary appears to be in possession of Prof. N. H. Torczyner of the Hebrew University in Jerusalem: v. "Mi-Miktabe Shimeon de Geldern Al Nesioto be-Erez Yisroel" in the Luncz memorial issue of *Yerushalayim*, pp. 106-110 (Jerusalem, 1928) which includes three letters written by G. during his stay in Palestine. The most recent sketch of G. is the first essay in F. Heymann's *Der Chevalier von Geldern* (Amsterdam, 1937).

VICTORY FOR JUSTICE: B.'s memoirs were brought out simultaneously in Hebrew (*Zikronot R. Dob mi-Bolehov*, Berlin, 1922) and English (*The Memoirs of Ber of Bolechow*, London, 1922) by M. Vishnitzer. From the latter the selection here comprises pp. 60-67. For contemporary portraits v. M. Wasserzug's *Memoiren eines polnischen Juden*, edited by H. Loewe (Berlin, 1911), and Isaac Berens'—related to David Oppenheimer—"Eine Familien-Megillah" edited by I. M. Jost in *Jahrbuch für die Geschichte der Juden und des Judenthums*, vol. II, pp. 39-82 (Leipzig, 1861).

PIONEER IN SWEDEN: The ms. written in Judeo-German was first brought out by the Israelitiska Litteratur-Sällkapet edited by J. Seligmann, with a reproduction of a fine oil portrait which hung in the Stockholm Public Gallery: *Aron Isaks Sjelfbiografi* (Stockholm, 1897), the selection here comprising substantially pp. 9-39, translated by Leo W. Schwarz. There are two German versions, *Aaron Isaacs Minnen*, edited by A. Brody and H. Valentin (Stockholm, 1932) and *Denkwürdigkeiten des Aron Isak*, edited by Z. Holm, pseud. (Berlin, 1930); and a Yiddish version edited by N. Shtif, *Aaron Isaacs Autobiografia* (Berlin, 1922). An informative account of seal-engravers is given in "The Jewish Artist before the Time of Emancipation" by F. Landsberger in *The Hebrew Union College Annual*, vol. XVI, pp. 321-414 (1941). Very few memoirs of Scandinavian Jews have been published: v. the lively recollections of M. A. Goldschmidt in the last vol. of his *Collected Works* (Copenhagen, 1887), and the note on the reminiscences of G. Brandes below.

A KABBALIST IN PARIS: The autograph ms. of A.'s diary is in the Library of the Jewish Theological Seminary of New York and has been reproduced in full in *Sefer Maagal Tob ha-Shalem*, edited by A. Freimann, 2 vols. (Jerusalem, 1934): part of it was published by the same editor in the publications of the Mekize Nirdamim (Berlin, 1921) and extracts from 1755-1778 published in E. Adler, *op. cit.*, pp. 345-368 from which the selection here is reprinted. Other contemporary accounts have been made available in J. D. Eisenstein, *op. cit.* The material from the diaries of Ezra Stiles, the first president of Yale University, relating to that picturesque traveler Rabbi Isaac Karrigal is assembled in G. A. Kohut's *Ezra Stiles and the Jews* (New York, 1902). The diary of another observant traveler a generation earlier, one Abraham Levy, written in

Judeo-German, has been preserved: v. *Israelitische Letterbode,* p. 148 ff. (Amsterdam, 1884-1885). As for the Baalshem of London known as Dr. Falk (1708-1782), a ms. diary is preserved in the Beth ha-Midrash of the United Synagogue of London as well as of his valet, Zwi Hirsch of Kalisch. For the latter v. E. N. Adler's *Hebrew Manuscripts,* p. 46, ms. no. 2441 (Cambridge, 1921).

A TRIP WITH ISRAEL BAALSHEM: While hasidic literature is rich in more or less legendary biographical materials, memoirs of the zaddikim are rare. M.'s reminiscences from the text in A. Kahana's *Sefer ha-Hasiduth,* p. 62 (Warsaw, 1922) translated by Leo W. Schwarz. M.'s father, Zwi Hirsch, apparently also knew the Baalshem: v. "Beth Zaddikim" in *Sefer Niflaoth ha-Yehudi* (Warsaw, n.d.) p. 84 ff. Unique in hasidic literature is the autobiography of Nahman of Brazlav's amanuensis, Nathan of Nemerow: *Sefer Yeme Maharnath* (Lublin, 1919) and his volume of correspondence *Sefer Alim li-Terufah* (Berditchev, 1896), and an enlarged edition (Warsaw, 1900). The best sources for personal experiences are the thousands of letters, many of them still in manuscript, written by the zaddikim. Kahana's anthology gives a fair sampling, but even since the publication of his book a batch of the Baalshem's letters have been brought to light.

MY STRUGGLE WITH AMAZONS: M.'s work was first published in 3 vols. (Berlin, 1792-93) and was translated into English by J. C. Murray, *Solomon Maimon: An Autobiography* (Boston, 1888) from which the selection was revised. It is high time that this masterpiece was again made available to the English-reading public. Sidelights on M.'s character in S. J. Wolff *Maimoniana; oder Rhapsodien zur Characteristik Solomon Maimon's* (Berlin, 1813). For M.'s Berlin contemporaries of the Enlightenment, v. L. Bendavid, *Selbstbiographie* (Berlin, 1804) who appears with others in *Bildnisse jetzt-lebende Berliner Gelehrten mit ihren Selbstbiographien* (Berlin, 1805-06) with portraits by J. M. S. Lowe. Of Moses Mendelssohn, who left no memoirs but appears in almost all contemporary memoirs, there is a batch of letters exchanged with Fromet M., largely written in Judeo-German, together with other correspondence in the Jubilee edition of his writings, *Gesammelte Schriften,* vol. XVI (Berlin, 1929) and vol. XI (Berlin, 1932) where the above-mentioned batch is printed in German script; v. also Moses Mendelssohn, *Brautbriefe,* edited by I. Elbogen in the Schocken series (Berlin, 1936). A descendant has gathered the traditions in *The Mendelssohn Family* by S. Hensel (English edition, New York, 1882). V. notes on Heine, Zunz, Herz, below.

WEDDED TO THE MUSE: Some of the latter portions of M.'s self-portrait, which are of especial interest to the literary historian, have been omitted here. The text was printed in *Sefer Zikkaron,* pp. 117-126, edited by N. Sokolow (Warsaw, 1889). V. also M.'s *Mein Leben* (Warsaw, 192?). A batch of ten letters of M.'s were edited by I. Rivkind, "Iggaroth" in

Reshumoth, vol. V, pp. 408-434 (Tel Aviv, 1927). Life in the Russian and Polish villages and cities of that period is recorded in numerous memoirs: e.g., A. Cahan's *Blätter fun mein Leben,* vol. I (New York, 1926); P. Wengeroff's *Memoiren einer Grossmutter; Bilder aus der Kulturgeschichte der Juden Russlands im 19. Jahrhundert* (Berlin, 1908); I. Kopeloff's *Amol is Geven,* with a Preface by H. Zhitlovsky (New York, 1926); G. Lewin's *Das Buch fun mein Leben* (Warsaw, 1937); Shmarya Levin's *Childhood in Exile,* the first of 3 vols. also in Yiddish and Hebrew, translated by Maurice Samuel (New York, 1929); M. Berlin's *Fun Volozhin bis Yerushalyim; Episoden,* 2 vols. (New York, 1933; Hebrew ed. Tel Aviv, 1939); H. Zhitlovsky's *Zichroines fun mein Leben,* 3 vols. (especially II and III) (New York, 1935, 1940); S. Dubnow's *Sefer ha-Hayyim,* vol. I (Tel Aviv, 1936); Dob Stock's (real name: Berl Stock-Sperber) *Mi-Mahoz ha-Yalduth* (Tel Aviv, 1938); A. A. Friedman's *Sefer ha-Zikronoth* (1858-1926) (Tel Aviv, 1926).

HOW I WROTE MY SONGS: Appearing first serially in the *Morgen Journal,* the complete Yiddish text together with an English rendering by S. Hirsdansky and a foreword by M. Rosenfeld was published by the Zunzer Jubilee Committee (New York, 1905). Reprinted here, somewhat revised, are substantially pp. 10-41. V. also M. S. Zunzer's *Yesterday* (New York, 1939). Memoirs of *badhanim, hazzanim, meshorrerim,* etc. are rare, even for our own times. There are some personal notes in Solomon Lifschütz' *Teudath Shlomo* (Offenbach, 1718), a book about cantorial music by a relative of the famed Josef Süss Oppenheimer; v. also the reminiscences of Elkan Cohen in *Oesterreichisch-ungarische Cantoren-Zeitung,* vol. III, nos. 6-8 (Vienna, 1882) and M. Rosenfeld, a cantor in Pisek, *ibid.,* vols. XI-XII (1891-92); A. J. Paperna's *Meine Erinnerungen an A. Goldfaden* (Warsaw, 1923); G. Levin's *Das Buch fun mein Leben; Frülings-johren in Lublin* is replete with musical recollections; P. Minkowsky's "Mi-Sefer Hayyai" in *Reshumoth,* vols. I-V; and A. Friedman's *Fünfzig Yahre in Berlin* (Berlin, 1929).

LOVE FOUND A WAY: Most of the memoirs out of Eastern Europe during the past 75 years mention experiences with hasidism. None are more graphic than K.'s *Meine Zichroines* (2 vols., Berlin, 1922) from which the selection, translated by Samuel Kreiter, comprises substantially vol. I, pp. 185-305.

LIFE OF A HUMORIST: The translation of this fragment is by Tamara Berkowitz Kahana: v. *Das Sholem-Aleichem Buch,* edited by I. D. Berkowitz (New York, 1926). Recollections of S. A. by his son-in-law in *Ha-Rishonim de-Bene Adam,* 2 vols. (Tel Aviv, 1938), and by his brother, W. Rabinovitch, *Mein Bruder Sholem Aleichem* (Kiev, 1939). Of the memoirs of the Yiddish writers, v. those of J. L. Perez, first published in *Die Jüdische Welt* (Vilna) and a Hebrew rendering by M. Z. Wolfobsky, *Zikronotai* (Tel Aviv, 1928), and Sholem Asch's

"Rückblick" in *Menorah: jüdisches Familienblatt für Wissenschaft-Kunst und Literatur,* vol. VIII, pp. 511-538 (Vienna-Berlin, 1930).

MEMORIES OF CHILDHOOD: This selection from "Pirke Zikronoth," which was published in pp. 86-144, vol. V of *Reshumoth,* and translated by I. M. Lask. A. H.'s voluminous correspondence is also revealing: *Iggaroth A. H.,* 6 vols. (Jerusalem, 1923-25). Another recollection of South Russian hasidism by a contemporary writer, A. B. Gottlober, *Zikronoth mi-Me Yalduti,* 3 vols. (Warsaw, 1880-1881).

BEFORE THIRTY: From a posthumously published ms. "Ketaim Autobiografiim," pp. 6-17, edited by J. Cohen and F. Lahower in vol. VI *Keneseth* (Tel Aviv, 1941). "Sapiah" was published in vol. II, pp. 129-167 of *Kitbe H. N. Bialik* (Berlin, 1923), and translated into English by I. M. Lask, pp. 39-140 in *Aftergrowth and Other Stories* by H. N. Bialik (Phila., 1939). B.'s letters are published in *Iggaroth,* edited by F. Lahower in 4 vols. (Tel Aviv, 1938). The agony of spiritual readjustment, stimulated by the Enlightenment, runs like a red thread through the memoirs of creative spirits: v. J. L. Gordon's *Kitabe J. L. Gordon,* vol. I (Tel Aviv, 1928); P. Smolenskin's *Ha-Toeh be-Darche ha-Hayyim,* with an introduction by R. Brainin, 4 vols. (Warsaw, 1905), R. Brainin's *Kol Kitbe R. B.,* vol. III (New York, 1940), and M. Ben-Ami, a writer's recollections of S. "Perez Smolenskin" pp. 447-458, 556-573, vol. XLIV (Jerusalem, 1925); M. L. Lilienblum's *Hatot Neurim* (Vienna, 1876); S. Tchernichowsky's brief "Autobiographia" in *Ha-Shiloah,* vol. XXXV, pp. 97-103 (Odessa, 1918).

CHILDHOOD IN LITHUANIA: The ms. is still in progress, and the selection was Englished by the writer's son, Louis Berg. A fascinating portrait of childhood in Lithuania will be found in I. A. Kasovich's *Sechsig Johr Leben* (New York, 1924) which has been rendered into English by Maximilian Hurwitz, *The Days of Our Years* (New York, 1929). V. also E. S. Brudno's *The Fugitive* (New York, 1917).

MY ROAD TO HASIDISM: From "Mein Weg zum Chassidismus", pp. 659-672 in *Die Chassidischen Bücher,* translated by Libby Benedict (Hellerau, 1928). H. Kohn has written a full biography, *Martin Buber, sein Werk und seine Zeit* (Hellerau, 1930). Cp. B.'s preeminent collaborator F. Rosenzweig's *Briefe* (Berlin, 1935).

INDEX

SCHOCKEN PAPERBACKS

ACTON, LORD	Renaissance to Revolution SB7
AYALTI, HANAN J., ed.	Yiddish Proverbs SB50
AYRES, C. E.	The Theory of Economic Progress SB33
BAECK, LEO	The Essence of Judaism SB6
BERENSON, BERNARD	Rudiments of Connoisseurship SB37
BERENSON, BERNARD	The Sense of Quality SB29
BERNSTEIN, EDUARD	Evolutionary Socialism SB11
BICKERMAN, ELIAS	Ezra to the Last of the Maccabees SB36
BOWRA, C. M.	The Heritage of Symbolism SB10
BROD, MAX	Franz Kafka—A Biography SB47
BROGAN, D. W.	Abraham Lincoln SB48
BRYCE, JAMES	The Holy Roman Empire SB3
BUBER, MARTIN	Tales of the Hasidim: Early Masters SB1
BUBER, MARTIN	Tales of the Hasidim: Later Masters SB2
BUBER, MARTIN	Ten Rungs: Hasidic Sayings SB18
CHAGALL, BELLA & MARC	Burning Lights SB35
CHARLES, R. H.	Eschatology SB49
COHON, S. S.	Judaism: A Way of Life SB38
COOLEY, CHARLES HORTON	Social Organization SB22
EHRENBERG, VICTOR	The People of Aristophanes SB27
FRANK, JEROME D.	Persuasion and Healing SB44
FRIEDLÄNDER, MAX J.	Landscape, Portrait, Still-Life SB43
GANDHI, M. K.	Non-Violent Resistance SB17
GLATZER, NAHUM N.	Franz Rosenzweig: His Life and Thought SB21
GLATZER, NAHUM N., ed.	Hammer on the Rock: A Midrash Reader SB32
GLATZER, NAHUM N., ed.	A Jewish Reader: In Time and Eternity SB16
GUYAU, M.	The Non-Religion of the Future SB39
HALLIDAY, F. E.	Shakespeare and His Critics SB41
HERFORD, R. TRAVERS	The Ethics of the Talmud (*Pirke Aboth*) SB23
KAFKA, FRANZ	Amerika SB28
KAFKA, FRANZ	Letters to Milena SB24
KAFKA, FRANZ	Parables and Paradoxes SB12
KAFKA, FRANZ	The Penal Colony SB4
KATZ, JACOB	Exclusiveness and Tolerance SB40
MALINOWSKI, BRONISLAW	The Family Among Australian Aborigines SB52
NEWMAN, LOUIS I.	The Hasidic Anthology SB46
NILSSON, MARTIN	Imperial Rome SB30
PARES, BERNARD	Russia: Between Reform and Revolution SB34
PENROSE, ROLAND	Picasso: His Life and Work SB31
ROTH, CECIL	A History of the Jews SB9
SCHAUSS, HAYYIM	Guide to the Jewish Holy Days SB26
SCHECHTER, SOLOMON	Aspects of Rabbinic Theology SB15
SCHOLEM, GERSHOM G.	Major Trends in Jewish Mysticism SB5
SCHOLEM, GERSHOM G., ed.	Zohar: The Book of Splendor SB45
SCHÜRER, EMIL	Jewish People in the Time of Jesus SB8
SCHWARZ, LEO W., ed.	Memoirs of My People SB51
SUTTON et al.	The American Business Creed SB25
TOCQUEVILLE, ALEXIS DE	Democracy in America (*unabridged, with introductions by John Stuart Mill*) 2 v., SB13/14
WÖLFFLIN, HEINRICH	Art of the Italian Renaissance SB42
ZBOROWSKI & HERZOG	Life Is With People: Culture of Shtetl SB20

At your bookstore. For complete catalog write to:
SCHOCKEN BOOKS 67 PARK AVENUE, NEW YORK 16, N. Y.